3D Graphics & Animation

Second Edition

Contents At a Glance

On the CD-ROM

E Hardware and Software Selection

F Hardware and Software Products

G Planning and Organization

3D Graphics & Animation

Second Edition

Mark Giambruno

New Riders

1249 Eighth Street, Berkeley, California 94710

An Imprint of Peachpit, A Division of Pearson Education

3D Graphics & Animation, Second Edition

Trademarks

All terms mentioned in this book that are known to be trademarks or service marks have been appropriately capitalized. New Riders Publishing cannot attest to the accuracy of this information. Use of a term in this book should not be regarded as affecting the validity of any trademark or service mark.

Warning and Disclaimer

This book is designed to provide information about 3D graphics and animation. Every effort has been made to make this book as complete and as accurate as possible, but no warranty or fitness is implied.

The information is provided on an as-is basis. The authors and New Riders Publishing shall have neither liability nor responsibility to any person or entity with respect to any loss or damages arising from the information contained in this book or from the use of the discs or programs that may accompany it.

Publisher
David Dwyer

Associate Publisher
Stephanie Wall

Production Manager
Gina Kanouse

Managing Editor
Kristy Knoop

Senior Acquisitions Editor
Linda Bump

Acquisitions Editor
Victoria Elzey

Product Marketing Manager
Kathy Malmoff

Publicity Manager
Susan Nixon

Senior Editor
Lori Lyons

Copy Editor
Margo Catts

Indexer
Chris Morris

Manufacturing Coordinator
Jim Conway

Cover Designer
Aren Howell

Composition
Gloria Schurick

Media Developer
Jay Payne

For my family and friends.

❖

Table of Contents

About the Author

Mark Giambruno was born in 1957 in the small California foothills town of Placerville. He grew up in Sacramento, where he enjoyed annoying his teachers with epic space battles drawn—during class—in the margins of his schoolwork. In high school and college he pursued classes in art and electronics, but found the display-less computers of the time utterly boring.

In 1982, he used his younger brother's need for computer access at home as an excuse to buy his first microcomputer—an Atari 800—and has been heavily involved with computing ever since. He started his own computer graphics firm in 1990 and took on San Francisco-based Mondo Media as one of his main clients. When he was free to relocate, Mondo offered him a full-time position, and he become one of their lead artists and project directors. He conceptualized, managed, and created graphics for many of the company's projects, including those for such clients as Microsoft, Sierra Semiconductor, and Compaq.

After a few years of doing business-oriented multimedia, he went on to head up Mechadeus's first two CD-ROM games, *Critical Path* and *The Daedalus Encounter* (featuring Tia Carerre of *Wayne's World* fame). His responsibilities on *Daedalus* included design, co-writing the script, art direction, and editing. He also wrote *The Official Guide to The Daedalus Encounter* for BradyGAMES, which chronicles the project and provides hints and tips for completing the game.

Later projects for Mondo Media included art direction of game cinematics for *Mechwarrior 3*, *Under Cover*, and *Alpha Centauri: Alien Crossfire*, as well as creating and art directing in-game assets for both *Star Fleet Command* releases. He also art directed *Spiral*, a Flash-based Mondo Mini Show with character designs by Toshihiro Kawamoto (*Cowboy Bebop*, *Gundam*, *Golden Boy*).

Currently, he is an independent contractor providing writing, 3D modeling, design, and animation services through his Binary Arts company. His most recent projects include co-writing the English adaptations of two Japanese detective novels, *Under Cover* and *Angel's Fang*, both by #1 best-selling author Arimasa Osawa.

His favorite diversions include watching *subtitled* anime and playing FPS games like *Unreal Tournament* and *Return to Castle Wolfenstein*.

About the Technical Reviewers

These reviewers contributed their considerable hands-on expertise to the entire development process for *3D Graphics & Animation*. As the book was being written, these dedicated professionals reviewed all the material for technical content, organization, and flow. Their feedback was critical to ensuring that *3D Graphics & Animation* fits our reader's need for the highest-quality technical information.

 **Paul J. Baccash** is a freelance 3D animator in New York City, primarily working on the Broadcast side of the industry. His work includes commercials for such clients as AT&T, FOX, HASBRO Toys, Y.E.S. (Yankee Entertainment Sports) Network, and Power Rangers, to name a few. Paul is also a partner and co-founder of Clique Design Group LLC, a multimedia company providing cutting-edge web design services inclusive of a state-of-the-art recording studio (Clique Sound Design) for voiceovers, commercial jingles, and various other music genres.

Paul is well-versed in 3ds max and Maya. He is also the technical editor for the highly acclaimed book *Inside 3ds max 4* (New Rider's Publishing, Kim Lee author and editor). In addition, Paul also does compositing work using Combustion. In the recording studio, he is senior engineer, utilizing a combination Pro-tools software and ADAT hardware to create superb recordings. In his spare time, Paul plays guitar and sings with an up-and-coming band called Fried Rice & the White Guys (www.friedricewhiteguys.com). Paul can be reached at pbaccash@cliquedesign.com or clique.design@verizon.net.

Paul would like to thank Luis Cataldi, Sheldon Whittaker, and Kim Lee for valuable information, priceless inspiration, and minimizing his perspiration! Thanks Guys!

 **Douglas J. Nakakihara** is the documentation manager for NewTek. Although he graduated with a degree in accounting and gained a CPA certificate, his real interest was always computers. He freelances as a web designer and has written several PC utilities. He has worked as a 3D animator and has written for many computer publications throughout the years. For more information, see www.dougworld.com.

Acknowledgments

I'd like to take this opportunity to thank everyone at New Riders Publishing who put forth their time and effort to see this book through to completion:

Senior acquisitions editors Steve Weiss and Linda Bump, for making the initial contacts and meetings that paved the way for this revised edition.

Victoria Elzey, acquisitions editor, for taking up the reins and guiding the project over the long haul.

Lori Lyons, project editor, for managing the technical editors and me, and for wrangling with all the files.

Paul Baccash, technical editor, for checking my work for accuracy and handling the Maya version of the tutorials.

Douglas Nakakihara, technical editor, for making sure I had my facts straight and for creating the LightWave version of the tutorials.

Margo Catts, copy editor, for making sure I wasn't inventing too many new spelling or grammar rules.

Mike LaBonne, graphics editor, for providing me with information and assistance in preparing the diagrams and illustrations for the book.

Stacey Beheler, acquisitions coordinator, for handling document distribution and getting those all-important paychecks processed.

All the designers, artists, specialists, coordinators, managers, proofreaders, and technicians who I'll never know, but who brought their skills and experience to the development and production process.

I'd also like to acknowledge and thank the people who helped create or contributed to the original edition of this book: John Kane, Simon Knights, Linda Laflamme, Howard Jones, Jennifer Eberhardt, Stacey Beheler, Ruieta Da Silva, Deanan Da Silva, Stephanie Pellegrine, Jim Giambruno, Eva Giambruno, Laura Hainke, and Drew Vinciguerra.

In addition, I'd like to thank some other companies and individuals who helped to widen the scope of this project and make it go more smoothly:

Marco Patrito, Maurizio Manzieri, and the entire Virtual Views team for the beautiful images from the graphic novels *Sinkha* and *Hyleyn* that grace the cover, the color gallery, and many other pages of the book.

Interviewees Sheldon Whittaker, Cindy Yamauchi, Mike Jones, Richard Green, Eric Chadwick, Leila Noorani, Kelly Kleider, Bob Jeffery, Laura Hainke, Eric Ronay, Gustavo "Goose" Ramirez, Derek Thompson, Marco Bertoldo, Andy Murdock, and Marco Patrito for sharing their thoughts and experiences as 3D artists.

Dominic Milano and Lea Anne Bantsari of the late, great *InterActivity* magazine, as well as Miller Freeman Publishing for allowing me to use excerpts from the 3D Tools and Animata articles in this book.

Discreet for providing me with the newest release of their excellent 3ds max 4.2, which was used throughout the book for creating the tutorials and sample figures.

Mondo Media/Mechadeus for providing info for the job interview portion of the book and allowing me to use images and animation from their portfolio as examples of top-quality 3D work.

Special thanks to all the other companies and individual contributors who sent or otherwise assisted in providing images for the book, including: Per Abrahamsen, Activeworlds, Activision, Adobe Systems, Alias|Wavefront, AniMagicians, Laurent Antoine, Artbeats, Ascension Technology Corporation, Den Beauvais, Marco Bertoldo, Kenn Brown, Eric Chadwick, Jeff Cantin, Cody Chancellor, Curious Labs, Digital Art Zone, Digital Illusion, Discreet, James Edwards, Foundation Imaging, GameSpy Industries, Richard Green, Laura Hainke, Terry Halladay, Marshall Hash and Ken Baer of Hash, Inc., Akira Iketani, Masa Ishikawa of InSpark, Inc., Interplay, Mike Jones, Masaru Kakiyama, Jussi Kemppainen, Simon Knights, Guillermo M. Leal Llaguno, Jared Lim, Richard Mans, Momentum Animation Studios, Mondo Media/Mechadeus, Darrin Mossor, Andy Murdock, Martin Murphy, The National Center for Atmospheric Research, Paramount Pictures, Marco Patrito of Virtual Views, Vadim Pietrzynski, Carles Piles, Pixar, Brian Prince, "Goose" Ramirez, Frank Rivera, Softimage, Stefan Schmidt, Adrian Skilling, Stratasys, Erik Bethke of Taldren, TruFlite, Turner Broadcasting, Viewpoint, Virgin Interactive, Terrence Walker of Studio ArtFX, Sheldon Whittaker, and ZINK. (Please see Appendix B, "Contributors," for contact information.)

Thanks also to Yuki Yoshioka, Kenn Navarro, Nikki Arias, Alan Lau, and the California Department of Motor Vehicles for their patience and/or assistance.

Last, but far from least, my thanks to my family and friends, for their support and understanding, and especially to my Mom, for her part in making my existence possible, her support and concern, and those delicious home-cooked CARE packages which ensured that not everything I ate came from a cardboard box or a drive-through window.

Once again, thank you all for your help, advice, inspiration, and support.

Tell Us What You Think

As the reader of this book, you are the most important critic and commentator. We value your opinion and want to know what we're doing right, what we could do better, what areas you'd like to see us publish in, and any other words of wisdom you're willing to pass our way.

When you contact us, please be sure to include this book's title and author as well as your name and email address. We will carefully review your comments and share them with the author and editors who worked on the book.

Email: errata@newriders.com

Introduction

When John Kane of New Riders Publishing first contacted me in 1996 about writing a book, he told me that they had two titles in mind. One was a non-product-specific "essential guide to 3D," and the other, also non-product-specific, was a beginner's guide. The latter seemed like the best choice for me, because I've always tried to help others who were interested in getting into the field. There were a number of people who helped me out when I first got started, and I like to carry on that tradition.

I was somewhat concerned about the fact that the book would not focus on any particular program, however. After all, how could I explain a procedure or write a tutorial when every product on the market does things differently and may even use different terminology for a given operation? On the other hand, even if the book were written specifically for the product I had the most experience with at the time, the DOS version of 3D Studio, what could I cover that hadn't already been detailed in more thorough tomes like *Inside 3D Studio*? After quite a bit of consideration, I realized there were quite a number of things I'd learned that were rarely talked about in other 3D books, and sharing them could really help newcomers to the field.

I also wanted to make the book unique in that I wanted to cover *all* aspects of getting into 3D graphics, from understanding what 3D is up to and including advice on getting a job. I felt that my experiences as both an employee and contractor in the field for a number of years—as well as having held both staff artist and art/creative director positions—would help give the readers a better idea of what would be expected of them if they pursue a career in 3D.

Besides covering 3D theory and common tools and techniques, I also wanted to point out the things that help to set work apart from the pack. In other words, I wanted to focus on the solid design, the mapping, the small details, and the other things that catch an art director's eye. I also wanted to explore the creative process as a whole, getting into the design, storyboarding, and scriptwriting aspects of modeling and animation. I felt that most 3D books and very few manuals touch on the important aspects of creating a reel, such as telling a story, directing the action, editing, and adding music and sound to finish it off.

In addition, I noted that most software manuals take a very piecemeal approach to their tutorials, giving the reader some basic task to perform to demonstrate an idea, and then discarding that work when they move on to the next tool. The result is a collection of unusable micro-projects, leaving the newcomer to start from scratch in order to make something presentable. With this book, nearly all the tutorials are interrelated and build on each other to help produce a finished portfolio piece.

Finally, I wanted to explore all these subjects in a comfortable, casual tone that would make reading the book seem less like a college lecture and more like a conversation about a mutual interest. I also decided to inject some of what I try to pass off as humor to ease the reader into the subject matter and occasionally provide relief from the monotony of highly technical information.

Revisiting the material six years later as I write this second edition, I've been surprised by how much has changed, particularly in the capabilities of the hardware and software and the overall quality of 3D work these days. In addition to updating the book to keep pace with new products and techniques, I've also tried to avoid information that seems likely to become dated in the near future. Interviews with other 3D artists on all types of subjects have been added, and I've asked them to share their experiences and advice on getting into the business as well as tips on specific tasks. My intention is to ensure that this book will remain a valuable part of your library even after you have established yourself as an experienced 3D artist.

The result of my efforts, and the efforts of many others, now rests in your hands. I hope you will find this book to be a useful resource in answering your questions, teaching you new techniques, and achieving your goals.

Getting the Most from 3DGA

There are a couple of different ways to use this book. If you read it prior to ever seeing 3D software in action, it provides a valuable overview of the 3D field, theory, tools, and filmmaking techniques that would aid you in any program you end up using. An alternative is to use it in conjunction with the manuals that come with your 3D package, as a second reference and real-world guide. You can do the tutorials as an alternative to some of the ones in your manuals, or as a way to confirm that you've learned the material thoroughly.

In either case, your best bet is to read through each chapter in a comfortable chair, then move to your computer to do any tutorials. The tutorials have been organized into the final sections of key chapters so that you don't have to read at your workstation (something many people find uncomfortable).

Using Your Manuals with the Book

With the exception of the tutorials for 3ds max, LightWave 3D, and Maya located on the companion CD-ROM, this book is not product-specific, so it can't give detailed lists of the steps you must take to accomplish things with your particular 3D software. Therefore, you need to work with your 3D software's manuals to learn how a given tool or operation is used in your package. However, the principles presented here remain the same throughout most programs, and alternative methods can be found for tools or techniques your package may not offer. In addition, this book offers alternative viewpoints and explanations of 3D theory and tools, along with a lot of tips and practical advice.

The best way to use the tutorials is as an addendum to any tutorials provided in your manuals, or as an alternative tutorial after you understand the necessary commands for your software. In other words, consider it a self-test to make sure you have learned the principles, not just a bunch of steps.

For those who are new to 3D, it's a good idea to start from the beginning and work your way through your software's User Guide. If you have read the earlier chapters of this book, you may find some of the introductory information about 3D applications and theory redundant, so feel free to skim through it. It never hurts to read a second resource, however, and you may find some uncertainties cleared up by reading a different presentation of the material.

Users with at least one other 3D package under their belts will probably just scan through the manuals to get a sense of how the program operates, and then launch into a couple of the tutorials. Because the 3D principles are similar across most packages, the Quick Reference card and Reference Manual portions of the documentation will probably be their tools of choice.

Overview of Chapters

The book has been arranged in a fairly straightforward manner, from "What is 3D?" to modeling and animation techniques, to developing a reel and landing a job. The ends of Chapters 3–10 contain the tutorial sections for the topics covered. The appendixes provide additional information and resources, such as a Glossary, lists of organizations, reference materials and publications, information on planning and organizing your 3D projects, and a list of image contributors. It also has a guide to hardware and software with special attention to the needs of the 3D artist—it's worth looking over if you plan to upgrade or replace your computer system.

Here's a brief look at the contents of each chapter and appendix:

Chapter 1, "The Virtual Path," gives a quick introduction to 3D graphics and examines the broad range of applications that utilize 3D. It also looks at the kinds of jobs available in the field and has suggestions about how to learn more about computer graphics.

Chapter 2, "Delving into Cyberspace," provides tips on making the transition from 2D to 3D graphics and explores the principles of 3D graphics in depth. Topics include coordinate systems, polylines, polygons, objects, viewpoints, and axes, to name a few.

Chapter 3, "3D Modeling," looks at the different kinds of modelers available and discusses good work habits. It covers the creation of 2D shapes and different methods of turning them into 3D objects, as well as 3D primitives and transforms. This chapter is the starting point for a series of tutorials that build on each other throughout the book.

Chapter 4, "Modeling: Beyond the Basics," gets into some of the tips and techniques that will help set your work apart from the crowd. It includes information on bevels, deform modifiers, vertex-level editing, subdivision surfaces, face extrusion, and other techniques for accurate and advanced modeling.

Chapter 5, "Low-Poly Modeling," is new to this edition and looks at the special needs of models intended for use in real-time applications like games and the web. It builds on the vertex-level editing introduced in Chapter 4 and provides helpful hints for modeling characters and vehicles for game applications.

Chapter 6, "Texture Mapping," demonstrates how mapping can be used to enhance the realism of mesh objects by giving them color and texture. The topics examined include the following: how mapping can be used in place of mesh for creating the illusion of detail, the basics of material creation, mapping coordinate systems, and various techniques for obtaining and creating custom maps.

Chapter 7, "Lighting," explores the principles of light in the real world and how they apply to the 3D environment, along with the basics of photographic lighting techniques and how they can be used to add drama and interesting effects to your 3D objects and scenes. This chapter also covers the kinds of light sources and controls available in the virtual world, and discusses the special capabilities and options available with 3D lighting tools.

Chapter 8, "The Camera," contains a look at camera terminology, comparing virtual cameras to their real-world counterparts, and shows how the position and focal length settings of the camera can increase the drama in a 3D scene. It also examines the use of the camera for storytelling purposes, based on the principles developed by filmmakers over several decades.

Chapter 9, "Animation," delves into animation terms and techniques, including timelines, motion paths, forward and inverse kinematics, and so forth. It looks at the tools and techniques of character animation, and shows how the storytelling process is advanced by turning objects into performers.

Chapter 10, "Rendering and Output," explores render time issues such as resolution, aspect ratios, color depth, palettes, and atmosphere. The chapter covers the uses and creation of postproduction effects like glows and lens flares, and includes an overview of the different types of output, from digital to slides to videotape.

Chapter 11, "The Reel," begins with a look at the creative process and examines ways to generate and develop ideas. It discusses the value of adding story elements to a reel, and goes through the pre-production processes of script writing, designing, and storyboarding a piece, along with other aspects of doing a reel, including postproduction, editing, visual effects, and audio.

Appendix A, "Glossary," is a compilation of 3D terminology used throughout the book and covers related topics, along with concise definitions.

Appendix B, "Contributors," is a full list of the companies and individuals who have contributed interviews and images for this book and/or CD-ROM. Those individuals who are available for contract 3D work have additional contact information listed for use by recruiters or producers looking for outside talent.

Overview of CD Chapters

Chapter 12, "Getting the Job," covers the challenges of starting a career in 3D graphics, including researching companies, preparing a resume and portfolio, and securing an interview. It looks at the differences between being an employee or a contractor, what art directors are looking for, the interview process, salaries, benefits, and ways to further your career.

Appendix C, "Recommended Reference," contains suggested reading, image collections, and reference material to help you find answers to your questions, get your creative juices flowing, or just plain entertain you.

Appendix D, "Resources," has web site addresses for schools, organizations, and companies that can help you learn more about 3D animation and/or provide valuable information or services for artists and companies in the field.

Appendix E, "Hardware and Software Selection," takes a look at nearly all the components of a typical computer system and what you, as a 3D artist, should look for when purchasing equipment. It also includes information on graphics programs and utilities that can be helpful in creating your work.

Appendix F, "Hardware and Software Products," contains contact information for all the gear and programs discussed Appendix E and throughout the book.

Appendix G, "Planning and Organization," deals with the finer points of researching, designing, and producing animation. It looks at how to gather reference and ensure accuracy in your models, tips for organizing your directories, object and file-naming conventions, budgeting, scheduling, and a host of other subjects.

Using the 3DGA CD-ROM

Included with the book is a companion CD-ROM usable on both PC and Mac systems. The CD-ROM contains the tutorial files and instructions specific to 3ds max 4 or higher, LightWave 7, and Maya 4. (To run these tutorials, your system should meet the minimum requirements of these software packages.) In addition, you'll find color versions of some of the black-and-white figures in the book as well as sample animations and artwork from 3D artists all over the world.

Using the Tutorial Files

With the exception of the low-poly modeling chapter, the tutorial design of the book has the user working from start to finish on a single project, a *Blade Runner*-style advertising blimp. Although this approach has the benefit of moving the user toward a completed portfolio piece, the nature of the tutorials makes it difficult to jump in at a later point because each depends on work done in earlier chapters.

In order to make it easier for users to get around problems or skip over tutorials they aren't interested in, multiple versions of the model in various stages of completion have been included. In addition to the Maya, max, and LightWave files that contain all the mapping and animation work done to the model, the model is also provided in DXF, the standard interchange format readable by nearly every 3D program. Unfortunately, DXF doesn't support animation, mapping coordinates, or textures, so you would have to re-apply these if you use the DXF files instead of building your own.

The tutorial model files have been divided up by software format, and then by chapter number. Within each directory for a given chapter you will find the following directories containing the illustrated tutorials in HTML format, the model (geometry) files, and the texture maps.

Note that the DXF files are not saved in small increments like the other formats—they are saved as the major sub-assemblies, such as the thrusters, gondola, and so forth, as well as in completed project form.

Viewing the Images and Animation

The IMAGES and ANIMATIONS directories on the CD-ROM contain work created by artists from all over the world. They are here for you to use as study examples and inspiration, but you may NOT redistribute or reproduce them without the express written consent of the artists or companies that hold the copyright.

The images and animations are stored by artist or company name, in the JPEG (.JPG) format. Virtually all the still image formats can be read directly off the disc by Photoshop or any good image utility, such as ACDSee, Thumbs Plus, Paint Shop Pro, and others. The animations come in two formats, Microsoft AVI, and Apple QuickTime. Whenever possible, I have tried to acquire the animation in the superior (and cross-platform) QuickTime format. If you don't have QuickTime installed on your PC, you can download it from `www.apple.com`.

All right! Now go forth and conquer. The first chapter awaits!

1

The Virtual Path

A virtual dragon flaps its wings amidst a computer-generated background.
Image ©1996 Vadim Pietrzynski.

*T*he student watched from the shadows as the Master muttered strange incantations over a glowing pool of light. Slowly, mist-like tendrils rose from the pool and flowed into place, forming the outline of a dragon. The Master paused for a moment, considering the result, then played his gnarled hands across its surface, replacing the ethereal outline with thick, textured scales awash in iridescent colors. Pleased, the Master smiled a toothless grin and waved his arms in a swirling motion.

"Go forth!" the old man cried. "Take to the skies!" With that, the dragon shuddered, spread its leathern wings, and leapt into the air. The creature hovered for a moment, and then began soaring around the room. Awestruck, the student's knees buckled, and he tumbled into the chamber, collapsing in a heap on the stone floor. He looked up at the wondrous dragon just in time to see it advance toward him, belching jets of flame. The student tried to move, but it was too late! The blaze struck him full on, then…

Nothing.

A moment later, the dragon itself dissolved into a shower of tiny sparks, and was gone. Stunned, the student gazed up at the Master, who chuckled and offered the young man his hand.

"An illusion," the old man proclaimed, "existing only to your eyes. I conjure them to illustrate and entertain." He turned and walked back toward the glowing pool, taking a seat nearby. "Now, what brings you here?"

"Forgive my intrusion, Master," the student replied, "but I came seeking the Virtual Path."

"Indeed? Well, I should say you have found it!" The Master laughed. "That creature was but one of a universe of possibilities, limited only by one's skills and imagination as a conjurer. But tell me, why do you seek this path? It's not an easy one, and will require much time and effort. The glowing pool will require your undivided attention for hours at a time."

"Yes," the student replied with a smile, "but it's sooo cool!"

What Is 3D, Anyway?

As with the curious student in this somewhat anachronistic tale, many of you may know that you want to create computer graphics, but don't fully understand what they are. Well, my notes for this section say, "Explain 3D graphics in a simple manner," so here goes…

As you probably know, 3D stands for *three-dimensional*. That means that things have three…uh…dimensions: namely width, height, and depth. If you look around the room, everything you see is three-dimensional—the chair, the desk, the TV, the walls, your dog, everything.

"Now, wait a minute," you say. "If everything in the room, like this rather heavy book in my hands, is three dimensional, then how come the '3D graphics' I've seen on computer screens are *flat*?"

Well, that's because the term "3D graphics" is a lie. A falsehood. A distortion of the truth. In actuality, 3D graphics should be refered to as "Two-dimensional *representations* of three dimensional objects." 2D, of course, means two-dimensional, or having only width and height, but no depth. In other words, *flat*.

"Okay, I sort of get it," you say, "but give me an example."

Fair enough. Go grab a camcorder and I'll show you. Don't worry—I'll wait.

Oh, prefer to use your imagination, huh? Very well. Imagine that you're now videotaping the room. You get up from your comfortable seat and wander around, taping things from all angles. You stub your toe on a chair, a painful reminder that you're moving through a three-dimensional world.

Now imagine that you pop the tape into your VCR and play it back on the TV. Yes, there's your three-dimensional room, but now it's *flat*. Pause the tape and look at the scene—the objects seem realistic enough, and have texture and color and shadow. You can see the sides of some objects, but no matter how you move your head around, you can't see behind anything. To put it *flatly*, you are looking at a two-dimensional *representation* of three-dimensional objects.

In computer graphics, objects exist only in the memory of the computer. They have no physical form—they're just long lists of numbers and mathematical formulas and little electrons running around inside the computer. Because the objects don't exist outside the computer, the only way to record them is to add more formulas to represent lights and cameras.

Thankfully, the software takes care of most of the nasty math stuff, enabling the user to view the non-existent scene on the computer monitor and manipulate it with mouse and keyboard commands (see Figure 1.1).

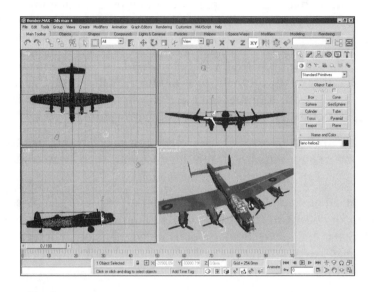
Basics of 3D Software

In many ways, using 3D modeling and animation software is like building a room full of objects from scratch and then videotaping the scene as you move the objects around. 3D software enables you to design the room and its contents using a variety of basic geometric objects such as cubes, spheres, cylinders, and cones, which you can select and add to the scene. The program also gives you the tools needed to define custom objects by drawing cross-sections and turning them into 3D objects, or by sculpting and manipulating the basic ones.

After all the objects have been created and positioned, you can choose from a library of predefined materials, such as plastic, stone, wood, and glass, and apply them to your objects. You can also create your own materials by adjusting controls such as color, shininess, and transparency, and even use painted or scanned images to make the surfaces of your objects appear any way you like.

Lighting is another aspect of creating a 3D scene, and the software enables you to choose from several different kinds of lights, as well as to define their color, brightness, shadow characteristics, and so forth. By positioning lights in the virtual space, you can control how the objects are illuminated.

Next, you set up the virtual cameras to record the scene. By adjusting the settings on the camera, you can get wide-angle effects or zoom in on a small detail. Positioning the cameras in interesting ways also adds to the drama of the scene.

The scene is brought to life by moving any of the objects in the room, including the lights and cameras. You can make the objects move mechanically, or appear to take on human characteristics. You can use filmmaking techniques to tell a story with your animation, or simply create something that looks cool.

Finally, you can record the animation onto videotape or as a digital video file, allowing you to view the finished results and share them with others. Using 3D graphics software, you can create just about anything you can imagine, and then use the result as a portfolio piece, a portion of a computer game, a scene from a sci-fi epic, or any number of other possibilities.

How Are 3D Graphics Used?

3D graphics have a surprisingly broad range of uses in all sorts of different businesses and fields of study. Some, like the multimedia, film, broadcast, and game businesses, have more need of 3D modelers and animators than some of the research fields. Still, it's good to be aware that the opportunities are so numerous and varied.

Film

The film industry has traditionally used matte paintings, hand-built miniature models, and full-sized props for most of its special effects (SFX) work. The myriad of spacecraft in the original *Star Wars* trilogy, the deserted terraforming complex from *Aliens*, and the incredibly atmospheric cityscapes of *Blade Runner* were painstakingly constructed from wood, metal and fiberglass, decorated with plastic model parts, and outfitted with tiny lights. Likewise, fantastic creatures were usually portrayed by people in foam rubber suits, by stop-motion models, or even puppets (perhaps the most famous being the gnarled, green-skinned Jedi Master Yoda, from *The Empire Strikes Back*).

Although 3D animation had its first substantial role on the big screen in Disney's 1982 film *TRON*, it was not until the monster success of *Jurassic Park* in 1993 that it became recognized as a practical alternative to traditional effects work in certain situations. After *Jurassic Park*, the use of 3D animation in films rapidly increased to its logical conclusion: 1995's entirely computer-generated feature film *Toy Story*. This feature was partially inspired by the Academy Award®–winning short film *Tin Toy*, an earlier work from the same director, John Lasseter of Pixar Animation Studios (see Figure 1.2).

In addition to the clearly CG (computer graphics) style of the characters in *Toy Story*, filmmakers have strived to portray realistic human characters in 3D as well. Many of the human "extras" in *Titanic* were computer animated, and the stunningly realistic characters in the *Final Fantasy* movie are pointing the way to a future when the audience will be unable to tell a CG actor from a flesh-and-blood one.

3D animation also found its way into traditional 2D animated features as reference for the hand-drawn work. An example of this is the carriage from Disney's *The Little Mermaid*, which was created as a 3D model, then animated to make the complex motions of rolling along a winding country road. The resulting 3D animation was then redrawn by hand so that it matched the look of the characters and backgrounds.

Nowadays, improvements in 3D rendering technology have enabled Disney animators to blend 3D elements directly into their otherwise 2D films without redrawing them. Examples of this include the computer-generated Hun on horseback in *Mulan*, CG crowds in *The Hunchback of Notre Dame*, and the moss-covered trees that serve as a natural skate park in *Tarzan*. Other good examples of incorporating 3D imagery into 2D films include the robot from *The Iron Giant* and the possessed Boar-god in *The Princess Mononoke (Mononoke Hime)*.

In addition to 3D, there are other applications for computer graphics in films as well, but these often go unnoticed in the final film. For example, *digital retouching* is a process that uses *2D paint* programs (software for drawing, painting, and manipulating 2D images) to modify photographic stills and movies. This method is often used to remove wires from suspended actors (such as Keanu Reeves and Hugo Weaving during their mid-air gun battle in *The Matrix*), or to erase television antennas from a cityscape that is supposed to represent the 1940s. The script for *102 Dalmatians* called for an all-white Dalmatian puppy. Because pups old enough to be trained to do stunts for the movie always had some spots, digital artists had to paint out the black spots on every shot. Incredibly real 3D dogs were also used in some scenes. Finally, one of the most dramatic and unique uses of digital retouching technology in films was the removal of Gary Sinese's legs for his role as a double amputee in *Forrest Gump*.

In addition to modifying certain elements of a shot, 2D paint systems can be used to alter or re-compose entire scenes. For example, during post-production work on *Terminator 2*, director James Cameron decided that he preferred the semi truck plunging into the drainage canal from right to left instead of the way it was originally filmed. Digital artists complied by flipping the scene, then reversing the street signs and vehicle license plates frame-by-frame. Because there are 24 frames for every second of film, these digital retouching efforts are a lot of work!

Some effects shots are a literal collage of different elements. Consider the shot in *Titanic* where the ship leaves port, for example. The scene consisted of live actors standing on a real dock, clusters of real actors shot against a solid color background, a forty-four foot scale miniature of the Titanic, a miniature tugboat, computer-generated people, birds, water, and smoke, and some 2D matte paintings to fill out the background. All these elements were filmed or created separately, and were blended together into a seamless whole using sophisticated 2D paint and compositing systems.

Other examples of 2D digital effects include the submarine wakes (water disturbances) in *The Hunt for Red October* and Woody Harrelson's demonic morph in *Natural Born Killers*. Digital retouching is not limited to 2D graphics, however. For the film *Primal Fear*, a church was constructed with 3D graphics and superimposed over an existing structure (see Figure 1.3).

> **definition**
>
> *morph* Animated 2D and/or 3D effect that makes one image or form smoothly transform into another by mapping an image onto a 2D grid and then progressively distorting the grid while cross-fading the image. The first commercial use of the technique was in the film *Willow*.

FIGURE 1.3

3D graphics and image compositing software enable filmmakers to change the look of a location shot to suit their needs. Here, a church is superimposed over an existing structure. Image created with Alias|Wavefront's Composer for *Primal Fear*, courtesy of Dream Quest Images. ©1996 Paramount Pictures.

The *Star Wars* trilogy re-release, which marked the 20th anniversary of the first film, includes a unique showcasing of computer graphics. First, portions of the films had to be restored and digitally remastered from numerous copies, including foreign ones, because the negatives had deteriorated in storage. Next, 3D animation was used to add new elements to the film, such as more air and ground traffic around Mos Eisley spaceport. In addition, some scenes that were cut from the original film because of timing, budget, or other concerns were restored, including one featuring Han Solo chatting with Jabba the Hut. In the original footage, Jabba was played by a human actor, which naturally doesn't jive with his appearance as a giant slug in *Return of the Jedi*. For the restored scene, then, a 3D version of Jabba was animated and composited together with the decades-old footage of Harrison Ford.

Although film special effects remains one of the most prestigious forms that 3D graphics can take, it is by no means the only application for CG in the entertainment field. In fact, for sheer volume, television series and advertisements probably win out.

Broadcast Television

Back in the early nineties, the popular science fiction series *Babylon 5* set the standard for broadcast 3D animation effects with its impressive ships and alien vistas. It also raised some eyebrows, because the production house, Foundation Imaging, used personal computers and relatively low-cost *LightWave 3D* software for creating the work (see Figure. 1.4). Indeed, the show became a prime example of what could be accomplished without resorting to *Silicon Graphics, Inc. (SGI) workstations* and $60,000 software. Of course, the high-end systems and software are still the industry's standard, and are well represented in other shows, such as the breathtaking opening animation for *Star Trek: Voyager*.

Hypernauts © 1996, ABC and Foundation Imaging

FIGURE 1.4

A shot from the television show *Hypernauts*, which featured 3D animated ships and mechs created by Foundation Imaging. Image ©1996, ABC and Foundation Imaging.

One of the most interesting trends in television series has been the appearance of 3D animated cartoons among the usual Saturday morning lineup. Shows such as *Reboot*, *Beast Wars*, and *Shadow Raiders* are refreshing not only because of their 3D look, but because they offer something many of the other contemporary 2D animated shows don't: lots of movement.

Commercials are fertile ground for the eye-catching visuals made possible with CG. Morphs appear to be particularly popular, sucking kids into soda bottles or turning a car into a running tiger. In addition, character animation ranging from dancing automobiles and gas pumps to wisecracking M&Ms has become a commonplace addition to (and welcome relief from) the hordes of human product pushers.

Less apparent to the casual observer is the use of 3D models for product shots in commercials. Using CG instead of traditional (and possibly more expensive) studio photography, even a mundane bottle of dishwashing liquid achieves perfection, with nary a plastic seam, creased label, or air bubble out of place.

Although not as glamorous as some of the other applications just discussed, station IDs and news graphics are also popular uses for CG in broadcast television (see Figure 1.5). These are usually updated every season to keep the look fresh and try to outdo the competition.

FIGURE 1.5

3D graphics are often used to create station IDs, news graphics, and opening sequences for broadcast television. Image courtesy of Turner Production Effects.

Although the flashiest 3D animation is usually reserved for network and station identification, the idea of having virtual sets for news and talk shows is starting to catch on. The idea is that because the sets can be generated with 3D programs, they can be frequently and cost-effectively upgraded to keep the look of the show fresh. This method also enables effects that would be impossible in a real studio environment.

> **definition**
>
> *real time* The immediate processing of input data and graphics, so that any changes result in near-instantaneous adjustments to the image.

In this kind of application, the newspeople or show hosts and guests are videotaped on a *bluescreen* set, which is a mostly empty stage painted a particular shade of blue. The blue areas of the image are then rendered transparent and replaced with the 3D background. With some systems, the sets are generated in *real time*, enabling the camera to follow the live performers as they walk around.

A variation on this "virtual set" idea was used during the filming of *A.I.: Artificial Intelligence*. For some of the shots of Rouge City, a 3D representation of the city was built and loaded into a computer on the set where the actors were being filmed against a bluescreen background. By tying the computer into a system that calculated the position of the camera, the software was able to generate 3D images of the city as it would appear behind the actors at any given angle. The 3D images were then fed, along with the video of the live actors, to another system that combined the two, enabling director Stephen Spielberg to get a good idea of how a shot would look long before the final background effects were added weeks or months later.

The bluescreen technique was also used in combination with 3D graphics to create some of the heavily damaged humanoid *mecha* in *A.I.*, including the cook and the nanny.

Multimedia

Some of my first paying 3D work came as point-of-sale (POS) and trade show demos for high-tech companies. I did most of this work for Mondo Media, which was located along with a lot of other multimedia companies in San Francisco's SOMA (South Of MArket) district at the time. In fact, there was such a concentration of multimedia companies there that it became known as *Multimedia Gulch*.

Point-of-sale demos are intended to run on kiosks or computer systems in a retail store environment, attracting the customer's attention and providing information about the product. Often these demos are used for advertising the computer system itself, and virtually every hardware manufacturer uses them to espouse the features, capabilities, and user-friendliness of its PC clone over the clearly inferior PC clone on the shelf next to it.

Trade show demos tend to be much flashier than POS demos and cover a much broader variety of products and services. If you've ever been to a big trade show, you know how every booth tries to scream for your attention, using everything from free doodads to celebrities to three-story-tall video walls equipped with deafening sound systems. Here, the idea is not so much to talk about features (which would be lost on the typical harried showgoer), but to make an impression in the viewer's mind about the product and company.

Usually, the impressions the demos try to sear into the viewer's brain are

◆ THIS is a HOT company

◆ THIS is a COOL product

◆ THIS is more IMPORTANT than breathing

To this end, trade show demos pull out all the stops, combining video of performers, special effects, and, of course, 3D animation into MTV-style eye candy tuned for a three-second attention span. In other words, working on these projects can be a lot of fun!

Far more staid and evenly paced are the presentations and speaker support projects that make up much of the corporate work created in-house or by multimedia companies. These include the typical bullet-point slides and graphs, along with 2D and 3D animation to jazz things up. Presentations are usually made one-on-one or to a small group with a laptop system, whereas speaker support jobs are often big-time affairs where the presentation is made to hundreds of people using big-screen projection systems.

On the subject of speaker support presentations, companies often want the multimedia firm to provide someone to run the computer during the speaker's talk, just in case of a software glitch. I handled this task for the first time at a big National Semiconductor presentation, and the experience can be pretty scary. Just before the presentation started, somebody ran around to all the speaker support stations and dumped an unfamiliar style of intercom headset on the desk. I put mine on, and the presentation started. After a couple of minutes, I started to hear static, and people began asking where it was coming from. I suddenly realized that it was *my* intercom that was causing the problem, and I couldn't figure out how to get the transmitter to work so that I could respond to the screaming director! One of those "character-building" situations, for sure. In the end, it all worked out fine—my intercom was replaced, and every cue was hit.

Web and VRML

The World Wide Web (WWW) is another spot where 3D graphics are often used. In this environment, 3D graphics may range from simple buttons or other graphical elements on the page to integrated VRML (Virtual Reality Markup Language) applications. *VRML* is a web browser technology that enables the user to explore simple 3D environments online (see Figure 1.6), and is used for such things as graphical chat rooms such as those found at www.activeworlds.com, or for evaluating the location of some concert seats before you buy them.

Another growing use of 3D on the web can be seen at some online retail sites. Interactive virtual products enable the shopper to examine the features of a camcorder or peek inside a box of chocolates. Check out www.viewpoint.com for some examples.

Games

To my mind, doing graphics for game projects is one of the most enjoyable applications of 3D. Depending on the type of game, you may end up working with near-broadcast quality images and animation, and probably with more freedom than an individual artist would have when working on a film or broadcast project.

3D seems to run rampant in today's games, used for everything from generating the detailed characters and environments of *Quake III*, *Unreal Tournament*, and *Max Payne* to the video or real-time *cut scenes* (also called *cinematics*) in various games that suspend gameplay in order to show plot developments in a movie-like way (see Figure 1.7).

definitions

pre-rendered   In games, 3D graphics that have been rendered during the game's development process as images or movies. Contrast this with real-time 3D graphics, which are rendered "live" on the user's computer.

surround node   A 360-degree panoramic image that is rendered at selected locations within a 3D model. The viewing software enables the user to scroll around the image, which creates the illusion that the user is inside a 3D space.

Before real-time 3D graphics became fast and detailed enough to build a visually rich game around, multi-CD motion video games such as *The 11th Hour*, *Zork: Nemesis*, and *The Daedalus Encounter* made heavy use of *pre-rendered* 3D graphics as a way to provide backgrounds for the live actors. In addition, *Zork: Nemesis* and the *Star Trek Technical Manual* provided virtual environments to explore by making use of 360-degree high-resolution *surround nodes* (see Figure 1.8). This panoramic technology, called QuickTime VR on the Macintosh, uses a specially rendered still image that enables the player to look all around a particular area before moving on to another "explorable" node.

Despite the quality and richness of the animation in motion video games, the biggest impact 3D has made in gaming is the real-time play afforded by the *Quake*-style *engines*. Here, some detail in the models and mapping are sacrificed to achieve the speed and responsiveness that a First Person Shooter (FPS), flight simulator, fighting game, or space battle simulation requires (see Figure 1.9). As computer systems and game consoles continue to increase in power and more sophisticated software appears, the quality of these games will continue to improve to the point where they will be nearly indistinguishable from pre-rendered animation, and eventually, perhaps even rival video footage of the real world!

FIGURE 1.8

3D graphics were used to create the highly detailed environments in Zork: Nemesis, and special rendering techniques yielded 360-degree surround nodes that the player could explore. Image by Mondo Media ©1996 Activision.

> **definition**
>
> *engine*   The portion of a software program that manages and renders real-time 3D graphics.

FIGURE 1.9

The Open Doors real-time engine realistically models environmental changes and physical interactions by using "self-aware" data. Hill scene created with 3ds max, Photoshop, and Open Doors. ©2002 Whatif Productions LLC.

Illustration and Fine Art

Taking a break from animation for a moment, the illustration and fine arts fields have seen a slow but steady influence coming from the 3D world (see Figure 1.10). All-3D illustration work is still rare compared to 2D work, but at least it's no longer restricted to technology and gaming magazines. More common are works that integrate 2D and 3D, or that use 3D as a starting point and are then substantially reworked in a paint program.

As far as fine art goes, some *avant-garde* types have been doing CG work since the late '70s. As with photography at the end of the 19th century, however, some people are having trouble accepting 3D as a valid form of fine art. Eventually, of course, this will change and 3D modeling software will be seen as just another tool for the artist, not the source of the work itself. For now, even games are crossing over into the realm of art books, with hardbound coffee table books such as *From Myst to Riven* offering imagery from the CD-ROM adventure game series.

In the comics and graphic novels arena, 2D paint programs such as *Photoshop* are routinely used for coloring work, and 3D is starting to show up more and more. Back in 1990, Pepe Moreno's *Batman: Digital Justice* broke new ground for 3D in graphic novels, and today, comics such as *Gear Station* use 3D backgrounds for every issue. In addition, a new type of CD-ROM-based multimedia graphic novel appeared in the mid-nineties—it was called *Sinkha,* and it featured some of the most stunning 3D work seen at that time (see Figure. 1.11).

Research, Forensics, and Training

Business and marketing people have recognized the value of graphics to represent complex data for a long time, and this holds true for those in the scientific fields as well. Whereas a static bar chart is often adequate to communicate a page full of sales figures, that isn't always enough to represent research data. It may take the most sophisticated systems, gigabytes of data, and cutting edge programming to create a 3D animation representing a mathematical principle, natural phenomenon, or biological structure. One application of CG in a research environment is the modeling of weather systems. 3D graphics represent high and low pressure areas, air currents, precipitation, and other factors to accurately model a storm.

Medical research and techniques also benefit from new CG technology. One of the most impressive efforts has been the development of an amazingly accurate 3D model of the human body, with a level of detail never before imagined (see Figure 1.12). The process involved freezing cadavers and cutting them into extremely thin 1mm cross-sectional slices. The next step was to *digitize* the cross-sections, then use custom software to reassemble the sections into a completed model. This kind of imagery may have been the inspiration for the "sectioned horse" scene in the film *The Cell.*

> **definition**
>
> *digitize* The process of transforming images, objects, or sounds into a digital form that a computer can manipulate.

FIGURE 1.12

Body cross-section from the Visible Human™ Project, a digital database of volumetric data representing a complete adult male and female. Produced by the University of Colorado Center for Human Simulation.

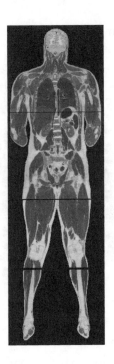

Forensic animation, which is usually a re-creation of an automobile accident or plane crash, has become very popular for demonstrating a complex series of events in courtroom situations. This type of animation uses evidence from a scene, eyewitness reports, and real-world physics to generate a simple (but as accurate as possible) representation of what happened.

The 3D images in *Time* magazine that showed the extent and range of the damage to and around the World Trade Centers are a good example of using 3D stills to clearly illustrate a point. Take a look at the print section of the gallery at www.lightwave3d.com to see the image.

Forensic animation is also becoming popular for reconstructing murders as well, but concern is being raised about this. Despite the fact that this type of animation is very simplistic, seeing a murder scene played out can still be very compelling to a jury, and they may give the explanation presented in this manner more weight in their deliberations than the same information presented in another manner.

Taking to the air for a moment, flight simulators make use of the latest real-time 3D technologies to accurately re-create the experience of piloting an aircraft. These systems are invaluable for training, particularly because dangerous weather conditions or mechanical failures can be programmed to occur. This enables the pilots to have an opportunity to experience an emergency situation that they may someday face in real life.

In keeping with the high-tech trend in weaponry, military training is also being done in simulators. For example, tank crews can maneuver on realistic battlefields that simulate conditions and enemy tactics half a world away.

Finally, no discussion of 3D research would be complete without mentioning *virtual reality (VR)*. The possibilities for this immersive technology are truly immense, ranging from remote control brain surgery to the most awesome movies and games imaginable. Unfortunately, the overblown hype that VR received early in its development has left it looking like a fever dream to many. Still, there is no insurmountable problem to prevent its full implementation some day, and in the mean time, it remains an interesting field with vast potential.

One of the most interesting novels about the potential of VR is Neal Stephenson's cyberpunk classic, *Snow Crash*. It's excellent reading for anyone interested in virtual reality and the future of online VR communities, or for anyone just hungry for some great science fiction. His novel *The Diamond Age* is another interesting read that's packed with imaginative technology.

Design and Engineering

3D modeling and animation have become popular in the field of architecture, as well. Much of the drawing work is still done with pencil or 2D drafting software, but some projects are realized in 3D as well. The resulting stills or animation are used as presentation materials and walkthroughs for clients, investors, and planning departments (see Figure 1.13). In some cases, 3D models are combined with background photos of the actual site, creating a very realistic rendering of how the building would look in its planned environment.

Figure 1.13

3D programs are often used to create architectural renderings. Buildings can be visualized accurately with the program, and the renderings composited with photographs of the site. Image courtesy of Guillermo M. Leal Llaguno, created in Discreet 3ds max.

3D modeling is very popular in product design companies, because it's possible to easily revise the models to meet a client's ever-changing tastes in color, style, and detail. Automobile designers frequently use 3D software for designing car bodies because it enables them to evaluate the complex interactions of light and shadow on the contours of the vehicle.

Solid modeling is a special form of 3D for engineering applications. It adds information about the material's weight, density, and tensile strength, as well as other real-world facts, to the model's *dataset*. Because all the physical information on the "real" materials is available, the bridge, ship hull, or machine part being modeled can be subjected to computer-simulated stresses. This enables engineers to evaluate the design and see whether it will perform as desired without having to build a physical prototype.

Also extensively used in the engineering field are *CAD/CAM* (Computer Aided Design/Computer Aided Manufacturing) programs, which enable the designer's drawings to be programmed directly into the machines that manufacture the parts. In addition, through the use of rapid prototyping techniques such as *laser stereo lithography*, actual physical prototypes of complex objects can be built quickly, layer by layer, out of a tank full of plastic goo. Another technique, *Fused Deposition Modeling (FDM)*, uses spools of thin plastic filament, which are fed into a heated computer-controlled tip and applied in thin layers to build up a part (see Figure 1.14). There is even talk of installing an FDM system like this in the International Space Station to

definition

dataset A collection of information that describes a 3D object. A dataset may contain 3D coordinates, material attributes, textures, and even animation.

definition

CAD/CAM CAD (Computer Aided Design) is the use of the computer and a drawing program to design a wide range of industrial products, ranging from machine parts to homes. CAM (Computer Aided Manufacturing) uses CAD drawings to control the equipment that manufactures the final object.

create simple replacement parts on-site. Who says *Star Trek's* replicators are science fiction?

FIGURE 1.14

Rapid prototyping devices like the Stratasys FDM Titan generate solid physical models of 3D objects out of polycarbonate, ABS plastic, and other materials. Depending on the method and materials used, the objects can be surprisingly durable. Image ©2000 Stratasys.

What Kinds of Jobs Are Available?

There are a lot of different job positions in the 3D field, and not all of them are artist positions. This can actually work for you if you're trying to break into the business. You may have the skills to get one of the other positions right away, and then get more CG experience working with the people and systems at hand. The following sections discuss the various available roles, starting with management.

Producer/Director

The titles and responsibilities of those working in the project management aspect of 3D vary widely, but in general, they break down as follows:

The *producer* is responsible for project schedules, budget, and communicating with the client. Producers may have been artists at one time, or they may come from project management positions in other fields and have gotten up to speed on the basics of 3D graphics.

The *director* is responsible for the creative vision behind the project and often manages the artists. Directors are usually experienced senior artists who are familiar with all aspects of graphics production.

Note that these positions are sometimes combined, or that certain responsibilities may fall onto others. For example, there may be a *creative director* who's in change of the project's overall look and feel, whereas an *art director* handles the day-to-day management of the artists. Depending on the situation, producers and directors may or may not actually do some of the artwork themselves.

Designer

Sometimes, the producer or director may designate a *designer* who is responsible for developing the visual look of the project. The designer may conceptualize the user interface, character designs, environments, mechanical devices, and so forth. Usually, the designer makes sketches that other artists use as a guide for their 3D constructions, and then may go on to execute some modeling work as well (see Figure 1.15).

FIGURE 1.15

Design sketch for the Terran Alliance fighters from the CD-ROM game *The Daedalus Encounter.* Drawing by Cody Chancellor, ©1995 Mechadeus.

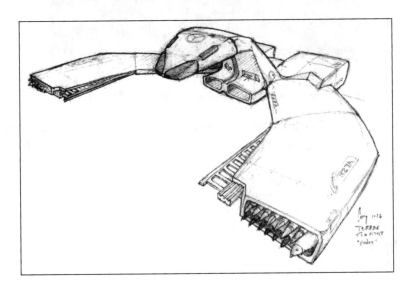

Modeler

The next three positions—modeler, mapper, and animator—are usually combined into modeler/animator or simply 3D artist. Still, they require different skill sets, and most artists are better at one aspect than the others. Also, they may be entirely different positions on some projects or in some companies, so they are presented separately here.

The *modeler* can be thought of as the sculptor (or construction worker) of the group, building 3D models according to the designer's sketches, or based on his or her own ideas (see Figure 1.16). Modelers have to be able to think in 3D terms, envisioning how to construct the desired object with the tools and techniques at hand. Some high school math and trigonometry may be useful now and then, but don't let that bother you—having an artist's sense of proportion and composition is far more important than knowing what a cosine is.

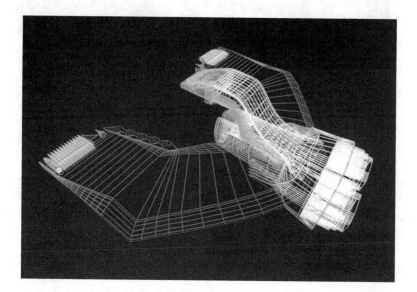

FIGURE 1.16

Modelers use 3D software, design sketches, and their own ideas to construct complex objects such as this fighter, which is based on the design shown in the previous figure. Image by Andy Murdock, ©1995 Mechadeus.

Mapper

Painting skills are the key to being a successful *mapper*, because the job requires creating textures (also called *maps*) in a 2D paint program such as Photoshop, applying the textures to 3D objects, and then evaluating and tweaking the results (see Figure 1.17). Good mappers are highly sought after for real-time 3D games of the *Quake III* or *Soul Calibur* variety. The models have to be kept relatively simple for speed, so much of the work of making them look detailed and interesting is up to the mapper.

FIGURE 1.17

Mappers use products such as Photoshop and Fractal Painter to create the surface textures that give 3D models a realistic appearance. Image by Andy Murdock, ©1995 Mechadeus.

Note that even in situations where mapping is handled by a separate artist, the modeler is often responsible for doing preliminary texture work to define the materials, and to confirm that the model is properly prepared for mapping.

Animator

Next to mapping, animation is probably one of the hardest skills to develop. On the surface, it can be said that the *animator* defines the motion of the models, cameras, and lighting according to storyboards and experience (see Figure 1.18). But in fact, the animator must

◆ Understand the structure and intricacies of the model

◆ Be familiar with the principles and practice of photography, lighting, and film direction

◆ Have the ability to breathe life into the scene through dramatic timing and realistic, fluid motion

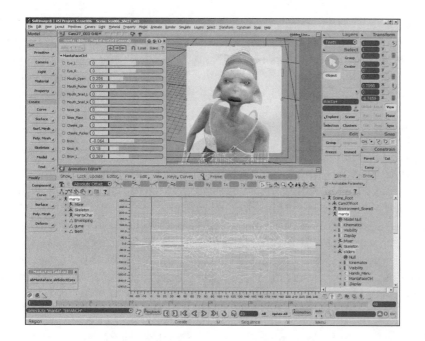

FIGURE 1.18

Using animation software
such as Softimage XSI,
animators breathe life
into scenes by imbuing
3D models—such as this
Manta alien—with char-
acter and personality.
Image courtesy of
Softimage Co.

To this end, the animator often becomes something of a performer, lum-
bering around his desk to get the feel for a giant's gait, or contorting her
face in a mirror to find just the right expression for a character.

These skills are so important that companies will often choose people with traditional *cel animation* experience over those with computer graphics training, preferring to teach experienced animators
about using 3D tools instead of the other way around.

Production Assistant

As with any business endeavor, there are always unglamorous jobs
like managing documents and files, running errands (usually
involving lunch), and making calls. In the CG industry, these tasks
often fall into the hands of the *production assistant*.

Now, you're probably wondering, "Why is he talking about this
job? I want to do animation, not go pick up somebody's lunch!"
Well, the fact is that some companies out there get their pick of top applicants with lots of experience, and it's almost impossible to get a job there
unless you have an "in." Becoming a production assistant, or even an

> **definition**
>
> *cel animation* The pro-
> cess of drawing and painting
> images on individual sheets of
> transparent celluloid that are
> later combined with back-
> ground art and photographed
> one at a time to make a
> traditional animated film.

unpaid intern, can get your foot in the door and your hands on some high-end gear. In a crunch (and *if* you know the tools), you may even find yourself doing some modeling or animation work to help the staff meet a deadline. This can lead to your name popping up when a new position appears. Hey, it happens!

Programmer

Although *programmers* obviously have very different training and responsibilities than artists, there is a surprising amount of overlap in some fields of computer graphics. In games, for example, artists have to work with programmers to ensure that the graphics meet the proper specifications. In other cases, the programmers may create custom tools for the artists to use, either as stand-alone software or as *plug-ins* that give commercial 3D software new features and effects. Come to think of it, where would 3D artists be if programmers hadn't developed the modeling and animation software in the first place?

What's It Like to Be a 3D Artist?

Now that you've been introduced to some of the different jobs in the CG field, let's take a look at what life as a 3D artist is all about. My employment experience is mostly in the multimedia and game development arena, so keep in mind that the conditions in other fields are likely to be somewhat different.

People and Environment

There are all kinds of people in the world, and you'll find a representative sample in the graphics industry as well. Yes, everything from people who never emerge from their darkened offices unless their systems go down, to iron-fisted, whip-cracking tyrants (not me, of course). Mutants aside, however, 3D artists tend to be a fairly homogenous group, usually ranging from their early 20s to late 30s, and many have similar interests. These may include computer gaming, comics, action figures, Tim Burton films, motorcycles, *anime*, rock bands, and eating ethnic foods, to name a few.

Back in 1994 when I was directing *The Daedalus Encounter*, I was introduced to Japanese animation—*anime*—by one of the artists on the project. I was immediately taken in by the great look, unique stories, and mysterious culture portrayed in many of the shows. I watched hundreds (if not thousands) of different anime titles and studied the Japanese approach to filmmaking, its culture and language. My hobby eventually paid off professionally as well—I was able to direct some game cinematics for a Japanese game project as well as work with top character designer Toshihiro Kawamoto on an original animated show for the Web.

As far as workplaces go, it depends on the company, but art departments tend to be mostly weird, fun environments. Desks and systems are cluttered with action figures, generally non-lethal projectile weapons, and stacks of manuals, magazines, and unread memos (see Figure 1.19). Music plays, bizarre newspaper clippings, posters, and photos adorn the walls, and leftover pizza lurks atop the microwave (but usually not for long).

FIGURE 1.19

3D artist "Goose" Ramirez ponders a project at his toy-laden Mondo Media workstation.

One of the best things about a good art environment is that the artists can learn from each other and get answers to questions much more quickly and easily than by searching through a manual. On the other hand, there may be times when you need to work in a quiet or solitary office, and a good workplace provides for this as well. With this in mind, some companies allow you to work at home on occasion, so you can spend that extra hour or two with your nose pressed against the monitor.

In any business that has deadlines, the hours tend to be long from time to time, with 40-50 hour weeks being typical. During a serious end-of project crunch, that figure can rise to 90 hours or more, and I can recall at least one occasion where I put in a 36-hour "day." Still, if you're determined and stay productive all day, it's possible to keep a normal schedule.

For those with nasty commutes, children, or other responsibilities, companies may make flexible schedules available. At times, this can even be a very desirable thing for the company itself, because those working a late shift can make use of equipment that might otherwise sit idle.

So, you're probably wondering, "When I'm a 3D artist, will I be able to afford a Ferrari like all those id software guys?" Well, if you come up with the next *Doom* or *Quake*, maybe. Pay runs the gamut, but artists can expect to make between $30-60K or more depending on experience. In some cases, art directors, producers, and other art management types can pull down $60-120K or more.

The Production Process

Although much of the following information will be discussed in much greater detail later in the book, this seems like an appropriate spot to talk about what goes on in a production environment. First of all, most production houses are *service businesses*—that is, they bid on work that a client brings in.

To explain what they want, clients may have a script, storyboards, and designs that they present, or they may simply have a basic idea of what they want and need the production house to help design it as part of the job.

Much of the time, what clients want would cost far more than what they're willing to pay, so there's usually a period where the client's expectations are brought more in line with reality, and negotiations over the budget, timeline, and scope of work take place. The people usually involved in such negotiations are the client and the producer and director that the production house assigns to the project. At the end of such negotiations, the project has been pared down to a manageable and budgetary feasible size— at least sometimes, anyway.

After the script and storyboards have been created or revised, the producer and/or director select the team and get started on the project. In some cases, outside talent has to be brought in for some specialized role or simply because there aren't enough people on staff to handle the project.

The producer carefully watches the budget and timeline, and the weight often falls on the artists to get the shots or models the producer has assigned to them done more quickly than they would like. During this process, the director sometimes has to decide how to reallocate resources or adjust the shot list to keep the project on track.

At various points in the production process, the client may come into the studio to review the work done so far. The director and producer often accompany the client around to the artists' workstations and have them show off their work in various stages of completion. Usually, the client asks for this or that to be changed, and it's up to the producer to see whether the requests are the responsibility of the production house, or whether they're outside the original scope of the bid and require a "change order," which means an extra charge to the client.

As the artists generate shots, an editor (sometimes the director himself) takes the shots and assembles them together to ensure that the piece flows properly and is telling the story in an interesting and understandable way. This "rough cut" continues to improve as the shots get more refined and complete.

When the rough cut is far enough along so that the director and client are confident that the shots will not be changed, it may go off to the Sound Department for music and effects. After all the shots are finalized, they're combined with the completed audio and presented to the client for final approval. The staff makes a few tweaks, and it's a wrap!

Interviews with Two Production Artists

Now that you have a grounding in the kind of people, jobs, and project workflow you're likely to encounter in a production environment, let's spend some time talking to two production artists who have conquered the CG learning curve and have made it into the ranks of professional 3D artists: Sheldon Whittaker and Cindy Yamauchi.

Interview with 3D Artist Sheldon Whittaker

Sheldon Whittaker was born in 1975 in Christchurch, New Zealand. (In case your geography is a bit rusty, New Zealand is made up of a group of three islands in the southern Pacific Ocean). As a child, he showed his interest in art by drawing Smurfs on the walls of his parents' home. His interest in drawing and painting continued through the years, and at the time of this writing, he had just started his first full-time job in 3D as a Maya animator in Wellington, New Zealand.

I came into contact with Sheldon when he wrote me an email about the first edition of this book. We chatted about breaking into the business, discussed software and techniques, and continued to keep in touch over the years. I'm very pleased to have him share his experiences and examples of his work in this new edition.

Q: What made you want to get into 3D?

A: Star Wars! My first memorable cinematic experience was when I was just a little boy, and my father took me to see *The Empire Strikes Back*. It was so cool! All I can remember of that night was bright lights, snow, a snow monster, and some guy with asthma, but it made a huge impression on me. From that day on, I was drawn to science fiction like a moth to a porch light. I went for anything that had blazing special effects and "impossible" cinematography…anything that made me wonder, 'How did they *do* that?' I would look for any behind-the-scenes specials on TV, especially ones featuring George Lucas films. But in those days, I was resigned to the fact that I would never learn special effects or filmmaking in quaint little New Zealand.

At least, that was until a few years back, when a new show appeared on New Zealand television, called *Babylon 5*. It was obvious that the effects were done with 3D graphics, but it looked good in its day. Around that time I had purchased a new PC—a Pentium 75 with a whopping 16MB of RAM. Man, it seemed so incredibly fast! I began to buy PC magazines, and in one article I saw a write-up on Babylon 5 and how they were doing the effects with LightWave 3D. "That's cool," I thought. Following the article was an advertisement for LightWave, which cost around $1500.00 at the time. Suddenly I realized then that the hardware and software needed to get into 3D animation were becoming accessible, and that I would finally be able to experiment with making the movie-style special effects I was so passionate about, even if it was just as a hobby.

Not one to be easily intimidated, I contacted various professionals and picked their brains for info on getting started. They told me that it would take me at least three to four years to get to a professional level, and that if it was something I really wanted to do, I should pursue it with passion and vigor.

Q: How did you learn to do 3D modeling and animation? What software packages were you attracted to, and why?

A: Four years ago, learning 3D modeling and animation in a place like New Zealand was no easy task. First I checked the colleges and polytechnic institutes, but none of them were offering any kind of substantial course in computer graphics. As a result, I had to teach myself.

I bought a book called *3D Graphics & Animation: From Starting Up to Standing Out* by some guy named Mark Giambruno. The book was very well structured for a beginner, as it walked me through system and software choices. It also laid out a methodical learning process, from theory to hardware and software to tools—one that I still use when learning new software.

I feel as though I made some poor choices in choosing software at first, but I think those experiences helped to improve the way I work today. I could not afford LightWave, so I started off with a free copy of Macromedia Extreme 3D. I had moved up to a Mac 5500/250 603e with 128MB RAM at that time, but there still wasn't a lot of 3D software available for Macs back then. It had a scan-line renderer and spline-based surface modeling tools that enabled me to start learning about 3D modeling, animation, and rendering.

Within a few months, I had outgrown Extreme 3D and was seduced by the salesman at the local Mac store into buying Strata Studio Pro. I chose this package mainly because it had very nice ray-tracing and radiosity rendering capabilities. It felt like a definite step up in quality over the results I was getting with Extreme 3D, but unfortunately it lacked a robust set of modeling and animation tools. I was very interested in organic modeling, which the package was ill equipped for, so I became frustrated with Strata Studio after about a year. Still, I do give it credit for forcing me to find unique solutions to problems, instead of just looking for some plug-in or a magic button that creates the desired result for you. Yes, I had discovered "workarounds," the magnificent process by which you learn to use the tools you have to invent new ways of getting the results you want.

After Studio Strata Pro, I moved on to another Mac software package, Electric Image, which suited my needs until sometime in 2000. That was when I read that a college in town was offering a general multimedia and web design course that included a brief taste of Alias|Wavefront Maya v2.5. I approached the head of the multimedia department and asked if there was any way I could learn Maya on a full-time basis. He told me that they were planning to run a four-day intensive introductory course in Maya, and I jumped at the chance. It was my first taste of what a full-blown professional modeling and animation system could do. The next year, I heard that another local school, Christchurch Polytechnic, was offering a year-long, full-time certificate course in 3D animation. They had a few seats of Maya there, and I happily enrolled. I loved having so much access to a Maya-equipped system, but was a bit disappointed that the instructor was more of a 3D Studio MAX guy and didn't know Maya as well as I would have liked.

I like Maya because it has a complete set of NURBS and polygonal modeling tools, including subdivided surfaces. With its full and integrated set of animation tools, the potential is there to do just about anything you want. Compared to the packages I used before, Maya's capabilities seem truly limitless to me right now. If there's something I want to do, I know that there are at least four ways to approach it, and if the tools aren't there, I can easily come up with a workaround to accomplish the task. Maya also has a very powerful renderer that enables users to create fantastic images with superb quality if they know how to use it. I have heard many people remark that the render quality isn't that great, but I think that's maybe because they're looking for a magic button.

Q: What was the most difficult part of learning process for you?

A: Getting my head around 3D space. The whole process of doing 3D has really required me to access a lot more of my own "RAM." I've learned about planning ahead, moving a project through the production pipeline, and keeping track of every object and process within a scene so I know what everything does. I found this kind of mental discipline was the hardest part for me.

Q: You've learned a lot of different 3D programs. What methods of learning new software are most effective for you?

A: I find that a very methodical method of learning suits me best. I've been told that I have a logical, sort of mechanical approach to planning. There are five steps I take when learning a new package:

1. *Study the manuals.* This is basically an overview and refresher course in 3D to help learn the program's workflow. Each 3D package is pretty much the same in that they all enable you to model, texture, animate, and render in one way or another. Of course, they all have a unique flow and approach to these processes, so the first thing I like to do is to figure out where the tools are, what they do in theory, and what the packages' overall strengths and capabilities are.

2. *Select a project.* I always attack a formidable project that scares me a bit, so I force myself to learn. I also tell people what I'm working on so that I feel like I have to get on with it or appear as though I'm procrastinating.

3. *Do some modeling.* I build all the models for the project so that I learn about all the modeling tools. The manuals come into play all the time, and I actually think they're cool because I sometimes find a function mentioned in one line here or there that I might never have found just by skimming the book or by playing around with the program.

4. *Texture the models.* Some people seem to prefer animating before they do the texture work, or do it at the same time as the animation. I like to do textures before animating, so I can learn all the texture tools and spot any rendering issues.

5. *Do the animation.* This step improves my overall animation skills, as well as shows me how the package approaches the animation process.

Q: What was it like preparing for and finding a job?

A: It was nerve-racking. I had all kinds of thoughts going through my head, like, "What if, after all my time and effort, nobody likes my work?" and, "What if I can't hack it in a competitive industry?" Stuff like that. Yeah, preparing was a tough job. I kept asking myself whether I was ready. I was aware that many people try to enter the industry too quickly and get freaked out, or they just can't cut it and end up making matters worse for themselves when they are ready. Personally, I felt that I was ready, but that's not to say that I didn't have any doubts. I think that you just know when you're finally ready—when you get past your own ego, and can just be honest with yourself and say, "Yes!" or, "No, not yet."

Landing my first job was actually a combination of boldness and a stroke of luck. I basically started looking around out there while I was still studying in college, and approached a few postproduction houses. One of them saw some potential in my work, and gave me a chance to prove myself by giving me a freelance job modeling and animating a character for an advertisement. I felt really lucky to get an opportunity like that, as I knew they were taking a chance on me. Over the course of the project, they decided to employ me full time as their primary Maya animator.

Q: So where do you work now, and what's it like?

A: A postproduction facility called 2D Post. We do video editing for film productions, corporate presentations, television advertising, and 2D and 3D animation and special effects for film and broadcast. My bosses are David Tingy and Darren Smith. I know what you must be thinking: "2D? I thought you did 3D!" Well, the 3D department of 2D Post consists of one seat of Maya and one seat of LightWave. We're pretty new, but are making a pretty good go of getting new 3D work around these parts.

So, what is it like? It's a madhouse! At first I was a little shocked by the pace of things and the fact that my little ego had no real play in a production environment. Still, after an adjustment period where I mellowed out and learned to work in a team situation, I've found that having a group giving their input and skills on a project really pushes the quality up.

It's so awesome to be doing this kind of work, and I'm learning heaps of new things. I have access to the edit suites so I can expand my skill base, not to mention learning from the editors, producers, directors, and designers here. We also have a fabulous espresso machine to keep the juices flowing.

Q: Once you started working, what sort of things did you find surprising, or didn't know you would be dealing with?

A: Dealing with communication issues between supervisors, other 3D guys, and the client. For example, learning to understand and visualize what they want to see, as opposed to what I want to see. Of course, as the guy doing the work, I can slip a little of what I want to see in here and there. Artistic license, you know.

The other thing that surprised me was the speed at which you have to work on certain jobs. You don't always get to have a big budget and the relaxed deadline; sometimes, you have to rush a job and work around the clock. At times like that, you just have to plug an I.V. bottle full of caffeine into the old vein and keep rolling.

Q: If you had to prepare for a job in 3D all over again, would you do anything different?

A: I would try to put together better ammo for my interviews. My reel was almost nonexistent before, but it's filling up nicely now as I tackle newer and more sophisticated jobs.

Q: Do you have a "dream project" that you'd like to see completed?

A: Yes, I have a few kick-ass story ideas that I'm beginning to put down on paper, and I would love to get a team of people together with funding to create an all-3D motion picture. The other thing I'd like to do is develop a revolutionary PS/2 game I've been planning.

Q: Where would you like to be in five years?

A: Five years? Well, right now my plan is to remain here for the next two years to gain experience and learn all I can in that time to level up my skills. I'd also like to save up some money and take the Maya instructor certification courses so I can learn all there is to learn about it (assuming I don't run into a program I like even better). After that, I'd like to work in the film industry in either the U.S. or China for a few years, after which I would like to return to New Zealand to start a family, teach a new generation what I have learned in my years, and start a business. That last part exceeds five years a bit, but that's the plan for now!

Thanks again for taking the time to share your thoughts and experiences with us, Sheldon.

Interview with Animator Cindy Yamauchi

Cindy H. Yamauchi was born in Hawaii and is one of the few Americans that have actually worked as an animator in Japan. She started working part-time as an animator while she was still in high school, and spent the next twelve years in the anime industry, working on well-known titles such as *Akira, Record of Lodoss War,* and *Ranma 1/2.* She then returned home to Hawaii, where she landed a job doing 3D character animation on *Final Fantasy: The Spirits Within.* She currently resides in San Francisco, working as a freelance artist and running her own artist referral and representative business. One of her current projects involves helping an anime studio in

Japan interface with a U.S. anime publishing company that has licensed some of its titles.

I met Cindy just as she was wrapping up her work on the *Final Fantasy* movie. At the time, I was working on developing the look and feel for a 2D Flash series for the web called *Spiral*. I wanted the show to have an authentic anime look, and Cindy's skills were perfect for the job. Although neither of us work for Mondo Media anymore, we've kept in touch and hope to collaborate on some anime-related projects in the future.

Q: How did you get into 2D animation, and particularly into doing anime?

A: I was a military brat—my dad had been in the service, then worked as a civilian in Japan after that. Looking back, I suppose that environment had a great influence on me. I grew up watching a lot of Japanese TV programs, including anime.

I drew a lot as a kid. I've always been into creating stories, and for me, drawing was just another tool for telling a story. My parents mistook my sketching for artistic talent and enrolled me into several art classes. To this day, I rarely draw for the sake of drawing—I like to have some project that I'm clearly focused on before I break out the pencils.

When I was in high school, my friends and I started a manga club—it's a group that gets together to make their own comics—but it didn't last too long. At the time, I totally lacked the discipline to meet deadlines. I'm good at meeting deadlines now, though!

About that time, one of my friends—a fifteen-year-old who was a big *Grandizer* anime fan—decided to get into the business instead of attending high school (attending high school is not mandatory in Japan). One day she went to interview for an animation studio job, and I tagged along just for fun (hey, I was just a kid). Anyway, she was hired full-time as an in-betweener—an animator who "fills in" the missing poses between the ones the key animators draw. Much to my surprise, I ended up getting hired as a part-timer doing the same thing. The funny thing is, I didn't have any art samples or even a resume with me. There's not much to write on your resume when you're sixteen anyway, and I was totally clueless—and therefore fearless—when it came to job interviews. I can't recall what their requirements were, but I passed the interview. All of a sudden, I was an animator!

Q: What anime projects did you work on in Japan?

A: I was a key animator on *Akira*, *Ranma 1/2*, and *Venus Wars*, and worked as either a key animator or assistant animation director on *Dirty Pair TV*, *Youtouden*, *Tokyo Vice*, *Gundam ZZ*, *Onisama e... (Brother, Dear Brother)*, *Cleopatra D.C.*, *Hokuto no Ken TV (Fist of the Northstar)*, and many others. The last anime project I worked on was *Record of Lodoss Wars*. I was the animation director on the first OVA episode, and a key animator for the other episodes. When these titles were released in English, I went out and bought them, but I was crushed to discover that the translators almost always had my name spelled wrong in the credits. It should read "Hideko Yamauchi," you guys! Very depressing.

Q: What made you decide to get into 3D animation?

A: I never really "decided" to get into 3D; it just happened. To me, 3D is just another tool that I happened to be introduced to during my animation career, when I went to work on the *Final Fantasy* movie. My interest lies in filmmaking, particularly animated films, so I'm open to any new tools that help me do that. All that matters is that I enjoy the process and am happy with the results.

Q: How did you end up working on the *Final Fantasy* movie?

A: After spending good part of my youth doing "slave labor" on anime productions, I decided to leave my 2D animation career behind. I moved back to my home state of Hawaii and had started a whole new career in the travel industry. A few years went by, and one day I got a phone call from Kimura-san, who I met once back in my animation days. He had gotten my number from my old boss back when I was working as an animation instructor in Indonesia. Kimura-san told me that he was living in Hawaii now and working for a company called Square USA, and just wanted to let me know they were looking for animators. Later, I got a call from another person at Square, Yaginuma-san, who I worked with as a key animator on *Battle Royal High School* and *Gosenzo-sama Ban Banzai*. He wanted to see whether I might be interested in coming on board with Square. The next day, the producer called me, and I promised that I'd drop by to say hello, take a tour of the company, and talk about their job opening.

At that time, I had no experience in 3D at all—and consequently no demo reel—so I dug out some of my old animation work and walked into the studio without really taking the whole thing too seriously. As it turned out, Square was looking for anime-style animators and would train them to use

Maya 3D software. This was based on an assumption that it is easier to teach animators how to use a software package then to train someone who knows the software how to be a good animator. Anyway, one of the interviewers was a well-known anime artist who had worked on *Akira*. He seemed to like the artwork I brought with me, and I was hired that day. Eventually, I ended up doing animation on various characters for the film.

The whole thing grew out of a series of lucky coincidences, as well as knowing people. Who would have guessed that a Japanese game company would build an animation studio in Hawaii, and that people I'd worked with back in my anime days would end up working there? I was just at the right place at the right time. It also shows the importance of networking with people in your industry.

Q: So did you find that your experience in traditional 2D cel animation made it easier for you to make the transition to 3D?

A: Yes, I think so. The fundamentals of animation—timing, movement, weight, and so on—are the same regardless of the technique. That's probably why a lot of companies doing 3D animation prefer to hire artists with experience in traditional animation. 3D also shares the same terminology with 2D when it comes to animation and camerawork, and that made the overall process easier to understand.

Q: You said you had no experience in 3D at the time you interviewed at Square. How did you learn to do 3D animation, and which software packages did you study?

A: I learned everything I know about 3D through on-the-job training in preparation for working on the *Final Fantasy* movie. I had no idea how to use the Maya 3D software or Unix-based computers back then, and the only real training tool I received was a set of manuals. In my case, plodding through the manuals was the most difficult part of learning process. Fortunately, I was always surrounded by a group of 3D geniuses who provided me with answers whenever I was stumped. It was an ideal environment for a beginner.

Q: After you started working in 3D, what sort of things did you find surprising?

A: In 2D animation, especially in anime style, there is a lot of exaggeration involved in both timing and drawing actions. The same methods can be applied to 3D, but I found it rather difficult to get the same kinds of results.

3D isn't as malleable as 2D, where you can tweak a character or movement around quite a bit to get the desired effect.

Q: What are your thoughts on the future of 3D animated television and films?

A: For television, I'm just hoping the producers of 3D shows will not make the same mistakes 2D did in terms of budget and scheduling. Most 2D television series are outsourced to production overseas, and hardly anything is animated here in the U.S. I suppose it makes business sense to cut the costs, but it's a sad situation for creators and artists here.

Oh, and I would definitely like to see more 3D films that *don't* feature talking animals or babies.

My thanks go out to Cindy for sharing her knowledge and experiences with us in this interview.

How Do I Learn More about the Field?

Thankfully, 3D graphics is still a field where what you can do is more important than where you went to school or who you worked for in the past. This makes options like learning on your own feasible and practical, although professional training can open some doors for you, as you'll see in the following sections.

Teaching Yourself

The fact that you're reading this book indicates that you're planning to learn at least some of the aspects of 3D on your own, so let me tell you about my own experience with this method.

I started out in computer graphics by purchasing some low-cost hardware and software back in 1982 and just playing with it. My system of choice was the Atari 800, a graphics powerhouse with an 8-bit processor running at 1.7MHz and featuring four on-screen colors from a palette of sixteen, plus a whopping 48K of RAM. I spent the first weekend learning BASIC, and then wrote a little program that made an animated UFO zap a plane. Later, my younger brother reworked my code for the final project in his programming class, resulting in the seminal *Nuclear Destruction of Elko, Nevada*, wherein my UFO obliterated a sleepy desert town. The effort netted the admiration of his teacher and classmates, not to mention an A.

By the way, *my* contribution to the project was never mentioned, teaching me an early and valuable lesson about copyrights and intellectual property. To be fair, he did make up for it later by springing for half of a cassette data recorder (floppy drives were over $400 at the time). After that, we didn't have to write down our code and manually re-enter it every time the machine was rebooted. Whoo-hoo!

At any rate, by simply messing around with the Atari 800, and later with an Atari 512 ST and an Apple Macintosh IIcx, I was able to teach myself the principles of computer graphics and 2D/3D animation. I used them to create some portfolio pieces as well, and all that gave me a good start when I decided to enter CG as a career.

Videos

Instructional videos are videotaped courses in using a given software package, and are a good alternative to taking classes if no school teaches 3D in your area. Although you'll have to hunt around in trade magazines or online for instructional videos, you can also find lots of useful information in the documentaries and commentaries provided with many films released in DVD format. These "making-of" documentaries are good tools for learning about all phases of feature film production and effects, much of which is applicable to professional 3D animation work.

Schools

These days, a number of private and public schools offer computer graphics and 3D modeling classes. Although the equipment isn't always state of the art, schools do offer the advantages of having professionals available to answer questions, and they provide the student access to a number of different software packages. They also offer training in related subjects such as storyboarding, design for multimedia, and videographics, which help to round out your knowledge of the field.

Public schools, such as community colleges, tend to be less expensive and more accessible to most, with the downside being that they may require prerequisites before you can take the classes you want. It also may take longer to work through a CG curriculum in a semester-based system. Private schools, although more expensive and much less common than community colleges, usually offer more intensive, shorter-term classes.

In some cases, the schools act as a pipeline to businesses that look for new talent. While I was attending the Computer Arts Institute (CAI) in San Francisco, the staff at the school recommended me to a local multimedia company that was looking for more artists. As a result of portfolio work I had done on my own and at the school, I secured Mondo Media as one of my first clients, and they later hired me full-time.

For a list of public and private schools offering 3D training, see Appendix D, "Resources," on the companion CD-ROM.

Seminars, Shows, and Organizations

For the fledgling 3D artist, going to a CG-related convention is *de rigueur*. Such conventions usually offer hands-on workshops, seminars, and trade shows. The seminars are often very expensive, running hundreds or even thousands of dollars, but they can be an excellent source for the most current information and training. If you can't manage the bucks to attend all the seminars, getting a pass to the trade show floor usually costs less than a hundred dollars (and you may even be able to get free or discount passes if you subscribe to some of the CG trade magazines). The show floor can provide a wealth of interesting presentations, contact information, four-color brochures, and kitschy souvenirs.

Most of the CG conventions are sponsored by organizations involved in or related to the computer graphics field. Membership in these organizations may provide you with free publications, discounts on the shows and travel, and other benefits. They also may guarantee you a lifetime of CG-related direct mail offers.

There are a lot of different conventions, so here are some of my suggestions:

◆ **SIGGRAPH.** Everyone should try to attend this computer graphics Mecca, which is sponsored twice a year in various locations by the ACM (Association for Computing Machinery). Here, you will see the latest in hardware, software, and animation from all over the world. The ACM also has local SIGGRAPH (Special Interest Group GRAPHics) chapters that offer special presentations by pros in the field.

◆ **CGDC.** The Computer Game Developers Conference is a must-see for those in the gaming field. It's pretty expensive to attend, but well worth the money if you're in the biz.

- **E3.** Infotainment World (associated with *PC Games* magazine) sponsors the Electronic Entertainment Expo, which is another great show to attend if you're in the video game biz. It doesn't offer the conferences or contacts that the CGDC does, and it is mostly a massive trade show for showcasing new games and platforms. It is also, without a doubt, the loudest convention I've ever attended; be sure to bring earplugs to this one.

- **NAB.** For those interested in the television industry, the National Association of Broadcasters show pays a fair amount of attention to computer graphics.

In addition to these shows, platform-specific events such as MacWorld, PCWorld, and others have a lot to offer as well, and are worth attending for getting an overview of what's out there. They also are a good place to pick up hardware and software bargains.

Finally, local user groups are a good source of information and contacts in your area. These groups often meet at public auditoriums or at local software stores. If you happen to live near large hardware or software firms, you also may find corporate user groups that meet at the facility. Frequently, these groups get the opportunity to see and hear about the company's latest offerings.

Books and Periodicals

When it comes to getting concentrated, current information at an economical price, it's tough to beat books and magazines. In addition to the broadly scoped 3D book you hold in your hands, you may want to get a meaty product-specific reference after you have settled on a software package. For those who plan to work as freelance artists and contractors, you can find small business guides that specifically deal with the graphic arts field. In addition, collections of CG artwork are available to provide ideas and inspiration.

As far as magazines go, everyone should get *Computer Graphics World (CGW)*, which provides excellent coverage of the CG field. I also recommend *Animation* magazine for a broader picture of animation news. *Next Generation* and *PC Gamer* are good for people in the games biz, and *Wired* covers a broad spectrum of technology issues. If you're interested in special effects for film or broadcast applications, then *Cinefantastique*, *Starlog*, and

Cinescape are worth looking into. If you want the real nuts-and-bolts of the SFX field, however, you can't beat *Cinefex*—it's what the industry pros read.

See Appendix C, "Recommended References," (on the CD-ROM) for a list of suggested books and magazines, as well as publisher information.

The Web

Over the past few years, the web has exploded as a ready source of information about every subject imaginable, including 3D graphics. Information about 3D hardware, software, and techniques is plentiful, and there are tons of webzines, user forums, tutorials, online galleries, and personal websites to browse and learn from. Where to start? Here are some suggestions to get you started:

◆ 3D Site (www.3dsite.com) is a fast link site to resources on the web.

◆ CG Channel (www.cgchannel.com) is an attractive site with news, reviews, articles, and tutorials.

◆ Renderosity (www.renderosity.com) offers program-specific user files and a large collection of reasonably priced models, maps, and animation files offered up for sale by users of the site.

◆ VFXPro (www.vfxpro.com) has news and job listings for industry professionals.

See Appendix D on the CD-ROM for a lot more sites.

Internships

Sometimes, students or others with knowledge but little practical experience opt for an *internship* with a company. *Intern* positions offer either little or no pay, and mix production assistant-type jobs with graphics work. This situation can be a good way to get started if you can get along for a while without much money. Still, take advantage of every opportunity to develop your skills and portfolio so that you can move into a paid position as quickly as possible.

Summary

In this first chapter, you've had a look behind the computer screen at what 3D graphics are, as well as seen the broad range of applications that use 3D. You've also learned about the kinds of jobs that are available in the field, what it's like to be a 3D artist, and some different ways to learn more about computer graphics. The overview provided in this chapter gives you a good foundation from which to explore the more specific issues of 3D that you'll be looking at shortly.

In the next chapter, you'll learn about making the leap from 2D to 3D and explore the principles of 3D graphics. The next chapter includes a bunch of theory and graphs and stuff, but don't worry. After you have a good grounding in the fundamentals, you'll be getting into the cool parts!

CHAPTER 2

Delving into Cyberspace

"Darcron ship above Shadoowm City." Image from the book *Hyleyn* ©2000
Marco Patrito/Virtual Views.

"*N*ow then, lad—as I was saying, the navigational references along The Virtual Path are akin to the cardinal points of the compass. Here, you can see that the Northern direction is not unlike the…*"

The student's mind wandered as the Master continued with his tutelage, drawing diagrams and formulae on the large slate at the front of the chamber. The student was eager to get back to working with his Glowing Pool, where he had conjured some simple forms earlier that morning.

The Master was still facing the slate, so the student turned to watch the Pool as the primitive forms floated gently above it. Simply experimenting with the Pool had taught him much, and he was ready to try making a more complex object, perhaps a castle turret…

Suddenly, a large amber globe struck the table in front of him, jarring the student out of his reverie. His eyes followed the gnarled wooden staff attached to the globe until he saw the even more gnarled hand of the Master holding it. The old man scowled at him, obviously displeased.

"So, eager to return to the practical, are we?" the Master said, lifting the end of the staff from the table and absent-mindedly examining the translucent globe for scratches. "No need of all this boring theory and background have you."

The student swallowed hard and tried to blurt out an apology, but the Master interrupted him.

"No, no…perhaps you're right," the old man said, walking slowly toward the student's Glowing Pool. "Here, why not show me your skills? Conjure something for me." With that, the Master settled heavily in a chair near the Pool and gazed, unblinking, at the student.

The lad got up and hurried to the Glowing Pool. "Uh, how about a…castle turret?" he asked. The Master nodded with an oddly crooked smile and waited.

Beads of sweat began forming on the student's forehead as he dispelled the basic forms he had built before. Forcing himself to be calm, he began to summon a cylinder that would form the walls of the turret. Wisps of light emerged from the Pool, weaving a gossamer tube that towered above their heads. Pleased, the student stole a glance at the Master, who only grunted. His confidence building, the student started to summon a roof for the structure.

"Wha..." gasped the student as the roof appeared, but tipped on its side, as though it had fallen from the turret. He tried to rotate it into an upright position, but it only spun around like a top. The beads of sweat turned into rivulets as the student attempted numerous adjustments to turn the roof, then gave up and tried to simply move the roof to the top of the cylinder instead. He commanded it to rise up, but instead it skidded sideways, ending up a few inches from the Master's nose. He tried to pull it back toward the tower, but this time it flew up to the ceiling. Adjustment after adjustment sent the wayward roof zigzagging around the room. Finally, an ill-chosen command sent it hurtling back into the Glowing Pool, where it shattered into a spray of brilliant lights.

The Master turned toward the student and raised a solitary eyebrow.

"I..." stammered the lad, "I...believe you were talking about cardinal points, Master?"

Expanding from 2D to 3D

As our unfortunate student found out, working with 3D graphics can be frustrating if you don't have a solid handle on the principles and theory involved. True, it's nowhere near as interesting as playing around with the software, but understanding it now will save you a lot of time and trouble later on.

The easiest way to start is to examine how 2D and 3D skills overlap. If you have experience with Adobe Illustrator or another drawing program, you can make good use of what you already know about working with 2D shapes. As you recall from Chapter 1, the main difference between 2D and 3D is depth. 2D drawings have only height and width—no depth whatsoever. Although objects can be drawn in 2D so that they *appear* as though they are 3D, if you want to change the perspective or viewpoint in any way, you have to redraw the object from scratch (see Figure 2.1).

FIGURE 2.1

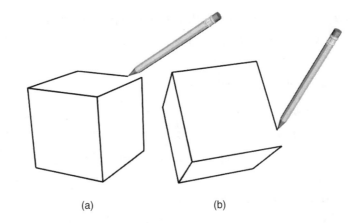

(a)   (b)

Because 3D objects have depth (at least inside your computer), you have to "draw" them only once; then you can view them from any angle or perspective without starting from scratch. Also, 3D programs automatically calculate the proper highlight and shadow information for a scene based on how you arrange the objects and lighting (see Figure 2.2).

FIGURE 2.2

After an object has been constructed in a 3D program, it can be given color and texture, lit, and then rendered from any angle.

In a sense, then, 3D programs not only redraw your subject from any angle you choose, they also create a painting of it based on the colors, textures, and lighting that you decided upon when you built and texture-mapped the model. With all those benefits, it's no wonder many artists rarely go back to traditional drawing and painting after they've gotten into 3D.

Now, although there are some major differences between 2D and 3D, many of the 2D drawing tools you may be familiar with are implemented in 3D programs as well. Tools such as the freehand pencil, Bezier pen, circles, arcs, polylines, polygons, lassos, and so forth are usually available, and work in much the same way as their 2D counterparts. The difference here is that instead of being used to create a finished shape in a 2D environment, these tools are used as a starting point for creating a 3D object. Some of the most common 3D forms that start with a 2D shape are lofts, sweeps, lathes, and extrudes. Exactly what they are and how they are constructed is discussed in Chapter 3, but the important thing to remember for now is that they rely heavily on 2D drawing techniques.

Another similarity between 2D and 3D software is the concept of layers. A *layer* in the 2D world is like a clear acetate sheet that you draw or paint on. By adding other layers (or sheets of acetate) to a 2D image, you can add additional elements in front of or behind the initial layer (see Figure 2.3).

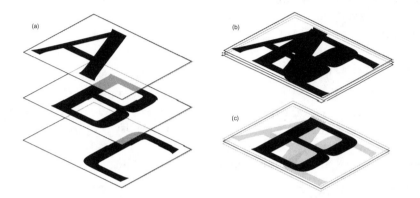

FIGURE 2.3

2D programs enable you to create drawings in layers, which is not unlike drawing on sheets of acetate. Elements can then be edited individually, without the visual clutter of unnecessary layers.

Because the layers are all separate, you also can change things on one layer without affecting any of the others. You also can place reference images in the background layer and trace over them in the foreground, a bit like using a light box to trace over a sketch. One of the biggest advantages to working with layers is that you can turn them on or off to reduce clutter on the screen. You can also "gray out" (make translucent) a layer to keep it visible for reference but make it less obtrusive.

Although 3D programs don't usually have layers in the way that a 2D program does, they do enable you to hide or "lock" objects to make isolating and editing a single object easier.

As with their 2D cousins, 3D programs use *groups* to define a collection of objects that can be dealt with as a whole. Grouping enables the user to choose a related collection of objects, and then temporarily combine them into a single unit. This makes it much easier to move, scale, or do other operations to the group, because you don't have to choose each element individually every time you want to do something to them all. The user can also add, remove, and reassign objects to or from a particular group as desired.

Principles of 3D Graphics

In Chapter 1, an imaginary camcorder was used to record the video of a room full of objects as an analogy for how 3D graphics are presented on a 2D screen. You may recall that 3D was defined as a "two-dimensional *representation* of three-dimensional objects."

In computer graphics, objects exist only in the memory of the computer. So how does the computer generate such convincing visual illusions using only mathematical formulas? Dust off those precious high school memories of plotting points on graph paper, and I'll show you.

3D Space Defined

Basically, 3D space is a mathematically defined cube of cyberspace inside your computer's memory. *Cyberspace* differs from real physical space because it's a mathematical universe that can exist only inside the computer. In addition, the system's software and user can manipulate this virtual space to simulate anything imaginable.

Like real space, however, 3D space is *vast*. Even with modern 3D software, it's easy to get disoriented or "lose" an object out in some cyber-backwater. So, if it's so big, how do you find anything? Luckily, 3D space comes with its own sort of built-in Global Positioning System (GPS), called coordinates.

Coordinates

In 3D space, the smallest area that can possibly be occupied is called a *point*. Each point is defined by a unique set of three numbers, called *coordinates* (see Figure 2.4). An example would be the coordinates 0, 0, 0, which define the center point of the cyberspace universe, also called the *origin point*. The first number is the value for X, the second is the value for Y, and the third is the value for Z. In the case of the origin point, all three values are 0. Other examples of coordinates could be 12, 31, 57 or 359, -2315, 143.

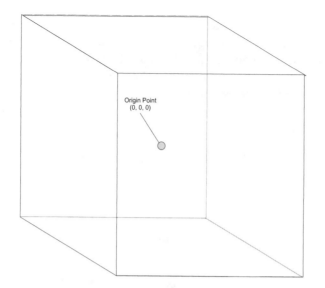

Origin Point
(0, 0, 0)

FIGURE 2.4

Every point in 3D space is defined by a set of three coordinates. At the very center of this cube-shaped "cyberspace" universe is the origin point, which is assigned the coordinates 0, 0, 0.

You can think of coordinates as a "street address" for every point in cyberspace. 3D software makes use of these addresses to define objects and their locations. So have you figured out why there are *three* sets of numbers, rather than two or four? Right—because they're related to the three dimensions: width, height, and depth. In cyberspace terms, these dimensions can also be thought of as directions, and the signposts that point to them are referred to as axes (that's pronounced "ax-sees," not "ax-ez").

Axes

An *axis* is an imaginary line in cyberspace that defines a direction. There are three standard *axes* in 3D programs, which are referred to as X, Y, and Z (see Figure 2.5). For reasons discussed later, terms like *up*, *left*, and *in* are difficult to apply to 3D space, but they can be used to explain the X, Y, and Z axes if you remember that this description *is applicable only from a given perspective*. The "width" axis, X, runs horizontally (left to right and vice-versa). The "height" axis, Y, is vertical, going from top to bottom and bottom to top. The Z-axis is related to "depth." It travels from the front to the back of cyberspace and vice-versa (or toward and away from the viewer's perspective). In the examples shown here, imagine that the cyberspace cube resides inside your computer monitor, and that you generally view it looking directly down the Z-axis. Note that the cyberspace cube is represented in the figures throughout this chapter from above and slightly to the left of this "viewer's perspective" so that the Z-axis can be seen more clearly.

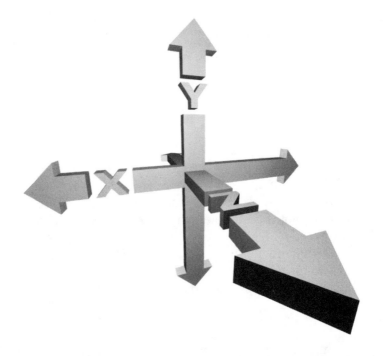

3D programs don't always orient the X, Y, and Z axes and coordinate their systems as shown here. For example, in 3ds max, the user is perceived as looking down at the cyberspace cube from above, so the Y and Z axes are reversed from what is shown in the examples used throughout the book. The principles remain the same, however, despite how the axes are oriented.

Now that you know what axes and coordinates are, how do they work together when you're navigating in cyberspace? Let's start by combining the two systems into a single diagram (see Figure 2.6).

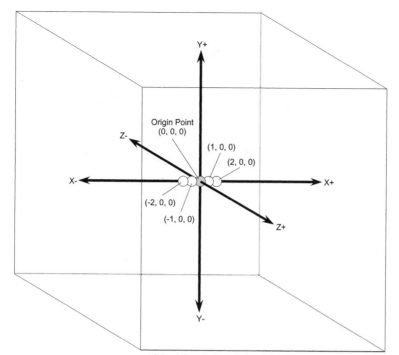

FIGURE 2.6

Coordinates and axes
are interrelated.
Coordinates on the pos-
itive side of a main axis
are greater than 0.
Those on the negative
side are less than 0.

Cube defines the boundaries of the 3D universe (not to scale)

As you can see, if you center the X, Y, and Z axes within 3D space, the coordinate at the intersection of all three axes is the origin point, 0, 0, 0. If you
plot—meaning draw a dot at—the point immediately adjacent to the origin
along the "right" side of the X-axis, the point would be identified as 1, 0,
0. The next point in the same direction would be 2, 0, 0 and so forth. On
the other hand, if you move toward the "left" side of the X-axis, the numbers would be negative: -1, 0, 0 followed by -2, 0, 0 and so on.

The same holds true for the Y-axis as well, with numbers going positive
when traveling "up" the Y-axis, and negative when going "down."
Therefore, plotting the point immediately "above" the origin would yield
0, 1, 0, and the one below it would be 0, -1, 0. Likewise, the Z-axis also has
positive and negative directions. In the right-hand coordinate system, positive is toward the viewer, and negative is away, toward the "back" of cyberspace. So, the point in "front" of the origin would be 0, 0, 1, and the point
"behind" it would be 0, 0, -1.

So, if you were trying to determine where coordinate 128, -16, 25 was, you would find it 128 points to the "right" of the origin (X-axis), 16 points "below" it (Y-axis), and 25 points closer to you (Z-axis).

It's easy to get confused about which direction is positive or negative in 3D space, but fortunately, many 3D coordinate systems are based on the *right-hand rule*, in which you use the thumb, index, and middle fingers of your right hand to help remember the positive directions of the X, Y and Z axes. To use the right-hand rule, make a fist with your right hand and hold it up in front of your face, your lower arm vertical. Stick out your thumb so it points to the right; this is the positive direction of the X-axis. Stick out your index finger so it points up at the ceiling. This is the positive direction of the Y-axis. Finally, stick out your middle finger so it points towards your face; this is the positive direction of the Z-axis.

You can use another variation on the right-hand rule to determine which direction is positive when rotating an object around an axis. Hold up your fist and stick out just your thumb. Point it in the positive direction of whatever axis you're interested in; X, Y, or Z. Now note the direction in which the rest of your fingers are curled. They point in the direction that a positive rotation would revolve an object.

As mentioned earlier, not all 3D packages use the same coordinate orientation, and by the same token, they may not use the right-hand rule, either. LightWave is a good example—it uses the *left-hand rule* to determine the positive direction of the axes. Each finger still represents the positive directions of the same axes, but you use your left hand. As a result, your middle finger will point away from your face, meaning that the positive direction of the Z-axis is away from the viewer with that particular package.

Lines, Polylines, and Polygons

Okay, so you have this vast cyberspace universe filled with zillions of points, each with its own set of coordinates, but right now, it's just a huge virtual box full of nothing. To make it useful, some shapes and objects need to be defined. Let's start with a simple line.

Suppose you played connect-the-dots with some of those cyberspace points by drawing a line (sometimes called a *segment*) between 0, 0, 0 and 5, 5, 0 (see Figure 2.7). If you continue the line to 9, 3, 0, you have what is called a *polyline*, which is a continuous line that consists of multiple segments. Finally, draw the last line right back to the origin point, 0, 0, 0.

The result is a *closed shape*, which means the shape has an "inside" and "outside." This is also a simple three-sided *polygon*, and is the basis of objects created in the 3D environment.

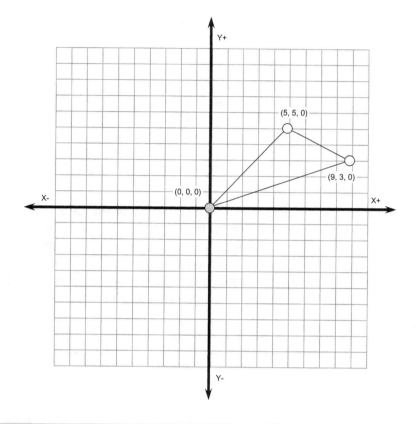

FIGURE 2.7

When a connection is made between two points, a line is formed. If that line is extended to additional points, it is a polyline. If the line is further extended to the starting point—enclosing the shape—it forms a polygon.

As with many commands in 3D graphics, your software may use different or conflicting terms to describe the components that make up a polygon: vertices, edges, faces, and so on.

Try dissecting a polygon, breaking it down into the basic components that 3D programs can manipulate: namely, vertices, edges, and faces (see Figure 2.8). A *vertex* is a point where any number of lines come together and connect to each other. The plural of vertex is *vertices*. In the example you saw in Figure 2.7, each one of the points you drew became one of the vertices in the polygon. Similarly, each one of the lines you drew formed a boundary, or *edge*, of the polygon. Finally, when the shape was closed, it created an "inside" and an "outside" to the form. The area enclosed by the edges of the polygon, the "inside," is called a *face*.

FIGURE 2.8

Polygons are composed of vertices, edges, and faces. Much of the time, the vertices are not actually visible, but you know where they are because the visible edges form "bridges" between the vertices.

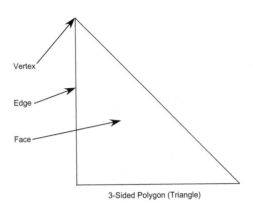

Although three-sided polygons (also called *triangles* or simply *tris*) are among the most common types of polygons in 3D graphics, they are by no means the only type. Four-sided polygons (called *quads*) are also common, but a poly can have any number of sides, up to a practical limit (see Figure 2.9). Although these simple-looking polygons don't look like much by themselves, when they're combined, they can form complex objects.

FIGURE 2.9

Most polygons in 3D programs are either (a) triangles, or (b) quads. However, there is no theoretical limit to the number of sides a polygon can have (c).

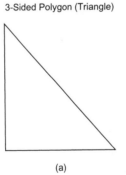

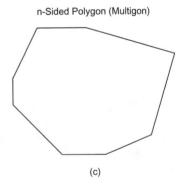

3D Objects

In many 3D applications, objects are made up of polygons, which are arranged by the computer into the form you desire. In some cases, only a few polygons are needed to construct a convincing object. Most of the time, however, hundreds or thousands are needed, creating a massive amount of data to keep track of. Thankfully, because the computer is so good at handling tons of complex numbers, it's able to keep track of all the polygons, points, edges, and faces in the scene.

For example, in the case of a simple cube, the software has to keep track of eight vertices, the twelve edges that connect them, and the six faces they form, assuming the cube is made up of quads (see Figure 2.10). If the cube were constructed with triangles instead of quads, the number of edges and faces would double. For more complex objects, the number of polygon elements can soar into the tens of thousands.

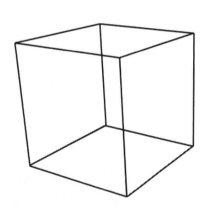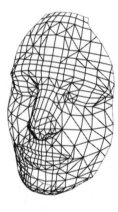

FIGURE 2.10

A simple cube has eight vertices that define the corners of the object. Complex objects can have hundreds or thousands of vertices.

Because these objects are made up of polygons, which are in turn defined by coordinates in cyberspace, the objects themselves take up space in your mathematical universe. For example, a cube may have one corner resting at the origin point 0, 0, 0, and be 5 units wide in each direction (see Figure 2.11). That would mean that the corner of the cube immediately "above" the origin point would reside at coordinates 0, 5, 0, which should be considered the "upper-left front" of the cube. Because the cube is on the positive ("right") side of the X-axis (the horizontal one), the next set of corners is at 5, 5, 0 (upper-right front) and 5, 0, 0 (lower-right front). Finally, because the cube is positioned "behind" the origin point along the Z-axis (depth), the final sets of corners would be at 0, 0, -5 (lower-left rear), 0, 5, -5 (upper-left rear), 5, 5, -5 (upper-right rear), and 5, 0, -5 (lower-right rear).

FIGURE 2.11

The construction of a cube in cyberspace demonstrates how linking coordinate points together can form a 3D object out of polygons.

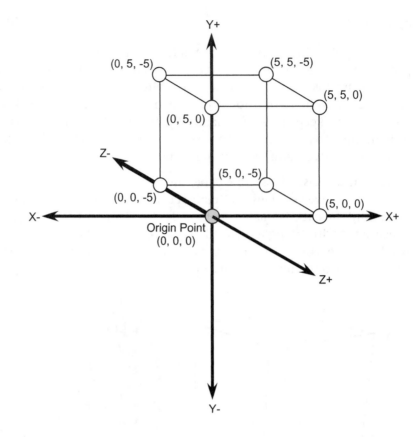

Modeling

The process of creating and manipulating objects in 3D space is called *modeling*. In many ways, it's a lot like sculpting something out of clay, or building a structure out of wood, concrete, and glass. The 3D software gives you basic objects to work with—the building materials, if you will—and you put them together into whatever you want. You also get a set of tools that enable you to modify the basic objects or build your own from scratch.

Texture Mapping

If modeling is like building a house out of wood and mortar, then *texture mapping* is like decorating it. Your 3D package gives you the ability to choose any color of "paint" to apply to your objects, and you can also use "wallpaper" made out of photographs or 2D painted images. In addition, you can control the transparency, shininess, and bumpiness of 3d objects, as well as many other surface characteristics.

Viewpoints

Just as it would be rather challenging to drive your car if it didn't have windows, manipulating the objects in 3D space is much easier when you can define a viewpoint (see Figure 2.12). A *viewpoint* is a position in cyberspace that represents the user's location. Most programs use a default viewpoint that has the X-axis running horizontally, the Y-axis vertical, and the Z-axis indicating depth as discussed. Usually, this default viewpoint is located at the extreme positive Z-axis (the "front") of cyberspace, and is focused on the origin point.

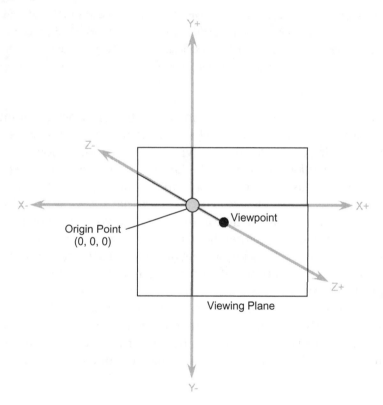

FIGURE 2.12

The viewpoint represents the current vantage point of the user. The viewing plane indicates the limits of the user's view, because only objects in front of that plane are visible.

Surrounding the viewpoint at a perpendicular angle is the *viewing plane*, which is an imaginary flat panel that defines the limits of the user's "sight." Just as a racehorse may wear blinders to keep its attention focused on the course ahead, the viewing plane defines which part of the 3D universe the user can see at a given time. Only objects that lie on the inside of the viewing plane are visible to the user, and everything else is "clipped off." In fact, another name for the viewing plane is the *clipping plane*.

To see something that lies outside the viewing plane, the user must change his or her viewpoint. In a sense, the viewing plane is like the limits of your own eyes' peripheral vision. If you want to see something that's behind you, you either have to turn your head (in other words, rotate the viewing plane) or step backward until the object is in front of you (the equivalent of moving the viewing plane). By the way, if the viewing plane happens to intersect an object, the object may suddenly disappear from sight, or look as though it were cut in half ("clipped") by the plane.

At this point, perhaps you've realized why the earlier references to "up, left, and behind" were used with caution. Whether something is left or right depends on the viewer's perspective. In the 3D universe, the viewer can be virtually anywhere, so what is "left" from one viewpoint may be "up" or "right" from another.

The windows in your software that look into the 3D space are sometimes called *viewports*. Your view into cyberspace is bound on the sides by the size of this viewport. Default 3D viewports typically show objects as *orthographic projections*, which will be familiar if you've ever looked at the blueprint for a house. There is always an overhead (top) view that shows the floor plan, as well as elevation (side) views that show the walls from the front, back, and sides of the house. In each view, you are "looking" at the building down a single, perpendicular axis. All these views are drawn to scale so that the carpenters know how big all the parts are and their proper relationships to each other. 3D software generally uses this same kind of "blueprint" layout for presenting objects in the 3D world. In addition to the typical three orthographic views, a fourth view shows the object from a user-defined off-axis viewpoint, either as a perspective view or an axonometric one. *Axonometric* means that the viewer's location is infinitely distant from the object, so that all lines along the same axis are parallel (see Figure 2.13).

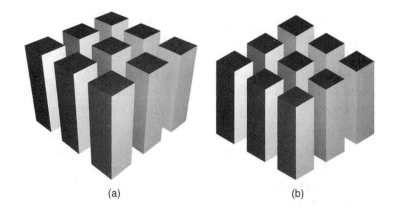

(a)   (b)

FIGURE 2.13

A comparison of perspective and axonometric views of identical sets of objects. (a) A perspective view provides cues to the size and distance of a form; it sees objects as a camera lens does. (b) Axonometric views, often used for modeling, ignore the effects of perspective.

Display Modes

So, just what *do* you see when peering into cyberspace from your chosen viewpoint? That depends on the capabilities of your software and its current settings. Because it takes time to convert all those polygons and other data into a form that you can see, there are several different ways of viewing 3D objects to enable the screen to be updated at a reasonable pace (see Figure 2.14).

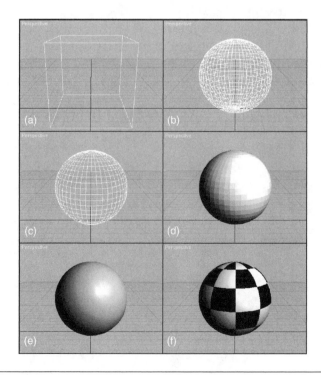

FIGURE 2.14

A texture-mapped sphere can appear in many different ways depending on the 3D software's display mode. (a)Bounding Box, (b)Wireframe, (c)Hidden Line, (d)Flat Shaded, (e)Smooth Shaded, (f)Smooth Textured.

The fastest and simplest display format is the *bounding box*, which is a box that has the same overall dimensions as the object. This is a very fast way to indicate an object's position and rough volume, and is frequently used by the software when the user is moving an object around in the scene. The problem is that all forms—from cubes to spheres to humans—are represented as a box, which makes the scene difficult to compose or edit while in this mode.

Wireframe mode draws the object using lines to represent the edges of the polygons, which makes it resemble a sculpture made of wire mesh. This enables the user to see the true form of the object and have access to individual vertices for editing and modification. Unfortunately, because every edge is visible (even the ones on the far side of the object), wireframe mode can sometimes be confusing. The remedy is to use *hidden line* mode, which draws the edges as in a wireframe display, but only the ones that would be visible to the user if the object were opaque. The result is much less confusing to the eye.

For a higher level of realism, you can opt for a shaded or textured display mode. *Flat shaded* mode shows off the surface and color of the object in a course manner. The objects appear faceted, but the effects of lighting can be seen for the first time. *Smooth shaded* mode (which shows the surface of the object with color and smoothing) has become very popular now that lots of video cards are able to support it. It is still very computationally intensive, however, and may not be practical to use with polygon-heavy scenes. *Smooth textured* mode starts to look like a finished rendering. This mode is great for previewing a shot and setting up lighting, but requires lots of CPU and video card horsepower and memory.

The more accurate or detailed the display mode, the longer it takes to redraw the viewport when something is changed. This can amount to quite a bit of time over the course of a project, especially ones with complex models or a scene with a lot of objects. If you find things bogging down, hide unneeded objects or switch to a simpler display mode.

Alternative Coordinate Systems

Until now, the focus has been on the fundamental coordinate system of 3D space, also called the *world coordinate system* (see Figure 2.15). Although the software always uses world coordinates to keep track of everything in 3D space, you may want to switch to different coordinate systems for convenience and control. Two of the most common alternatives are view coordinates and local coordinates.

Although coordinate systems are being referred to in this section, remember that coordinates and axes are interrelated, so you can consider these to be alternative axis systems as well.

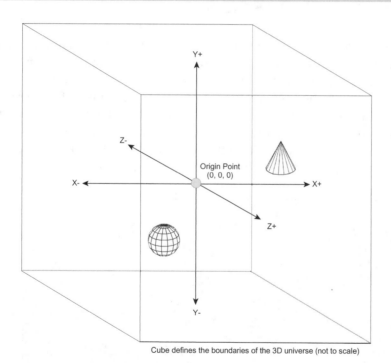

Cube defines the boundaries of the 3D universe (not to scale)

FIGURE 2.15

The fundamental coordinate system of 3D space is world coordinates. They remain the same regardless of the viewpoint.

Screen coordinates use the viewport window as the basis for the X, Y, and Z axes, and remain the same no matter how your viewpoint on the 3D scene changes (see Figure 2.16). This can be convenient for repositioning objects. For example, to move an object to the right in your scene, you always know that you have to move it positively along the X-axis when you use screen coordinates.

FIGURE 2.16

Screen coordinates are tied to the viewport window and remain the same regardless of how the viewpoint is changed.

Local coordinates use the object itself as the basis for the axes, and each object can have its own coordinate system. The exact manner in which the local axes are assigned to an object varies, but is often related to the viewpoint from which the user creates the object. For example, if you create a cone from an off-axis viewpoint, the local axes will be different from the world axes; in other words, the local X axis may be pointing the same direction as the world Y axis. In addition, after you reorient an object, the local axes are no longer aligned with the world axes (see Figure 2.17).

FIGURE 2.17

Every object can have its own unique local axes, which are usually related to the viewpoint at the time the object was created. The local axes are locked to the object and come together at the object's pivot point.

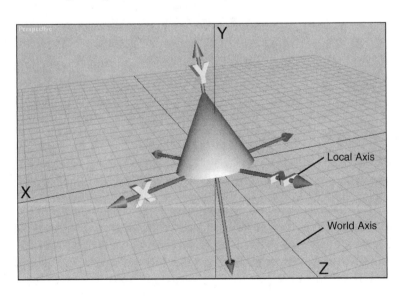

It's a good idea to use local axes to rotate an object, because using other coordinate systems may produce unexpected results. To see why, let's look at how rotation works in cyberspace.

Coordinate Systems and Rotation

When you rotate an object, three factors influence the way it turns:

◆ Which coordinate system (world, view, local, or user) is currently active

◆ The location of the rotational center point (pivot point)

◆ Which axis you choose to rotate the object around

As you know, the current coordinate system setting can have a big impact on how the axes are oriented, so this is the first thing that should be decided. In general, you'll want to use the local coordinate system when rotating an object around one of its own axes.

When local coordinates are selected, the *pivot point* is the spot where the three local axes meet. This is something like the origin point of the world coordinate system. However, whereas the world axes and origin point are fixed, the local axes (and therefore the pivot point) can be relocated anywhere in 3D space—it doesn't even have to be near the object itself.

The final factor, the selected axis, determines which of the three axes to spin the object around.

To illustrate why you must often switch to using the local coordinate system for rotation, imagine that you built a simple cone from an overhead viewpoint at the center of the 3D universe. In this situation, the cone would be perfectly aligned with the world coordinate system, its local X-axis pointing to the left, just like the world X-axis (see Figure 2.18).

FIGURE 2.18

When an object is created so that its local axes are in alignment with the world axes, the world axes can be used to manipulate it predictably (at first, anyway).

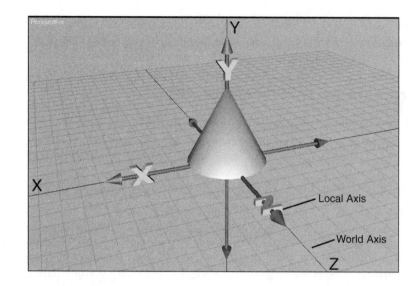

At this point, you could use the world axes or the local axes to rotate the cone -45° on its X-axis and get identical results (see Figure 2.19). After rotating the cone, however, the local axes are no longer aligned to the world axes—you would get very different results if you rotated the cone around the local Y-axis (the cone would spin like a top) versus rotating it around the world Y-axis (the cone would wobble).

FIGURE 2.19

After an object is no longer aligned with the world coordinates, you usually need to switch to using the local axis system in order to have the object revolve in the same manner as before.

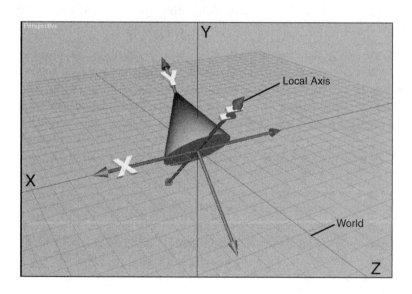

There are some ways to accomplish a controlled rotation without relying on the local axis, however. One is to carefully position the viewpoint so that it is in alignment with the local axes (some programs have a command for doing this), and then rotate the object using the screen coordinate system.

A *user axis* is just what it sounds like—an axis that you define. A user axis can be configured independently of the world, screen, and local axes (see Figure 2.20). It is very useful during modeling if you want to rotate an object at an oddball angle without disturbing the local coordinate system.

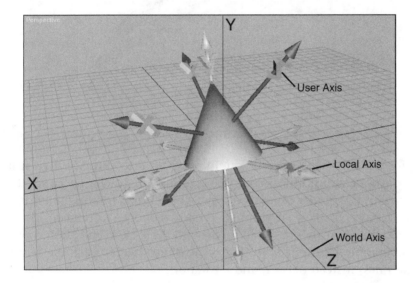

FIGURE 2.20

A user axis can be set up at any angle, completely independently of all other axes systems. User axes are often used for defining joint rotation points.

Sometimes it can be confusing to decide which axis you want to rotate an object around to get the desired results. As a memory aid, the terms used for flying a plane (pitch, yaw, and roll) are often applied to axis rotation (see Figure 2.21).

FIGURE 2.21

The maneuvering of an aircraft can help you visualize which axis you want to affect. Here, the X, Y, and Z axes are shown for an imaginary plane.

Imagine a plane flying toward you. In order for it to climb or dive, it must *pitch*, or rotate around the X-axis (see Figure 2.22). To change course to the left or right, the rudder causes it to *yaw*, which is like rotating it around the Y-axis. Finally, to make it through a narrow mountain chasm, the pilot must *roll* the plane, which rotates it around the Z-axis. The pitch, yaw, and roll mnemonic is so effective that some 3D software use these terms (or similar ones) instead of X, Y, and Z rotation.

FIGURE 2.22

X-axis (pitch) rotation makes the plane climb or dive. Y-axis (yaw) makes it change heading, and Z-axis (roll) rotation makes it bank.

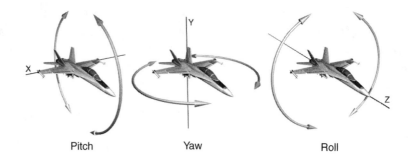

Pitch　　　　　Yaw　　　　　Roll

Lights

So far, we've been wandering around this 3D universe in the dark. We need some lights to illuminate these rotating objects so you can see them in the finished render.

3D lights work very much like real photography studio lights, except that you can position them anywhere (including inside the object) *and* they use less electricity. Just like the real ones, most 3D lights can cast shadows, which adds a great deal of realism to a scene. Four main kinds of lights are used in 3D software:

◆ *Omni lights* or *point lights*, which are like bare bulbs, illuminate things in all directions.

◆ *Spot lights*, which are directional sources, are often used to highlight portions of an object or provide the main source of illumination for a scene.

◆ *Distant lights* or *direct lights*, which are also directional, are used to simulate very distant light sources such as the sun, which casts parallel shadows.

◆ *Ambient light* is present everywhere in the 3D space, illuminating all surfaces equally. It's used as a way to very roughly simulate the illumination objects would receive from light bouncing off other objects.

Most 3D software enables the user to define any number of lights in a scene, but adding more lights increases the time it takes the software to render it. Chapter 7, "Lighting," gets into the characteristics and use of lights in much greater detail.

Cameras

Cameras are non-rendering objects that you can position in the 3D scene. They work like real cameras in that they provide a viewpoint on the scene that can be adjusted and animated. This camera viewpoint is different from most of the ones users employ for modeling, because it enables the scene to be viewed in a more realistic and natural perspective mode. Just like real cameras, the 3D kind often have different lens settings, formats (film sizes), and the like.

3D cameras may also have *targets*, which are positioning aids that enable you to see where a camera is pointed from a non-camera viewport. You can usually define and position as many cameras as you need, although some programs may allow you to have only one. These issues and more are discussed in depth in Chapter 8, "The Camera."

Animation

Modern 3D software enables you to animate just about everything: You can move and alter objects, lights, cameras, and even textures. Although computer animation can be a very involved process for complicated objects such as 3D people, much of the time it is fairly straightforward. You select how long you want a particular movement to take, and then reposition the object, light, or camera to the new location. The computer takes care of moving the object smoothly from its original location to the new spot you've selected, subject to your controls. Chapter 9 deals with the techniques of computer animation.

Rendering

Rendering is the process wherein the computer interprets all the object and light data and creates a finished image from the viewport you have selected. The final result may be either a single still image or one frame of an animated sequence.

To understand how the computer takes a bunch of polygons and turns them into a finished rendering, you have to examine how the computer interprets polygon surfaces. First of all, to be "seen" by the computer as a surface, a polygon face must have a normal. A *normal*, usually represented by a little line or arrow sticking out of a face, indicates which side of the polygon is visible, and what direction it's facing (see Figure 2.23). When the 3D software begins rendering, it calculates how much (and from which direction) light is striking a particular polygon face, based on the orientation of this normal.

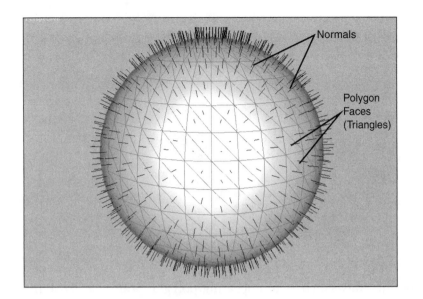

FIGURE 2.23

Normals are imaginary lines extending from polygon faces. The software uses them to calculate the intensity and direction of light striking the face.

Most of the time in 3D graphics applications, only one side of a polygon face has a normal, making it a *single-sided polygon*. Single-sided polygons can only be "seen" from the side with the normal, which can cause problems in some rendering situations (such as when a camera passes through the inside of an object). Therefore, the software also can be instructed to make a polygon *double-sided*, so that it can be viewed from either side. Take a look at the three cubes in Figure 2.24. The one on the left is a plain old cube, with all the normals facing away from the center. The middle cube has one triangular poly flipped around so that the normal faces the interior. The result is that we can see through the flipped normal. Not only that, but because we're seeing inside the cube, all the faces on the far side appear to be missing as well, because the normals are facing the opposite direction. The cube on the right has the flopped poly as well, but because the polys have been made double-sided, we can't see the problem.

FIGURE 2.24

Three cubes
demonstrate the differ-
ences between single
and double-sided
polys. (a) Normal
cube, (b) Cube with
flipped poly, (c) Cube
with flipped poly, but
made double-sided.

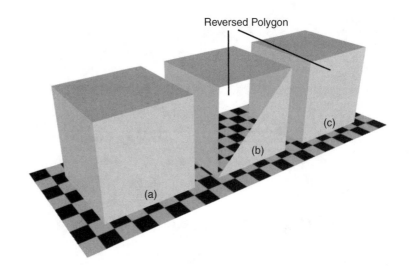

Rendering bugs—such as disappearing polygons—also can arise if a polygon is non-planar. Using a four-sided polygon (a quad) as an example,
imagine that it's resting on a flat plane (see Figure 2.25a). If you take the
right front vertex and pull it up away from the rest, the polygon becomes
"bent," or *non-planar* (see Figure 2.25b). Although it is still an acceptable
polygon (remember, polygons can have any number of sides), part of it
may not render properly, because the normal won't be in the right position. One solution to this kind of problem is to convert all the objects to
triangular polygons   (see Figure 2.25c). Because they have only three
vertices, it is impossible for them to be "bent" or become non-planar.

FIGURE 2.25

Planar and non-planar
polygons. (a) Planar
quad polygon, (b) Non-
planar quad polygon,
(c) Triangular polygons
cannot be made non-
planar.

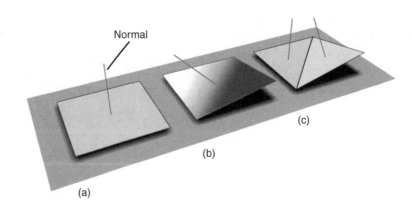

In addition to taking into account the position of normals, when the computer renders a scene, it considers any color or texture that has been applied to that polygon, the light positions, intensity, and color, and many other factors. Then, the computer "paints" the results of these calculations on the screen as an image. Most packages support several different rendering modes, and each mode produces a different look for the finished image (see Figure 2.26).

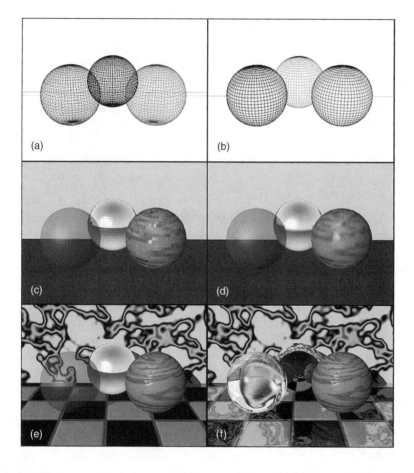

(a)

(b)

(c)

(d)

(e)

(f)

FIGURE 2.26

Common rendering types: (a) Wireframe, (b) Hidden Line, (c) Flat shaded, (d) Gouraud Shaded, (e) Phong Shaded, (f) Ray Traced.

The most basic, and fastest, rendering mode is wireframe, which is similar to the wireframe display mode discussed earlier. It is rarely used except for animation tests or when a "computery" look is desired for the image. Likewise, hidden line is just like the display mode also discussed earlier, and again is rarely used for output anymore.

For a *flat render*, the computer calculates the color and value of a polygon face based on a single normal in the center of the face. The resulting image is a collection of sharply defined polygon surfaces, each with one solid color. Texture information is ignored, and the image has a faceted appearance. This is a very quick way to render a scene, and is occasionally used for making test renders of animation sequences.

The next level of quality is called *Gouraud* or *smooth render*. The software calculates the color and value at each vertex of the face and then interpolates the result across the polygon face. The effect is smoothly blended object surfaces that are much more realistic than a flat rendering's surfaces. Smooth shading also incorporates textures that may have been applied to the objects. Many real-time 3D games and flight simulators use Gouraud shading.

Phong rendering retains the smoothness of Gouraud shading and adds specular highlights for even more realism. *Specular highlights* are the bright reflections of light seen on glossy objects. In Phong renders, the computer calculates the surface normal for every pixel on the screen that represents an object. Phong rendering is probably the most common mode used for finished images and animation.

One of the highest levels of rendering quality available from most desktop 3D packages is called ray tracing. *Ray tracing* is a method where the color and value of each pixel on the screen is calculated by casting an imaginary ray backward from the viewer's perspective into the model, to determine what light and surface factors influence it. The difference between ray tracing and the other methods mentioned earlier (collectively called *scanline rendering* techniques) is that the ray can be bounced off surfaces and bent, just like real light. The result is very realistic, with extremely accurate shadows, reflections, and even refraction.

Refraction is the bending of light waves that occurs when they move through different types of materials, and is noticeable in things like eyeglasses and water. In a ray-traced render, a transparent 3D object shaped like a magnifying glass lens actually magnifies what's behind it, whereas a similar lens in a scanline render would not. The packages that offer refraction mapping are an exception to this rule, because they can simulate the refraction effect despite using a scanline renderer.

Finally, the pinnacle of rendering quality is radiosity rendering, but it is only standard in a few packages and is extremely time consuming. Even a relatively simple scene may take hours to render on a desktop system.

Radiosity rendering takes into account light bouncing off all surfaces in the scene, instead of just the illumination produced by the light sources themselves. Even the color and shape of the objects are part of the calculations. Radiosity rendering can produce images of near-photographic realism.

Additional information on rendering modes and settings can be found in Chapter 10, "Rendering and Output."

Summary

Congratulations! You've successfully made it through the worst of the 3D theory. You can now hold the rapt attention of others at parties by telling them all about the principles of 3D graphics, from coordinate systems, to user axes, to rendering modes. In any case, this chapter has prepared you to take the first step in practical application of all this theory—building some models!

Chapter 3 finally gets into the thick of it, showing you the particulars of a 3D software package while embarking on a series of basic modeling tutorials. Ultimately, these tutorials will lead toward a finished portfolio piece. Whoo-hoo!

Modeling Basics

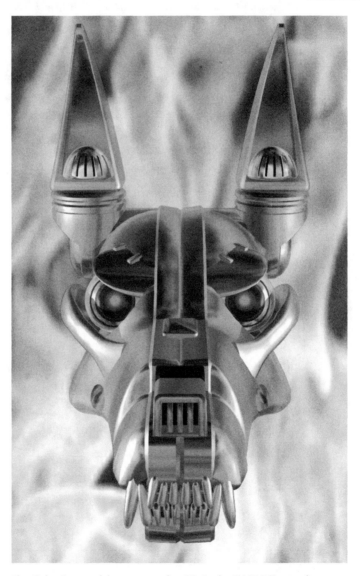

This CyberDog model was created in 3D Studio R4 (DOS) using basic lofts and modified 3D primitives. Image ©1996 Mark Giambruno.

"*A*t last!" *The student sighed as he finished the day's spell book studies. "Now I can add some more detail to my castle project." He got up from his chair and stretched, then wandered over to the Glowing Pool to admire his work. Before him floated an impressive castle tower, its walls dotted with windows. He smiled at the fine roof, finally perched properly atop the turret.*

"Not bad," the student said to himself. "I think I'll build an inner gate next...a wrought iron one." With that, he sat down to work. It was nigh on two hours later when the Master returned from his errands and approached to examine his student's work.

"Very good, lad," the Master remarked. "But aren't those iron bars usually twisted? Say, here and there?"

"Oh, I forgot about that. I guess I should have looked at the ones downstairs first." The student frowned thoughtfully. "Well, I can fix them easily enough." A few incantations later, the vertical iron bars were endowed with decorative twists.

"Now for the arched ones..." The student turned his attention to the bent iron bars that formed a decorative bridge between the vertical pieces. He spoke the Words of Deformation, but something went terribly wrong. The arches wrapped around themselves like Olde Gold pretzels!

"Aargh!" groaned the student, realizing the problem. "I can't twist them after they've been bent. The axis..."

"Quite so," interrupted the Master. "Seems you forgot one of the key principles of conjuring, lad," he sighed, tapping on a large wooden sign on the wall. It read simply:

Laying the Groundwork

As our hapless student just discovered, it isn't enough to know how to use a tool. You have to be able to see the project as a whole and plan a strategy for accomplishing it. Through theory and then tutorials, this chapter not only introduces you to the basic modeling tools, with tips on when to use them, but also offers suggestions for planning out the best modeling approach and developing good work habits.

The first step in planning any project is to sit down and decide exactly what you want to accomplish. For example, say your project involves animating two modern fighter jets in an aerial dogfight. Well, right off you know you're going to need 3D models of the planes, as well as imagery of the sky and ground to use for the backgrounds. Because we're dealing with modeling at this point, let's focus on one of the planes—say, an F-14 Tomcat like the one Tom Cruise "flew" in the movie Top Gun. Because this is a fairly well-known craft, there's a good chance that others have already built models of this jet that you could find free or purchase for a fee on the web. I can tell you from working in a production environment that this is one of the first possibilities I check on when bidding out a project—it's usually a lot cheaper and faster to buy a complex model from a *stock mesh* outfit (or find a freebie on CD-ROM or the web) than it is to build one. The only downside is that stock mesh tends to have a high polygon count, and it's difficult to modify. Take a look at Chapter 4, "Modeling: Beyond the Basics," for more information on stock mesh.

At any rate, because we're here to learn about modeling, let's presume that you want to scratch-build the F-14 model. Now that you've identified the kind of plane you want to build, you're going to need some reference materials to serve as a guide. You may start off by searching for images from the web, going to the library or bookstore to find pictures and specifications, and even watching a few movies to study how they look in action. Ideally, you'll find some detailed line art of the plane that you can scan and load into your 3D program and use as a template. For more tips on finding and using reference materials, take a look at Appendix G, "Planning and Organization," which you can find on the CD-ROM.

Now that you have a reference, study the plane. Identify the tricky parts, like spots where curved surfaces join together. Some of these areas may look a bit complex even to an experienced modeler, but remember that there's always more than one way to solve a problem, so if an aspect of the project seems particularly daunting, try to find a creative alternative.

Modeling Approaches

Whenever possible, take the simplest path to success when figuring out how a model will be constructed. The KISS (Keep It Simple, Stupid) principle applies very nicely to 3D work, because complicated models and operations tend to bog down the system and are more likely to cause trouble later on.

Bump and diffusion mapping (discussed in Chapter 6, "Texture Mapping") uses bitmapped images and normals manipulation to give the impression that there are additional mesh details on an object. Because of this, mapping can often substitute for lots of detailed mesh, particularly with objects that aren't the focus of attention or are distant in the scene. So, think about whether a texture could be used on a simpler object (even a single flat polygon) and still achieve satisfactory results.

In addition, think about how the model will be animated in the scene. If you never see the far side of an object, you may not need to bother modeling it.

If you're uncertain about whether a given modeling approach will work, do a test run with a quickly defined version of the object to find out. Experimenting in this way will often turn up alternatives that you may not have thought of otherwise.

Organizing Your Project

Before you start to build a model, take a little time to set up some directories (folders) to hold the files in an organized manner. I recommend creating a "3D Projects" directory and keeping all your original work in that, organized by the name of the individual project or model. In this case, you might call the subdirectory "F14 Jet." Inside that directory, create an additional folder called "Mesh" and another called "Maps." Then, when you go to build the model, you can save the 3D object files in the 3D Projects\F14 Jet\Mesh directory and the texture maps in the 3D Projects\F14 Jet\Maps directory. This will keep all the files related to the project in one easy-to-find directory. Keeping your files organized and grouped together this way also makes the projects easier to back up, because you don't have to hunt all over the hard drive to find the mesh and maps.

When you start texturing your models, you may find that you'll often use images that came free with your 3D program. I recommend that you make copies of any of these that you use on a given model and put them in the Maps directory for that project. Not only does this enable you to customize the maps for your project, but it also ensures that you'll have all the files you need if you ever try to open the project on a different system (one that may not have all the stock maps installed).

Now that you have a place for all the files, what about the filenames themselves? Use a clear, descriptive name and add a number (with a leading zero) to the end so you can save off different versions as you work. F14Jet_01.xxx would be a good one to start with for the mesh file. Apply the same logic to the texture maps as well—F14 Canopy Glass.jpg, F14 Tire Tread.bmp, and so on.

Properly naming the hundreds of individual objects that may make up a model is also important. When a model starts to get complex, selecting parts by eye can be difficult. Also, there are situations when you have to choose from an alphabetized list of objects to perform some process on them. This will be pretty tough if your list of objects contains entries like Sphere27, Line155, and Cube82—names that may be automatically assigned by the program as you create objects. Selecting from a list that includes items such as F14Rudder, F14WheelRight, and F14Missile03 would be a bit easier.

You'll find a more in-depth guide to object and file naming conventions in Appendix G, "Planning and Organization." I strongly recommend you read it before starting on any modeling project.

Modeler Concepts

Now that you've gotten organized, it's time to move on to the software itself. As you know, modeling is the process of creating objects with a 3D software program. The term *modeler* was defined in Chapter 1 as the person who performs this work, but it is also used to describe that portion of the 3D package that deals with object creation, as well.

Types of Modelers

Portions of the following material dealing with 3D software information and reviews originally appeared in an article I wrote for *InterActivity* magazine (Copyright 1996, Miller Freeman, Inc.) and is used with permission.

There are four basic types of modeling systems: polygonal, spline, patch, and parametric. Many packages combine these systems because each has its strengths and weaknesses. Polygonal is the most basic, and deals with 3D objects as groups of polygons only. Spline modelers are more sophisticated, and allow the user to work with resolution-independent objects. Patch modelers are well suited to sculpting organic objects, and parametric modelers allow the parameters of an object to be changed later in the process for maximum flexibility. Although each program takes a different approach, many of them incorporate two or more of these different modelers for flexibility.

Polygonal Modelers

Polygonal modeling is the oldest type of 3D modeling, harkening back to the days when people had to define points in 3D space by manually typing in X, Y, and Z coordinates from the keyboard. As you know, when three or more of these coordinate points are specified as vertices and connected by edges, they form a polygon, which can have color and texture. When you put a bunch of these polygons together, you can fashion a representation of just about any object. A downside to polygonal modeling is that everything is made up of these tiny, flat surfaces, and the polygons need to be fairly small or your object may appear faceted along the edges (see Figure 3.1). This means that if you will be zooming in on an object in a scene, you have to model it at a high *polygon resolution* (density), even though most of the polys will be unnecessary when you move farther from the object.

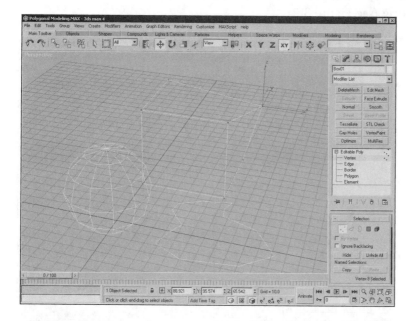

For consistency, all of the interface screen grabs in this book are from Discreet 3ds max 4.2. Like many 3D software offerings, max has several different modelers integrated into the package.

Because of the overall increases in processor and display speed over the years, 3D software began to migrate from polygon-based to spline-based modeling, and some packages practically ignored polygonal modeling completely. Interestingly, though, polygonal modeling has made a big comeback because of the incredible popularity of real-time 3D games, so more robust polygon editing tools have made their way into what were primarily spline-based products.

Spline Modelers

If you've ever used a 2D drawing program such as Illustrator or CorelDraw, you're familiar with splines, one of the main tools that these programs use. Technically speaking, a *spline* is a (usually curved) line that is defined by control points. One of the main advantages of spline-based modeling over polygonal modeling is that it is *resolution-independent*, meaning that (in theory) you can get as close as you want to an object and never see any faceting (see Figure 3.2).

FIGURE 3.2

Spline modelers, like the NURBS-based one shown here, use resolution-independent splines to define objects, and tend to produce smoother results than polygonal modelers. Also, the final polygonal resolution of spline-based objects can be adjusted at any time.

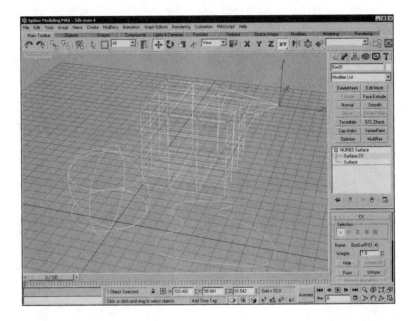

Spline modelers are well suited to creating complex organic shapes such as human faces, Tyrannosaurs, and alien spacecraft. Splines are often better for applications like this because their method of building forms uses smooth and natural curves, rather than jagged and artificial polygonal shapes. There are several different types of splines, with modelers commonly using the B-spline, the Bezier, and NURBS. Spline types and the differences between them are discussed later in the chapter.

Patch Modelers

Patch modelers use a network of control points to define and modify the shape of the patch, which is usually a lattice of either splines or polygons (see Figure 3.3). These control points, called *control vertices (CVs)*, exert a magnet-like influence on the flexible surface of the patch, stretching and tugging it in one direction or another. In addition, patches can be subdivided to allow for more detail and can be "stitched" together to form large, complex surfaces. Like spline modelers, patch modelers are very suitable for building organic forms.

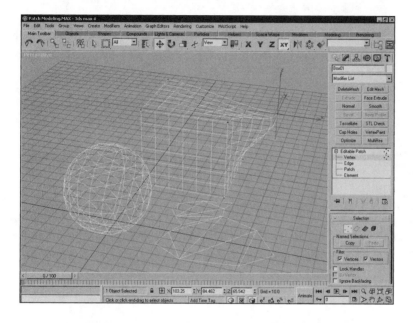

FIGURE 3.3

Patch modelers use magnet-like Control Vertices to affect the surface of an object, and can produce very smooth results. Like spline-based modelers, they are particularly well suited for organic modeling.

Parametric Modelers

Parametric modeling features objects that retain their base geometry information, such as their default shape, their current size, and how many segments their forms comprise. Because this information can still be accessed and changed even after the objects are modified, it allows the user to change or undo alterations to the object later on, and even increase or decrease its resolution (see Figure 3.4). Although parametric modeling is usually spline-based, not all spline modelers are parametric.

FIGURE 3.4

Parametric modelers
are also spline-based,
but allow operations to
be adjusted or undone
even after several
modifications have
been made to an
object. Among other
things, this enables
the object's resolution
to be adjusted
after creation and
modification.

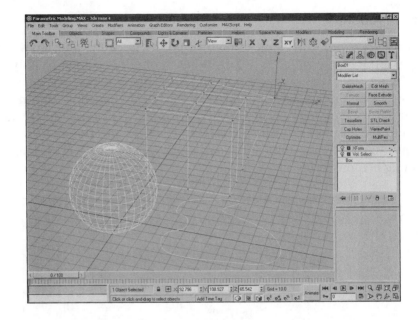

Deformations applied to parametric objects can often be adjusted at any time, even though they may have been applied several operations ago. (The student in the opening tale could have benefited from this.) Contrast this to polygonal modeling, where after an object is created, its resolution is fixed (unless you tessellate or optimize it). Likewise, deforming a polygonal object permanently modifies it, so if you bend an object, then later want to reduce that bend significantly, you probably have to start over again with an unbent object.

If a parametric model is destined for use outside the 3D program—in a game, for example—the model usually needs to be converted to a polygonal model. This is often referred to as *collapsing* the mesh.

The fact that so many different types of modeling approaches exist is another reason it's difficult to give specific instructions for the tutorials at the end of this chapter, which are designed to be program-independent. (Max, LightWave, and Maya-specific tutorials are included on the CD-ROM, however.) Although a spline or parametric modeler works best for the rounded organic forms in the tutorial, such as the helium bag, you can use a polygonal modeler as well, making sure that you set the mesh density to a reasonable level when you create the objects. Regardless of which type of modeler you have, however, all the tutorials can be accomplished in one way or another.

Working in the 3D World

Because each program is unique and does things a little differently, it's up to you to get up to speed on the user interface for your product, learning about how to move around, change the viewports, and so forth. However, they all have some things in common. Each has viewports into the 3D universe, sets of mouse-selected and type-in commands and parameters, dialogs or text files where you can set options, and so forth. Let's take a look at some of the things to be concerned with.

Getting Around

You'll probably be using a mouse to construct and modify objects, as well as navigate your way through the 3D universe. Familiarize yourself with any special functions the mouse performs through the use of the mouse button or key combinations. In particular, look for shortcuts that enable you to manipulate frequently used controls, such as selecting axes and switching between move, rotate, and scale functions.

To modify a shape or object, you have to select it, which usually highlights it somehow to set it apart from the rest. You can select things in the typical ways, by clicking on them with the cursor or dragging a marquee around a cluster of objects. In addition, many products allow you to open a dialog box and select objects by name, type, or color, which is very useful for picking out groups of related objects quickly (especially if you've followed a good object-naming convention).

You'll spend a lot of time peering at viewports, so get familiar with their controls. Most programs provide a way to *pan* (slide around the viewpoint) so that you can see things that are off to one side. You can also *zoom* in for detail work or zoom out to see more of the scene. There may also be a *zoom all* control that will automatically zoom out to show you everything in the scene. This is very helpful when you're trying to locate and move wayward pieces that were imported or created somewhere away from the rest of the model.

Most programs allow you to customize your viewports, selecting where you want the top view, the left view, the perspective view, and so on to be located. You may also be able change the size of these windows in some cases. If you can't select a new viewport with a mouse click, learn the hotkeys for changing views so you don't have to resort to using a drop-down menu.

Units and Scale

3D software uses coordinates to keep track of the size and location of objects, but these numbers are extremely long and rather awkward for users to work with directly. It's much more practical to use measurement systems you're familiar with, like inches or centimeters. Because of this, 3D programs often allow users to select the type of *units* they want to use for measuring: English (feet and inches), Metric (meters and centimeters), or Generic (decimal numbers, but much shorter than coordinates). In addition, they may let the user choose between fractional (1/2) or decimal (0.5) display.

Just as blueprints and engineering drawings use a *scale*—such as 1/8"=1'-0" or 1cm=1m—3D programs often allow you to set a scaling factor as well. It's important to set both units and scale when you first start a project, and be sure you use the same ones when building other models to combine with the first. That way, you're using a consistent measurement system, and when you merge the models into a single project, they'll be the proper sizes relative to each other.

Grids and Snaps

Grids are cross-hatched lines that can be seen in the viewport and used like graph paper for determining scale when creating objects (see Figure 3.5). When you build a 3D object, part of it usually ends up on a default grid that radiates out of the origin point, in the center of the 3D universe. However, you can change the spot at which an object will appear through the use of *construction planes* or *construction grids*, which are alternate, movable planes that move the default location for new objects to other parts of the universe. These are useful when you have a large scene and are working in a particular section only, or if you want objects to appear already aligned to a particular plane.

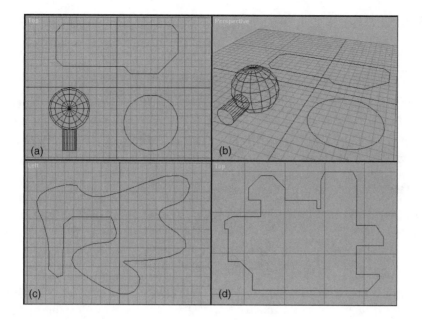

FIGURE 3.5

Using grids and snaps:
(a) Grids and snaps make the creation and alignment of shapes and objects easier. (b) Because both objects are active regardless of viewpoint, you can align objects from any perspective. (c) For creating free-form shapes or objects, turn snap off. (d) Snaps can be set independently of the grid, making it easier to handle adjustments that are smaller than the grid.

The *snap* feature usually is employed in conjunction with a grid and causes the cursor to snap from one position to another, usually at the intersection of two grid lines. Depending on the program, you may be able to snap to the vertices or faces on objects as well. Note that the snap setting can be different from the grid setting, which is convenient for creating or moving objects precisely without having to alter the grid setting.

It's a good idea to use grids and snaps whenever possible, because it makes your shapes and alignments more exact, and you probably will find that it makes the modeling process go faster.

Hide and Unhide

Hide enables you to make a shape or object disappear from the scene; use *Unhide* to make it reappear later. This pair of commands is great for clearing out mesh that you don't need to see at the present time (as well as preventing that mesh from being accidentally modified), and it makes the scene render faster, as well. Sometimes, however, you want to see the object, but don't want it to be selected or modified accidentally. That's where a command that is commonly called either Freeze or Ghost comes in.

Freeze/Ghost

When you apply *Freeze* or *Ghost* to a shape or object, it still appears in the scene, but you cannot select it while it's frozen. This is a very useful feature, because 3D scenes tend to get quite complex, and it's easy to pick or transform the wrong object. Frozen objects usually change color, letting you know the object is frozen so you don't get frustrated trying to figure out why you can't select it. When you want to modify the object, you can *Unfreeze* or *Unghost* it.

Groups

Grouping is a convenient way to attach a number of different shapes or objects together temporarily. This enables you to deal with them as a whole for transforms, mapping, and other operations, but still tweak them on an individual basis if need be.

Creating a group is easy—just select the objects you want, Group them, and give the group a name. In addition, some programs enable you to manipulate individual objects within a group without using *Ungroup* first.

2D Shapes

Because many of the upcoming 3D operations use 2D shapes as a starting point, a good understanding of how to create and manipulate them is fundamental.

You probably had your fill of 2D polygon theory in the last chapter, so I'll keep this recap brief. 2D shapes can consist of lines, polylines, polygons, or splines. As you recall, a polyline is a type of line with more than one segment (in other words, containing three or more vertices). A polygon is an enclosed shape with three or more edges. Polygons have faces that show up when rendered in a 3D program, whereas lines and polylines generally don't.

Why Use 2D Shapes?

Building 2D shapes is an excellent way to begin creating a complex 3D object. If you create 2D outlines of some of the forms, it's possible to use the software tools to convert them into 3D objects.

Working in 2D first makes it possible to visualize and define cross-sections, and to establish the proper composition and scale of the components. In addition, 2D polygons serve as *cheap mesh,* which is a slang term for an object that has a low polygon count or is very efficient and quick to render. An example would be constructing the walls of a room scene out of flat polygons, rather than using several 3D boxes, which contain six times as many faces.

A good example of using 2D shapes to develop a 3D object is the "Gizmo" model I constructed for Mplayer Interactive, an Internet gaming company. The Gizmo is a device that looks like a high-tech portable TV and serves as the user interface for the Mplayer service (see Figure 3.6).

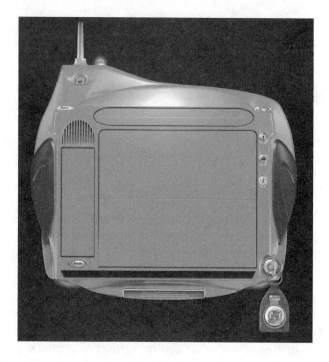

FIGURE 3.6

This 3D model of the Mplayer "Gizmo" was constructed with 3ds max. Image by Mark Giambruno and Laura Hainke, ©1996 Mplayer.

As a starting point, I imported the original 2D Illustrator drawing (by Tom Gooden of Good Dog Design) of the Gizmo into 3D Studio. Next, I broke down the complex, flowing design into a few key cross-sections, which I drew as 2D shapes (see Figure 3.7). I used a modified version of the original Illustrator drawings in conjunction with the additional cross-sections to form the skeleton of the object. I then "skinned" (covered later in the chapter) these 2D forms to create the finished object.

FIGURE 3.7

The Gizmo's basic form was developed out of spline-based cross-sections. The initial shape was imported from an Illustrator drawing, and then additional cross-sections were defined to outline the shape at various depths. Mplayer Gizmo, ©1996 Mplayer.

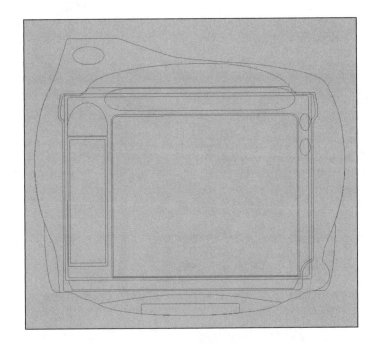

The 2D cross-sections in this case weren't polylines. They were splines, which are much more appropriate for the required curved shapes.

Splines

As discussed earlier, a spline is a (usually curved) line that is defined by control points. There are several different types of splines. Modelers commonly use the B-spline, the Bezier, and NURBS (see Figure 3.8).

All splines are similar in that they consist of a line or shape that's controlled by a polyline or polygon. The controlling polyline or polygon itself (also called a *control line, control polygon,* or *hull*) isn't seen—it merely serves to define the curvature of the resulting spline. Depending on the type of spline, there are *control points* or *control vertices* that mark key positions along the control lines, and *tangent points* or *weights* that act like little magnets to attract the spline in their direction. By manipulating these points, the user modifies the shape of the spline.

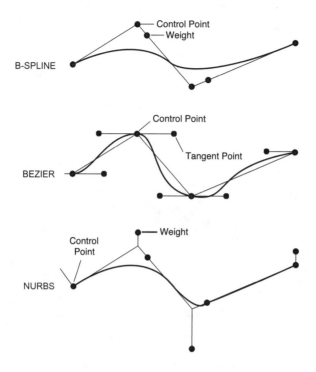

FIGURE 3.8

Three types of splines commonly used in 3D programs: B-spline, Bezier spline, and NURBS (Non-Uniform Rational B-Spline). Each uses a unique method to control the shape of the spline.

B-splines use control points with equal weights to adjust the shape of the spline. Control points rarely reside on the resulting curve in this type of spline.

Bezier splines have control points that always reside on the resulting curve. Extending out from the control points are tangent points or handles, which enable the curve to be modified without moving the control points. These tangent points also can be operated independently of each other, which may detract from the smoothness of the curve, but allows for a great deal of control.

NURBS (Non-Uniform Rational B-Splines) also have control points that reside away from the resulting curve, but rather than tangent points, they have weights to control the curve. In addition, there are knots that define the number of control points on a given portion of the curve.

Sounds a bit complicated, huh? Well, the best way to understand splines is to create a few different styles and experiment with them. If you move the control points around you can see how they influence the spline, and the finer points of controlling these shapes will quickly become apparent.

Editing 2D Shapes

2D shapes are easily modified, which is another advantage to using them as the basis for 3D objects. How a shape is modified depends on whether it's polygonal or spline-based, but some operations are common to both. In addition, note that splines can have polyline segments, or that some of the control points can be different from the others. Figure 3.9 shows some of the different control point or vertex types.

FIGURE 3.9

Control point types:
(a) Standard Bezier.
(b) Bezier Corner.
(c) Smooth. (d) Corner.

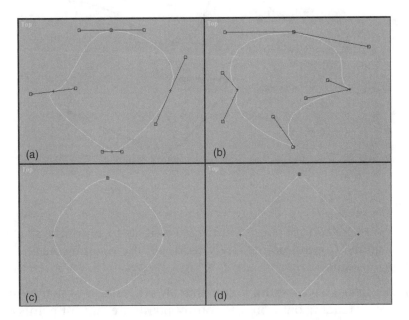

The following list describes these control points or vertex types.

Standard Bezier control points have handles that are tangent from the curve, and move as a unit when they are rotated or their lengths adjusted. This tends to keep the curves fairly smooth.

Bezier corner control points have handles that can be adjusted independently of each other, which enables you to define much sharper and more angular curves.

Smooth control points don't have handles—they use a set formula to calculate how the spline curves between control points.

Corner control points apply no curvature to the spline, making segments between them straight lines.

By mixing these different control point types, you can make virtually any 2D shape. These control points and vertices can be further modified with editing operations.

The basic line and polyline editing operations include moving, adding or deleting lines, vertices, or edges (see Figure 3.10). Note that there may not be specific commands for these operations, because they're usually selected through the use of the mouse buttons or modifier keys such as Shift, Ctrl, and Alt.

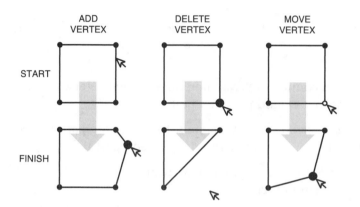

FIGURE 3.10

Basic line and polyline or polygon vertex editing operations. Add creates a new vertex, whereas Delete and Move directly affect existing ones.

Add Vertex creates a new vertex, either along an existing edge or as an extension of the last point of a line or polyline.

Delete Vertex removes a vertex and its adjacent edges, and causes a new edge to be formed between any vertices to which it was connected.

Move Vertex enables you to reposition the selected vertex and the edges to which it's connected.

Note that many programs may indicate the *first vertex* (the one that was created first) by surrounding it with a box or making it a different color during editing. This isn't important for most operations, but it does affect skinning, which is discussed later in the chapter. For now, remember that any vertex can be reassigned as the first vertex if you use the appropriate poly or spline editing tool, which may be called First or First Vertex.

Although less common than basic line and vertex editing commands, some programs offer useful 2D trimming and rounding (filleting) operations (see Figure 3.11). Trims are often applied by hitting a button to start the operation, then selecting the lines in a certain order, but this varies by program.

FIGURE 3.11

Trim connects lines at the point of intersection, whereas Bevel and Round (Fillet) create a new segment or curve to bridge the selected points. Note that the process by which these functions are applied to a shape in a given program may vary substantially from the method shown here.

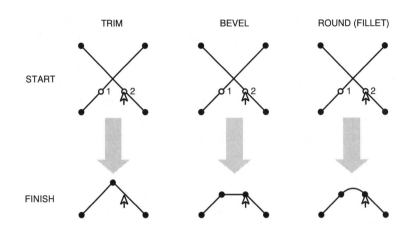

Trim Lines connects overlapping lines at their intersection, and deletes portions that extend past that point.

Bevel Lines creates a new segment to bridge the gap between selected points. It also deletes portions that extend past the selections.

Round or *Fillet Lines* create a new segment like Bevel Lines, but in this case, it's a smooth curve.

The basic modifications for splines include moving, adding or deleting control points, and adjusting tangent controls or weights (see Figure 3.12). As with the line, polyline and polygon modifications, there may not be specific commands for these operations. They are usually done through the use of the mouse buttons or modifier keys such as Shift, Ctrl, or Alt.

FIGURE 3.12

Common Bezier spline modifications. Control point adjustments (upper row). Tangent point adjustments (lower row).

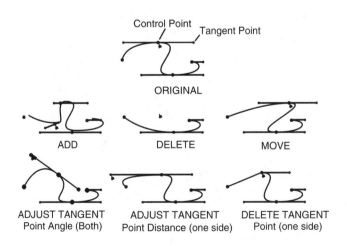

Add Control Point creates a new vertex, either along an existing curve or as an extension of the last point on the curve.

Delete Control Point removes a vertex and its adjacent curves, and causes a new curve to be formed between any vertices to which it was connected.

Move Control Point enables you to reposition the selected vertex and the curves to which it is connected.

On standard Bezier curves, the tangent points are locked together most of the time. If you move one, the other moves in a mirror fashion. Through the use of modifier keys or by changing the control point type, it becomes possible to adjust them independently, varying the distance (and sometimes the angle) of one side while leaving the other side undisturbed.

In addition to these common modifications, many programs enable you to convert polygonal lines or objects to splines, and vice versa. Drawing an outline with a polyline and then converting the shape to a spline can make it easier to create a smooth, complex object, because many people find it easier to rough out a shape with polylines (see Figure 3.13).

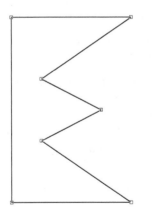 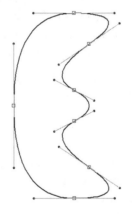

FIGURE 3.13

Some programs enable you to convert a poly into a smoothed spline. This can make it quicker and easier to create complex organic shapes.

Shape Resolution

As you know, image resolution relates to the number of pixels on a screen or image, allowing for more or less detail. Similarly, polygon resolution specifies the density of line segments and polygons for mesh, and therefore defines the amount of detail and smoothness in the object (see Figure 3.14).

FIGURE 3.14

Effects of resolution
on objects and open
splines: (a) High
resolution. (b) Medium
resolution. (c) Low
resolution.

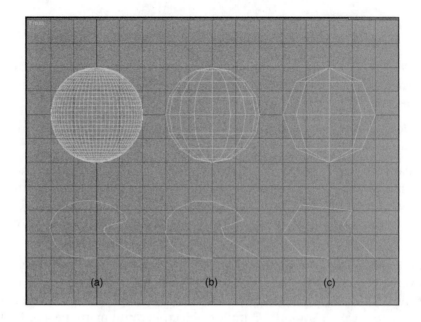

Although a polyline or polygon's resolution is usually set at the time you create it, it's sometimes possible to increase or decrease the resolution later on. Splines, on the other hand, must go through a conversion process when they're used in a polygonal modeler, and their resolution setting has a major effect on how smooth the curves remain.

A common term for indicating a shape or object's resolution is how many steps it contains. *Steps* refers to the number of additional vertices generated between control points on a spline or vertices on a poly. For example, a setting of 0 steps would mean no subdividing vertices would be added, because the line travels between the original control points or vertices in a single step. If the object had a step setting of 3, however, there would be three additional vertices added, making the line between the original points break into four segments.

It's important to note that resolution settings affect the shape or object as a whole, so if you increase the number of steps to smooth out a curve, the program may also subdivide the straight portions of the object as well, creating unnecessary vertices. Some programs may offer you an optimizing option to delete these extra vertices automatically, however.

2D Attach/Detach

Often, it's useful to attach 2D shapes together to join separately drawn elements, or to form a composite shape. *Attach* is a common command for 3D programs that enable you to join separate elements into one object (see Figure 3.15). Implementation varies, with some programs prompting to see whether you want to attach whenever 2D vertices are moved within range of each other. Other programs require you to select the elements and specifically command the software to attach them.

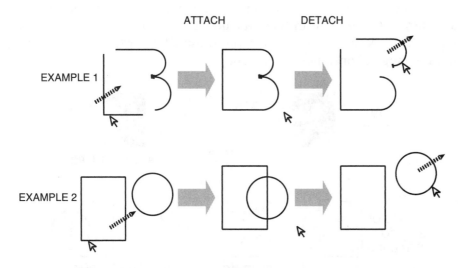

ATTACH   DETACH

EXAMPLE 1

EXAMPLE 2

FIGURE 3.15

Attach and Detach: (upper row) Attaching and detaching line segments makes it easier to create complex 2D shapes or to use portions of one shape elsewhere. (lower row) Attaching objects together is similar to grouping them. They can be detached at a later point.

Note

> Attaching two polylines together doesn't necessarily mean that they form a single *closed shape*. In some cases, you may have to *weld* (combine) the endpoints of the shapes together in a separate operation.

Likewise, you may want to *detach* part of a shape that divides the original object into two elements for use elsewhere—essentially the opposite of attach. Doing this usually requires you to select the elements you want, and then use the command Detach or something similar.

2D Booleans

Boolean operations (named for 19th century mathematician George Boole) enable you to build onto a shape by combining it with a second shape, or carve away at a shape by subtracting a second shape from the first. Booleans are very powerful and useful tools, because they enable you to create shapes that would take much longer if you made the changes by manipulating the vertices.

Shapes selected for Boolean operations are called *operands*, and the order in which you choose them will affect the outcome in some operations, such as Subtract. Other Boolean types include Add, Intersection, and Split (see Figure 3.16). Note that programs tend to use different terms for Booleans, but the range of operations is similar.

FIGURE 3.16

The 2D Boolean operations Add, Subtract, Intersection, and Split. When using Subtract, the second object selected is subtracted from the first.

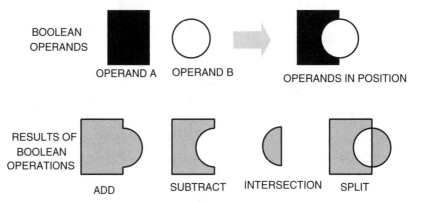

Boolean Add combines the shapes into one, adding their volumes together and deleting any overlaps. Add is great for building a very complex shape out of lots of simpler ones, like the cross-section of a gear made out of some circles and rectangles.

Boolean Subtract removes from the first shape any portions of the second shape that overlap it. Use subtract to carve away pieces of a shape or "cut holes" for creating hollow objects.

Boolean Intersection deletes any portion of either shape that isn't overlapping. This can be useful for creating shapes that "fit" snugly inside other shapes, like liquid inside a jar.

Boolean Split deletes any portion of both shapes that overlaps. You probably won't use this one much, but it's nice to know it's available.

Importing/Exporting Shapes

Another advantage of working with 2D shapes is that they're readily transportable from 2D drawing programs to 3D modelers, and vice versa. This means you can *export* (save in a compatible format) existing work created in Adobe Illustrator or CorelDRAW!, for example, and import it into your 3D program.

Most 3D programs support at least one 2D import/export format. DXF (Drawing eXchange Format) is a common one, along with AI (Adobe Illustrator) and IGES (Initial Graphics Exchange Specification). See Chapter 10, "Rendering and Output," for more information.

Turning 2D Shapes into 3D Objects

You've seen how to create and edit 2D shapes, but how are they turned into 3D objects? Actually, you can apply several different operations to one or more shapes, with a surprisingly broad range of results. The most commonly used operations are extrudes, lathes, sweeps, and skins. Shape resolution plays a part in these operations as well, because the software usually enables you to define how many increments (steps or segments) are used when converting a shape from 2D to 3D. By the way, shapes don't have to have depth in order to be useful in 3D scenes. As long as a 2D shape is converted into a flat polygon with a face, it can be mapped and used in a model just like any other object.

Most 3D programs make heavy use of the mouse for defining and moving shapes and objects, but most offer numerical entry as well, enabling you to enter precise coordinates, distances, or transformation percentages.

Extrusions

The most straightforward way of making a 2D shape into a 3D object is by extruding it. An *extrusion* is simply pushing the 2D shape into the third dimension by giving it a Z-axis depth (see Figure 3.17). The result of an extrusion is a 3D object with width, height, and now, depth.

FIGURE 3.17

Extrude process: (a) 2D shapes are defined using polylines or splines. (b–d) Extrude is applied to the 2D shapes, giving them whatever depth is desired.

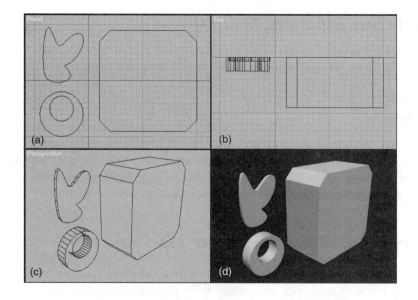

Extrusions are very useful for creating block-like shapes, columns, panels, and the like, but the sharp-edged result definitely has a CG look to it. In Chapter 5 you'll learn how to modify the Extrude operation to make this less obvious.

To create an extruded object, first define the 2D shapes with polylines or splines. Note that if you create shapes within shapes, such as the two circles in the figure, the inner ones will create holes in the object. Next, select the desired shapes and apply an Extrude operation to them, setting the depth of the object with mouse movement or numerical entry.

Lathing

The next method of forming a 3D object is lathing. In woodworking, a lathe is a device that rotates a block of wood at high speed, enabling you to trim away at the wood with a sharp gouge. Lathes are used to create intricately carved cylindrical objects such as chair legs and bedposts. In 3D modeling, a *Lathe* command spins a 2D shape around an axis, extruding it in small steps as it rotates (see Figure 3.18).

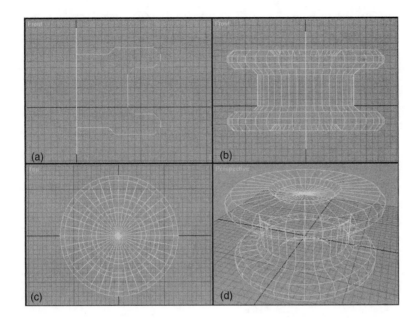

FIGURE 3.18

Lathe process:
(a) A 2D cross-section
is created, and the
lathe axis selected.
(b–d) The Lathe
operation spins the
cross-section around
the axis, extruding it
in small steps.

Lathe is ideal for creating any kind of radial object, such as pulleys, reels, pipe flanges, and of course, *wine glasses*. Along with extrude, it's one of the fundamental operations in 3D graphics.

To create a lathed object, define a 2D object or objects with polylines or splines to use as a cross-section. Selecting the Lathe command enables you to define the axis around which the cross-section will be spun. The result is a radially symmetrical 3D object.

Like many 3D tools, lathe offers significantly different results depending on how you set your axis. If the axis is located in the center of the cross-section, it results in a *closed lathe*, whereas an *open lathe* results if the axis is moved away from the center point (see Figure 3.19).

Lathes don't have to be a full 360°—they could just as easily be 90°, 180°, or 272°, resulting in a *partial lathe*. Partial lathes are useful for creating cut-away views of objects, or for eliminating unnecessary portions of the form, such as when part of the lathed object will be inside of another object.

FIGURE 3.19

Lathe types: (a) Closed
lathe. (b) Open lathe.
(c) Closed partial
lathe. (d) Open partial
lathe.

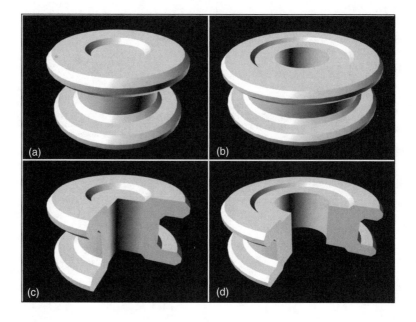

Sweeping

Although common, the next two 2D-to-3D operations have different (and
sometimes contradictory) terms applied to them depending on the software being used. For example, 3D Studio refers to these operations as lofts,
but many other products refer to them as sweeps, and that's what they'll
be called here. A *sweep* is a single 2D cross-section that is extruded along a
path (see Figure 3.20).

To create a swept object, start by defining a 2D cross-section with polylines
or splines. Next, create a path for the cross-section to follow by using polylines or splines. Note that this path can be open or closed. Assign the
cross-section to the path or vice-versa, adjusting its orientation. The cross-
section doesn't have to be centered on the path, nor does it need to be
perpendicular. Of course, the orientation will affect the final result. Finally,
performing the Sweep operation extrudes the cross-section along the path
to create a 3D object.

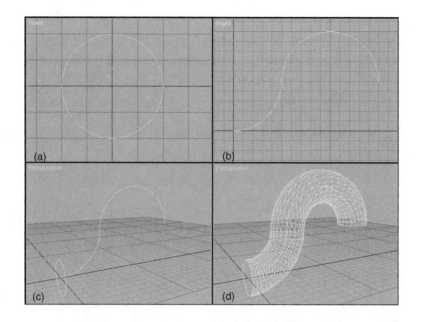

FIGURE 3.20

Sweep process:
(a) Define a 2D cross-section. (b) Create a path using polylines or splines. (c) Assign the cross-section to the path or vice-versa, adjusting its orientation. (d) Sweep the cross-section along the path to create a 3D object.

Sweeps come in three basic flavors, defined by the path: open, closed, and helical (see Figure 3.21). Although helical could just be considered another open sweep, it is used so often that it deserves special mention.

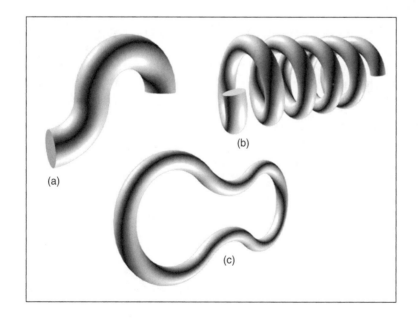

FIGURE 3.21

Sweep types:
(a) Open sweep.
(b) Helical sweep.
(c) Closed sweep.

Open sweeps are created with paths that have two ends, and are ideal for creating a curved extrusion, which the standard Extrude command can't do. Obvious uses are creating wires, rope, and tubing, plant stalks, snakes, or any sort of bent stock used in manufactured items.

Helical sweeps are a form of open sweep in which the path coils around like a spring, which happens to be the most common use for this type. It's also useful for creating screw threads. Most programs offer controls for generating the helical path for this sweep easily.

Closed sweeps are created by closing the path, so that the cross-section meets up with itself as it is swept along. Closed sweeps are good for creating such things as fan belts, picture frames, trim, or bumpers around other objects.

Although we won't be getting into texture mapping until Chapter 6, "Texture Mapping," it's worth noting that sweeps are one of the types of objects that can be tricky to texture map properly if you don't assign mapping coordinates at the time you make them.

Skinning

The final common way of converting 2D shapes into 3D objects is by *skinning,* which is similar to an open sweep, except that you can use different cross-sectional shapes along the path (see Figure 3.22). In essence, the program creates a "skin" to wrap over this framework, something like the way fabric or plastic is stretched over metal tines to create an umbrella.

Depending on your program, skinning operations may require some extra preparation. For example, your program may demand that each cross-section (CS) have the same number of vertices. If this is the case, you need to add vertices to some shapes so that they all have the same quantity.

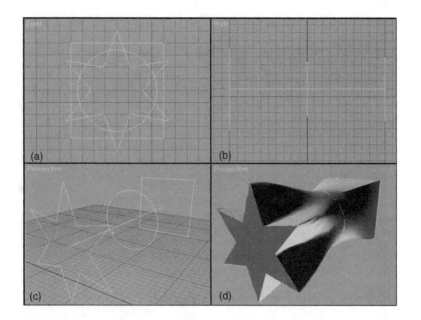

FIGURE 3.22

Skinning process:
(a) Define the 2D
cross-sectional shapes.
(b[en]c) Create a path
and determine where
the cross-sections will
be located. (d) Perform
the Skin operation,
which creates a sur-
face to bridge the
cross-sections.

In many cases, skinning operations are sensitive to the orientation of the first vertex (discussed earlier) on each cross-section, because the program starts the skin by connecting these first vertices. In general, you want the first vertex of each CS to be more or less in line with the others. Otherwise, the object may appear to be twisted (see Figure 3.23). This will require some planning on your part to arrive at a good combination of vertex quantity and placement.

After the cross-sections are ready, you create a path (straight or curved) to define the depth of the final skinned object. The last step is to assign the cross-sections to the path, which may be done in different ways, depending on the software. Some products require you to position the cross-sections at their appropriate depths, then do the Sweep operation by selecting each CS in order. Other programs enable you to leave the cross-sections in their original location, then assign them by distance or per-centage to the path. In either case, the process is a good way of creating models of machine parts, rifle stocks, toy cars, and other moderately complex objects.

FIGURE 3.23

(a)   (b)

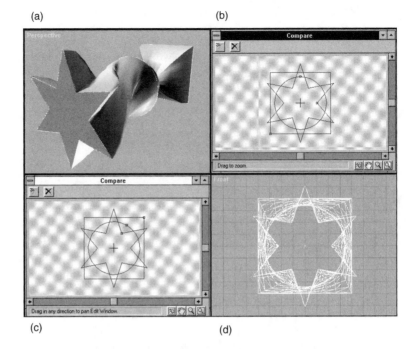

Skinning gone awry:
(a) Problem: the 3D
object appears twisted.
(b) Examining the cross-
sections shows that the
first vertices are not
aligned. (c) Rotating the
cross-sections creates a
better alignment. (d) The
skin on the adjusted
object is now much
less twisted.

(c)   (d)

3D Primitives

Primitives are the building blocks of 3D—basic geometric forms that you can use as is or modify with transforms and Booleans (see Figure 3.24). Although it's possible to create most of these objects by lathing or extruding 2D shapes, most software packages build them in for speed and convenience.

The most common 3D primitives are cubes, pyramids, cones, spheres, and tori. Like 2D shapes, these primitives can have a resolution level assigned to them so that you can make them look smoother by boosting the number of sides and steps used to define them.

Some primitives, such as cylinders, cones, and hemispheres, have a flat, "cut-off" section called a *cap*. Some programs enable you to select from different styles of caps, and even omit the caps altogether.

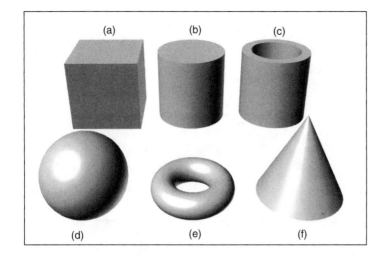

FIGURE 3.24

Common 3D Primitives:
(a) Cube. (b) Cylinder.
(c) Tube. (d) Sphere.
(e) Torus. (f) Cone.

Inappropriate use of unmodified primitives is probably one of the most common novice mistakes. By their very nature, primitives have a mathematically perfect appearance that screams, "I am a 3D object!" As you will learn in Chapter 5, you're generally better off using less perfect 2D shapes as the basis for your 3D objects. Primitives are best suited as building blocks for more complex forms or for use in your scene's background, where any extra detail will be lost anyway. Also, primitives can be very useful as foreground objects when they're altered through the use of transforms and modifiers (more on this in Chapter 5).

Some programs may offer an array of additional, more sophisticated primitives that may be better suited to foreground use because they offer beveled or rounded edges instead of that "chopped-off 3D look" (see Figure 3.25). A number of these extended primitives would be a real chore to create from scratch, so they can be a time-saver in that regard as well.

That about does it for building basic 3D objects. It's time to move on to the particulars of positioning these objects in 3D space. It's a big universe in there, so it's essential to know how to get around.

FIGURE 3.25

"Extended" 3D primitives available in some programs provide beveled and radius edges as well as difficult-to-model shapes: (a) Filleted Cube. (b) Spindle. (c) Beveled Cylinder. (d) Torus Knot. (e) Capsule. (f) Star Polyhedron.

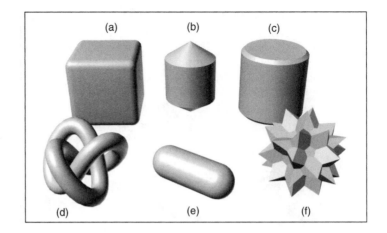

Transforms

In general, *transforms* are operations that alter the position, size, or orientation of an object. Such basic transforms as Move, Scale, and Rotate are essential to any modeling task, because you have to be able to adjust the position and orientation of the separate objects to make a scene.

Every program uses a different interface for controlling transforms, but many of them involve having some sort of gizmo appear inside or around a 3D object when it is selected. The gizmo usually includes a visual axis indicator representing the local axes of the object and its pivot point, and has some sort of handles you drag with the mouse to perform the selected transform.

Transforms may be affected by *axis locks* or *axis constraints*, which are controls in the software that enable you to turn off movement along the X, Y or Z-axis, or any combination of them. Axis constraints enable you to transform objects along the desired axis only, which prevents accidental movement in unwanted directions.

Because so many things affect axis orientation, what is the correct axis one minute might be wrong the next. So, if your object stubbornly refuses to move, rotate, or do any other transform in the desired direction, check to see whether axis constraints or some other types of locks are active.

The current coordinate system (view, world, local) in use can have a big impact on transforms. Transforms may also be affected by the pivot point location, because they use it as the center of the transform operation. The pivot point may be centered in the object or offset into the boonies somewhere. Usually an indicator of some kind shows you whether the program is set to use the object's pivot point or whether it is using one that the software sets in the center of the object.

Move

It comes as no surprise that *Move* relocates objects, allowing you to place shapes and objects anywhere in the 3D universe. In most cases, this is done with the mouse, but many programs also provide a way to enter this data numerically for precise adjustments.

Move may be affected by the current coordinate system and axis constraints only, unless inverse kinematics (see Chapter 9, "Animation") are in effect. The pivot point setting has no effect on Move.

Rotate

Rotate makes an object revolve around the selected axis. The tricky part about Rotate is making sure everything is set up so that the object revolves in the way you want. For example, do you want to rotate using the Screen, World, or Local axes? Which pivot point are you using, and is it centered in the object, or offset somewhere? The *pivot point* of an object is located at the junction of its local axes, similar to the way the origin point resides at the center of the three world axes. When you rotate the object, it revolves around this pivot point. Your 3D software will probably have some sort of controls for defining multiple pivot points and selecting which pivot point you want to use for a given Rotate operation.

Imagine you were making a simple model of the solar system. For the sphere representing Earth, you would want to set the pivot point at its center and rotate it around the Y (up/down) axis, so it spins around more or less like it should. (Ignore the fact that the Earth is tilted slightly off-axis for the moment.) In addition to spinning around like a top, the Earth also has to orbit around the Sun, which means you also need to have another pivot point in the center of the sphere representing old Sol. When you rotate around that center point, the Earth sphere will move in a broad circle around the Sun sphere.

When doing rotation or other transforms, make sure your software's visual axis indicator is turned on, if it has one. This will tell you where and which way the axes are located before you do the rotation. As you would expect, the axis you choose to rotate the object around has a dramatic effect on the results (see Figure 3.26).

FIGURE 3.26

Rotate revolves objects around the desired axis. (a) The base object. (b) Rotation around the X-axis. (c) Rotation around the Y-axis. (d) Rotation around the Z-axis.

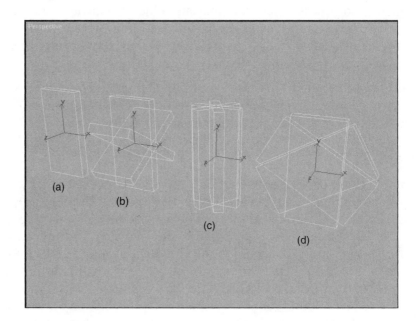

Scale

Use *Scale* to adjust the overall size of an object. Like other transforms, the results of a scale operation may vary according to the coordinate system, axis constraint settings, and pivot point. For example, if the X-axis is the only one active, a scale stretches the object horizontally only. If all three axes are active, scale re-sizes the object in all directions (see Figure 3.27).

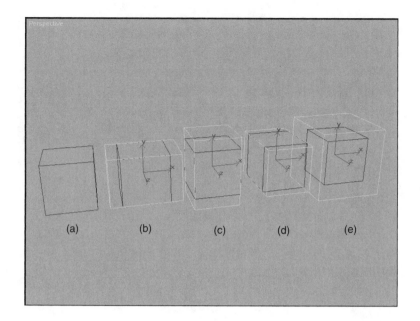

FIGURE 3.27

The Scale command re-sizes objects along the desired axes.
(a) The base object.
(b) Scaling the X-axis.
(c) Scaling the Y-axis.
(d) Scaling the Z-axis.
(e) Scaling all axes simultaneously.

If the scale operation is set to use the object's non-centered pivot point, the scale will transform the object toward or away from that point. For example, if the pivot point is located on the left face of a cube, a scale operation will leave the left face in the same position while scaling all of the other faces away from it.

Mirror

The transform command *Mirror* either reverses an object or copies a reversed version of it along the selected axis (see Figure 3.28). Some programs enable you to select multiple axes to mirror around as well. Mirror may be affected by the coordinate system and axis constraints.

In addition to making reversed copies of entire objects, Mirror can be a great help when dealing with complex symmetrical objects, like human faces. If you work with only the right or left half of the face when editing, you reduce the clutter of having all those extra vertices. When you want to check your work, Mirror-copy the face to create the missing side.

FIGURE 3.28

Effects of mirror: (a) The object is selected, and a mirror axis defined. (b) If the user elects to Mirror-copy the object, a second reversed version is created.

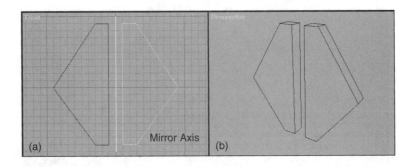

Mirror Axis

(a)   (b)

Align

Align enables you to bring object surfaces flush with each other or center multiple objects along one or more axes. Align is great for getting objects lined up the way you want them without tedious zooming and repositioning. Align is also useful for quickly bringing an object into the appropriate area of a scene if it has been accidentally created or imported into some obscure corner of 3D space. Align may be affected by the axis constraints.

There are quite a few different Align settings, depending on your software. The basic ones are *Align Center*, *Align Left*, and *Align Right,* which do exactly what they say (see Figure 3.29). The alignment can take place on one or more axes, and some products enable you to align to any object, face, edge, or vertex to another.

FIGURE 3.29

Typical Align types: (a) The base objects are currently centered on the Z-axis, and the bottoms are aligned with each other. In the following examples, the small cube will be aligned to the larger one. (b) Align Center, on both the X- and Y-axis. (c) Align Left on the X-axis. (d) Align Left on the X-axis, plus Align Center on the Y-axis.

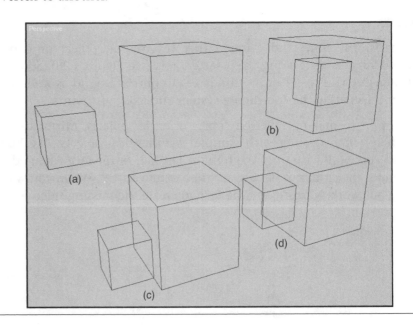

(a)   (b)   (c)   (d)

Deforms

You've learned how to move, scale, and rotate things; now it's time to apply some torque to them. *Deforms* such as Bend, Twist, Skew, and so forth, enable you to easily alter primitives and other objects in subtle or dramatic ways.

> If you aren't using a parametric modeler to do your deforms—or if you plan to collapse the object down to editable mesh—you may want to save off a version of an object before you apply a bend or twist to it. These sorts of deforms are very difficult to alter later in the modeling process if you find you need to make an adjustment.

Like transforms, deforms may be affected by axis constraints, the current coordinate system, and the pivot point settings. They may have additional parameters of their own that also affect outcome, such as an independent center point. In addition, deforms are affected by the resolution of an object. If the object on which you're performing a deform operation doesn't have enough steps or segments, the result won't be satisfactory (see Figure 3.30). This means you have to think about how you will be modifying an object at the time you create it to ensure that you will be happy with the results later on, when you apply the deform. Clearly, this is one of the reasons why spline and parametric modeling is so popular—they enable you to adjust the resolution of an object at just about any point.

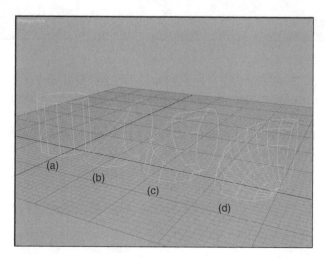

FIGURE 3.30

The effects of object resolution during a deform. (a) Cylindrical primitive with no deformation applied. (b) Bend performed on a single-segment cylinder. (c) Bend on a 3-segment cylinder. (d) Bend on a 10-segment cylinder.

Bend

The *Bend* deform distorts an object evenly around the selected axis. As the student in this chapter's opening story discovered, Bend requires some planning if you expect to do other deforms on the same object. This is because when you bend an object, it no longer conforms to one or more of the axes you might need for a later deform, such as a Twist. Therefore, Bend is often one of the last deforms you do to an object to distort it into the finished form. Also, Bend may be affected by the coordinate system, the axes constraints, and the position of the object's pivot point (see Figure 3.31).

FIGURE 3.31

Bend distorts an object around an axis.
(a) The base object.
(b) 90-degree bend with pivot point at base of object.
(c) 90-degree bend with pivot point in center of object.

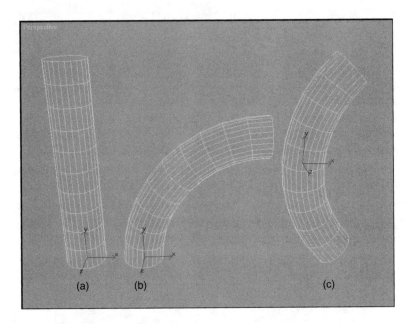

Taper

The *Taper* command compresses and expands an object along the selected axis. Taper may be sensitive to coordinate setting and axis constraints, as well as the position of the object's pivot point, because Taper uses it as a sort of fulcrum for the operation (see Figure 3.32).

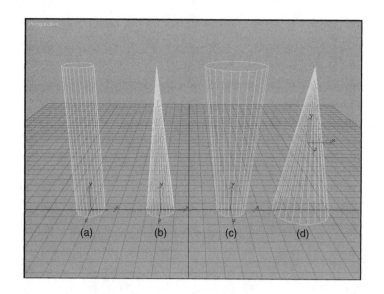

FIGURE 3.32

Effects of pivot point location on Taper:
(a) The base object.
(b–c) If the pivot is at one end of the object, that end is unaffected.
(d) If the pivot is centered in the object, both ends are affected in opposite ways.

Skew

Skew forces one side of the object in one direction along the selected axis, and the other side in the opposite direction. This is akin to putting your hands on the sides of your face and pushing up with your right hand while pulling down with your left. Like the other deforms, Skew may be affected by the coordinate system, the axis you have selected, and the pivot position (see Figure 3.33).

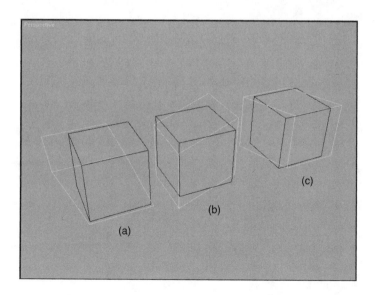

FIGURE 3.33

The effects of Skew (the affected object has been scaled a bit larger than the original for clarity): (a) Skewing on the X-axis. (b) Skewing on the Y-axis.
(c) Skewing on the Z-axis.

To be sure, Skew probably isn't going to be one of your most commonly used operations. It does have its uses, although you can often attain the same results with other tools, instead.

Twist

Twist winds an object around an axis like the stripes on a barber's pole (see Figure 3.34). Twist may be affected by coordinates, axes constraints, and the pivot point. Twist makes heavy demands on the affected faces of the object, so setting the proper mesh resolution is important.

FIGURE 3.34

Twist winds an object around the selected axis. It requires an object with substantial mesh resolution along the twist axis, or the results may be disappointing.

Squash and Stretch

The transforms *Squash* and *Stretch* are modified scale operations that treat the object as though it has liquid inside it. Instead of merely expanding or collapsing an object to any degree you select, they make it act as if it were made of bubble gum. Squashing the object makes it spread out around the edges, and stretching makes the object get thin in the middle (see Figure 3.35). Squash and Stretch may be affected by coordinate settings, axes constraints, and the pivot point.

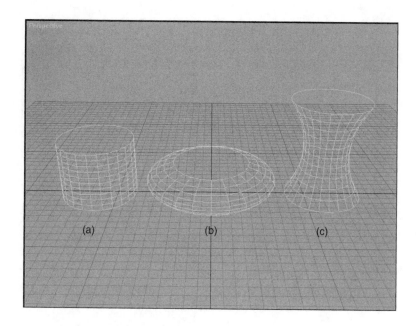

FIGURE 3.35

Squash and stretch in action: (a) The base object. (b) Squash makes the object spread out around the edges. (c) Stretch makes the object thinner in the middle, as if you were pulling gum apart.

Duplicating Mesh

Shapes and objects often have to be duplicated in the process of modeling, and there are several ways to do this. Many programs allow you to duplicate shapes and objects easily when doing a transform operation by holding down a modifier key like Shift as you move, scale, or rotate the object. This generates a copy that you continue to transform while leaving the original intact. As with the transform and deform operations, the current coordinate system, axis constraints, and pivot point may have an effect on the outcome.

Copying and Instancing

Most of the time, you'll use a *clone* or *copy* operation similar to the method just outlined to create an identical duplicate of the selected object. There are a couple of variations on the cloning theme, however. Straightforward clones are simply copies of the original, and become objects in their own right, just as if you had made them from scratch. Each of them can be modified independently of its mesh brethren (see Figure 3.36). Naturally, this is desirable if you're trying to create variation between the objects.

FIGURE 3.36

Cloning and instancing:
(a) The original object.
(b) Duplicated made by
Move-copy or some other
operation. (c) With regu-
lar copies, each duplicate
can be modified inde-
pendently. (d) With
instanced copies, modifi-
cations made to any of
the copies affect them all.

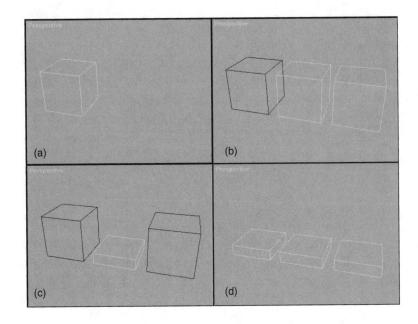

On the other hand, there will be times when you want to be able to affect a large number of objects in the same fashion, without working on them one by one. In these cases, you can opt to create *instanced objects*, which appear to be copies, but are actually the same object seen at different points in space. It's sort of like going into a house of mirrors—there's only one *you*, but there seem to be a small army of clones about. In addition, instanced objects consume very little memory, so your system tends to operate and render faster than if the copies were straight clones.

Instanced objects are a real time-saver when dealing with scenes that use lots of identical objects, like a structure made up of identical columns. If you decide to make an adjustment to the columns' shape, you need adjust only one and the rest will change automatically. One caveat, though—transforms such as scale and rotate may or may not affect an instance depending on the program and how you set the parameters.

Arrays

A convenient way to create a series of clones, instanced or otherwise, is to use the Array command. *Array* creates a matrix or pattern of objects based on the one you have selected.

A *linear array* is a series of copies made in a line along a selected axis (see Figure 3.37). To create a linear array, you select an object, then define an axis, distance, and number of duplicates desired. The duplicates can either be identical to the original, but simply offset, or they can have additional transforms done to them, such as Rotate or Scale.

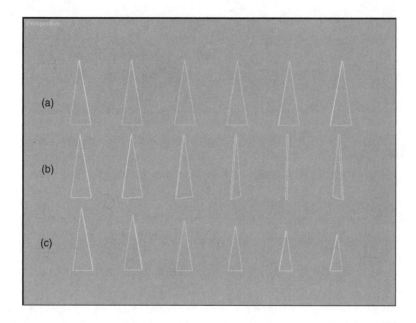

FIGURE 3.37

Examples of linear Arrays: (a) A basic linear array. (b) A linear array with rotation applied. (c) A linear array with scaling applied.

Arrays don't have to be linear, however. They also can be rotation-based, resulting in a *radial array* (see Figure 3.38). The process here is very similar, except that you select a rotation axis and specify the number of copies along with the angle in degrees that you want them offset from each other.

FIGURE 3.38

Rotational arrays:
(a) Object with pivot point
offset along Y and Z axes.
(b) X-axis array. (c) Y-axis
array. (d) Z-axis array.

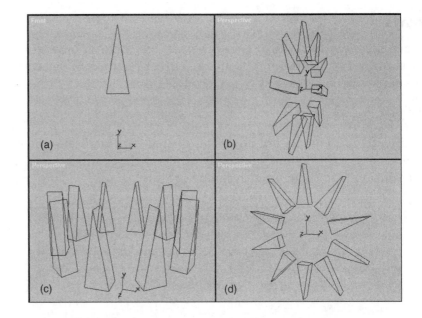

Digging In

All right! It's time to think about *building something.*

Because this book doesn't focus on a single 3D product, the tutorials that follow provide general instructions rather than details about the specific tools you must use for each step. (Note, however, that this new edition of the book has product-specific tutorials for Max, Maya, and LightWave located on the included CD-ROM.) For example, the steps will tell you to "make a rectangle and extrude it" rather than "press Ctrl-R to make a rectangle and Ctrl-E to extrude it." I've made every effort to ensure that the operations presented are available in most programs or that you will be able to use alternative methods for tools or techniques your package doesn't offer.

If you are learning a NURBS-based package, such as Maya or the Rhino modeler, the steps will probably vary quite a bit from this generic tutorial, which is based primarily on polygonal modeling techniques. Users of these types of packages should use the Maya-specific tutorial located on the CD-ROM, but should take a look at the other tutorials to see how the process works for polygonal modeling. By the same token, I recommend that users who follow the generic, max, or LightWave tutorials take a look at the Maya tutorials to get an idea of the advantages and disadvantages of NURBS modeling. Having a good handle on different modeling approaches helps you to select the best approach for constructing a given object.

If you've already spent some time with 3D programs, you may be able to plunge right in and use the reference guide section of your manuals to get over any rough spots. If you are totally new to this or are using a brand-new package, you'll need to learn how a given tool or operation is implemented in your software. In this case, you may be better off going through sections of the user's guide in your manuals, and perhaps do the basic tutorials as well. After doing the software manual's tutorials and learning the necessary commands, try the ones in this chapter. Think of them as an addendum to your manual or as tests to make sure you thoroughly understand the tools.

Note that most manuals take a very piecemeal approach to their tutorials, giving you a basic task to perform that demonstrates an idea, and then discarding that work when you move on to the next tool. The result is a collection of unusable micro-projects, leaving you to start from scratch to make something presentable. With this book, the tutorials are interrelated and build on each other toward producing a finished portfolio piece.

The tutorial subject is an advertising blimp, inspired by Ridley Scott's futuristic *film noir* masterpiece, *Blade Runner* (see Figure 3.39). Due to copyright restrictions, I couldn't use the film's exact blimp design, but this version offers more of an opportunity to try out the tools in more or less the order in which they were presented in the text. In addition, this project should be challenging enough for most of you just starting out, and you are highly encouraged to customize and enhance it with additional details anyway.

FIGURE 3.39

The Blade Runner-
esque advertising
blimp, which you can
construct with the help
of the tutorials. By cus-
tomizing and adding
additional details and
mapping, you can turn
it into a real portfolio
piece.

The blimp is ideal for a tutorial of this type because it is a subject that encompasses just about every tool and technique presented, from basic 3D shapes to deform modifiers. More importantly, it can be customized easily, so you can modify it to your own taste and showcase your creative strengths and style, not to mention your new-found 3D skills. For example, you could give it a 1950s or Victorian look, or make it totally *Alien*. You could incorporate it into your demo reel and plaster the sides with "billboards" of your contact information or the reel's credits. (If you decide to alter the blimp, you may want to first read the section on concept and design, "The Reel," in Chapter 11.)

3D Modeling Tutorials

Topics covered:

> **Using Extrude**
>
> **Using Lathe (Closed, Open, and Partial)**
>
> **Using Sweep (Closed, Open)**
>
> **Using Skinning**
>
> **Using Transforms (Move, Scale, Rotate, Taper, Twist, Align)**
>
> **Using Duplication and Instancing (Mirror, Array)**

About the Tutorials

In the following tutorials, you will begin to construct portions of the blimp model. At this point, you should either have tried out the following techniques, or be working with your software manuals to see how your package accomplishes each one of these operations.

If you run into difficulties, review the section of the book that deals with the problem operation, paying particular attention to tips that may help you figure out the problem. The life of a modeler/animator is filled with challenges both artistic and technical, so consider this as part of your training and try to find a creative way around the problem.

The tutorial steps presented here are generic and can be adapted to work with nearly any program. However, if you are using one of the more popular 3D packages on the market, including discreet 3ds max 4.2, Alias|Wavefront Maya 4, or NewTek LightWave 7, there are program-specific tutorials and mesh files of the project at various stages on the companion CD-ROM in the back of this book. If you are using one of these packages, I strongly recommend you use the version of the tutorials on the disc rather than the ones in the book.

At the start of the chapter, the basic strategies of planning out a 3D project were presented. For the blimp, the logical overall strategy would be to construct the gas bag first, then add the large video screens. Next would come the other major sub-assemblies, such as the engines and spires. The logos and other details would come last. Unfortunately, the construction of the gas bag is an advanced chapter project, so you'll be doing the monitor screens and engines first. The individual object strategies will become apparent when you do the tutorials.

There will probably be several occasions during the course of these tutorials where objects don't materialize in the 3D universe quite where you expect them. Read up on construction grids and planes in your manual to help you build objects where you want them. To help locate and move wayward pieces, use the Zoom All command, which adjusts the viewpoint to show all the mesh in the 3D universe. Most of the time, you'll find "missing" mesh off in the virtual boondocks somewhere. You'll probably use Zoom continually to make the objects large enough to work with.

Using Extrude

All units used to specify distances in the tutorials are generic—they don't represent any real-world measurements. Set your software to use generic units and decimal numbers if possible.

Start the tutorials by using a simple extrusion to create the monitor screen for the side of the blimp. Here's the procedure:

1. Turn on Grids and Snaps. In the right viewport, use lines and arcs to create the 2D monitor shape 575 units wide × 460 units high (see Figure 3.40a).

   If your software requires it, Attach the shapes together and/or Weld their vertices to create a single closed shape. Name it MonSHP01.

2. If your software doesn't leave the original shape intact when doing an Extrude, copy the shape and move the copy out of the way. You'll need it later on for another operation.

3. Select the first shape and Extrude it 15 units deep into a thin 3D panel, with one step or segment (see Figure 3.40b). Name the object MonScn01.

4. Save your file as B_MON01 and close it.

FIGURE 3.40

Creating an extruded object: (a) Draw the outline of the shape in 2D. (b) Use Extrude to give the shape the desired depth.

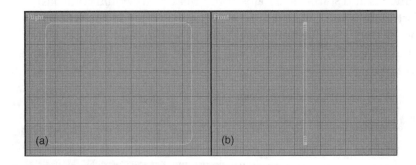

Using Lathe (Closed, Open, and Partial)

To try out the different lathe operations, switch over to working on the engines of the blimp, which are called thrusters (see Figure 3.41). The thrusters are enclosed propellers that move the blimp around.

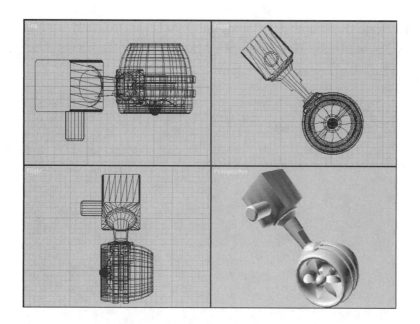

FIGURE 3.41

The completed thruster assembly. The cylindrical strut the thruster is attached to will rotate to allow the thrusters to operate at different angles.

Creating a Closed Lathe

Here are the steps for creating the nose cone in the center of the prop. Note that this shape could also be created by scaling a 3D hemisphere primitive, but this is a *lathe* tutorial, so you're going to use a lathe operation instead.

1. Create a new document. In the front viewport, draw three circles (with radii of 10, 45, and 56 units) to use as a reference in setting the scale of the thruster shroud and nose cone (see Figure 3.42a).

   These lines will not be used to create the 3D objects, but are useful for "roughing out" a shape before modeling. If your software doesn't support the creation of 2D shapes in the 3D environment like this, ignore these references.

2. In the right viewport, offset the circles from each other by 10 units so that you can see them from this view, then Freeze or Ghost them so that they stay put (see Figure 3.42b).

3. In the right viewport, create an arc that is the same radius as the small reference circle you drew in the last step, 10 units (thickened here for clarity). Add a polyline that connects to the endpoints of the arc.

   If your software requires it, Attach the shapes together and/or Weld their vertices to create a single shape (see Figure 3.42c).

4. Scale the shape 150% along the X-axis (horizontally) to give it a more graceful appearance (see Figure 3.42d).

5. Save your work as B_THR02.

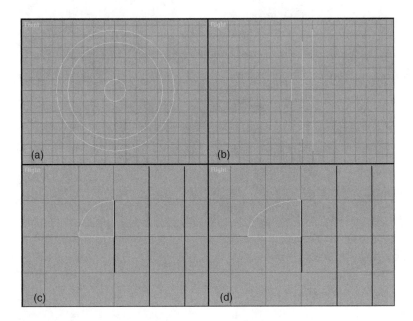

In most programs, choosing the Lathe command enables you to define the axis that you want to serve as the centerline of the lathing operation. In some products, however, you may need to define the object's axis in advance.

6. Choose Lathe and set the axis along the lower edge of the shape (see Figure 3.43a). This will determine the centerline around which the shape will be spun.

   This is a closed lathe because the axis touches the shape, creating a "solid" result.

7. Complete the Lathe operation, spinning the shape 360° into a 3D object with 16 segments (see Figure 3.43b).

8. Examine the results in a Camera or Perspective viewport (see Figure 3.43c). Does the object appear to have the right shape and proportions? If you were experimenting, this would be the point to Undo the operation and adjust the shape before lathing it again.

9. Render a close-up of the nose cone (see Figure 3.43d).

    Some programs have trouble with lathes like this, and may create odd artifacts near the centerline. Your software may offer a Weld Core command to correct this—if not, doing a Smooth operation (discussed in Chapter 5) should take care of any problems.

10. Name the object ThrNos01 and save your work as B_THR.

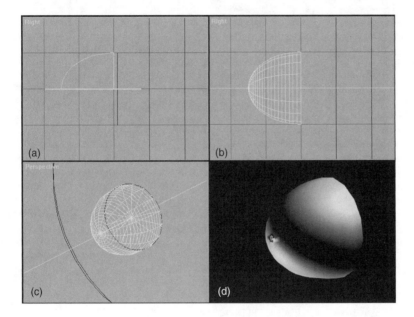

FIGURE 3.43

Steps for lathing the nose cone object:
(a) Set the axis for the lathe. (b) Spin the shape 360 degrees around the axis.
(c–d) Examine the resulting object for proper appearance. You may have to apply a smoothing operation to correct artifacts.

Creating an Open Lathe

To create the propeller shroud, use another lathe operation, this time with the axis some distance from the shape. Here are the steps:

1. Using the reference circles as a guide, create a closed spline cross-section of the shroud 102.5 units long (see Figure 3.44). Use five control points to define the spline.

    You may find it easier to create the rough shape with straight lines first, and then use the Bezier control points to adjust the curves.

FIGURE 3.44

Use a Bezier spline to create a cross-section of the
thruster's engine shroud.
Use polylines if your software doesn't support
splines.

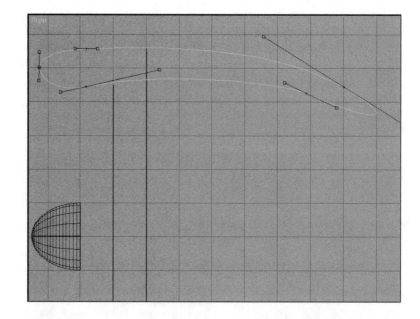

2. Choose Lathe (set to 16 steps or segments) and set the axis along
   the centerline of the nose cone. This will spin the shroud around
   the same axis as the cone. Complete the Lathe operation, spin
   ning the shape 360° into a 3D object (see Figure 3.45a).

3. Render the results in a Camera or Perspective viewport (see Figure
   3.45b). Name the object ThrShr01.

4. Save your work as B_THR04.

FIGURE 3.45

Steps for lathing the
engine shroud object.
(a) Set the axis for the
lathe in the center of the
thruster and spin the
shape 360 degrees
around it. (b) Examine the
resulting object for proper
appearance.

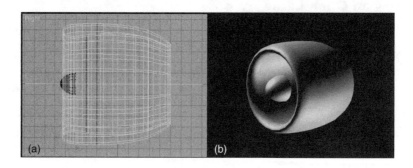

Creating a Partial Lathe

Next, create the reinforcing bands that partially surround the shroud.
Follow this procedure:

1. In the right viewport, draw a polyline cross-section of the band 11 units wide × 3.25 units high (see Figure 3.46a).

2. Position the cross-section as shown and set the axis to the same place as the previous lathes—the center of the thruster (see Figure 3.46b).

3. Lathe the object around the axis, but limit it to 300° rather than the full 360° (see Figure 3.46c).

4. The result is a partial lathe with a 60° gap starting at the top of the engine. If your software puts the gap on the opposite side, rotate the band around so that it matches the figure. Name the object ThrBnd01 (see Figure 3.46d).

5. Save your work as B_THR05 and close the file.

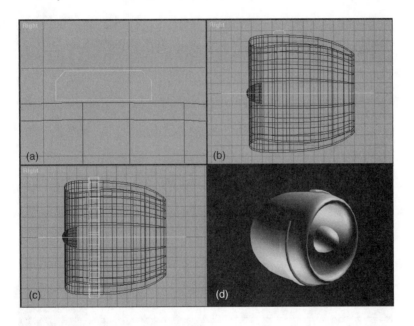

FIGURE 3.46

Doing a partial lathe of the support band:
(a) Create a polyline cross-section.
(b) Position the cross-section and set the axis. (c) Spin the shape 300° around the axis. (d) Make sure the gap is in the position shown.

Using Sweep (Closed, Open)

This is an opportunity to get experience with two kinds of sweeps: open and closed.

Closed Sweep

To try out a closed sweep, go back to the blimp monitor project and add a frame around it. Here are the steps:

1. Open the file B_MON01.

2. Draw a polyline cross-section of the monitor frame 26 units wide × 32 units high (see Figure 3.47a).

3. If necessary, position the cross-section along the spline MonSHP01 (or its duplicate) that you made earlier.

   Note that some programs may be sensitive to where the object is positioned for an operation like this, whereas others allow you to position it independently when doing the sweep (see Figure 3.47b).

4. Perform the Sweep operation, using the spline MonSHP01 as the path. Set shape segments to 0 and path segments to 1. The resulting sweep object should be centered around the screen. Name it MonFrm01 (see Figure 3.47c).

5. Render the monitor from a perspective view and check for proper appearance (see Figure 4.47d).

6. Save your file as B_MON02.

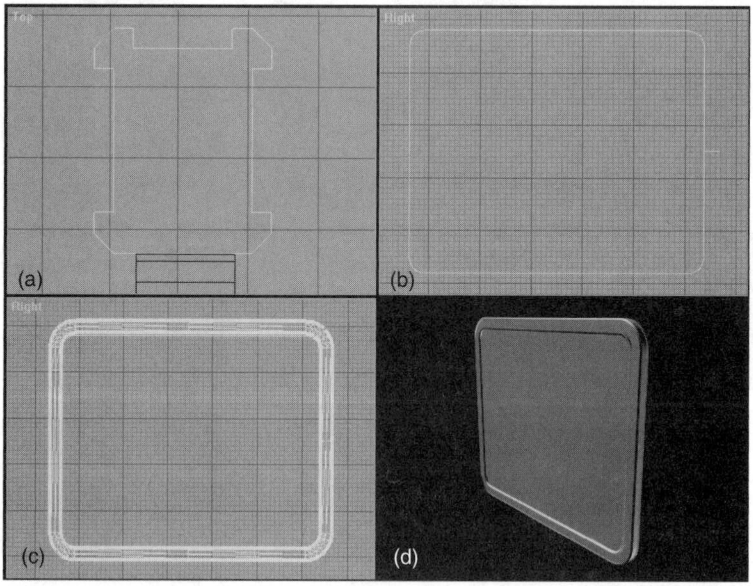

FIGURE 3.47

Create a closed sweep for the monitor frame:
(a) Draw a polyline cross-section.
(b) Position the cross-section up against the screen edge if your program requires that.
(c) Sweep the object using the monitor shape as the path.
(d) Check your results.

Open Sweep

Next, an open sweep is used to create a cable coming off the edge of the screen and connecting to a control box. Here are the steps:

1. Create a box 200 units wide × 70 units high × 40 units deep and position it on the far side of the object MonPnl01.

    This will be an electrical box for the monitor. Name it MonBox01 (see Figure 3.48a).

2. To make a cable running from the electrical box to the monitor frame, draw a spline coming out the end of the box, dropping down, then curving back up toward the MonFrm01 object. Create a circular cross-section nearby, with a radius of 5 units (see Figure 3.48b). Make sure the shapes are centered on the box depth-wise by checking the Front viewport.

3. Create a swept object with the circle, using the spline as a path. Name it MonCab01 (see Figure 3.48c).

4. Render a perspective view of the box and cable.

    Note that the end of the cable is hanging out in space right now. It will get fixed later on (see Figure 3.48d).

5. Save your file as B_MON03.

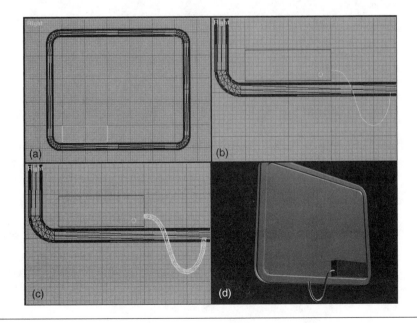

FIGURE 3.48

Creating an electrical box and cable:
(a) Create and position the box. (b) Create an open spline path and circular cross-section.
(c) Sweep the circle along the path.
(d) Check your work.

At this point, things may start to get a little busy on your screen. Use the Hide command to get unneeded mesh out of the way. Also, remember to use Freeze or Ghost if you need the mesh, but are having trouble selecting the right objects when other mesh is in the way.

Using Skinning

This is a tricky spot, so make sure you understand how your program deals with skinning before you do the tutorial. When you're ready, use skinning to create the bracket where the thruster attaches to the strut:

1. Open the file B_THR05.

2. In the Right view, create a closed polyline (50 units square) and two circles (radii 20 and 16 units) that will form the shape of the mounting bracket (see Figure 3.49a).

3. If your program requires that you use the same number of vertices for each cross-section, add four more vertices to each of the circles. Align the First Vertices of each of the shapes as closely as possible, using Rotate (see Figure 3.49b).

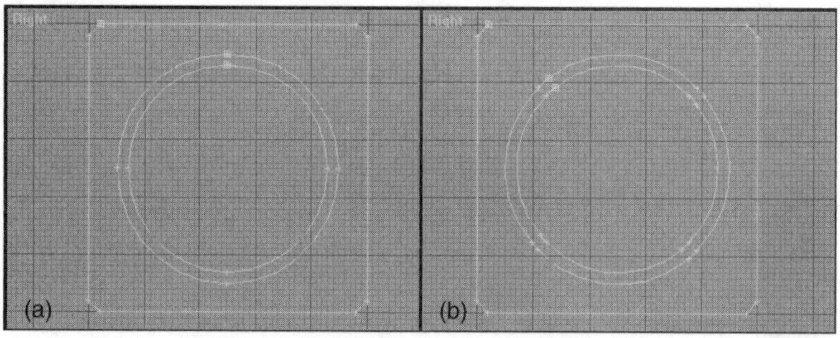

FIGURE 3.49

Create a skin object by drawing cross-sections: (a) Make sure that the first vertices are aligned now or during the skinning process. (b) If your program requires an equal number of vertices in each cross-section, add additional ones to the circles.

4. In the Front view, create a straight path 15 units long to define the depth of the skinned object. Position it in the center of the other shapes (see Figure 3.50a).

5. Using the method outlined by your program, assign the cross-sections to the path. The outermost shape should be used twice, once at the back (the point where the cross-sections reside) of the object and again at the 50% point on the path. The larger circle is used at the 75% and 90% points, and the smaller circle at 100% (see Figure 3.50b).

6. If the first vertices were properly aligned, the polygons in the object should not appear to be overly twisted (see Figure 3.50c).

7. Render the object to check for proper appearance. The shape and/or path step settings may have to be adjusted for a smooth result. Name the object ThrMnt01 (see Figure 3.50d).

8. Save the file as B_THR06.

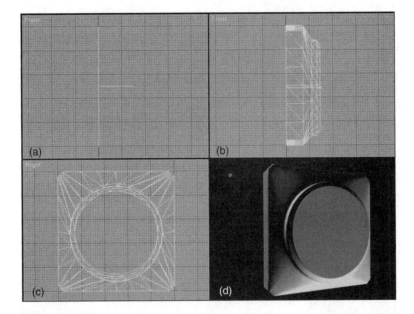

FIGURE 3.50

Creating the mounting bracket: (a) Draw a straight path defining the depth of the skinned object. (b) Skin the object by assigning the cross-sections to the appropriate points along the path. (c) Check for overly twisted cross-sections. (d) Check your work.

Move

Here, use Move to reposition the mounting bracket you made in the last tutorial into position on the side of the thruster:

1. In the Front viewport, select the mounting bracket and Move it to a point midway between the ends of the partially lathed band (see Figure 3.51a).

2. In the Right view, Move the mounting bracket horizontally until it is positioned as shown (see Figure 3.51b).

3. Save the file as B_THR07.

FIGURE 3.51

Moving the mounting bracket: (a) Move the bracket midway between the ends of the partially lathed band created earlier. (b) Adjust the horizontal position of the bracket as shown.

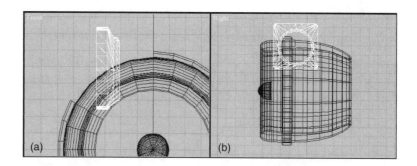

Rotate

Now, use Rotate to orient the mounting bracket:

1. In the Front viewport, Rotate the object 120 degrees counter-clockwise around its center until both ends intersect the engine shroud evenly, (see Figure 3.52).

    In the figure, the rotation is made on the Z-axis, but this may be different in your software.

2. Save the file as B_THR08.

FIGURE 3.52

Rotate the bracket (around the Z-axis in this example) until both ends intersect the engine shroud equally.

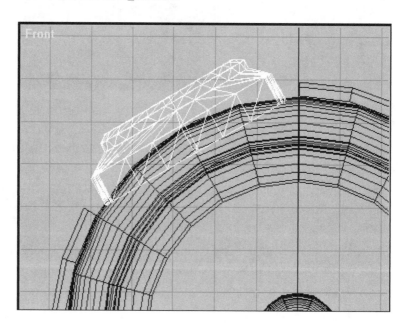

Bend

Returning to the monitor project for a moment, you can take care of that loose cable with a Bend.

1. Open the file B_MON03.

2. From the Top view, select the cable object MonCab01 and examine the axis indicator, which is probably centered in the object (see Figure 3.53a).

3. Use Axis Move or the appropriate command for your software to relocate the axis to the point where the cable meets the box. Because the bend occurs around the axis, it needs to be relocated or both ends of the cable would be affected (see Figure 3.53b).

4. Apply a Bend to the object until the end of the cable is centered in the monitor frame (see Figure 3.53c–d).

5. Save the file as B_MON04.

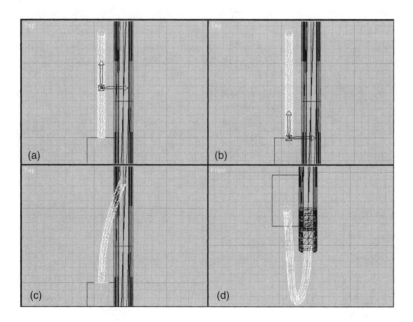

FIGURE 3.53

Bending the monitor cable: (a) The default position of the axis is the center of the object. (b) Relocate the axis to the end of the cable. (c–d) Apply Bend until the end of the cable is centered in the frame.

Scale

Y'know, that cable looks a little too big (how very convenient). Give Scale a try by re-sizing the monitor cable:

1. Make sure your software is set to scale along all three axes at once.

2. Check to make sure the axis of the object MonCab01 is centered along all three axes at the point where the cable meets the box. Scale the object MonCab01 down to 75% of its original size, noting that because the axis was at the end of the cable, it is scaled in that direction rather than toward the center of the object (see Figure 3.54a).

3. From the Front view, Move the cable horizontally until it is centered in the monitor frame again (see Figure 3.54b).

4. Save the file as B_MON05 and close it.

FIGURE 3.54

Scaling the monitor cable:
(a) Scale the cable down
by 25%. (b) Move it so
that the cable is centered
in the monitor frame.

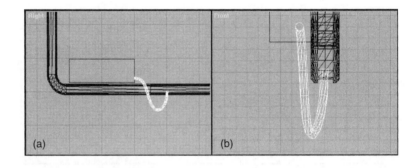

Taper

Next, use Taper to create a connector between the mounting base and the reinforcing band:

1. Open the file B_THR08.

2. Working near the top of the thruster, draw a polyline slightly larger than the cross-section of the band created earlier (see Figure 3.55a).

3. Extrude the connector outline until it bridges the gap between the mounting bracket and the band (see Figure 3.55b).

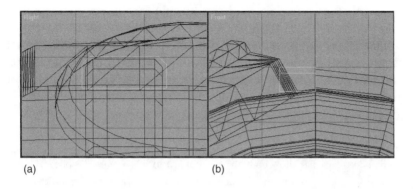

(a) (b)

FIGURE 3.55

Creating the connector: (a) Draw a polyline around the band cross-section.
(b) Extrude the polyline to bridge the gap between the bracket and band.

4. With the object's axis set at the band end of the connector, Taper the opposite end out about 30° along both available axes (see Figure 3.56a–c).

5. Render the model to check for proper appearance (see Figure 3.56d). Name the object ThrCon01.

6. Save the file as B_THR09.

(a) (b)

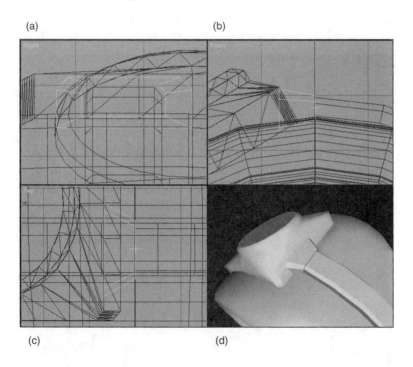

FIGURE 3.56

Tapering the connector: (a–c) Set the pivot point flush with the band end of the connector. Taper the object along both available axes. (d) Compare your result to this image.

(c) (d)

Twist

Twist makes heavy demands on the affected faces of the object, so setting the proper mesh resolution is important here. If trouble shows up, you may also want to increase the number of polygons on the object by increasing the number of steps in the propeller object before you extrude it.

 Some odd things may show up in the tutorial figures when twist is applied. This is because of low mesh resolution, but is unavoidable in this case because the figures would be too confusing and unclear if the mesh were made denser.

To demonstrate Twist, go ahead and make some propellers for the thruster:

1. In the front view create a cylinder (radius 7.5 units, 10 units deep) in the center of the thruster, behind the nose cone. (Check your placement in the right view.) Name the object ThrPrp01 (see Figure 3.57).

2. Create a spline outline of a propeller blade (45 units wide × 17 units high) with a total of 4 vertices.

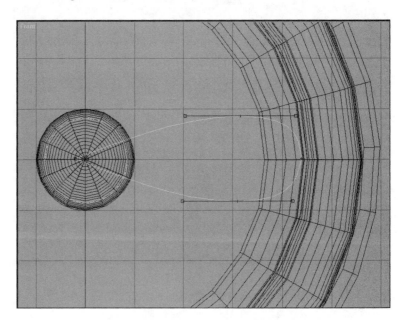

3. Move the propeller blade spline out in front of the thruster so it is easier to see and work with (see Figure 3.58a).

4. Extrude the spline 1 unit to make a thin blade (see Figure 3.58b).

5. Twist the blade about 30° around the long axis (see Figure 3.58c).

6. Render the blade and look for smoothing problems. Subdividing or tessellating the object before applying the twist may help (see Figure 3.58d). Save the object as ThrBdA01.

   By using letters as part of the object name, you can keep a "01" designation for all the blades in the first thruster.

7. Save the file as B_THR10.

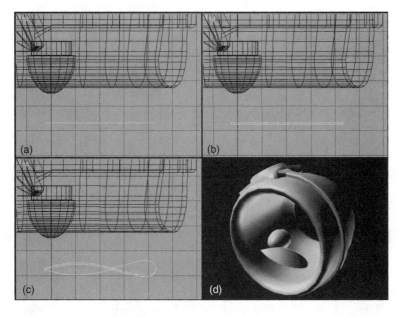

FIGURE 3.58

Twisting the propeller blade: (a) Move the spline away from the thruster. (b) Extrude it to create a thin blade. (c) Twist it 30 degrees around the long axis. (d) Examine the result for flaws.

Mirror

Normally, it's a good idea to apply mapping coordinates and texture to a single object before duplicating it, because it saves you time later on. Unfortunately, it would be disruptive to the tutorial to get into mapping issues at this point. You may, however, want to look over the mapping coordinate section of Chapter 6, "Texture Mapping," and do that work at this point.

For this tutorial, use Mirror to generate a reversed copy of the connector built earlier:

1. Select the connector (object ThrCon01) and Mirror copy it along the appropriate axis so that a reversed version appears (see Figure 3.59a).

   You may need to use a Shift key or other modifier to make Mirror create a copy rather than just reverse the original.

2. Set the connector copy to use the center of the thruster as the rotation axis. Rotate the copy counterclockwise about 55° into position on the opposite side of the mounting bracket (see Figure 3.59b).

3. Save the file as B_THR11.

FIGURE 3.59

Mirroring the connector: (a) Mirror copy the connector. (b) Rotate it into position on the opposite side of the mounting bracket.

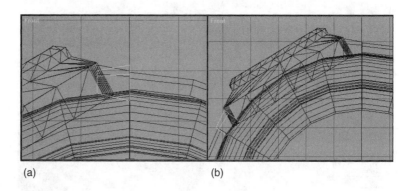

(a)   (b)

Copy

At this point, balance things out by copying the band and connectors:

1. Select the band and connectors (see Figure 3.60a).

2. Use the modifier key (usually Shift) for your software to do a Move-Copy operation. Drag the copy about 20 units into the position shown (see Figure 3.60b). Name the new object ThrBdA01 (ThrusterBandAssembly01).

3. Save the file as B_THR12.

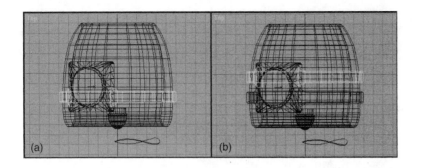

FIGURE 3.60

Copying the band and connectors: (a) Select all three objects. (b) Use a Move command with the correct modifier key (check your manual) to create a copy and position it as shown.

Align

Getting back to the propeller blades, use Align to position the first blade on the thruster model:

1. In the Top viewport, select the blade, ThrBdA01. Choose Align, and then select the prop object ThrPrp01 (see Figure 3.61a).

2. Choose the appropriate Align options to center the blade on the hub along the thruster's central axis (see Figure 3.61b).

3. Save the file as B_THR13.

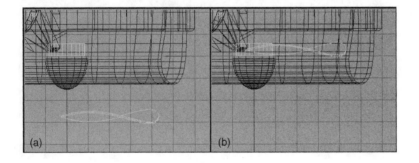

FIGURE 3.61

Aligning the blade: (a) Choose the blade, then Align. Select the prop hub object as the destination. (b) Set the Align options to center the blade as shown.

Arrays

Next, use a radial array to make the rest of the propeller blades:

1. From the Front viewport, select the propeller blade ThrBdA01, and make sure the pivot point is set to the center of the prop hub, ThrPrp01 (see Figure 3.62a).

2. Choose Array and set the rotation angle to 60°, the number of duplicates to 5, and the type of duplicate to "instanced." The result should be a radial array of six blades (see Figure 3.62b–c).

3. Render the model and observe the results. You may notice oddities in the blades now that you are seeing them from different angles (see Figure 3.62d).

4. Save the file as B_THR14.

FIGURE 3.62

Using Array to create the rest of the propeller: (a) Choose the blade and check that the pivot point is aligned with the center of the hub. (b–c) Use Array to make 5 more instanced duplicates rotated 60°. (d) Check the results to see whether any new anomalies have shown up in the blades.

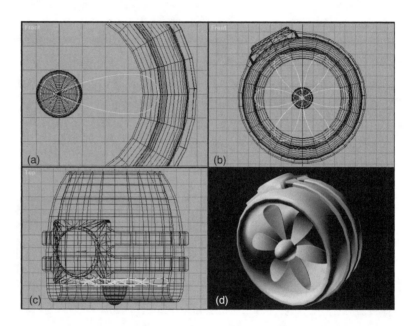

Adjusting Instanced Objects

In the last tutorial, you created a radial array, using instanced objects, so that any adjustments made to any one of the blades are made to them all. To demonstrate this, adjust the pitch (angle) of the blades in the thruster model:

1. In the Top view, select one of the blades and increase the Twist setting (or apply an additional one), to increase it by another 30° (see Figure 3.63a).

2. Render and examine the results. Looks a lot more high-tech now, doesn't it (see Figure 3.63b)?

3. Save your work as B_THR15 and close the file.

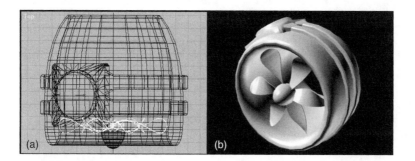

FIGURE 3.63

Adjusting the blade pitch with instanced objects: (a) Select a blade and increase the Twist to a total of 60 degrees. All the blades are twisted by the same amount, because they are instance objects. (b) Render the result.

Summary

The functions you learned about in this chapter—from working with 2D shapes to creating 3D objects to instanced arrays—are the foundation for most of your modeling work. The basic tutorials have helped you to create the beginning of an interesting model, and you can continue to add to it—and learn from it—in the chapters ahead.

Speaking of the next chapter, it will build on the modeling basics from this chapter and move you toward some more advanced operations. You'll also find tips and techniques that will help to set your work apart from the crowd. This is where you'll start to discover the things that few manuals will tell you: the importance of bevels, techniques for accurate and advanced modeling, cool tricks, and more.

CHAPTER 4

Modeling: Beyond the Basics

This De Tomaso Mangusta was created with polygonal "box modeling" techniques in 3ds max.
Image ©2000 Michael Jones.

"*Mithrak's bane!*" cried out the student. "*This still looks terrible.*" He sighed heavily and regarded the form floating above his Glowing Pool. He had been trying for nigh on the entire day to build a guard, one that could populate the ramparts of his otherwise unoccupied castle model. Unfortunately, the crude objects he had assembled to build the artificial sentry resulted in unrealistic lumps and seams covering the entire surface. "*It looks like one of those nut-crackers from the Rhinelands,*" he muttered to himself.

"*Problems, lad?*" the Master called from across the chambers. "*I did warn you about such an advanced undertaking...*"

"*Yes, but I'd like to try anyway. That's the only way to learn, right?*" The student rose and walked over to where the old man was working.

"*Rightly so,*" said the Master with a chuckle. "*Say, perhaps if I showed you one of my own human models, you could gain some insights.*"

"*Oh, that would be great!*" The lad plunked himself down in front of the Master's Glowing Pool.

"*Very well, then,*" the Master replied, closing his eyes and taking a breath. "*Dizkmann Eemayl Kolecktkall.*" The master waved his arms mystically. Suddenly, a human figure appeared, floating in midair before them.

The student was stunned. He expected a disgustingly detailed and precise model, but this...this wasn't much better than his own piecemeal effort. The figure had more details and was better proportioned to be sure, but it still looked like a cross between a jigsaw puzzle and the Frankenstein monster.

"*Well, does this help?*" the Master asked with a toothless grin. "*It was an early effort, but still pleases me.*"

"*Why, yes, Master.*" The lad got up from his seat and prepared to beat a hasty retreat to his own Pool. "*I don't feel so bad...I—I mean, I think I understand now,*" he finished, edging away with a smile.

"Ah, do you indeed?" The Master raised one of his bushy brows. "Then why are you leaving before I finish?

"Huh?"

"Heetlampp Kuizinarte Vaasoleen," the old man whispered, and the seams and bulges on the human figure began to blend together and disappear, resulting in a disgustingly detailed and precise model.

"D'oh!" cried the student, slapping his forehead.

Reference and Accuracy

There are many paths to a destination, and as our student discovered, some may be right in front of us, yet hidden because it may not occur to us to use a tool or technique in a certain way. This chapter looks beyond some of the basic modeling tools and techniques, and finds some different paths to building complex models.

Just as an accurate map is useful when hiking a mountain path, good reference is very useful to the 3D modeler. As proof, try an experiment: Close your eyes and imagine you have to model and map an ordinary pen. Think about the brand you use most of the time. Try to visualize the overall form, details, and material colors in detail. Now look at the real pen. Chances are, you'll see details that you forgot about, like subtle chamfers and indentations. The materials probably look different as well, perhaps glossier than you thought, or with interesting reflections and refractions. The point is, you probably don't remember a lot of the details about objects, even ones that you look at every day, *but it's these details that make the difference between ordinary 3D work and true professional-quality models.*

Using reference materials when designing, building, and mapping your projects can improve the quality of the results immensely. Your reference may consist of the actual object, photographs, drawings, video—any kind of visual record. Of course, you don't have to follow the reference precisely, but seeing the kinds of details that are there can help you to determine how much additional mesh or mapping is required to get a professional result, or give you ideas about how to change the design but still keep it believable.

For specific recommendations on finding and using reference materials, look on the CD-ROM at Appendix G, "Planning and Organization."

Mesh Tessellation and Optimization

Tessellation and optimization are two sides of the same coin. They involve either increasing or decreasing the number of faces on an object.

Tessellation subdivides the faces in the selected area, dividing single polygons into two or more to add more resolution to a surface (see Figure 4.1). Although tessellation adds more resolution, it doesn't necessarily smooth out a corner or make a curve more graceful. That often requires other tools that are covered later in the chapter.

FIGURE 4.1

Effects of tessellation: (a) Original polygons. (b) Edge tessellation adds vertices to the middles of the existing edges and connects them with new edges to subdivide the polygon. (c) Face-center tessellation adds a new vertex in the center of the polygon and adds edges extending back to the original vertices.

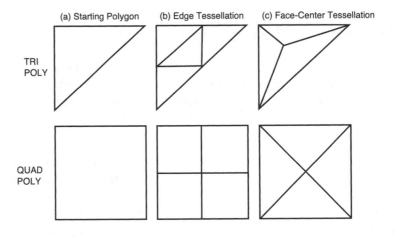

In the quest for accuracy, you may sometimes "over-model" an object. Although lots of detail definitely adds to a scene and helps to make your work more professional, too much mesh can slow the modeling process—and rendering—down substantially.

Managing mesh resolution at the time you create the object is best, but you have another option—*optimization*, which can reduce the number of vertices and faces on an object substantially without having too much of an impact on the rendered results (see Figure 4.2). This feature, either built in or added on to your program as a plug-in, also comes in handy when a particular modeling process ends up producing extra faces that could be consolidated. At other times, you may need both high-res and medium- or lowres versions of the same object for use in long shots or as placeholders.

FIGURE 4.2

Effects of mesh optimization: (a) Original mesh. (b) Original mapping. (c) Original render. (d) Mesh reduced 50% by optimization. (e) Scrambled mapping due to optimization. (f) Optimized render.

Optimizers work by combining faces that fall within a user-defined angle of one another. If these faces have very little variation in angle between them, they can often be combined without causing any significant amount of change in the model. The overall results, however—especially on a mesh-intensive scene—can be dramatic.

Depending on your software, an optimizer may function in a parametric manner, enabling you to vary the amount of optimization on the fly. It may also let you view an object in optimized form for viewing speed, but then render it with all or most of the polygons intact.

The downside is that optimization wreaks havoc with the mapping coordinates, so you can't rely on parametric or loft coordinates to remain intact. Of course, if you have applied spherical, cylindrical, cubic, or one of the other post-modeling coordinate systems, you need only reapply them after optimization.

Radius Edges and Bevels

One of the most fundamental, yet often overlooked, tenets of better modeling is that you should avoid having perfectly square edges in your mesh whenever feasible. The reason is that few objects in the real world have razor-sharp corners, and having them in your models makes the result look very CG. Instead of using sharp corners, dull them by using bevels or radius edges and corners (see Figure 4.3).

FIGURE 4.3

Non-squared edges help catch the light and look more realistic. (a) Flat bevel. (b) Bevel with smoothed normals. (c) Radius edges.

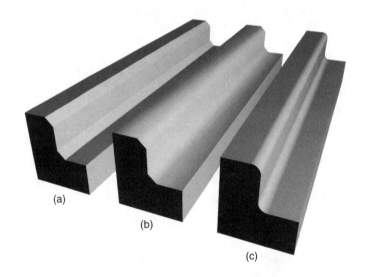

(a)

(b)

(c)

A *bevel* or *chamfer* is a flat transitional plane located between two other planes, usually set at an angle that is half the difference between the two. In other words, if you had a 90-degree corner, the bevel would be 45 degrees.

A *radius edge* uses an arc to transition between the planes, resulting in a smoother transition when the object is seen close up, or when the transition is very large. A *radius corner* follows the same principle as a bevel, except that it uses an arc to round off a square corner.

The extra surfaces you create with beveled or radius corners also tend to catch the light, making the object more interesting visually. Of course, it's impractical to round off edges all the time, but adding even a few bevels to an object can create the illusion that it's modeled at a much higher resolution, and your results will look more professional (see Figure 4.4).

FIGURE 4.4

The use of bevels on the blades and cylindrical trim rings make this mace look as if it was created at a higher resolution than it really was. Image by Mark Giambruno/Mondo Media for Zork:Nemesis ©1996 Activision.

If your software offers extended primitives like the ones discussed in Chapter 3, chances are good that they include beveled or radius cornered cubes and cylinders. Using these primitives instead of the "squared off" standard ones will make a mechanical model look more realistic and professional with little extra effort.

Although some programs may have built-in automatic bevel tools or options, many do not, leaving you to generate the bevel as part of a deform modifier (which the next section explains), or to draw two cross-sections, one slightly larger than the other, for skinning. Note that your software may offer an outline tool that you can use to create the second cross-section easily.

Another option for creating bevels is to leave an extra step or segment in the loft or extrusion that you can manually edit by manipulating the faces or vertices. The problem with creating bevels by scaling vertices or faces is that unless the object is symmetrical, the scaling won't be even (see Figure 4.5). The only option you will probably have is to do a lot of tweaking to small groups of vertices to even out the bevel.

FIGURE 4.5

Using Bevel modifier versus scaling vertices: (a-c) Bevel modified shapes. (d) Symmetrical shapes work fine for vertex scaling, but (e) oblong or (f) freeform shapes require additional vertex-level tweaking to even the outline.

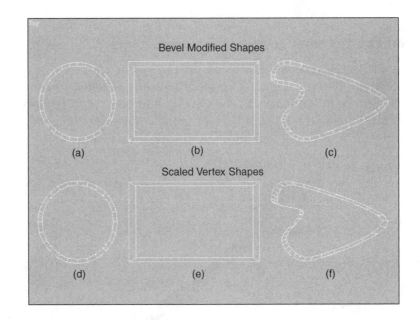

Deform Modifiers

Deform modifiers are transform settings (such as scale, twist, bevel, teeter, and deform/fit) that are applied to cross-sectional shapes as they are swept along a path. In other words, they modify an otherwise straightforward sweep object. This enables you to vary the size and orientation of the cross-sections, as in the bellows of the accordion-like Wertmizer musical instrument from *Zork:Nemesis* (see Figure 4.6).

FIGURE 4.6

The bellows of the accordion-like Wertmizer were created using a scale modifier on the cross-section as it was swept along a curved path. Image by Mark Giambruno/Mondo Media for Zork:Nemesis ©1996 Activision.

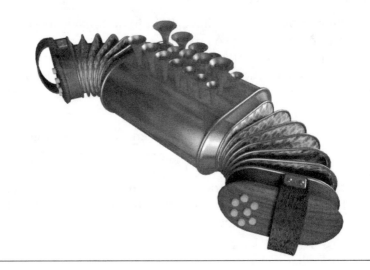

You've already had a look at what bevel deform modifiers would be used for from the preceding section, so next it's time to take a look at some of the other deforms available.

Scale Deform Modifier

The *scale deform* and other modifier controls usually take the form of a graph, which you adjust to set the amount of deformation desired as a generic value or percentage (see Figure 4.7). In this scale deform example, the swept cross-section (in this case, a circle) remains unaffected (that is, at 100% scale) until one-quarter along the path, then the scale of the cross-section is increased to 150% as it moves along to the midway point. The scale is dropped to -50% at three-quarters of the way down the path, then returns to 100% at the end. In addition, the deformations can be either symmetrical, affecting both the X- and Y-axes, or asymmetrical, and affect only one axis.

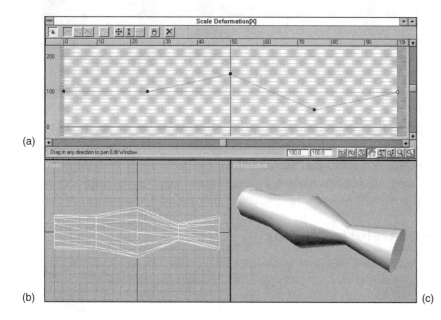

(a)

(b)

(c)

FIGURE 4.7

Scale deformed object: (a) The graph defining the position and scale percentage of the cross-section. (b–c) The resulting object.

As you can see, scale deform modifiers are capable of creating lathe-like variations in size on an object with a circular cross-section. Unlike lathe, however, they can be applied to *any* cross-sectional shape, and the X and Y scaling values can be set independently. Also, the path can be curved, whereas a lathe axis is always straight.

Twist (Rotate) Deform Modifier

Another deform modifier is often called either *twist* or *rotate*, and it spins the cross-sections around the path as they're extruded (see Figure 4.8).

FIGURE 4.8

Rotate (or twist) deformed object: (a) The graph defining the position and twist or rotate percentage of the cross-section. (b–d) The resulting object.

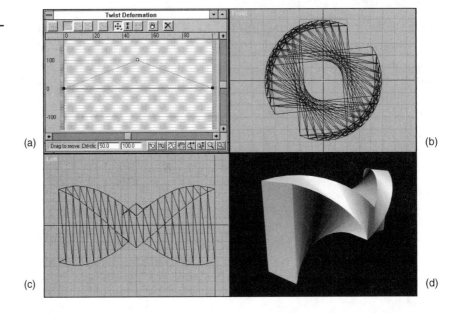

(a)   (b)   (c)   (d)

The results of the *twist deform* or *rotate deform* are not unlike the twist transform you learned about in the last chapter. The difference is that the amount of twist can be varied along the length of the object, which may be difficult to do with the whole-object transform version. Also, the path can be curved, whereas a twist axis is always straight.

Teeter Deform Modifier

Teeter is another deform modifier, which rotates the cross-section around its own local axis as it is extruded (see Figure 4.9).

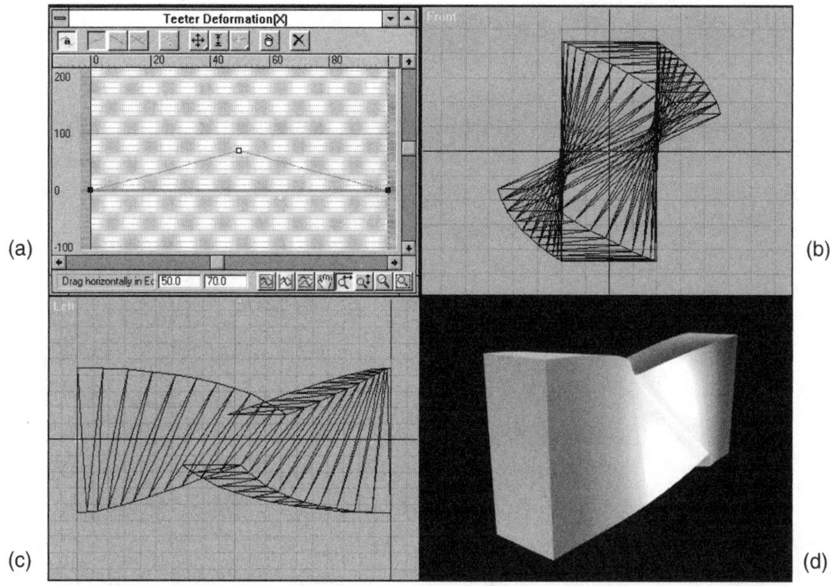

FIGURE 4.9

Teeter deformed object:
(a) The graph defining
the position and teeter
percentage of the cross-
section. (b–d) The resulting object.

The *teeter deform* is an odd one, and it's probably not a modifier you're likely to use often. It's useful for creating some odd, asymmetrical variations
along the swept object, so you might use it for creating an alien tree trunk
or something. Note that if the teeter settings are too high, the cross-
sections will overlap and result in creases or other mesh troubles.

Deform/Fit Modifier

Some programs have a *Deform/Fit* modifier that enables you to define the
shape of an object with an X-axis outline, a Y-axis outline, and one or more
cross-sections. Although this type of modeling may have some constraints
depending on your program, it can create some fairly complex forms quite
easily, such as the fuselage of an aircraft or the wooden stock of a musket
from *Zork:Nemesis* (see Figure 4.10).

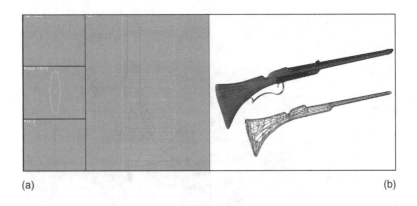

FIGURE 4.10

Using Deform/Fit: (a) The
X- and Y-axis outlines of
the musket stock are
defined, along with a
rounded cross-section.
(b) The cross-section is
swept along the straight
path, but forced to stay
within the outline bound-
aries, forming the finished
3D object. Image by
Mark Giambruno/Mondo
Media for Zork:Nemesis
©1996 Activision.

(a)   (b)

 Tip

It can be confusing to visualize how to set up a deform/fit. Here's a suggestion:
Imagine you're building a mold out of the X- and Y-axis shapes, and then "pouring"
the cross-sectional shape into it.

3D Booleans

Boolean operations are very powerful sculpting tools, enabling you to cut
or drill one form with another as well as combine multiple objects into
one, among other things. As such, they give the modeler a means for creating objects that are difficult or impossible to make with other tools. You
learned about 2D Booleans already, and 3D Booleans work in the same
way, except that they deal with three-dimensional volumes.

As you may recall, the objects used in Boolean operations are called
operands. In most cases, there will be two operands involved, and their
positioning and the type of operation performed determines the results.
The most common Boolean types are Add (Union), Subtract (Difference),
and Intersect (see Figure 4.11).

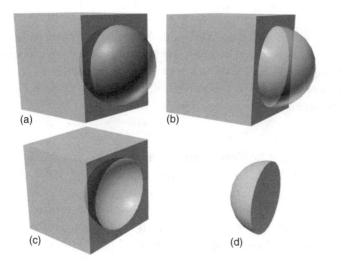

(a) (b) (c) (d)

FIGURE 4.11

Common 3D Booleans:
(a) The operands, a
cube and sphere.
(b) Add combines the
volumes together.
(c) Subtract removes
one volume from the
other. (d) Intersect
leaves only the
overlapping portion
of the two volumes.

Boolean Add combines the operands into one object, adding their volumes together and deleting any overlapping polygons. This is similar to simply attaching two objects together, except that the Boolean deletes any overlapping mesh, leaving only the polygons that form the surface of the combined object.

Boolean Subtract removes from the first volume any portions of the second volume that overlap it. This is like using the second object as a drill or scoop to carve away at the first object.

Boolean Intersect deletes any portion of either volume that *isn't* overlapping. In other words, a new object is formed out of those parts of the two objects that are overlapping.

When working with Boolean objects, it's important to remember that this operation is usually *destructive*, which means that the original operands are lost in the process, and you may not be able to undo a failed attempt. Therefore, it's very important to save a version of your project before attempting a Boolean operation, to make it easy to go back later and adjust the operands if you find the result wasn't to your liking.

Booleans sometimes fail, either because the computer is unable to deal with the complexities of the operation, or because their positions create vertex overlaps or other problems. If a Boolean fails, try adjusting the position of the operands slightly. As a last resort, you may need to either simplify the operands or tessellate the faces on one or both operands.

One last thing about Booleans—they may cause an automatic optimization of the affected faces, meaning that unnecessary faces are removed. Although this is often desirable, in some cases it causes polygons to become non-planar or other mesh troubles. Test render your Boolean results to look for problems like this, and consider turning off the optimization option and re-trying the Boolean if problems show up.

Editing Mesh

When you start to manipulate only *portions* of a given object, you've entered the realm of *sub-object operations* or *mesh editing*. This section deals with a variety of options for altering your models at this level.

You witnessed the use of vertex-level editing to adjust 2D shapes back in Chapter 2, "Delving into Cyberspace." Well, *sub-polygon operations* such as vertex-, edge-, and face-editing can also be employed on 3D objects. This process of vertex-level adjustment is often called *pulling points*, and is very useful for sculpting or refining objects, adding small integrated details, and fixing glitches in the mesh.

Vertex Operations

The tools and techniques used for vertex-level work are similar to those used for 2D shape editing: Vertices can be copied, moved, deleted, rotated, twisted, and otherwise manipulated with other standard transforms and operations. Of course, a few of these transforms can't be applied to a single vertex—some work on only a group of two or more.

Naturally, doing vertex-level editing work is tougher with 3D objects, because you have the added dimension of depth to contend with, and because the greater number of vertices makes it easier to accidentally select and manipulate the wrong ones.

Vertex-level editing is often used to make small adjustments on isolated sections of an object, or for fixing stray vertices or scrambled faces created by other modeling operations, particularly Booleans. But vertex editing, being very precise, also has applications for doing sculpting on objects. In fact, this is one of the methods suggested for doing organic models such as human heads, which are discussed later in the chapter.

Some programs provide *magnet tools* options designed to make sculpting easier by attracting or repelling vertices when the tool is brought close to the object. Using magnet tools is faster than selecting sets of points and adjusting them a group at a time, and they create smoother, more natural projections and depressions as well. The same principles apply with *soft selections*, in which additional points are moved around at different rates depending on how far they are from the core group of selected vertices (see Figure 4.12).

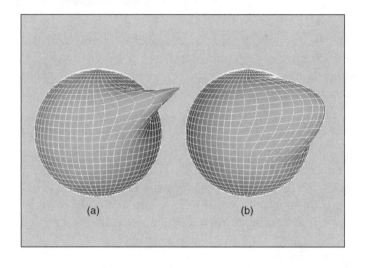

(a)   (b)

FIGURE 4.12

Soft selection or magnet tools enable the user to influence an entire region of vertices at different rates.
(a) Pinched result from a fast drop-off setting.
(b) Bell-curve result from a more gradual drop-off setting.

For an example of how vertex-level editing can be employed, consider the method I used to create some magical crystals for *Zork:Nemesis*. Because we were using 3D Studio R4 (DOS) for the project, the crystal effect had to be accomplished without relying on refraction effects, because the program didn't offer raytracing.

Starting with a sketch by Cody Chancellor, I created a number of leaf-like spline shapes, then extruded them with a bevel at each end to catch the light. This resulted in a very glassy-looking assembly of blocks, but without the internal "fire" you expect from gems. The reason is that gems have internal facets that catch the light, and those were missing from the mesh at that point. By using vertex-level editing to pull points on the faces inside the crystal, and by adding some additional internal polygons as well, I was able to make some internal structures that approximated the internal facets of a gem (see Figure 4.13).

FIGURE 4.13

The reflective surfaces inside these free-form crystals from Zork:Nemesis were created by pulling points and adding additional polygons. Image by Mark Giambruno/Mechadeus ©1996 Activision.

To finish off the crystals, I applied an additive, highly translucent bluish material (see Chapter 6, "Texture Mapping," for definitions) to the object, and then placed an omni light in the center to give them a glowing appearance and increase the intensity of the reflections.

For more conventional gems, the same principle of modeling the internal and external reflective structures still applies, but to do it accurately, you will need a reference book that describes these structures clearly so that you can duplicate them in 3D. For suggestions, see Appendix C, "Recommended References," located on the companion CD-COM. Also, if you're using a ray-tracing program, there are a host of other settings and considerations that can be applied to increase realism even more.

Edge Operations

Although most sub-polygon tweaking involves pulling points around, there are other useful operations that can be made at this level as well. The edges that delineate the boundaries of a polygon can be moved, rotated, deleted, and otherwise transformed just as vertices can. In addition, edges can have the following special operations performed on them:

Edge extrude pushes a copy of the selected edge away from the original and adds polygons to fill in the gap. The result is a fin-like projection extending away from the original edge (see Figure 4.14b).

Edge divide is a polygon-level form of tessellation that splits an edge by creating a new vertex at the point the user clicks, creating additional polygons in the process (see Figure 4.14c).

Edge turn rotates the selected edge between available vertices. This is usually done to influence the normals of the polygon so that the result seems to be smoother (see Figure 4.14d).

Edge visible/invisible toggles the visibility of the edge. Whether an edge is visible has an influence on the normals (and therefore the appearance of smoothness) of the rendered result. Visibility also helps to define which faces in a given area belong to a single polygon—now that the edge is invisible, the pair of triangular polygons has become a quad (see Figure 4.14e).

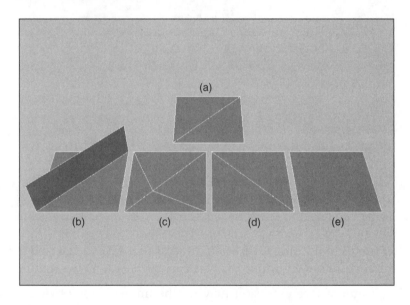

FIGURE 4.14

Edge operations: (a) The unaltered polygon, made up of two triangles. All operations are performed on the edge running diagonally from lower left to upper right. (b) Edge extrude creates a new set of faces that join the original and extruded edges. (c) Edge divide adds a vertex and splits the original two faces into four. (d) Edge turn rotates the edge. (e) Edge invisible hides the edge and turns the tris into a quad.

Many of the edge operations are rarely used during normal modeling; they are much more commonly used in low-poly modeling, where every aspect of a given poly can have a noticeable impact on the model. You'll learn more about this style of modeling in depth in the brilliantly titled Chapter 5, "Low-Poly Modeling."

Face Operations

Just like vertices and edges, transforms and editing can be done at the face level as well. Often, modelers will work at the face level to select and delete unneeded sections of mesh—like sections that end up inside or butted against other mesh—to lower a model's polygon count.

Face divide works just like edge divide, except that the user can select a point anywhere inside the polygon as the point for the new vertex to appear (see Figure 4.15).

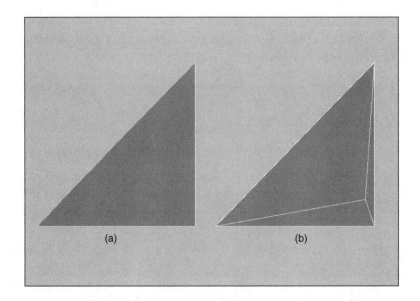

(a)   (b)

Another useful tool is *face extrusion*, a process that takes a selected face (or faces) and extrudes it in or out from its current position (see Figure 4.16).

The true value of face extrusion may not be immediately obvious, but it has a number of uses. First of all, it enables you to create additional surface details with the faces of an existing object, which can quickly result in effects that would take quite a bit of work to generate otherwise. Note that after you've extruded a face, you can extrude it again to create another step, or extrude some of the new faces that were created in the process.

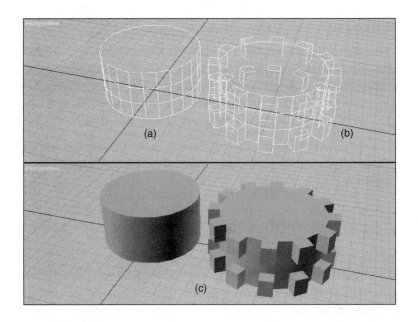

FIGURE 4.16

Effects of face extrusion:
(a) Cylinder showing
unmodified faces, (b) A
group of selected faces
extruded outward.
(c) The objects in
shaded view.

The fact that face extrusion enables you to build up additional mesh out of a single object makes it easier to create projections that are smoothly blended into a single form. For example, you could use repeated face extrusions to create the fins of a shark by drawing the extra needed mesh out of the smoothly swept body.

Face extrusions also are useful for building bevels from a squared-off surface, or for doing sweep-like work on an existing object. As you generate an extruded face, you can make use of the fact that it's already selected to scale, rotate, and move it into other positions.

Polygon Operations

Working our way up from sub-polygon manipulation, we'll now take a look at operations that deal with groups of faces and polygons. Because these still deal with portions of a single object, they too are considered sub-object operations.

The range of operations and transforms available for polygon ops is pretty similar to the ones that can be used at the face level. Having a polygon operations level is really more of a convenience feature, enabling the user to quickly select and deal with entire polygons, rather than trying to round up all their constituent faces.

Element Operations

Remember Attach and Detach? They work at both the 2D and 3D levels. When 3D objects are attached to one another, their component parts remain transformable and editable as *elements*. Chances are you won't use this level of editing very often—most of the time, you'll have adjusted an object just the way you want it before attaching it to another.

Element-level operations are virtually identical to the ones used for manipulating entire objects, except that some of the face operations may be available as well.

Displacement Mapping

Yet another tool in your arsenal of mesh manipulation weapons is displacement mapping. Unlike bump mapping, which is a material-level embellishment that affects the surface normals to make an object *appear* to have projections or depressions, *displacement mapping* or *deformation mapping* actually affects the mesh, extending it outward or inward (see Figure 4.17). It's applied the same way as a bump map is—as a grayscale image (refer to Chapter 6, "Texture Mapping," for more information). Depending on the program, black pixels may have no effect, whereas white ones cause the greatest amount of displacement, or vice-versa.

FIGURE 4.17

Displacement mapping:
(a) Grid object. (b) Radial gradient bitmap used to determine relative displacement of vertices.
(c) Deformed grid after displacement is performed.

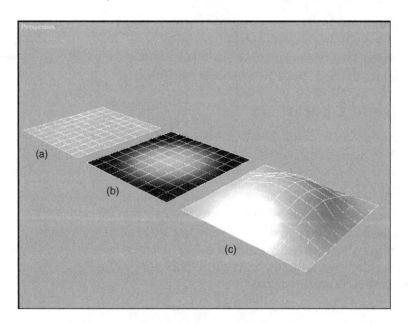

Displacement mapping can be used to solve a host of other modeling problems, from creating *bas-relief* (a style of sculpture where the subject projects only slightly out of a flat background) to doing patch modeling-like modifications to existing mesh. It is often used to create *terrain models* based on grayscale imagery (see Figure 4.18).

FIGURE 4.18

Terrain models are often created with displacement mapping. For more accurate results, some products, like TruFlite, can generate models directly from geological survey maps. Image ©1996 Martin D. Adamiker.

One thing to keep in mind if you're planning to use displacement mapping is that the base object should have a fairly substantial number of faces in order to create subtle curves and detail. The faces should also be triangles rather than quads to avoid planarity problems. If you're planning to deform an extruded object, set the cap style to grid, or use Boolean-cut grid shapes so that the objects have a uniform pattern of faces and vertices for displacement.

definition

grid object A flat polygon, subdivided into triangular or square faces.

The *displacement level* or *displacement strength* setting is the adjustment for how much displacement occurs to the mesh and multiplies the grayscale range provided by the displacement bitmap. Another factor that affects a displacement operation is the mapping coordinates. For information on how mapping coordinates work, see Chapter 6.

Tip

Using displacement to create terrain-style effects can be useful on a smaller scale as well. For example, displacement mapping can be used at a low-strength level to create rumpled sheets of paper from a simple flat rectangular grid object.

Building Organic Forms

Organic forms have always been a tricky subject for 3D modelers, especially if the form is something well known to the viewer, like a human. A face, for example, is so complex and has so many curves, hollows, and subtleties, that it's difficult to know where to start. It also requires that the user have a great deal of control over small areas, yet the use of a large number of vertices in the model makes editing difficult and confusing.

One of the most tedious but precise methods of building a complex form is to use relatively low-level tools such as edge extrusion and vertex pulling to construct it. This method was used to create some impressive 3D heads often seen in Animation Master advertising and demo reels, and for the model of Hyleyn from the *Sinkha* CD-ROM (see Figure 4.19).

FIGURE 4.19

The 3D model of Hyleyn (right) from the Sinkha CD-ROM was created by painstaking point-by-point creation and manipulation of individual vertices, coupled with extensive retouching. Image by Marco Patrito/Virtual Views ©1995 Virtual Views.

No matter what the technique, doing human figures requires excellent sculptural sensibilities, as well as good reference material showing the subject from several angles. This is a good example of where employing scans of the reference material as a background image would be invaluable. Refer to Appendix G, "Planning and Organization," for more details.

Skinning

For those of us without the time or patience for the vertex-by-vertex method, most 3D programs offer some software-assisted options. One such method of creating humanoid and sculptural forms involves using the skinning technique discussed in Chapter 3, "Modeling Basics." If you create a number of cross-sections of the figure, applying a skin results in a smooth, nearly seamless model (see Figure 4.20). Of course, designing and adjusting the cross-sections takes a lot of care and experimentation, especially if your program requires that all cross-sections have the same number of vertices.

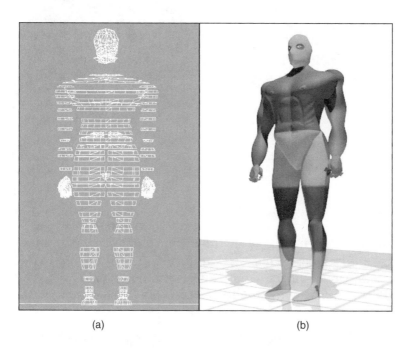

(a)   (b)

FIGURE 4.20

Example of a skinned figure: (a) The cross-sections defining the figure may be polylines, splines, or 3D objects, depending on the program. (b) The skinning process connects the cross-sections with a surface mesh, which can be virtually seamless depending on the methodology and limits of the software.

One caution about trying to use this method for articulated human faces, however: Because it produces polygons that are laid out like a grid, it's less than ideal for faces because of the ways in which they need to be deformed around the mouth and eyes to create expressions. Generally, artists tend to create faces with polygons arranged radially around those spots.

Metaballs

Metaballs is a form of modeling in which you build forms out of various-sized spheres. The software blends the spheres together into a single mass.

Metaballs are a popular way to make lots of different organic forms, even complex ones like human heads and animals.

To build a metaballs form, you scale and arrange spheres to follow the contours of the object you want to create. Different hardness settings can be assigned to the spheres, which tells the software how pliable that particular sphere is when the time comes to blend it with others at render time (see Figure 4.21). The harder the sphere, the less it will blend into the others.

FIGURE 4.21

Metaballs modeling: (a) Sphere-like metaballs scaled and grouped together to form a rough heart shape. (b) With some products, the resulting metaballs object may only be seen when rendered.

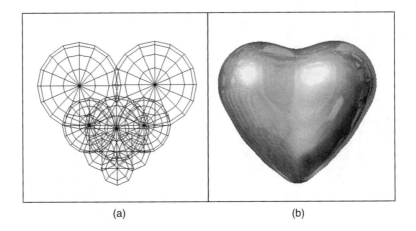

(a)   (b)

Although you can build some very impressive objects with Metaballs, it can be a tedious job, especially if your software limits you to using only spheres, and you can't stretch them or do other transforms other than moving and scaling. In those cases, to make a cylindrical form, for example, you have to line up a bunch of spheres. You may have to put a bunch of little spheres around the points where they meet to keep the finished mesh from having low spots.

With some of the newer metaballs packages, other primitives can be employed as well, making it much easier to get the forms you want quickly. Still, because it's generally not a "What You See Is What You Get" (WYSIWYG) modeling technique, you'll probably have to do a lot of experimenting and tweaking to get the results you want.

Mesh Relax

Some programs have *mesh relax* features that enable you to smooth out or blend pieces of mesh together, similar to the way metaballs blends spheres together. The difference is that the objects can be any kind of mesh, from primitives to lofts to what-have-you, so the user has much more control over which regions—and to what degree—the mesh is blended. These tools work by relaxing the vertices in the selected areas, averaging them out so that they appear to soften the sharp intersections where two pieces of mesh were joined together. The effect is a bit like holding a match close to a wax sculpture—it softens the wax and smoothes out the details.

These kinds of tools can be a real boon for organic work, especially if you use a polygonal modeler. A good example of this is the Foo Dog Cannon that I constructed in 3D Studio R4 as part of Mondo Media's contract artwork on the CD-ROM game *Zork:Nemesis* (see Figure 4.22).

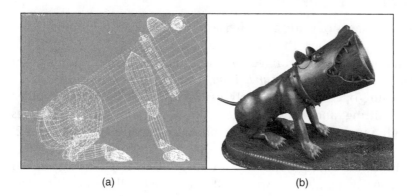

(a)   (b)

FIGURE 4.22

Modeling the Foo Dog Cannon: (a) 3D primitives were stretched and overlapped to rough out the form. (b) With the Smooth plug-in, the primitives were blended together with near-seamless results. Image by Mark Giambruno/Mondo Media for Zork:Nemesis ©1996 Activision.

To build the dog-shaped artillery piece, I started with a rounded-off tube for the barrel, then added the dog musculature to it with primitives that were squashed and bent. A leg, for example, consisted of a couple of elongated spheres for the upper and lower spheres, meeting at the elbow. The paw was a set of five or six squashed spheres forming the pads and toes. Bent cones were used to create the claws.

A fast way to get started with human figures is using Fractal Design Poser, which contains a library of different body types and ways to morph them. Be sure to use the thumbwheel-style fine-tuning controls to pose the models, or you may end up with human pretzels.

After a limb was completed, I would save it, Boolean Add the components together, and then use the Smooth plug-in from Bones Pro to smooth the mesh together. It took a fair amount of test runs and experiments, but the results were very fluid, and it was a pleasure to create.

In addition to mesh relax, there is a more sophisticated type of mesh blending called *mesh smooth*, which uses advanced tessellation techniques to add additional faces that smooth out the rough corners of a model. This technology also forms the core of one of the biggest advances in polygonal modeling—subdivision surfaces.

Subdivision Surfaces

The advantages of using a subdivision surfaces process for modeling is that this method enables the user to build and manipulate relatively low- to medium-poly mesh, yet have the mesh increase in resolution *and* smoothness at any time. The *subdivision surfaces* process consists of a mesh smoothing operation that analyzes the lower-resolution base object and uses splitting and averaging techniques to add additional faces that smooth out rough edges and emphasize details (see Figure 4.23). In essence, you work in a relatively low-poly manner, but get high-poly results. This technique has a lot of advantages, not the least of which is that it speeds up all your work and makes saved files smaller because you can work with lighter mesh.

FIGURE 4.23

Subdivision surfaces in action: (a) A single rectangular box was created. (b) The faces of the box were extruded to create this simple human form. (c) Additional face extrusion and some point pulling were used to refine the character. (d–e) Applying multiple iterations of mesh smooth added additional faces and smoothed out the form. (f) The resulting TV-headed character.

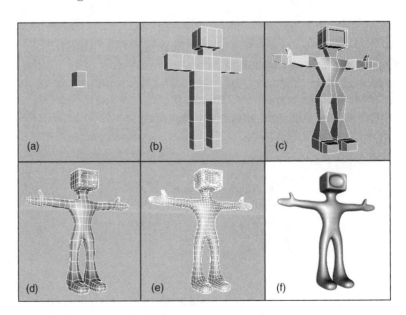

PIXAR experimented with subdivision surfaces in the Academy Award®–winning short film *Geri's Game* (directed by Pixar's Jan Pinkava), using the technique to create the hands and face of a gnarled old man playing a spirited game of chess against himself (see Figure 4.24). If Geri had been constructed with traditional high-poly techniques to bring out the lines and creases of his face and hands, the density of the model would have slowed the animation and rendering process significantly. The success of the technique on *Geri's Game* led PIXAR to use subdivided surfaces on their subsequent film releases *A Bug's Life*, *Toy Story 2*, and *Monsters, Inc.*

FIGURE 4.24

In *Geri's Game*, subdivision surface techniques were used to create the careworn features of the title character. The process enables artists and animators to use relatively simple mesh that is increased in resolution and detail at render time. Image ©1997 PIXAR.

Subdivision surfaces have big implications for the gaming industry as well. Support for this "variable resolution technology" is being built into computer hardware, which will enable games to rez-up low-poly mesh characters, vehicles, and environments on-the-fly, giving them greater detail and realism without making play speed suffer too much.

Another potential tool in your organic modeling arsenal is a *deformation cage*—a lattice-like network of control points that can be used to deform the mesh it surrounds. It works a bit like the control points on a NURBS modeling package, except that it operates on polygonal or parametric mesh.

3D Modeler Interviews

At this point, let's take a break from looking at tools and processes to hear from two different artists on the subject of advanced modeling, from sexy sports cars to *Star Wars* X-Wings.

Modeling Sports Cars and Spacecraft: An Interview with 3D Artist Mike Jones

Mike Jones was born in San Francisco in 1978 and grew up in the Bay Area. He currently works for Westwood Studios Pacific as a game cinematic artist. Mike has been working in the games industry for almost six years and has credits in a dozen published games, including *Hot Shots Golf 2*, *Motor City Online*, *Red Alert 2*, *Emperor: Battle for Dune*, and *Yuri's Revenge*. He finds it kind of ironic that he ended up pursuing a career in art when he spent most of his youth trying to avoid it; he originally was interested in becoming a writer.

I met Mike while directing the *Mechwarrior 3* cinematics. I had just hired 3D artist Eric Ronay to do animation on the project and was looking for one more artist, primarily to do the effects work. Eric told me about his former co-worker, Mike Jones, and I brought him in for an interview. He had some nice-looking work from an unpublished *Star Trek* game on his reel, including a planet explosion effect, so I hired him on the spot. In addition to *Mech*, we worked on a couple of other projects together while at Mondo Media, including *Under Cover* and *Alpha Centauri: Alien Crossfire*.

Q: What made you want to get into 3D?

A: In the middle of high school, I found my calling in computers and started taking programming classes in Basic, Pascal, C, C++, and a little bit of Assembly coding. Of course, the first thing that I wanted to code was a *game*. I started working on a role-playing game, and actually got farther along with it than I thought I would—far enough that it was time to come up with a way to visually represent the world I had created. A friend of mine, Andrew Backer, showed me a program called 3D Studio R4 (DOS), and I used it to create several very basic objects for the game. I was instantly hooked on the program and ended up spending all my spare time learning to use it.

Mrs. Farrin, my computer-programming teacher, saw how interested I was in the graphical aspect of computers and allowed me to use my programming class to teach myself art! She even went as far as calling the software publisher, Autodesk, and acquired an educational version of the program for me to work with. During the course of the next year, I signed up for three computer classes a day, and continued to learn the package and work on my portfolio.

During my last semester of high school, there was growing interest in digital multimedia among the students. As there were no CG-oriented art classes for people to take there, Mrs. Farrin and I created a curriculum that included Adobe Photoshop, Premiere, and several morphing tools. When I wasn't helping out as a teacher's assistant during class, I would work on my own projects.

After a few months of hard work and experimentation, I had a portfolio that I thought was worth showing around. Looking back now, I can see that I did almost everything wrong, though. It was just like every other *Star Wars* fanboy piece—bad animation, no shadows, no textures, and *way* too many lens flares. I'm still surprised that it got me a job in the industry.

Q: How did you learn to do 3D modeling and animation?

A: My first job in the industry was Quality Assurance (QA) for a company called Visionary Media Inc. Being in QA means that you play a game all day, and try doing things to make it crash. The game was called *Firewall*, and although it shipped only in Taiwan, it gave me enough time at the company to prove that I was able to handle any task thrown my way. At the time, VMI was bidding on a new game called *Star Trek: First Contact*. When we got the contract, I was hired on as an artist.

First Contact was a first person shooter using the Unreal 3D engine. My job was to model the interior environments of the USS Enterprise–E for various missions. The level-building tools for the Unreal engine were very different from the professional 3D packages, but they did teach me a lot about lighting. I set up an average of more than a thousand lights for each level. I taught myself basic color theory through trial and error, experimenting until an environment looked good. During that time, Autodesk released its new 3D Studio MAX product, and our studio got a promotional copy. I spent many nights there teaching myself MAX.

Although you may have heard of *Star Trek: First Contact* the movie, I assure you that you never saw the game. After two arduous years of production, it was canceled because of technical issues, and everyone on staff except one programmer and one artist were let go. I was fortunate enough to keep my job, and we started working on concepts for the next project. For obvious reasons, I started working on my portfolio again and looked around for new opportunities.

Q: What 3D software do you use, and why?

A: Although there are a lot of different 3D packages available today, Maya, Softimage, 3ds max, and LightWave are the most popular. I prefer the 3D Studio line because I have used it for many years, ever since the 3D Studio R4 (DOS) days. I like max because it gives me the flexibility to build some of my most complex projects with speed and simplicity, which I have found lacking in some of the other packages.

I've also worked with Maya and think that it has a better renderer than max, but Maya requires more knowledge of scripting and programming to use. Although it is extremely powerful, I feel that it is designed for larger teams, such as movie effects groups, that can afford a team of full-time programmers devoted to creating custom tools for it. For this reason and the fact that it's not that great for polygonal modeling, most game companies use 3ds max or LightWave for producing their work.

Speaking of the games industry, it increasingly matures into a larger and more complex medium, and the publishers are consolidating from dozens of small outfits into a few major players. Gone are the days when a teen with an idea, some computer knowledge, and a little space in his garage can write a game and start up his own company. Now there are investors, stockholders, marketing firms, and conglomerates that pour millions into development. Soon, we'll be seeing games that have the budgets of feature films. As that happens, we'll see more game companies opting for the more expensive programs and procedures that Hollywood employs today.

Q: How did you get in with Westwood Studios, and what do you do there now?

A: I worked for Mondo Media for about a year when they decided to switch their business focus from 3D work to 2D work. I was extended an invitation to learn 2D cel-style drawing and animation, but as I can't draw well at all, I decided that it was time to pack up and leave. Mondo really helped out with my transition to my current job; they let me use their systems to work on my new portfolio and helped me cut everything together for my reel. With a new reel in hand, I sent it off to all the game developers I knew. I then waited for a very disappointing two months, during which I didn't receive a reply from any of them.

It's sad but often true—getting into these companies requires that you have *contacts* as well as a good reel. You can have the best reel in the world, but if it gets buried in some pile in the Human Resources Department, it does you no good. When I came to finally understand that, I gave my reel to a headhunting firm. They have people within the game companies whom they talk to on a regular basis, and may even get first pick of positions before they're advertised. Anyway, my reel was sent around to the industry again, this time by the headhunter. I got six calls for interviews in the first week alone! In the end, there were two good offers that I had to choose from: one would have had me living in Hawaii, which is obviously a huge plus, and the other was Westwood Studios in Southern California. Although I would have loved to live in Hawaii, I felt that working for an established company was far more secure and would look better on my resume.

When I first got started at Westwood, I was brought in as an in-game asset artist for *Red Alert 2*. I modeled a lot of the interface and created some of the art assets for the cities. As soon as that project shipped, our parent company in Las Vegas requested some help on the cinematics for *Emperor: Battle for Dune*. Several in-game artists were pulled in to help, and I was one of them. They liked the work that I did on it so much that I was promoted to the cinematics department for our next project, *Red Alert 2: Yuri's Revenge*.

I was the only artist in the cinematics department using 3ds max; everyone else was using Maya. The reason was that there was no time to teach me Maya before the next project started, so I was allowed to use max to do my portion of it. Having grown up in the San Francisco Bay Area, I jumped at the chance to work on the intro cinematic because it featured a battle going on around the Golden Gate Bridge and Alcatraz Island.

Because no one else in the department knew 3ds max, I had to do all the modeling, texturing, animation, and effects for the intro by myself. It was some of the most fun I've had on a project yet. It took just under two months of hard work to produce, but I also think that it's some of my best work yet. The entire CG sequence was only a minute long, but in the end, it was totally worth all the long hours. Westwood was so happy with the quality that they decided to have the entire cinematic team switch over to 3ds max for the next project!

Q: What advice do you have for people who'd like to work at a game company?

A: First and foremost, you must *play games*. Although you don't have to be a hardcore gamer, you should know what makes a game fun and addictive. Game developers live or die by their products' quality. Computer hardware doubles in speed every 14 months, and the average development cycle for a game is 18 to 24 months. As a result, developers can only hope that in two years they will have correctly guessed what people are going to want in a game as well as what the hardware will support. If their game date slips, the hardware and their competition will leave them behind. This means that the game industry must continually push the boundaries of technology in an effort to be the best.

With the deadlines so concrete, you can expect to be working more than the usual forty hours a week when crunch mode comes around. On the other hand, it's all worth it see your name in the credits of a million-seller. Playing games on a regular basis will help keep you on track about what trends are evolving and what they mean for the future.

Q: What projects have you worked on over the years? How big were the teams?

A: I've worked on many projects in my career; most published, but some not. Most of the teams have been relatively small, usually less than six team members, and sometimes it's just me. I tend to like the smaller team environments because it makes you learn a little bit about everything. One of the Dreamcast titles I worked on allowed me to tackle animation, modeling, texturing, and lighting—the whole enchilada. It was probably the most educational project that I've worked on yet. I also enjoy working on larger teams, though. Although you do tend to specialize in a particular aspect of the project, when it's all done, you find out how rewarding it is to work on something much larger than yourself.

Q: You did some extremely detailed *Star Wars* models as posters—talk a bit about them.

A: Around the time that Mondo Media decided to switch their business focus to 2D work, I really started to get into making large poster-sized prints of my work. As an artist, I detest anything that compromises the vision that I want to share; for me such restrictions include rendering time and resolution. I tend to like posters more than video because prints can have incredibly high resolution. The resolution for animation is generally limited to 720 × 480 pixels, unless you are working in film. On the other hand, a print that's 24 × 36 inches can have a resolution of 7,200 × 10,800 pixels. This enables me to push the complexity of my artwork so much that I actually find myself wondering how I'm going to come up with that much detail.

I always wanted to do something *Star Wars*-related as a large print, but I needed a whole lot of reference to be able to pull it off. A friend from Mondo loaned me a book called *Star Wars: Chronicles*, which is probably the definitive book on the *Star Wars* trilogy. It has tons of pictures of all the physical models used in the movie, taken from every angle. I was inspired by the Star Destroyer and decided to start modeling it in extremely high resolution. You might think that it would be pretty easy to model because it is a fairly basic shape—until you take a closer look at the hull. The amount of tiny detail the original model makers applied to those ships is staggering. ILM (Industrial Light and Magic) even coined a term for it: *greeble*.

The hardest part of modeling the Star Destroyer was locking down the overall scale and proportions of the model. I started by creating a very rough version of the overall form and tweaking that until I thought the proportions were pretty close. Next, I created about 30 different pieces of "greeble," basing them off of the photo reference. After I had these built, I duplicated them and placed them in position all over the ship, always checking the photo reference to make them fit in properly. For the next three weeks, all I did was clone greeble and fit it onto my model. When I finished, the model consisted of over 300,000 polys. Although most of those were basic, boxlike primitives, the cumulative effect was incredible— all that detail showed up at print resolution and looked awesome.

Overall, the Star Destroyer poster took six weeks to create. That includes building all the assets from scratch and trying out different compositions until I was happy with the final look. Normally, I wouldn't spend that much time on one particular piece, but I was both inspired and unemployed at the time, so it worked out pretty well.

One other thing—when people ask me about the secret to modeling, I have to answer, "patience and attention to detail." Those two things will get you ninety percent of the way to becoming a great modeler. The actual modeling techniques themselves are not usually too difficult to learn; it's training yourself to look at the detail—and being able to see what makes an object unique—that's the hard part.

Q: How did you approach building the model of the De Tomaso Mangusta sports car?

A: The Mangusta model was done for a British Motors project back in '99. It was for a QuickTime VR rotation of the car on their web site. As you can imagine, that made it a little harder, because the entire model had to look correct from every angle; there wasn't any way to hide mistakes. My job was to build the model, and then rotate the camera around it, making a render at every 10-degree increment. The QuickTime VR software was used to combine the rendered frames and enable the user to interactively rotate the car to any angle.

I started the project trying to figure out which modeling technique was going to give me the flexibility and power needed to create the ultra-fine curves that car modeling requires. I considered three different approaches: NURBS, patch modeling, and polygonal "box modeling" combined with subdivision surfaces. Although NURBS lends itself very well to creating aerodynamic surfaces, I like to put the mesh detail where it is most required and leave other areas less complex. NURBS requires hulls and CVs to completely enclose the entire object, thereby adding complexity where it is not needed.

Patch modeling seemed like the way to go at first, and I went as far as modeling the entire back bumper as a patch before I realized that I needed an approach that would allow me to get even greater control over the final look. When you're working with a very detailed object, and each patch-modeled vertex has a Bezier spline that needs to be tweaked, modeling can quickly get very slow and cumbersome. So, I scrapped the patch-modeling route and went with a solution that was something of an unknown for me: box modeling. Although I had used box modeling before, I had never attempted anything of this scale and complexity.

Let me take a moment to explain the theory behind box modeling and subdivision surfaces. The reason that it's called box modeling is because you usually start with a cube and then start extruding and editing faces to create the form you want. Of course, you can start with any primitive that best represents your object; sometimes I even start with just a single polygon, and then pull and clone edges to create the hull.

Polygons are inherently flat, making smooth, organic objects very difficult to construct. The only way to get a polygonal object to look truly curved is to have each poly about one pixel in size; not something you could do by hand. What subdivision surface tools—such as the Mesh Smooth modifier in max—do is enable you to create a very basic, low-poly object that is representative of the final, high-poly object. The tool then tessellates the low poly "hull" and smooths out the rough edges at render time. This enables you to work on a model that shows up as ten thousand polys in the viewport, but is tessellated in the render to many times that amount. This may sound like a very inefficient way to render, but computers are fast enough now to handle hundreds of thousands of polys without much slowdown, especially if you're lucky enough to have a decent rendering farm to work with.

Getting back to the model, British Motors provided me with a ton of reference material on the Mangusta. They even gave me a file that contained the AutoDesk CAD model. Unfortunately, this model had been converted from NURBS to polys, and all the edges had buckled—none of them joined up properly anymore. I couldn't use any of the supplied mesh for the final renders, but it did give me excellent reference on which to base my model.

I spent six weeks modeling and texturing the Mangusta, and the client was very happy with the final product. British Motors signed off on it, and I sent all my final assets to them. Although they were very happy with what I sent, I have yet to see it anywhere on their website.

I decided to improve it even more for use as a portfolio piece, so I spent an additional four weeks just tweaking textures and moving vertices. By the end of the whole project, it had taken just under three months of part-time work to create a piece that I am very proud of, despite the fact that until now it has appeared only in my demo reel.

Q: Do you have any "dream project" that you'd like to work on?

A: I have always enjoyed sci-fi books, but my first love is the fantasy genre. The fantasy books I like best are the ones that take themselves seriously and have a darker story to tell. One of the books that I always thought would be awesome to do as a movie was *The Lord of the Rings*. Judging by the box office numbers and the fact that I have seen it four times now, that was a good choice. Because *The Lord of the Rings* is now being done in grand style, the other books I would like to see made into films are *The Wheel of Time* series by Robert Jordan. I think it has a unique vision and an engaging story filled with lots of character development and interaction. The first few books in particular had a perfect balance between action, adventure, character development, and story. Now, if he would just finish the epic in this decade, someone could start a script for it.

I'm currently working with my roommate to create a short original CG film that I hope to have done later this year. Although I would love to provide some shameless self-promotion for it here, we don't have a web site URL for it yet.

Q: Where would you like to be in five years?

A: I actually have trouble looking just six months into the future, let alone five years, but I would really like to get into doing special effects for movies. I have worked in the games industry for almost six years, and although I enjoy creating games and I love the freedom that I have when working on them, I'm starting to feel like I need to look to the next step. I feel that my artwork could benefit from new creative inspiration in a different field. As I mentioned before, I grew up near ILM and the whole *Star Wars* hype, which was the catalyst that got my imagination soaring. From the age of five, I would spend hours dreaming of the final assault on the Death Star and of the Millennium Falcon swooping in to save the day. It was a favorite pastime for me during those years, and it would be a great personal achievement to be able to work on the current series of Star Wars movies.

Therefore, at some point in my career I would like to work at either Industrial Light and Magic or Lucasfilm. I realize that the waiting list to get into such places is huge, and the competition is fierce. My chances are slim—and some would say impossible—but on the other hand, I wonder where I would be right now if I had not followed my own dreams and defined my career and myself in the process. For me, the point of following a dream is to not let any limitations govern your actions. It is to know your final destination without knowing the specific road to take; that way, you make your own road and grow to meet the demands that come of it.

I'd like to thank Mike for taking the time to share his thoughts and experiences with us. Mike's personal web site can be found at www.DigitalArtMonkey.com.

Modeling the *Star Wars* Universe: An Interview with 3D Artist Richard Green

Richard Green was born in 1963 and grew up in a "boring suburb" in Southern California. Finding little of interest going on in his general surroundings, he concentrated on creative endeavors. He became an avid model builder when he was around eight years old. He also liked to draw, although he didn't feel he was very good at it. While attending high school in the late '70s, he found he was better at technical illustration, and really enjoyed drafting as well. He actually *liked* technical pens, despite their tendency to clog up.

Filmmaking was another big interest, and Richard made dozens of short movies with lots of miniatures and special effects work in them. In his senior year he got a job as a draftsman with a small company and stayed there for four years while trying to figure out what he wanted to do for a living. He never took the job title "artist" very seriously, and couldn't imagine himself as a career artist; but deep down, he knew it was what he really wanted to do. He eventually attended the prestigious Art Center College of Design in Pasadena and studied industrial design, which he felt was a good blend of the artistic and the practical.

After school, he landed a short-term but lucrative design job, then used the money to move to San Francisco. He struggled for the first couple of years, and did a little of everything: some industrial design work, building miniature sets for movies, constructing some full-size dioramas for museums, and lots of 2D graphic design and illustration. Eventually, a colleague from Art Center hooked him up with a prototype-building job at small, little-known division of the Lucas Empire that dealt with site-based attractions and theme parks. When that division shut down, he went to work at an industrial design firm. Later on, he ended up at LucasArts, where he worked on *Star Wars* and other games for several years. After another stint doing freelance work, he went back to full-time employment at Totally Games.

I met Richard just after he left the industrial design firm and before he ended up at LucasArts. He came into Mondo Media to show his portfolio after we let it be known that we were looking for 3D artists. At the time, I was designing and directing a point-of-sale multimedia demo for Microsoft's upcoming Windows NT operating system. The demo featured a number of 3D animations, and I selected Richard to help out on the project. He also worked on the tunnel environment for *Critical Path* later on, as well as the hydroponics environment for *The Daedalus Encounter*. My sincere thanks to Richard for taking the time to share his knowledge and experiences here.

Q: How did you get into 3D modeling and animation?

A: I attended Art Center between 1985-88, and shortly after I started, they became one of the first design schools to put together a computer graphics lab. I spent a lot of time there. They had 2 PIXAR workstations—PIXAR used to be in the hardware biz—and an early version of the Alias modeling software. I got my first exposure to 3D at the school, and even got to take a class taught by 3D graphics pioneer Jim Blinn. He had actually written the 3D software we were being taught; it had no graphical interface, so everything had to be typed in as sets of coordinates. Jim was a quirky genius, but a very patient and thoughtful teacher. I talked to him years later at SIGGRAPH, and he was pleased to find out that I had gone on to work on one of his favorite games, *Full Throttle*.

Experimenting with 3D was a lot of fun, but the equipment was so expensive that I never thought it would be practical to own myself. I wrote it off and got into 2D graphics in the Mac lab. They had a room full of brand-new compact Macintoshes! Later on, I bought my own Mac, an SE/20 with a whole 20MB of hard drive space that cost me about $2600. I find it very amusing that I have fifty times as much memory in my current system as my Mac had in drive space. Anyway, it wasn't until a couple of years later, while working in an industrial design studio, that I was able to play around with Strata 3D software on the Mac. The output looked great, and a ray-traced 160×100 image only took four hours to render! Still, that was what really got me hooked on 3D—the software and hardware finally seemed within my reach.

Those experiences from college and afterward introduced me to the basics. I did only modeling at the time because animation was out of the question—the long render times and the high cost of frame-by-frame output to video made it impractical. My background in drafting and Jim Blinn's class built a very solid foundation for my understanding of the 3D world. 3D has some pretty abstract concepts that can be difficult to grasp, and were especially hard back in those days, when 3D was a real unknown to most people. My earlier forays into filmmaking also gave me a lot of experience in the areas of pacing, shot blocking, editing, and camera and light placement, all of which became invaluable later on.

Q: What 3D software do you use, and why?

A: I started using 3D Studio (DOS) around 1992. At that time, I believe LightWave 3D was available only on the Amiga, and PC hardware was much cheaper than Mac stuff. I needed to buy both a new machine and the software, and a PC with 3D Studio was the most affordable combination. It also seemed to be the most powerful tool at the time in its price range. I owned LightWave for a few months in the mid-nineties, but frankly could never get used to its archaic interface and modular design.

It seemed a huge step backwards from what I was used to, even if many of the tools it had were pretty advanced.

3ds max has been slow to integrate necessary features, and its reliance on plug-ins can be a blessing and a curse; but it's still the best all-around package for what I do. Although it does very few things *brilliantly*, it does almost everything pretty well.

Q: How did you get in with LucasArts and Totally Games?

A: I worked for a long-gone division of the Lucas empire called Rebel Art & Technology. They did location-based attractions and theme park designs, but were shut down in a big reorganization in 1990. The heads of the art departments of the other Lucas companies, ILM (Industrial Light and Magic) and LucasArts, were kind enough to look at my work to see if they could use me for any projects. They couldn't at the time, but I found out about a 3D *Star Wars* game they were working on at LucasArts called *Rebel Assault*. I decided my best shot at getting in with them was to get the same software they were using and teach myself to use it. Even if the LucasArts job never happened, I loved working on 3D art and was determined to switch careers when I felt capable enough to make a living at it.

For six grueling months, I worked during the day as an industrial designer, and then worked long hours on my 3D portfolio at night. Finally, an opening appeared at LucasArts, and I made my move. I was at the right place at the right time, and had the right skills. I became the third artist in their tiny 3D department; most of their products used 2D art at the time.

I worked for five years at LucasArts, until I got pretty burned out on the place. The company had grown very fast, and the office politics had become intolerable. I was bored with the kind of work we were getting, and there was an ongoing systematic purge of all the experienced—meaning expensive—senior artists like me.

I left LucasArts and lazily freelanced under the name Artbot (www.artbot.com) for a year and a half after that. I don't remember how I heard about it, but one of the clients I got hooked up with was Totally Games. Several of them had left LucasArts in the late eighties to start their own company—then called Peregrine—and had developed the hugely successful *Star Wars X-Wing* series of games. I freelanced for them for a few weeks, doing some wild TIE-fighter designs for the final game in the series, *X-Wing Alliance*. I liked the project and the people there, and I felt refreshed and ready to dive back into that world, so I went to work at

Totally Games full time. I got to design things more than ever before, and had a lot of freedom to devise and execute sequences however I wanted. Consequently, the intro cinematic cut scene for *X-Wing Alliance* was the best 3D work I had done to date, and it was a heck of a lot of fun. It was great working for a small, fast-moving company, especially compared to the 300+ employee behemoth LucasArts had become.

Q: What advice do you have for people who'd like to work at LucasArts or ILM?

A: The most important thing is to be *great* at what you do. That sounds obvious, but it wasn't always the case when I was at LucasArts. There were so few skilled 3D artists available at the time that we sometimes had to go with what we could find. It's not like that anymore, because the pool of 3D talent has exploded in the last few years. Competition for jobs is much more intense nowadays—you have to make sure your work is better than the next guy's.

Next, be original. A lot of people seem to think that just knowing 3D and being a *Star Wars* geek qualifies them for a job with LucasArts, but it doesn't. You need to be a truly creative person, not just someone who can re-create a vehicle or scene that someone else has already done. There's a good chance at LucasArts that you may not work on a *Star Wars* game at all, so being a walking encyclopedia on the subject won't help you. Versatility is a crucial quality—if you are good at many different things related to the job, you have a much better chance at staying on when times are lean.

Also, don't be influenced by the name "Lucas." It's a company, like any other, and their business is to produce products that make money. It's not in business as a place for fanboys to worship. I used to review reels and recommend new hires, and you wouldn't believe the mail I used to get. People offered to work for free, or who just wanted to sweep the floors or something, simply because it was LucasArts! Those people were always rejected, of course. Many applicants tend to forget that as exciting as LucasArts sounds, it's a business, and there's no room for hangers-on. Occasionally LucasArts did accept interns, but they pulled their own weight and then some—one college intern that was on my team turned out to be awesome at modeling and writing shaders. Eventually, he wound up at PIXAR.

Last, don't confuse ILM with LucasArts. They are distinctly different companies with different missions, methods, and resources. Do not attempt to use a job at LucasArts to springboard into ILM. They're in contact with one another and will not let it happen. Decide where you want to go, *and go there*. Don't "settle" for a games job if you can't get into ILM. Both companies need people who are dedicated to what they do, not someone who's scheming to make a lateral move in the Lucas organization.

Q: What projects have you worked on over the years? How big were the teams doing these projects?

A: I worked on seven *Star Wars* games over the years: *Rebel Assault* and *Rebel Assault II, Rebellion, DroidWorks, X-Wing Alliance,* a finished but never-released game called *Rebel Agent,* and a never-completed one called *The New Emperor.*

The type of game and its production schedule determines the size of the art team. Shorter production cycles meant we had to put more people on a project for a shorter amount of time, which was always a pain. The 3D team for *Rebel Assault* consisted of only four or five artists. *Rebel Assault II*— which I was the lead artist on—had as many as 15 3D artists on it at a given time. Pre-rendered games like that require a lot of artists, whereas a flight simulator game like *X-Wing Alliance* needed only about six artists.

In addition to all those *Star Wars* games, other titles I worked on in some capacity include *Full Throttle* and *Ballblazer Champions* for LucasArts, plus *Critical Path* and *The Daedalus Encounter* for Mondo Media/Virgin Interactive. At Totally Games, I've just finished working on *Star Trek: Bridge Commander* for Activision, and am now working on an Xbox title for Microsoft.

Q: Which models or animation have been the most interesting for you? Which have been the toughest, and why?

A: I was a huge *Star Wars* fan back in the days of the original trilogy— before the dark times of Episode 1—but my fondest memories were of my work on an adventure game called *Full Throttle*. It was great fun to work on something other than *Star Wars*, and to have a chance to do some "cartoony" character stuff in 3D. It was mostly a 2D game, but after I did a test to determine if we could use 3D animation for all the game's vehicles, they were sold. It was a blast modeling the vehicles and characters from Peter Chan's designs.

One of the challenges with *Full Throttle* was to figure out a way to match the look of the 3D elements to the 2D elements. I did this with a mix of special texture maps and carefully reducing the palettes to a very limited range of colors, then compositing them together. That sounds pretty straightforward now, but at the time, the tools for doing this were very poor. I think that our results were quite stunning for the time—or perhaps even now—and it's the game I'm the proudest to have worked on.

The toughest project ever I did was a level for *Rebel Assault II*. As the art and animation lead on the project, my days were filled with just about everything *except* doing 3D work. I promised myself that I would create at least one level of the game, but the only time I had to work on it was after 7:00 p.m., when all my lead-artist tasks were done, the day's fires were put out, and I was exhausted. In the end, I was disappointed with my work on that level. I'll leave it up to you to guess which level it was!

Q: Was there anything special for you about working on a *Star Wars* game?

A: Back in college, I never thought there would even *be* a *Star Wars* video game for the PC, much less that I would work on any of them. It's not something I had consciously aimed for; it just sort of happened as a logical extension of everything else I'd done. Ironically, I'm basically doing the same things I did back when I was 15—making little movies with spaceships in them. Of course, it's not *exactly* the same as then, and there was a *huge* amount of other stuff in between that made everything else possible.

Like many game artists my age, *Star Wars* had a huge influence on me when I was young. After seeing it, I wanted nothing more than to work on movie special effects, which is partly why I studied industrial design; many of the movie effects guys were industrial designers. Rather than turning me into a full-blown *Star Wars* geek—I was only partially "infected"—the movies opened up a new world of possibilities that I could creatively pursue. Instead of dwelling on *Star Wars* stuff, I drew and modeled and made movies with my *own* vehicles, characters, and places.

The most enjoyable part of working on the *Star Wars* games came when I got to design new vehicles and environments that had to fit into that universe. I was pleased that I was able to expand the limits of something that had such a strong influence on my career, instead of simply building existing designs.

Q: When doing models of *Star Wars* ships, were you able to get access to the original physical models?

A: Not at first. There was a lot of publicly available reference material for just about anything we needed, and we simply used that. For the bluescreen shoot on *Rebel Assault II,* we used the original costumes and helmets for the live actors, so we spent some time at the "archives" preparing for that.

Not everyone at LucasArts had access to the warehouse where the *Star Wars* props and models were stored, however, and security has gotten much tighter since I was there many years ago. I wound up visiting the archives four or five times during my days at LucasArts. It could be very nerve-wracking at times, because the building was overflowing with all kinds of *stuff*. Incredibly expensive models costing hundreds of thousands of dollars apiece were crammed together on rolling stands like a bizarre *Star Wars* traffic jam. I had to tiptoe my way through them, terrified of breaking anything. We shot photos of some of the ships for texture mapping purposes, and it was tremendous fun to be able to wander around freely, looking at all the amazing models and matte paintings and props close-up. Many of the props are very cheesy-looking in real-life, whereas others had more detail and intricacy than would ever be picked up on film. I'm a big fan of practical models—meaning physical ones—so there was almost nothing more exciting than having access to the real thing.

Back when LucasArts was located in the same industrial complex that ILM is currently in, the art department had its own building that contained some of the actual props and paintings from the archives. I had the deck cannon from Jabba's sail barge on top of the divider wall next to my desk! Others had original matte paintings hanging on the walls of their offices! It all seems shocking now that those items would be so casually placed around the office, and somebody finally had the good sense to move them into the safety of the archives with the rest of the stuff.

Amusingly, about a week after a photo trip to the archives, I went to see the public show of *Star Wars* models and props that had opened in San Francisco, just to see what the exhibit looked like. As I started to reach over a tall Plexiglas barrier to point out something on a model to a friend—the model itself was still four feet away from my hand—when a security guard practically jumped on me! I had to laugh, because I had been *handling* some of the models in the archive just days earlier. It was a great exhibit, though, and it was wonderful to see all the people getting to enjoy what only a few had seen before.

Q: Do you prefer a particular type of modeling (polygonal, spline, patch, NURBS...)?

A: Most of the modeling I've done has been polygonal, though recently I've experimented with subdivision surfaces modeling, which is actually quite a fun way to model. Most of the models I've worked on recently have had low- to mid-poly counts for use in our game engine, so it's important to keep close track of the number of faces. Simply deforming basic geometric shapes—which retains the objects' mapping coordinates—then stitching the parts together is often the fastest method.

I've done most of the pre-rendered cinematic cutscenes at Totally Games, and that often involves rebuilding low-poly models into medium- to high-poly models. Sometimes that means just adding rounded corners or more facets to curved surfaces so the flat edges don't show up in the rendered shots. Again, this is most easily done by simply "pulling points" around. Sometimes even that isn't necessary. Often the medium and even low-poly models can be used for otherwise high-res animation. It just depends on how close the ship is to the camera, whether motion blur is used, and what sort of effects are going on that can help obscure a low-poly model. It's all about saving time wherever you can.

I've seen models with insane amounts of detail in them that would never show up in a shot, even in the tightest close-up. A lot of modelers take pride in building a "perfect model," but it's really just a waste of valuable resources. I try to build just what's necessary for the project, and I know that's true of people at ILM, too. As an example, a few years ago at LucasArts we needed a 3D model of C-3PO. We knew that ILM had built one for the Special Editions of *Star Wars*, and it would save us a lot of time if we could just use their model—something we had done before on other projects. After we got the model from them and converted it, we were stunned to find it consisted of only a few simple boxes and cylinders with a detailed texture shader applied. The model just had to sit on the back of a heavily motion-blurred land speeder, so they had built only what they'd needed for the shot, nothing more.

Q: How did you approach building a *Star Wars* model like an X-Wing?

A: Modeling something from the *Star Wars* universe is pretty easy, because there's so much good reference around. First I'd start with a layout drawing, like a blueprint, and load it as a bitmapped mapped image onto a flat polygon, then start tracing the different parts with splines. These splines are mostly for reference—sort of like a wire-outline version of the model—but can sometimes be directly extruded to make parts.

On something like an X-Wing, the fuselage is the most complicated part, but even that is fairly straightforward. Being old-fashioned, I would probably create it by lofting cross-sections along a path. These cross-sections are like the bulkheads in a plane's fuselage. They're a very good way to create accurate proportions on something where people are likely to notice if it's out of whack, and believe me, *Star Wars* fans notice that stuff. Lofting cross-sections is also a good way of creating subtle rounded corners that would be difficult to add later. The rest of the parts are pretty much basic geometric shapes like cylinders and boxes, but with raised-panel details.

Razor-sharp corners don't usually appear in manufactured objects, and they're one of the things that make CG models *look* like CG models. Even where a part is clearly just a box, I try to use chamfered edges with at least one facet to help "break" the edge. This creates an almost subliminal roll-off of the shadow around the shape, plus a little highlight along the edge that just looks much more natural.

The last step is texture mapping. In the case of the X-Wing, we were lucky to be able to photograph the actual physical model used in the films. We scanned and cleaned up the photos, then applied them as texture maps. If we didn't have photo reference, then we would have had to paint realistic textures in Photoshop. It was worth spending the time to do the textures well, because so much of a model's character and sense of reality comes from its mapping.

Q: Do you have any other tips or tricks for modeling or animation to help people improve their work?

A: I look at a lot of 3D work on different web-boards and forums, and the most common problems I see are with lighting and composition. Most people don't pay enough attention to those aspects of their images and the results end up being far less dramatic or interesting than they could be. Ironically, composition and lighting are among the easiest things to learn to help you make your images look better. Read books on filmmaking or photography to learn all you need to know. Tens of thousands of people have spent the last 170 years experimenting with photography and refining these ideas, so it's all there for the taking.

The other thing is to not get caught up worrying about tools and features. I've seen great work from artists using very low-end tools and hardware, just as I've seen a *ton* of crap from people with $50,000 worth of equipment and software. If you have something worthwhile and interesting to share with the world, the tools you use should make little difference.

Q: Do you have any "dream project" that you'd like to work on?

A: I'd love to have the time to work on my own animation projects. I have several good ideas for animated shorts, and some have even progressed to the 3D animatic stage. I don't know when I'll get the time to finish them, though. When I get home after doing 3D work 8–12 hours a day for a living, it's hard to motivate myself into working on my own projects. I've actually worked hard the last few years at teaching myself ways *not* to work too hard. It's necessary to keep me from burning out. It really *is* possible to do something *too much*—even things you love to do.

Q: Where would you like to be in five years?

A: I have a real affection for animated shorts, and even though I don't fancy myself the next John Lasseter, I'd love to be working on my own ideas full time. After completing one, I'd sell it to television as a series, have it become a huge hit, and then write and executive-produce from semi-retirement in Hawaii. Hey, it could happen! After all, when I was fifteen years old, I never thought I'd end up working on six *Star Wars* games.

My thanks go to Richard for sharing his thought and experiences with us. Richard's web site is at www.artbot.com.

Modeling Alternatives

There may be times when it's just too difficult or impractical to model an object from scratch using only the tools provided by your software program. In this kind of situation, there are some alternatives.

On the CD-ROM, in Appendix E, "Hardware and Software," some peripherals mentioned are 3D scanners and digitizers. These are devices capable of creating 3D mesh from physical objects, including people. Although some of these systems (particularly the scanners) are often prohibitively expensive to own, there are service bureaus that will scan people or objects for you at whatever resolution you desire, clean them up, and export them in the proper file format (see Appendix D on the CD-ROM).

One of these service bureaus is Digital Delusion in Emeryville, CA., and they were kind enough to give me a demonstration of their CyberWare head scanner. The subject (yours truly) was seated on a platform, then remained relatively motionless while being scanned by a rotating laser and video camera. The scanner sent the data to a nearby computer, where the mesh version of the subject could be seen (see Figure 4.25). Shiny objects (like eyes) and wispy objects (like what's left of my hair) cause problems for the laser scanner, so these elements were cleaned up or removed in the 3D program. Because the video scan was created in tiny vertical increments as my head was being scanned, it created an interesting wrap-around texture map. The map was then applied to the mesh head, adjusted for scale and position (a time-consuming process), and the resulting 3D CyberMark was rendered.

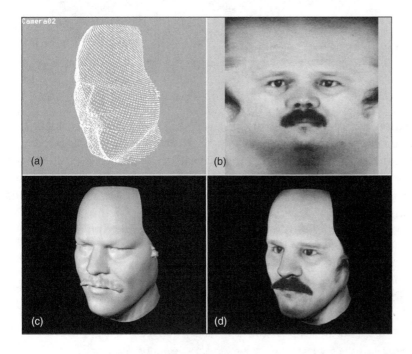

FIGURE 4.25

3D scan example:
(a) Medium-density mesh generated by the scanner, after clean-up.
(b) The very flattering video image capture performed at the same time. (c) Rendering of the mesh head.
(d) Rendering of the mesh head with the image map applied. Spooky.

Although 3D scanning is clearly a good way to go if you're trying to produce an accurate model of a human head and/or body, it's also advantageous for any complex character. *Maquettes* (small sculptures made of plaster or Super Sculpty) can be created of just about any sort of character, then scanned or digitized. This method was used to create the termites in the Orkin pest control commercials, for example.

Mesh Libraries

Finally, as I mentioned briefly in the last chapter, there may be times when modeling an object doesn't make sense from a time or budget standpoint. In these cases, the alternative may be to buy a model from one of the stock mesh providers such as Viewpoint, Zygote, or Acuris. These companies provide *mesh libraries* of mapped and unmapped 3D models in a variety of different formats and resolutions (see Figure 4.26).

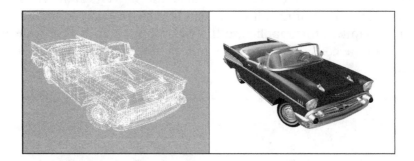

FIGURE 4.26

The classic '57 Chevy model from Viewpoint is a good example of the high-quality models available from mesh libraries. This is actually a sample mesh that was distributed with 3D Studio R4 (DOS).

The objects cost hundreds or thousands of dollars each, but in a pinch, or in a situation where a complex and accurate organic model is needed (such as realistic people or animals), they can be a very practical alternative. On top of the price tag, there are some other caveats to be aware of: First, unmapped objects may require quite a bit of work to map properly, because you may have to break them down into small elements to apply mapping coordinates. Second, objects with lots of individual pieces also may not be labeled properly, making it difficult to select the objects you want from a list.

Although most of the models sold by these companies are created using either 3D scanners or digitizers, some may be scratch-built objects that they buy from modelers. In fact, you may want to consider offering mesh to one of these companies if it's of a general interest nature (and you've retained the rights to it after producing the product or animation for which it was originally intended).

If the mesh library doesn't offer exactly what you want, consider using what's available as a starting point and adding modifications to it. We ran into this situation on *Zork:Nemesis*, because six or seven suits of armor were needed for one of the puzzles. Because the budget was too restrictive to model them all from scratch, we got a basic medieval suit of armor from Viewpoint, mapped it, then applied or removed pieces of mesh to make them more reminiscent of other eras. Although the results certainly weren't historically accurate by any means, they did do the trick (see Figure 4.27).

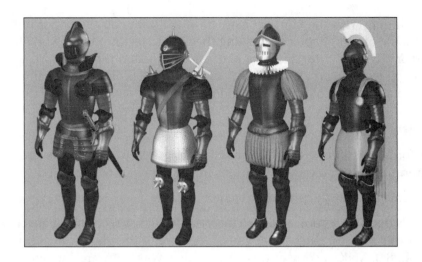

FIGURE 4.27

Using a basic medieval suit of armor, variations were made by adding or subtracting mesh details. Image by Mark Giambruno & Laura Hainke/Mondo Media for Zork:Nemesis ©1996 Activision.

Many mesh library producers offer free samples online or on their CD-ROMs for you to use and evaluate. Look at their web sites (listed in Appendix D) for more information. In addition, a fair amount of public domain 3D objects of all quality levels are available though the Internet or in online providers' libraries.

Intermediate Modeling Tutorials

Topics covered:

Using Deform Modifiers

Creating Bevels

Editing Mesh

Using Booleans

Completing the Model

The tutorials in this section are intermediate in difficulty and assume that you have developed enough familiarity with the basic tools to determine the best approach for constructing some of these objects. Therefore, some of the instructions are more general.

Continuing with the blimp construction will give you the opportunity to put some of this chapter's modeling theory and techniques to work. By the end of this set of tutorials, most of the mesh work on the blimp project will be complete. This is also a good time to take the project further and make it into a true portfolio piece by adding your own details and variations.

Using Deform Modifiers

To form the skin of the ship, build it as a sweep object. Use the Scale deform modifier to create variations in the diameter of the object.

1. Create a new document or scene.

2. Using the Arc tool, create a cloverleaf-like cross-sectional shape 440 units wide for the helium gasbag, or skin, of the blimp (see Figure 4.28a). Make a copy of this shape unless your software's sweep operation will leave it intact.

3. Define a straight path for the sweep 2500 units long, with the axis running through the center of the cloverleaf shape (see Figure 4.28b).

4. Sweep the cloverleaf cross-section along the path. The result should look similar to the lower figures (see Figure 4.28c–d).

FIGURE 4.28

Creating the helium bag for the blimp: (a) Use arcs to create a cloverleaf shape for the cross-section. (b) Make a straight path to define the length of the bag. (c–d) Sweep the shape along the path.

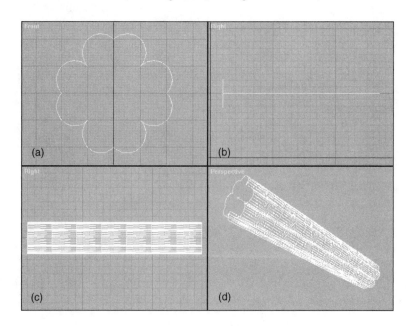

5. Apply a Scale Deform Modifier to the sweep so that you can create an "envelope" that defines the diameter of the cross-section. To control the shape of the envelope, use a Bezier spline or whatever control point type your software offers. Use the settings in the graph as a guide. The horizontal scale represents the length of the path, and the vertical scale is the percentage of scaling to apply to the cross-sectional shape (see Figure 4.29a).

6. The finished sweep should resemble Figure 4.29b. You may need to adjust the number of steps and segments to achieve a good balance between smoothness and mesh density.

7. Render the object from a perspective viewpoint and check for problems (see Figure 4.29c). Name the object GasBag.

8. Save the file as B_MAIN01.

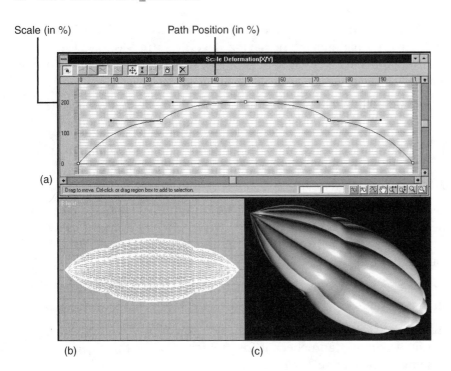

FIGURE 4.29

Using Scale Deform to shape the helium bag: (a) Set Scale Deform to create an envelope similar to this one. (b) Adjust the steps in the resulting mesh for a good compromise between detail and density. (c) Render and check the results.

Creating Bevels

This tutorial offers a couple of different options for creating supporting rings for the gas bag. Use whichever one is supported by your software or is the most convenient.

If your software doesn't offer either of the beveling options below, you can create the beveled object by sweeping the cloverleaf shape along a path 2 units long. Use the Scale Deform Modifier to create a roughly beveled sweep object, then use vertex-level editing to slide sections of the front and back faces around to even out the chamfer. Another method is to create two cloverleaf shapes—one slightly larger than the other—and then use the two cross-sections to create a skinned object, much as you did with the thruster mounting bracket.

Some programs offer either Bevel tools that directly manipulate an object according to the parameters, or have a Bevel Deform Modifier for use on swept objects. If your software offers one of these options, use it to do the following:

1. Hide the GasBag object. Select the clover-like cross-section used for the gas bag or the duplicate you made earlier (see Figure 4.30a)

2. If your software doesn't offer a Bevel tool to do the job directly, plan to make it into a sweep object by creating a path 20 units long. Otherwise, go to step 3.

3. Use the Bevel tool (if available) or Bevel Deform Modifier to create a beveled sweep object. Use the Bevel Deform Modifier in the same way as the Scale Modifier was used in the last tutorial to create this object (see Figure 4.30b).

4. Adjust the bevel to get results similar to the side view close-up shown in Figure 4.30c.

5. Adjust the steps for the shapes and path to control the mesh density. Render the object and check it for problems. Name the object BagRng01 (see Figure 4.30d).

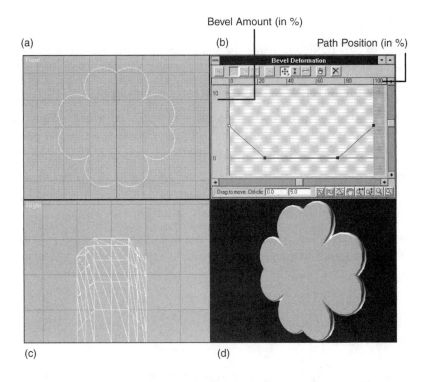

(a)

(b)

Bevel Amount (in %)

Path Position (in %)

(c)

(d)

FIGURE 4.30

Beveling a support ring for the blimp: (a) Select the cloverleaf cross-section. (b) Use a Bevel tool, or create a sweep object and use a Bevel Deform Modifier. (c) Adjust the bevel as shown. (d) Render the result and adjust step settings if necessary.

6. Unhide the GasBag object and use Move and Scale to position BagRng01 about 975 units from the end of the blimp. The BagRng01 object should extend out from the edges of the GasBag object slightly. Copy, move, and scale three duplicates into the positions shown (see Figure 4.31a).

7. Render the objects from a perspective view (see Figure 4.31b).

8. Save the file as B_MAIN02.

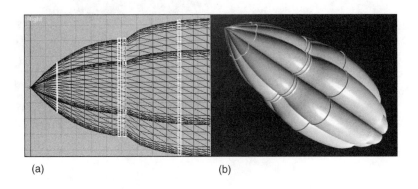

(a)

(b)

FIGURE 4.31

Positioning the support rings: (a) Use Copy, Move, and Scale to position the rings. The best positions will depend on the shape of the GasBag you created. (b) Render the result. You should see highlights kicked up by the bevels on the rings.

Editing Mesh

Mesh editing can be used rather than scale deformation to create simpler forms, such as the strut used to attach the thruster to the ship.

1. Open the file B_THR15. Hide the thruster components.

2. In the Right viewport, create a 16-sided cylinder 75 units long with a 15 unit radius and 3 segments that will be used as the strut. A perspective view is shown here for clarity (see Figure 4.32a).

3. In the Front viewport, enter vertex-level editing mode (if applicable) and scale the one set of mid-object vertices to 80% of their original diameter; then move them 20 units to the right (see Figure 4.32b).

4. Scale the other set of mid-object vertices to 110% of original diameter and move them 15 units to the left. Scale the leftmost set of vertices 160% (see Figure 4.32c).

5. Name the object ThrStr01. Render it from a perspective view to see the results (see Figure 4.32d).

6. Save the file as B_THR16.

FIGURE 4.32

Using vertex editing to create the strut: (a) Create a cylinder. (b) Use vertex editing to scale and move the first set of vertices into position. (c) Complete the strut by editing the other vertices. (d) Render the result.

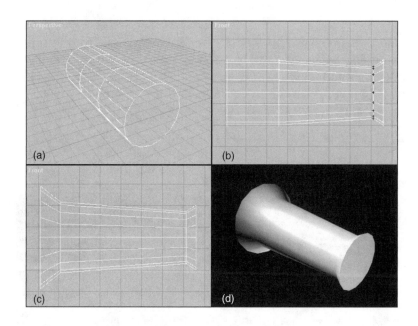

(a)　　(b)　　(c)　　(d)

Using Booleans

This tutorial uses Boolean subtraction to add interest to the strut created in the last exercise.

1. In the front view, create a box 28 units wide, 10 units high, and 32 units deep, and position it as shown (see Figure 4.33a).

2. Use Align or Move in the top view to make sure the box extends past the edges of the strut in both directions (see Figure 4.33b).

3. In the front view, rotate the box about 2° clockwise (see Figure 4.33c).

4. Mirror Copy the box and move the duplicate to the opposite side of the strut (see Figure 4.33d).

5. Save the file as B_THR16a before proceeding, but don't close the file.

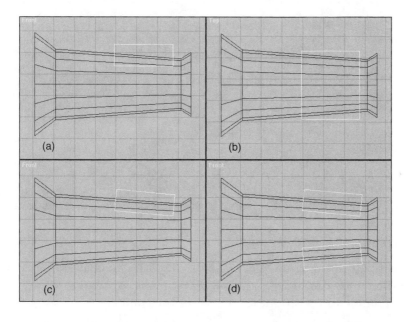

FIGURE 4.33

Preparing to Boolean the strut: (a) Create a box to use as a cutting object. (b) Make sure the box extends past the edges of the strut. (c) Rotate the box to match the strut. (d) Mirror Copy the box to the opposite side.

Because Boolean operations don't always work as expected, always save your work before you execute one. If the Boolean fails, try repositioning the mesh slightly. You may also need to tessellate one or both objects (as a last resort).

6. Following the methods outlined in your software manual, use Boolean Subtract to remove the first box's volume from the strut (see Figure 4.34a).

7. Repeat the use of Boolean Subtract to remove the second box's volume from the strut (see Figure 4.34b–c).

8. Render the object and check the results (see Figure 4.34d).

9. Save the file as B_THR17.

FIGURE 4.34

Performing a Boolean operation on the strut: (a) Referring to your manual for the steps, subtract the first box's volume from the strut. (b–c) Repeat the operation for the section box. (d) Render the results.

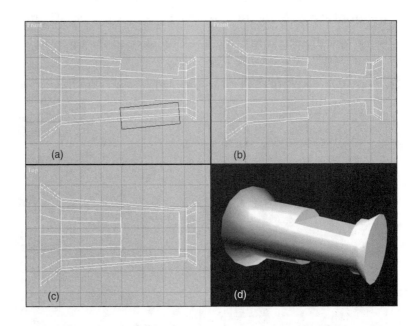

Completing the Model

Using the techniques you've learned in the last two chapters, and the general directions that follow, complete the modeling work on the blimp by constructing and positioning the rest of the components.

The figures and instructions will become less detailed at this point, and issues such as size, position, object naming, and so forth are up to you to determine from the figures, unless specifically noted. Because many of the remaining items are not critical, experiment and add additional detail, if desired.

Complete the Thruster Assembly

Complete the thruster assembly by rotating the strut into position and creating the base and other details.

1. From the Front viewport, Unhide the thruster assembly and rotate it counterclockwise 15° so that the ThrMnt01 object is now at a 45° angle. Move and rotate the ThrStr01 strut into position, making sure it is centered over the thruster mount (see Figure 4.35a).

2. Create an engine for the thruster (ThrEng01), using a beveled cylinder. Create a support (ThrSup01) to hold the motor in place with a simple cylinder (see Figure 4.35b).

3. Copy the mounting bracket ThrMnt01 from the thruster and rotate it 180°, positioning it as shown. Scale the bracket up until the circular face is a bit larger than the end of the strut. Use vertex-level editing to extend the end of the bracket. Name it ThrBas01 (see Figure 4.35c).

4. Create a cylinder and bevel one edge, positioning it so that it appears to be a motor mounted to the bracket. Name it ThrMtr01 (see Figure 4.35d).

5. Save the file as B_THR18 and close it.

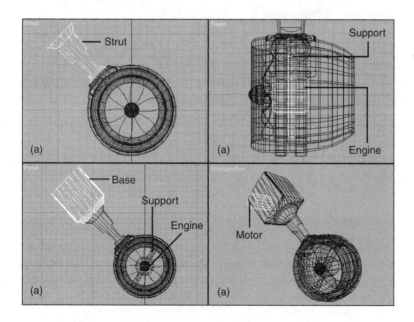

FIGURE 4.35

Finishing the thruster assembly: (a) Rotate the thruster and strut into position. (b) Add an engine and support to drive the propeller. (c) Copy and modify the thruster mount to use as a base. (d) Add a motor object on the side of the base.

Create the Gondola

Create the gondola by following these basic steps:

1. Open the file B_MAIN02, and use the GasBag mesh and the views in the figures to determine scale and proportion. Overall size of the gondola is about 400 units wide, 160 units high, and 500 units long (see Figure 4.36).

2. From the Top view, create a beveled rectangular shape to use as the outline of the gondola.

3. Using sweep and bevel modifier techniques, create the roof of the gondola (35 units high). Use Gon*Xxxnn* as the naming convention.

On the CD-ROM in Appendix G, "Planning and Organization," take a look at the section on object-naming conventions. It will help you select appropriate names for the parts you'll be adding.

4. Mirror the roof and position it directly below to form the base (75 units high) of the gondola. Extend the bottom of the floor downward with vertex editing.

5. Create a 4-sided cylinder for use as a window frame component, 50 units high. Use Array to create a row of identically placed window frame objects. Use Array again to create a second set perpendicular to the first. If necessary, center the assembly in the middle of the gondola.

6. Use a single box object to create the window glass, positioning it through the centers of all the window frame objects.

7. Create a thin box object to act as a trim/support piece. Use Array to duplicate it across the bottom of the gondola.

8. In the Front view, create a diamond-like shape and use sweep with a bevel modifier it to form a skid on the bottom of the gondola.

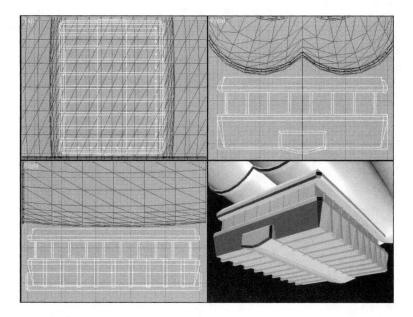

FIGURE 4.36

Construct the gondola using these views as a reference, or design your own. To make the ship look larger, make the human-sized gondola smaller.

Create the Catwalk Assemblies

Follow these basic steps to create the catwalk area adjacent to the gondola:

1. Use the previously constructed mesh and the views in the figures to determine scale and proportion. Overall size of the catwalk is about 300 units wide, and 400 units long (see Figure 4.37).

2. Create an I-beam-like cross-section shape and extrude it to make the beam that hangs from the bottom of the GasBag rings next to the gondola. Use Cat*Xxxnn* for the object-naming convention.

FIGURE 4.37

Construct the catwalk area using these views or invent your own layout. Consider adding additional details like railings, electrical conduits and equipment, and so on.

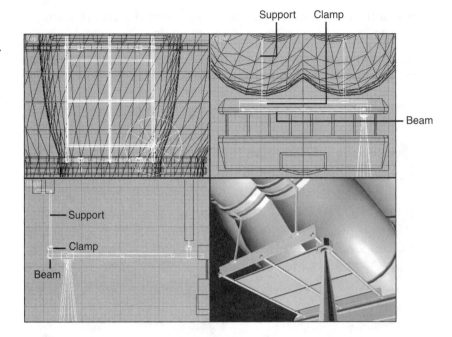

3. Create a clamp shape near the end of the beam and extrude it to be wider than the I-beam (see Figure 4.38).

4. Create a 4-sided cylinder to connect the clamp to the ring above. Copy the clamp and support and move it to the opposite end of the I-beam.

5. Copy the I-beam, clamps, and supports and move them directly under the adjacent ring. Adjust the supports to reach.

6. Use 8-sided cylinders to create a framework of six horizontal supports mounted to the I-beams.

7. Create a thin panel that covers the four large openings in the framework. Name it CatGrd01.

> The ship has a total of five searchlights with visible beams. This generic tutorial presumes that your software doesn't offer volumetric lighting, so the visible beams will be created with mesh and material settings. If your package does offer volumetric lighting, you can skip step 10 and create a similar look by adding a volumetric spotlight when doing the lighting tutorials instead.

8. Create a beveled 8-sided cylinder to form the base of the searchlight.

9. Create a hemisphere, then use vertex editing to pull the center portion toward the interior, creating a depression.

10. Create a cone that fits into the depression and extends downward.

11. Move the assembly into position on the catwalk. The assembly will be duplicated after mapping.

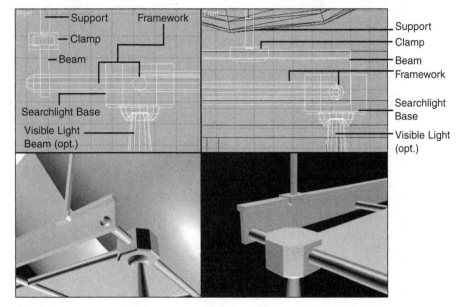

FIGURE 4.38

Detail of the catwalk areas. Remember to use bevels to catch the light on moderate to large objects.

Create the Spires

The spires are antenna-like probes extending outward from the ship, and they have small lights attached to them.

1. Use the previously constructed mesh and the views in the figures to determine scale and proportion. Overall length of the spire is about 400 units (see Figure 4.39).

2. Create a side view of the spire and fins as 2D polyline shapes.

3. Extrude or bevel all three shapes. Use Spr*Xxxnn* as the object-naming convention.

4. Rotate the fins 90° and center them on the main spire.

5. Add a sphere at the thick end of the spire to serve as a base.

6. Add some small low-res spheres to act as "lights." Use RunLit*nn* as the convention for all lights.

7. Group the objects together as SprGRP01 and move them into position on the ship.

FIGURE 4.39

Create spires to serve as antennae and to add extra interest to the form by extruding or beveling some 2D polyline shapes. Add small spheres to serve as non-illuminating "lights."

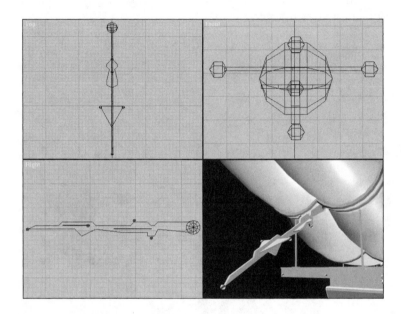

Position the Thrusters

Bring the thruster assembly into the model and position it.

1. Merge the contents of the latest B_THR*nn* file into the B_MAIN*nn* file you've been working with.

2. Move and rotate the thruster assembly as shown. Make sure the ThrMtr01 motor object doesn't go inside the GasBag object (see Figure 4.40).

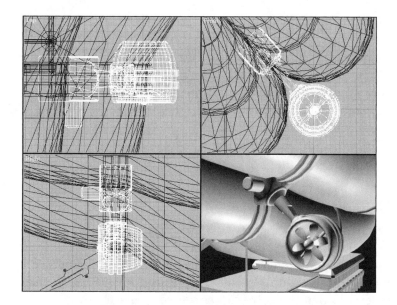

FIGURE 4.40

Merge the thruster
assembly file into the
main model and position
it as shown.

Position the Monitor

Bring the monitor assembly into the model and position it.

1. Merge the contents of the latest B_MON*nn* file into the B_MAIN*nn*
    file you've been working with.

2. Move and rotate the monitor assembly as shown (see Figure 4.41).

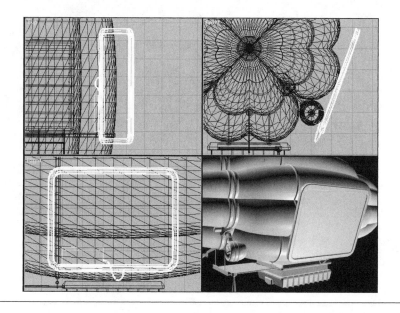

FIGURE 4.41

Merge the monitor
assembly file into the
main model and position
it as shown.

Add the Detail Mesh

At this point, add all the little detail mesh to the model, such as guy wires, supports, the nose cone on the end of the GasBag, and so forth.

1. Using the figures as a guide, add small-diameter cylinders as guy wires from the monitor to the BagRng01 object (see Figure 4.42).

2. Use a cone to cover the end of the GasBag object, and add a cylinder and sphere projecting off the end of it. They will be used in the animation tutorials as part of the docking sequence, so make sure the sphere has a radius of 10 units. Add a tube protruding near the base of the cone to add some interest.

3. Add more low-res spheres as "lights" onto the spires, rings, gondola, and other portions of the ship. As with the ones on the spires, use the name RunLit*nn* for the objects, so that they can be selected and modified as a group. You may also want to make them instance objects so that their size can be varied *en masse* as well.

4. Add, modify, or fix anything I forgot to mention.

FIGURE 4.42

Adding detail mesh like guy wires and fake lights makes the model more interesting and realistic. Small details also help establish scale, especially when the viewer can relate the objects to their "real life" sizes.

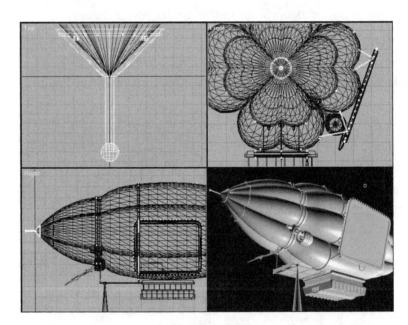

Because it will save time in the mapping and animation processes, we won't be duplicating the mesh assemblies to finish off the modeling at this point. That will occur in the tutorials for Chapter 9, "Animation."

By now, you've created almost enough mesh to pass for a completed modeling project. However, to turn this into a true portfolio piece, a great deal more modeling work is needed. The addition of more spires, additional guy wires, doorways, and escape hatches for the gondola, railings, electrical equipment, and so forth will take the model to the next level, and make it a truly professional work. Although it is impractical to cover all these additions in this tutorial, you are highly encouraged to customize and enhance the model in this way.

Summary

This chapter has moved beyond the basics of modeling and into some of the more intermediate (and perhaps even advanced) techniques. Despite the fact that it may be a while before you're ready to take on an advanced project like building a character, it's important to understand some of the approaches so that you can apply them to simpler objects, as well as note possible advanced applications of tools you already use.

The value of reference and how to make the most efficient use of it was discussed. You also looked at the importance of bevels, explored deform modifiers, vertex-level editing, face extrusion, and other techniques. Finally, you received some tips on doing crystals and examined some alternatives to modeling as well.

In the next chapter, you will see how mapping can be used to enhance the realism of mesh objects by giving them color and texture. You will also look at how mapping can be used in place of mesh to create the illusion of detail without bogging things down.

CHAPTER 5

Low-Poly Modeling

Low-poly characters like "Mole" are right at home in powerful new graphics cards and console game systems that accelerate 3D performance to new heights. Image ©2001 Barry Collins (model), Per Abrahamsen (mapping), James Edwards (design).

*T*he Master sat quietly all morning in his garden, admiring the gorgeous spring weather. The air was fresh, the sun warm, and all the flowers were in bloom; it felt like paradise.

Finally, knowing that he still had tasks to perform on the Glowing Pool, he reluctantly made his way up the stairs in the old stone keep. As he neared the top, he heard odd clattering sounds coming from the workroom, intermingled with the excited voices of his student and another young man. He entered the room to find the two lads bent over the Glowing Pool, feverishly manipulating some virtual swordsman in battle.

"What's this, then?" the old man asked as he made his way over to the source of the ruckus.

"Oh, Master...there you are," replied his student, still locked in virtual combat with the other lad. "This is my friend Nolan of Bushnell. He's an apprentice to a Spellwright!"

"A Spellwright, eh?" replied the Master. Spellwrights were powerful sorcerers who developed and refined the spells used by people like the Master and his student to summon illusions. Although the Spellwrights were not usually artisans themselves, they created the magical tools necessary for such work.

"Yes! And he's been working on new spells that allow the Glowing Pool to be used for playing games, like this one," the student replied, contorting himself strangely as he bade his virtual fighter to parry a blow. "I'm going to be helping him by making the fighters and arenas."

The Master sighed heavily. "Let me give you some important advice," he said.

The two boys stopped playing and gazed up at him.

The old man walked over to the window, letting a shaft of warm light fall on his aged face. To the boys, it looked as though he was being illuminated by the light of Heaven. "Lads," he said woefully, "Glowing Pools are not toys. They're powerful and expensive, and no one will want to use them for such foolishness. You're putting your energies into something that has no future at all. Now, go outside into this glorious day and think on that for a while."

The young men looked at each other, then made their way toward the door, heads bowed in depression. They spent the better part of the afternoon pondering the Master's words. When they finally made their way back up to the workroom, they were shocked to see the old man bent over the student's Glowing Pool, gyrating wildly as his virtual fighter delivered the final blow to his opponent. The Master started to cry out in joy, but suddenly realized that he was no longer alone.

The young men stared at him, arms folded. "No future, eh?" said the student.

"Busted..." the old man sheepishly muttered.

The Real-Time Explosion

It's impossible to walk the game aisles of Toys'R'Us or CompUSA and not see that real-time 3D is the technology of choice for most action and online Role Playing Games, and is steadily gaining on 2D for other types of games as well. All the new-generation consoles have powerful 3D capabilities, and video cards such as the nVidea GeForce line continue to push Mac and PC 3D graphics to new heights. As a result, the quality of real-time 3D characters and environments is improving rapidly (see Figure 5.1). The demand for real-time games has made the production of in-game, real-time 3D assets a focus for many artists in the field.

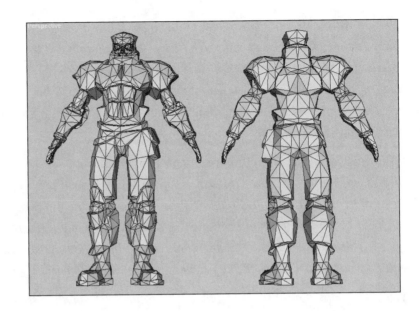

The use of 3D on the web is also increasing, due in part to the higher data throughput available with broadband connections such as DSL, cable modem, and satellite. Content ranges from web shows such as DotComix' *Dilbert* and *Sister Randy* to Brilliant Digital Entertainment's *Superman* and *Kiss: Immortals*. Both use web browsers linked to real-time 3D playback engines to deliver the content on your desktop. To check them out for yourself, go to www.dotcomix.com and www.brilliantdigital.com.

Web-based 3D holds an attraction for online retailers as well. Instead of merely featuring a photo of a product such as a camcorder, a 3D-enabled online store could offer an interactive 3D version of it, allowing the potential buyer to view it from any angle, and even watch an animation of the viewscreen unfolding for use. One of the companies offering the technology and content for such web commerce applications is Viewpoint, the same people who sell stock mesh online. You can see demos of their product at www.viewpoint.com.

Low-poly models have applications in hi-res animation as well. Although they tend to be constructed more crudely than their game counterparts, building a low-poly version of a character or vehicle and using it as a stand-in during animation can be a great time-saver. Using low-poly stand-ins may enable you to preview the animation in real-time, and test renders get done in a flash. When the animation is refined as much as possible with the stand-in, the animator can replace it with the hi-res mesh. Some programs may allow you to work with the stand-in during animation, but then substitute the hi-res mesh automatically when rendering. In some cases, you may not need to substitute the low-poly mesh at all; if the object is small enough in the scene, you can get away with the low-res version.

Nailing the Specs

Unlike high-res modeling, low-poly work is often very unforgiving. If you model something inefficiently for a high-res project, it still works; it just takes longer to render. If the poly count of models is too high in a 3D game, however, it can impact the performance of the game, even to the point where it is unplayable. A single vertex, slightly out of place, would probably never be noticed in a hi-res model; in a low-poly one, it can cause faces to disappear in the playback engine. Likewise, common hi-res modeling practices such as letting mesh overlap or neglecting to delete backfaces can have serious consequences for the appearance and performance of a low-poly model.

Therefore, planning is essential with low-poly projects, especially those intended for commercial use. The artist needs to be aware of the playback engine's requirements—what it can and can't do, and how far you can push things before they break. Before you tackle a low-poly project, be sure you get hold of all the important specifications for the models—their maximum poly counts, whether they need to be single objects, the texture budget, and so forth. The following list includes some of the common specifications:

♦ **File Format**. 3D engines generally have a very limited number of file formats they can either directly accept or provide conversion utilities for.

♦ **Polygon Limits and Restrictions**. The number and type of polygons allowed in the model have a specific limit.

♦ **Texture Map Specs**. The texture maps also need to be in a specific format, such as .BMP, and have a specific color depth, such as 8-bit or 16-bit. They probably also have to be a specific size. Some engines may also support alpha channel transparency, which can be useful for creating special effects like engine glows.

- **Filenames and Directories.** Specific file naming conventions and directory structures might need to be set up for your models to be imported properly.

- **Units and Scale.** Your models probably have to be built according to a certain scale so that they can fit in with other objects imported into the 3D engine.

- **World Coordinate System.** The 3D engine may or may not use the same world coordinate layout as your 3D package.

- **Mirrored and Instanced Geometry.** Some 3D engines may have problems with mesh that has been mirrored or instanced during the modeling process.

- **Mesh Structure.** Check to see whether long, skinny polygons or "T" intersections (where a vertex from one poly sits on top of a continuous edge of another poly) might be a problem for the engine.

- **Animation.** Can the objects be animated, and if so, by what process? For example, *Half-Life* uses real-time skeletal deformation, whereas *Quake II* stores animation as vertex transformations.

Many other considerations affect the way you construct and map low-poly mesh, but the point I want to make is that you really need to do your homework when you get into a low-poly project. Read the specifications thoroughly and dissect a sample model that works with the engine to see how it's put together.

The following sections look at some of these specifications in more detail, and examine some other low-poly concerns.

Poly Counts

A *poly count* is the total number of polygons that make up a given object. Most 3D engines prefer four-sided polys—quads—but work fine with 3-sided triangular polys as well. The difference is that it takes two triangular polys to make up a quad, so the artist can keep the poly count lower by using quads rather than tris wherever possible.

3D engines have limits as to how many polygons they can move around within a given time period, and this limit basically determines how complex the geometry can be in a given scene. Let's assume that an engine has a practical limit of moving 5000 polygons per frame of animation. If the gameplay calls for having only five objects in the scene, each can be modeled with 1000 polys apiece, or some other breakdown that doesn't exceed the limit. For example, two of the objects could be 1500 polys each, which would leave 2000 polys divided up among the remaining three objects. If the gameplay required 100 objects in the scene, each could be modeled at 500 polys, and so on. This is essentially how the poly count for a given model is determined.

Level of Detail

To milk more performance and the appearance of greater scene complexity out of a 3D engine, models are often created in two or three versions, each with a different poly count, or *level of detail (LOD)*. For example, you might have a 1000-polygon model for use when the object is large in the scene, then swap in a 300-polygon model if it gets far enough away from the camera that the viewer can't tell the difference (see Figure 5.2). By switching to a model with a lower level of detail, you free up the engine to handle additional objects without exceeding the total polygon limits.

(a) (b) (c)

FIGURE 5.2

3D assets for games are often produced with multiple mesh and mapping resolutions called levels of detail or LODs.
3D engines swap out objects farther from the camera with less-detailed versions.
(a) LOD-1: Full-res model with high-res maps.
(b) LOD-2: Full-res model with medium-res maps.
(c) LOD-3: Lower-res model and maps.

The best way to approach building different LODs for a given model is to make the highest-resolution version first, including texture mapping it, and make sure that it passes all the tests you throw at it, including client sign-off if you're doing the work for someone else. After the highest LOD is locked down, you can create the lower resolution versions by collapsing faces on the model until you've chipped it down to the desired poly count. If things go well, you won't even have to do a new texture map for the object.

One of the tricky parts about creating LODs is that reducing the poly count obviously means taking away mesh detail, and this can significantly change the object's shape as well. If the two LODs are a bit too different-looking, the transition between the two LODs will be very apparent. You may have to tweak the mesh and maps on the lower-res LOD to prevent or reduce this.

Texture Budget

Although texture mapping isn't discussed until the next chapter, some special considerations for low-poly mapping bear mentioning here. If you're totally unfamiliar with texture mapping at this point, you may want to return to this section after reading the next chapter.

Like the poly count, the *texture budget* is a maximum limit determined by the programmers for the number and size of the texture maps applied to a given object. The reason for this restriction is that the maps have to be held in RAM, which is often very limited in console games and video cards, especially older ones.

The individual texture maps for low-poly applications are often square and have a resolution that is a power of two, like 256×256 pixels. This specification helps the 3D engine calculate and apply the maps more quickly. Other common sizes for texture maps include: 1024×1024, 512×512, 128×128, 64×64, and 32×32.

Note that the texture budget may vary with the LODs, so lower-res models have half or a quarter of the total texture map real estate than the highest-resolution LODs do. In many cases, creating a lower-resolution texture map is as simple as shrinking down the overall dimensions of the largest maps. For the lowest-res LODs, though, you usually have to create a new texture map.

Texture Packing

Not only are there limits on the overall number and resolution of the texture maps, but the fact that there are so few of them means that you have to include the maps for several different parts of the model on a single image. The result resembles a patchwork quilt, with the textures for various unrelated parts of the model stuck side by side simply because they happen to fit there better than in some other arrangement (see Figure 5.3).

FIGURE 5.3

The packed texture maps for the "Mole" character demonstrate how textures for multiple parts of a model can be combined together into a single image. Image ©2001 Barry Collins (model), Per Abrahamsen (mapping), and James Edwards (design).

Because the dimensions of a given map affect how that part of the model looks when rendered in the 3D engine, the largest sections of the object—such as the wings on a aircraft model—require the largest chunks of the texture map, or the result looks fuzzy and stretched out. In some cases, the parts are oddly shaped, leaving the artist to "pack" the textures for other parts of the model into the odd-shaped open areas. This process of arranging and consolidating a number of different textures into a single texture map is appropriately called *texture packing*.

Note

One of the things that I think made the Starfleet Command models stand out was the use of "wall-washing" spotlight effects in the maps, which made the hull look like it was being illuminated by tiny but powerful lights on the ship. The spotlight effects were duplicated in the self-illumination maps so that those areas would appear lit even if the ship was not receiving any other source of illumination.

Low-Poly Techniques

Although low-poly modeling doesn't generally require any new modeling skills—you generally use some of the same techniques you would for hi-res vertex-level modeling—it does require that you use greater precision and make a lot of decisions about where to invest detail and where to simplify or just leave something out.

Box modeling is a popular way to approach low-poly modeling because it offers excellent control. It also enables you to rough out the entire model fairly quickly, so you can evaluate the poly count and decide where you can afford to add additional detail.

Maintaining Planarity

Because avoiding non-planar polygons is very important with low-poly modeling, there are a couple things you can do to help ensure that you don't mess up your quads while editing. First, use axis constraints when transforming vertices; this helps to ensure that the vertices aren't getting skewed off center the way they can if you just eyeball an adjustment. Second, keep an eye on your program's *model statistics information*—it's a readout that indicates how many quads, tris, and verts are making up your model at any given time. If your program doesn't feature something like this built-in, you can probably find a plug-in or a utility that will give you the same information.

If the number of quads drops and is replaced by tris, you have probably made some of the quads non-planar. Undo or go back to a previous version of the model and figure out what caused the problem.

Mesh Structure

Although a low-poly model depends on the 3D engine and other programming and animation considerations, it usually consists of several pieces of mesh attached together into a single object. In some cases, such as a character model, the object may have to be a single, seamless mesh so that it does not tear apart when animated. Mechanical devices, vehicles, and armor, however, may be constructed of individual collections of polys that lie very close to each other, but don't actually connect (see Figure 5.4). They're still "attached" together as a single object, however.

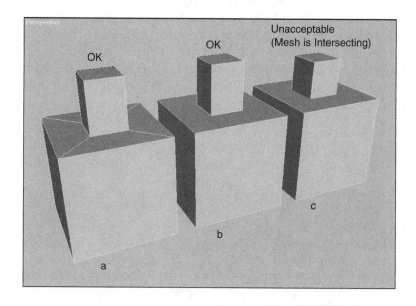

FIGURE 5.4

Samples of acceptable and unacceptable mesh construction. (a) Seamless mesh, used for deformation-animated objects. (b) Separate elements that don't intersect, combined into one object. (c) Separate elements that intersect can cause problems for 3D engines.

If you're building a model made up of multiple pieces, it may be important to ensure that none of the mesh passes through any other parts of the model. For example, if you were adding a little antenna to a low-poly model of a robot, you would want to position the bottom of the antenna very close to the top of the robot—so close you would have to view it magnified many times to see that it wasn't actually touching the model. If the base of the antenna "sinks into" the top of the robot, however, that may cause problems for the 3D engine.

Likewise, with a high-res model, you may not bother to delete the faces on the bottom of the antenna. With low-poly models, however, every polygon counts, so you want to delete anything that can't be seen or that the viewer won't miss. If some little detail can be created in the texture map rather than as a piece of mesh, do it in the texture map instead.

Smoothing

Real-time 3D engines often use Gouraud-level rendering, so that the angular polygons end up looking smooth and continuous. This is great for characters and rounded objects, but if you build a model of an Abrams tank, you may not appreciate having it looking soft and puffy. One common way to get around this is by detaching groups of polygons that you want to retain their flat, angular look. The detached groups remain in their same positions and are still part of the object, but the fact that their perimeter vertices are no longer attached to other sections of mesh means the smoothing calculations are done separately (see Figure 5.5). You can make use of this trick in high-res modeling as well; it's useful for helping to get nice highlights on beveled edges.

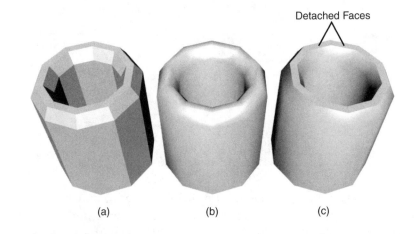

Detached Faces

FIGURE 5.5

Controlling smoothness by detaching faces: (a) Object as it is constructed. (b) Same object, as it might appear in a 3D engine that smooths normals. (c) Same object with end faces detached to break the smoothing process.

(a)　　　　(b)　　　　(c)

Although Curious Labs' Poser software is not a real-time 3D package, it uses the same sort of "smooth everything" approach to objects. Fortunately, the same technique of detaching mesh works well with Poser.

Game and Web Asset Artist Interviews

As you can see, low-poly modeling and animation offer some special challenges over hi-res work. For a bit more insight into the world of low-poly work, I spoke to four veterans: Eric Chadwick, Leila Noorani, Kelly Kleider, and Bob Jeffery. Here are their "war stories."

Low-Poly Modeling and Motion Capture for Games: An Interview with Eric Chadwick

Eric Chadwick was born in 1967 in the California central valley town of Modesto, the birthplace of George Lucas and the setting for his film "American Graffiti." As a child, Eric was always drawing, sculpting with clay, making roads and towns in the dirt, building toy airplanes with cardboard and glue, and putting together plastic models. He liked to doodle a lot, so he took art classes in school, and seemed to do well at it. After high school, he stumbled around a bit, trying to figure out what he wanted to do with himself. After a while, he enrolled in the Rhode Island School of Design, where he majored in Illustration (mostly because he could take classes in other departments and still get credit). The school was a real eye-opener for him, and helped to put a fine point on his conceptual and drawing skills.

Eric came on board with Mondo Media shortly after I did, back when we were still doing mostly point-of-sale retail demo work for high-tech companies. We worked together on various demos, as well as the *Mechadeus* game projects, and later a hockey game and the enhanced *Mechwarrior 3* cinematics. I've always found him to be a very talented, well-rounded and capable artist, one with a rare gift for organizing and documenting his projects.

Q: What made you want to get into 3D?

A: Groundbreaking partially-CG movies such as *Tron* and *The Last Starfighter* were a big draw. I was also interested in the technology behind some of the then-dazzling flying logos on TV.

Q: How did you learn to do 3D modeling and animation?

A: (Laughs) On the job! I had some Photoshop experience under my belt, but no 3D experience when I started at Mondo Media in 1991. I begged and cajoled my way into the place, and finally the owner sat me down in front of an early DOS version of 3D Studio—I think it was version 1.0—and asked me to build a replica of a remote control gizmo for a potential job. I think it was more to get me off his case than a real project, but it certainly got me going.

Q: What 3D software do you use, and why?

A: Although I used Alias a bit back in the *PowerAnimator* days, I've stuck with the 3D Studio line since I started. It was the primary 3D package used by Mondo Media's 3D graphics team, and later became the de facto standard for the game industry, so we stuck with it. I've played around with some of the others, but maybe I'm just too lazy to learn a new one.

Q: How did you get in with Whatif Productions, and what do you do there now?

A: I saw an ad online for a Lead Artist position with them. I checked out their work, and liked what I saw. I took the time to put together a very polished demo reel and a strong resume, and then did well in the interview. That was all it took. They specifically told me that the polished reel went a long way toward getting me the job.

Being the only artist at Whatif, it's my job to bring our technology to life with great graphics. I'm creating 3D scenes and characters for real-time 3D interactive demos that showcase our graphics technology.

Q: What projects have you worked on over the years?

A: I was an artist on *Starfleet Command II*, *Interstate '76*, *Rebel Assault II*, *The Daedalus Encounter*, and *Critical Path*. Projects I've directed include *Need For Speed: Motor City*, cinematics for *Mechwarrior 3*, and environments for Westwood's *Blade Runner* game. I also directed asset creation for two games that unfortunately never made it to market, *Spectacular Hockey '99* and *Aladdin and the Fate of Agrabah*.

Q: Which models or animation have been the most interesting for you? Which have been the toughest, and why?

A: If I had to pick just one project, the most interesting would be the *Aladdin* job. That's where I really cut my teeth on real-time 3D graphics. I learned so much on that job, and from then on, all I really wanted to do was real-time 3D work. The toughest job was probably *Hockey '99*, as I'm not really a fan of the sport, and the work was pretty grueling. We had a large number of moves we had to capture and clean up. The low-res player models were a pain to create, and the motion capture was done in a freezing cold ice rink. I'm happy with some of the work we did on it, but in the end, the publisher wasn't able to get the game into the stores due to some logistical headaches.

Q: What kinds of special challenges are presented by low-poly work over high-res work?

A: As I see it, the special challenges of low-poly work are basically that you need to be flexible and precise. You have to be flexible because your artwork often needs to work in a variety of situations; you have little control over the angle from which someone will see your model, unlike the fixed viewpoints used in film. You also have to be precise because the model needs to be rendered in real time on the client's computer, so it needs to be as lean and mean as possible, yet still convey what you intended. Artistic precision is also necessary to make sure the model works within the constraints of your target hardware. Computers load things faster and render things better when the model is carefully laid out than when it is produced haphazardly.

Q: Do you have any tips for someone doing low-poly modeling?

A: Learn all you can about vertices, edges, faces, and normals, the building blocks of modeling. Even now, with the higher-res poly counts afforded by the latest technology, this base-level knowledge is still essential. Study from the masters; there are a lot of great tutorials online. Bay Raitt has an excellent site at `http://cube.phlatt.net/home/spiraloid/tutorial/index.html`. Also, frequent the 3D software manufacturers' web boards; there's lots of useful knowledge there for the taking. Shane Caudle is a well-known real-time 3D artist whose `http://www.planetshane.com` site has lots of samples.

Know your target specs: the polygon count limits, texture budget, and whether it has to be quads or triangles. If the mesh will be animated, you need to make sure you put enough detail in at the points of articulation. If you're modeling a character for animation, create at least three edge loops at each joint. I recommend learning about edge loops and where to apply them; they're essential for good skin deformation. Check out `http://cube.phlatt.net/home/spiraloid/tutorial/modeling.html` for more info.

Q: The hockey game used motion capture for the player's moves. What are the advantages and disadvantages of using mocap over hand animation?

A: Mocap is great for accurate human motion, especially for sports or other situations where your characters need to match human movement as closely as possible. I've heard of some people getting mocap from animals as well, but there aren't many success stories there. The animals just tend to bite or scratch at the markers. It is also difficult to get a precise performance, unless you're working with a professional animal trainer.

Mocap is very dependent on the abilities of the performer and the experience of the director. The performers need the stamina for multiple takes—especially for sports mocap—and they also need to have an understanding of the needs and limitations of the final product. For example, in games the mocap is often looped, so that a short sequence can be used for an infinite duration. Performers need to be aware of their starting and ending motions—so that a nice smooth loop can be extracted from their motions—while still performing the motions so that they look natural. We had it easy in some ways with the hockey game mocap, because they were on skates in the first place, so a little foot-to-ground sliding was acceptable.

Animation is usually done by hand for all the non-human stuff in a game. For example, cartoon characters don't perform well if they're limited to natural human motion; they need squash and stretch, anticipation, follow-through, and all the other hallmarks of good hand animation. Other things in the game may also need hand animation too: props, cars, explosions, environmental objects, and so on.

Another good site to look at is `http://www.gamasutra.com/features/20000119/kines_01.htm`. There's some good info on mocap there.

Q: What kind of mocap setup and process did you employ during the hockey game capture setup?

A: We were fortunate to work with Industrial Light and Magic's motion capture unit, which is well known for their attention to detail. Even though they had never worked on ice before, we were both willing to give it a go. They wanted to test their setup in a challenging environment, in preparation for *The Mummy* location shooting later on in their schedule. We, of course, were very happy to be able to work with such a prestigious team.

They used a six-camera optical tracking system and used reflective white balls attached to the joints of the performer. We had several problems with the optical capture system, the most egregious of which was that ice shavings tended to obscure the markers, so we lost a lot of foot data. The ILM team rose to the occasion, though, and did what they could to clean up the motion. However, some of the motion we had to keyframe almost entirely by hand.

I can't remember which intermediate ASCII format we used to get the data out of their SGI systems and over to our PCs, but we eventually imported it into 3ds max through Character Studio's Biped plug-in. There were some problems and restrictions with Biped that also complicated matters. For example, we would calibrate the marker positions to the biped on one frame of the animation, but discovered that the markers would drift later in the animation, causing inaccurate translation. We also had some problems with how Biped stores animation data. The arm, for instance, stores all its motion in the hand bone, so if you try to animate just the upper arm, the lower arm gets a keyframe, too. This sometimes made it difficult to maintain a smoothly flowing motion, because we had to add keyframes on every frame to counteract the motion. Biped did make it easy to loop motions with the Motion Flow editor, though.

Adding hand-keyframed animation on top of mocap was a bit difficult in some cases because they tended to compete with each other, but we often simply deleted the mocap from a section or a limb and re-created the motion from scratch.

Q: Do you have any tips for someone trying to incorporate mocap into their work?

A: Get some sample mocap data from your mocap service bureau, and follow the entire process of getting the data into your software and working with your models. Try to get some extreme motion, like jumping jacks, or flips, or stretching exercises. These kinds of extreme motions will help you test the limits of your game characters' skin, as well as any motion translation idiosyncrasies, like skating feet. Going through the entire process should expose any problem areas.

On the setup side, make sure you come to the mocap session well prepared. Create a chart of all the motions, what each will be named, what each needs to transition to, who will perform the motion, how long the motion should last, whether there will be props the performer needs to interact with, and so on. The more you can plan out each motion, the better off you'll be. If the performers can be worked with beforehand, do a test run without the mocap setup to get them used to what they'll be doing, and to get your team acclimated to the process. Define who will direct the talent, who will check each performance for technical issues, and who will be responsible for signing off each motion on your chart. You should also think about who will take care of the performer's needs and who will create, manage, and repair any props.

Carefully measure the lengths of your performers' joints, positions of the markers, the thickness of their limbs and any other body dimensions that could be helpful when trying to set up the skeleton that will precisely mate the mocap with your digital character. Take photos of your performer in the mocap suit for reference later, and make sure to videotape the performance for reference. It helps to film each action from at least two different angles, and remember to have someone stick a slate into the footage to identify takes and filenames for each shot. You will need this footage later to help fix problem data or other mocap weirdness. Often the mocap service bureau will provide this footage for you.

The best advice, though, is to make sure you're working with people who really know their stuff. Thoroughly check the references given by the motion capture service bureau you're thinking about. Try to find a place that has done a mocap project similar to yours in the past—that should alleviate some of the "doing this for the first-time" problems you would probably encounter otherwise. Get sample data from the outfit and check it carefully against your animation setup. Refine your character setup to match the data, or work with them to change their output.

Q: What advice do you have for people who'd like to work at a game company?

A: Dream on! (Laughs). Just kidding. It's a blast—if you can get in—but it's also a lot of hard work. If you want to be a 3D artist, learn one of the industry-standard 3D programs, build some awesome artwork, and then show it off in a kick-ass demo reel. Also, strive to be a good "people person," and learn how to work in a team situation. Many people I know started out through internships—usually unpaid ones—but stayed long hours to learn the tools on site, picked the brains of their co-workers, then weaseled their way into a job. In fact, any position in the company can get you into the Art Department if you're dedicated enough, assuming the company is pretty open about that. I've seen financial guys become comedy writers, receptionists become artists, and producers become sound effects people.

Q: Do you have any "dream project" that you'd like to work on?

A: Actually, I'm doing it right now! For the last 5 years or so, I've wanted to work on a cutting-edge real-time 3D project. Last summer I was able to find a company in Massachusetts (oh, so far from my native California) that is doing just the kind of thing I've been interested in. All I can tell you is that we are basically creating a cross-platform multimedia engine, but the potential goes quite a bit deeper than that. There's a lot of high-level interest in what we're doing, and I would guess you'll see something from us before the end of 2002. Although it may sound like marketing hyperbole, what we're working on is very likely to have a profound impact on the way things will be done in the near future. I wish I could talk more about it, as it is actually quite exciting.

Q: Where would you like to be in five years?

A: Right here, challenging myself, creating the best real-time 3D graphics possible. I'd also like to be filthy rich and fabulously fit, but we'll see about that.

My thanks go out to Eric for taking the time and effort to share his experiences and insight here. Check out `http://www.whatif-productions.com` *to see what he's up to at work.*

Low-Poly Mapping: An Interview with Leila Noorani

Leila Noorani was born in Reigate, England in 1965, and grew up in Northern California. She had a keen interest in drawing ever since she was a kid, and her family and friends always assumed she would pursue a career as an artist. She wasn't so sure about that herself, but after a few years at a state university she realized art was the only thing that kept her interest, and she enrolled in art school.

I met Leila after returning to work at Mondo Media. We were rather busy at the time, and when we landed the big *Mechwarrior 3* cinematic job on top of that, I was told that the company could spare only one staff artist for the team (the rest would need to be recruited from outside). Fortunately, that artist was Leila Noorani. Her design and mapping skills were excellent, plus she could model and light scenes as well. Her skills were instrumental in making *Mechwarrior 3* one of the best-looking game cinematics at the time—it was even featured at the Computer Game Developer's Conference in "The Best of the Best" screening room.

Q: What made you want to get into 3D?

A: I first got interested in computers when I was working on my Master in Fine Arts degree at the University of Michigan and took a fundamental computer graphics course. The 3D segment of the course was really primitive—you had to type in the XYZ coordinates to plot the points and create very simple objects. I also started to combine digital media with printmaking, which was my primary focus at the time. I think that opened my mind to the possibilities of what an artist could do with computers; that working digitally could be far more interesting and interactive than using traditional media.

Q: How did you learn to do 2D paint, 3D modeling, and animation?

A: I took a course in Photoshop—it was enough to get me in the door at Mondo Media. I just hung around the office there, learning the software on my own time. When they started hiring designers for a big project, I showed the art director my fine arts portfolio. I think that he was looking for people with a good knowledge of art fundamentals and a creative portfolio over a lot of computer savvy. I was paid for a week of training on 3D Studio, working through the tutorials and teaching myself the package. I started working as a full-time contractor, which led to a salaried position. Most of my computer training occurred on the job.

Q: What 2D and 3D software do you use, and why?

A: Photoshop, Flash, Illustrator (when I have to), and 3ds max, because that was what we used at Mondo. I create all the maps in Photoshop. I like mapping that looks hand-created rather than relying on the material editor, so I use Photoshop to manipulate scanned images, or create a map from scratch.

I learned to use Flash for animation when Mondo Media was looking for people to animate their online mini shows, and ended up working on *Thugs on Film*. Later on, my Flash, Photoshop, and 3D experience came in handy when I applied to be a designer at a web and graphic design company, Pear Transmedia, a woman-owned web design and graphics company in downtown SF. The art director liked that I had a fine arts background, experience in the computer game world, and that I knew Flash. Even though I had little web design experience, she felt that I could pick it up and maybe bring a unique perspective to web design, because I was coming to it from something other than a graphic design background.

Having knowledge of all those programs turned out to be a real asset to me while working at that company. I was immediately put on a project to design a logo and website for a wireless company, and I used Flash for the website intro, Photoshop and Illustrator for the content pages, and 3ds max for the logo. I also made use of all three on another big project, designing and animating games for an English instructional CD-ROM. The games were designed in Photoshop, some text and icons created in Max, and the final game animated in Flash.

Q: How did you get in with Mondo Media?

A: I heard about the company through an old art school friend. He suggested I come in a few days a week and use their computers to train myself.

When I got there he handed me some tutorials and left me alone. It felt a little awkward, but just "being around" eventually led to a job there.

Q: What projects have you worked on over the years, and what was your role on each?

A: My first big project was an Aladdin real-time game for Disney Interactive. Mondo was doing the artwork, and I think I was on it six months or so—the entire project lasted well over a year. Unfortunately, like so many other games, it was never published, but the artwork we did for it is among my favorite of all the jobs I've worked on. We were issued some loose concept sketches, but we had a lot of freedom to create it in our own way. I got very good at painting cracks and wall textures (and pretty sick of it, too), but the end result was fun to see—very rich and colorful.

I did mostly real-time mapping and modeling my first year with the company, and then later I got more into the high-resolution 3D stuff, like the cinematic environments for *Mechwarrior 3* and *Undercover*. On those projects, I would create production paintings with a mixture of 3D and Photoshop to establish the look and feel of a scene, and show them to the art director and the clients for approval. Then, we would build the scenes in Max with this look in mind.

I also worked as an artist on some other games, including *High Heat Baseball*, the new version of *Centipede*, and a demo for *Prince of Persia*.

Q: Which 3D projects have been the most interesting for you? Which have been the toughest, and why?

A: I enjoy the low-poly projects the most, because there are more built-in parameters and limitations. The trick with low-poly work is to get the most interesting-looking objects using the least amount of memory; at the end, you know you've either done your job or not. And these games are more likely to get published, which brings a sense of completion. The high-res cinematic stuff is more creative, but also a lot more elaborate and labor intensive. It's sometimes hard to know when to call it "done" and go home at the end of a long day.

Q: What skills are important for texture mapping?

A: A basic understanding of the fundamentals: light, shadow, and color. The more you understand where to put your highlights, drop shadows, ambient light, and so on, the more convincing the map will look from different perspectives.

Q: What are the special challenges involved in doing low-poly mapping for games?

A: Fooling the viewer into thinking that there is a consistent light source illuminating the maps. This is especially challenging when re-using maps. The maps need to be generic enough so it isn't obvious they're being reused, but not so much that they lose all distinctiveness.

Another challenge is deciding when to simply map a plain surface, versus boosting its interest by adding additional mesh. The game programmers are always going to put speed first, so the artist must anticipate this and be very economical—keeping the poly count low, yet still making the object look good.

Q: How did you approach mapping the ships for *Starfleet Command*?

A: That was a fun project. The team designed the look and feel of the enemy fleets for the game with pencil sketches, and I painted mapping designs on top of those drawings in Photoshop. After building the ships in Max, I created one base map (a generic paneled texture) for the ship model. I also made a Photoshop file of reusable assets—a library of battle scars, panels, engine parts, buttons, gizmos, exhaust deposits, and other generic stuff created on different layers that could be used in the texture maps being created by different artists on the team. By using these two maps—sampling colors from the base map, and copying pieces from the asset file—I mapped the ship to look like the concept painting. Having a master map and assets map on file for everyone to use helped keep the look of the ships consistent, and saved time as well.

Q: Do you have any tips or tricks for texture mapping that would help a newbie or improve a more advanced user's work?

A: Create and maintain a good image library—not just the kind of stuff on CD-ROM made for texture mappers, but your own *personal* library. Save photographs, textures, images, and ideas. A rich library keeps the work looking fresh and unique. It reminds you of how things look in the real world, not just the gaming world. I use reference images and photo textures on just about every project—having them handy saves a lot of time not only during the research phase at the beginning, but throughout a project.

Whenever you come across a polygon that can be mapped with a solid color, use a stretched-out map only one pixel square to save memory. The size and number of maps you're allowed to use is always restricted, and tricks like this can help conserve map real estate that can be used for more important areas.

It's kind of obvious, but learning as many keyboard commands as possible in place of the mouse can be a huge time saver.

On large projects with several artists, it's really important to have someone designated to be the "File Nazi." That person organizes the file structure systems, and goes to great lengths to see that everyone adheres to it. For some of us more "unstructured" types, this may require insults and abuse, but it's worth it; I've experienced the pain of having a file disappear due to late-night exhaustion and the lack of a set naming and file convention.

Q: Do you have any "dream project" that you'd like to work on?

A: I would like to write and illustrate a book of my own stories.

Q: Where would you like to be in five years?

A: Living on a farm in the country. I'd just like to be sitting in the hay— among the chickens, cows and horses—*daydreaming*.

I'd like to thank Leila for taking the time and effort to share her thoughts and experience with us.

Creating 3D for the Web: An Interview with Kelly Kleider

Kelly Kleider was born in WoodStock in the province of Ontario, Canada in 1968, on the very day that the famous Canadian Prime Minister Pierre Trudeau was elected. He loved to paint and sculpt as a child, but unfortunately, his parents thought he should pursue a medical career, and would not allow him to take art classes in high school. He continued to feel that he was meant to be an artist, not a doctor, and when he made it into college, he succeeded in regaining control of the direction of his life. He is currently working as an artist at Frog City Software in San Francisco.

Kelly was working at Mondo Media when I returned there in 1998, and we worked together on *Mechwarrior 3*, *Starfleet Command 2*, and *Spiral*. He has a great deal of technical and modeling skill, and is one of those people who absorb facts like a sponge. If you're ever looking for some obscure bit of data, Kelly probably has it ferreted away somewhere in his head.

Q: **What made you want to get into 3D?**

A: Back in the mid-eighties, I had an Amiga 1000 with two and a half megabytes of RAM, which was a massive amount at the time. I was fascinated by computer graphics and games, and I wanted to get into sculpting in 3D. The Amiga was the first personal computer to offer cheap 3D software, so I bought a package called Silver and began teaching myself. I also got a 2D package called Deluxe Paint, which has since become a legend in the games industry. The tools were very primitive by today's standards, but I still applied myself to learning all I could about 3D, modeling, and computer graphics.

Q: **What was it like teaching yourself 3D modeling and animation at that time?**

A: It involved untold hours of pain and suffering. My first system didn't have a hard drive, which meant I had to render to *floppy disks*. As time progressed, the machines and software got better, and I was right there—hungry to learn and use the new features and capabilities. In the late eighties, I found myself at San Francisco State University studying animation. SF State had an SGI Personal Iris running Wavefront software—this was before their merger with Alias. Anyway, I was lucky enough to get into the advanced CG program, which was part of an inter-disciplinary department of the Liberal Arts School. I was in a class of eight students who learned Wavefront and fought over that poor old 20Mhz Unix box for a year. My humble beginnings made me realize just how much I still had to learn about 3D, and in all honesty, I still feel that way.

Q: **What 3D software do you use now, and why?**

A: Currently, I'm using 3ds max. It seems to be the most common 3D software for use in game development. Still, I'm not particularly brand-loyal; I use whatever's at hand and can do the job.

Q: **How did you get your job at Frog City Software, and what do you do there now?**

A: A friend was bidding on some cinematics for them and they asked if he knew any technical artist types. I'm a TD (Technical Director), but that really means I get to do a little—sometimes a *lot*—of just about everything.

Q: What projects have you worked on over the years, and what was your role?

A: Almost from the beginning of my career I was a TD of some sort. Early on at Colossal Pictures, I was an Assistant Technical Director, which is a euphemism for "whipping boy." I worked on a pile of commercials while at Colossal, including the first "Coke Sun" commercial, an Intel commercial, and a number of *Liquid Television* shows. More recently, at Mondo Media, I found myself on many projects, including the *Mechwarrior 3* cinematics, *Nerf: ArenaBlast* in-game art, and Mondo's own *Gone Bad*.

Q: Which models or animation have been the most interesting for you? Which have been the toughest, and why?

A: I really enjoyed modeling the zombie for the *Gone Bad* teaser, mostly because it's fun to do gore. Hmmm, that could be damning if taken out of context… (laughs).

Q: Speaking of which, how did you approach building the zombie character for the *Gone Bad* trailer?

A: Ironically, the zombie started out as just a *hand*. I was messing around with a model of a hand I had made a while ago, trying to make it look gory and decayed. The director, Marco Bertoldo, saw the hand, threw it in a scene, and started playing around with it. Marco asked if there was more to the zombie, so I started in on the head. The body wasn't that important, because you didn't really see much of it in the film. Technically, the most interesting part of the zombie's head is the scarring on the face; it was done with displacement mapping on a subdivided surface, so it required no additional modeling—just textures.

Q: Do you prefer a particular type of modeling?

A: I'm almost 100% a "poly boy." Although I personally prefer using polygonal modeling, I can see the value of other techniques. Sometimes parametric surfaces are needed, but in general, I find polys faster to work with.

Q: You've been an advocate of alternative modelers such as *Nendo*. Why do you like using these products at times, over doing everything in your primary package, 3ds max?

A: I love Nendo. Nendo is a simple yet very powerful little modeler. It only takes about fifteen minutes to explain every feature in Nendo, but some of the things you can do with it are really impressive.

I would be an advocate for Nendo's big brother, *Mirai*, but most studios don't want to spend $6495 on packages that are not part of the studio's core proficiency. Nendo, on the other hand, costs only $99. Most studios waste about a hundred bucks on donuts every Friday, so they'll okay that type of minor purchase. Nendo does clean OBJ export that imports very nicely into 3ds max without losing any quad information. When you're working on a project, it's nice to have a modeler with a different set of strengths available.

Q: You used to work on *Dilbert* and other real-time 3D shows for the web. What was the process for creating those shows?

A: *Dilbert* was produced at Protozoa in San Francisco, using their proprietary software, Alive! Like most productions at Protozoa, we started with motion capture performances that were then refined in the Alive! Package. Because Protozoa used Polhemus and Ascension-style magnetic tracking systems for the motion capture work, we were able to review the performances quickly and in real time. We could redo the moves if necessary until we got exactly what we were looking for.

The motion capture process is very much like recording something using a VCR; refining mocap data is a little tougher to explain. After a performance was captured, it became more like a segment of video than a key-framed function curve. In some cases, we could use sliders or joysticks (the high-precision variety, not a Sidewinder gaming stick) to tweak the performance or add lip-synched facial animation. If the performance just didn't work, we would have the performer get back into the sensor suit and redo the performance.

Q: What special challenges are presented by doing 3D for the web?

A: The *Dilbert* shows were done during the short-lived VRML boom. In some ways it was similar to the browser war between Microsoft and Netscape; two competing companies were vying for the VRML plug-in crown. The hardest part of the production was not the work itself, but getting everything working with two different plug-ins that had their own distinct peculiarities. The sad fact was that the public was not ready for VRML, and neither were the PCs of the day. Most machines at the time had CPUs in the 90-133MHz range, had no 3D acceleration, and sported wimpy 28.8Kbp/s modems. Today, the hardships are not with the computers or bandwidth, but with compelling content. If something's crap, no one's going to download it, no matter how fast their Internet connection.

Q: How do you feel about using motion capture over hand-keyframed animation?

A: They both are valid means to an end. If your production requires realistic human motion, "mocap" will give you that with minimal fuss. If your production needs a traditional, cartoon-like feel, you're better off with keyframing. Really, both techniques have advantages and disadvantages, and you need to do some research before starting down a particular path.

Q: What advice do you have for people who'd like to work in the 3D field?

A: It seems as if there are a lot of schools that offer training in computer graphics that were not around five years ago. The days when you could get on-the-job training are pretty much over, and most employers expect some form of formal training in CG or a related discipline.

If you want to teach yourself—and do it on the cheap—the web is also a great resource for tutorials, examples, advice, and free software.

Q: Do you have any "dream project" that you'd like to work on?

A: I have some game ideas I would like to see realized someday. The tough thing about doing a game is that almost everyone who plays games—and even some people who don't—have what they think are "great ideas" for games. Catching the eye of a publisher and getting funding are the toughest parts of getting a game made.

Q: Where would you like to be in five years?

A: If I fail at suddenly becoming independently wealthy, I guess being a principal in a game company would be all right.

My thanks go out to Kelly for taking the time and effort to share his experiences and opinions here. Kelly's website can be found at www.kleider.net.

Low-Poly Animation for Games: An Interview with Bob Jeffery

Bob Jeffery was born in 1972, in the small town of Malone, New York. While most kids were into sports, he preferred creative pursuits and hobbies, and art was always his favorite class. To him, art didn't seem like work—it was more like "fun-time," and he feels that's why he enjoys working as an artist so much. Currently, he's having fun at a game development company called Z-Axis.

I met Bob when I returned to Mondo Media in 1998. Bob and his significant other, Cindy Harrison, were both working there as production artists. Although we sat right across the aisle from each other, he was usually on low-poly game asset projects while I was working on cinematics. We didn't really get a chance to work together until *Under Cover* came along. I found Bob to be a very hard-working and dedicated artist with a sunny disposition and a willingness to help others. He even started up a little snack and soda concession called "Honest Bob's" for the employees, selling goodies at cost. That's just the kind of guy he is.

Q: What made you want to get into 3D?

A: Although I really enjoyed art, I was also very interested in math, science, and problem solving. In fact, I started college with plans of becoming an engineer. A couple of years into the program, though, I realized that I missed art too much and wanted to incorporate it into my career. 3D graphics turned out to be the perfect blend of art and technology.

Q: How did you learn to do 3D modeling and animation?

A: I transferred to the Savannah College of Art and Design, where I took courses that gave me a general knowledge of 3D packages even as I was developing my 2D art skills in drawing and animation classes.

Q: What 3D software do you use, and why?

A: Currently, I work with 3ds max. I use max because that's what we used at Mondo, and Z-Axis uses it for most of the games it develops for the PS2, Gamecube, and Xbox systems. I don't think the software matters all that much, though—a lot of the 3D programs out there are pretty decent. If you pick one package and can wrap your head around the general methodology of how it works, the knowledge is transferable to most other 3D software.

Q: What projects have you worked on over the years?

A: I've worked mostly in the games business. I started out modeling and texturing for a real-time game geared towards a younger audience, Disney's *Aladdin*. I also worked on Hasbro's remake of the classics *Centipede* and *Sorry!* With these projects, I got an opportunity to try my hand at 3D animation and found it to be very rewarding, but realized there was a *lot* to learn. I was lucky in that I could learn hands-on while working on cutscenes for more grown-up games, including *MechWarrior 3*, *Die Hard*, and *Aliens vs. Predator*. I then went on to work on *Hot Shots Golf 2*, where I got to do character animation full-time. Working on that project helped me confirm that I really wanted to specialize in animation.

Q: How did you get in with Z-Axis, and what do you do there now?

A: Contacts are everything in this business. Sure, talent is a must, but a company looking to hire is more likely to bring in someone recommended by an employee they trust. I happened to know three people working at Z-Axis who could vouch for me, and that helped get me in the door. Right now, I'm animating the cut-scenes for the next installment of Dave Mirra's Freestyle BMX for the PS2, Gamecube, and Xbox consoles. The work is a mix of character, camera, particle effects, and level animation. By "level animation," I mean objects in a given level (environment) that start in one state, then break, move, or explode during gameplay. There may also be environmental objects that loop continuously, like a rotating sign.

Q: Which models or animation have been the most interesting for you? Which have been the toughest, and why?

A: I like models that are stylized or that look really interesting even when standing still. Those kinds of models only look cooler after they are animated. I find human characters with lifelike motions to be not only the most difficult, but also the most uninteresting to work on. I would much rather start from a basis in realism, but add exaggeration to the timing, weight, and anticipation to make the movements clearer and more appealing. Cartoon action is just a lot more fun than realistic motion.

Q: What are the special challenges of doing animation for a low-poly character?

A: One of the big concerns is that your model may not be built in a way that allows it to be posed any way you want. Often, a limb may look pinched, or you might get intersecting polys because of the low number of vertices that you have to work with. Also, just as you have to keep the number of polygons very limited in game assets, you probably have a restriction on the number of keyframes that can be used as well. The challenge is to create a convincing, appealing motion with a low number of keyframes.

Q: What general process do you go through to animate characters for games?

A: Basically, everything should be planned out before you get to the animation stage. The model should be built with definition near the parts that will bend, and pivot points located in the places where they make the most sense, plus everything linked the way it needs to be for animation. In other words, make sure your character is finished and rigged properly before you start animating.

Before you touch the model, thought should be given to the motions that you'll be trying to achieve, either by acting them out, storyboarding the shots, or at the bare minimum, visualizing it in your head. After everything is planned, I generally put my character into the key poses that I want to hit throughout the animation. These poses should clearly convey what the action is.

Next, I space the key poses apart to adjust the timing of the sequence. This will give a general sense of the animation. Everything after that is "sweetening" the animation. I add additional poses and adjust timing to add weight, exaggeration, and anticipation to motions. Having *overlapping action* is important so that it doesn't look like your character is just popping between the poses you initially laid out. Overlapping action means to put a time lag between the motions of different parts of your character so that all the limbs, or whatever, don't start and stop their moves at the same time. For example, the shoulder might start moving before the elbow or hand, then the elbow would bend, and then the hand rotates and moves. The hand might get to its resting position first, and then the elbow and shoulder would overextend and settle.

Q: What sorts of things do you have to watch out for when setting up a character?

A: The movements that you want the character to perform will define how much mesh resolution needs to be located in particular areas of the model. Parts that bend or have a wide range of motion will need more detail to avoid pinching. Your character should be tested to make sure it can perform the motions your animation will call for *before* you get to that stage.

Q: What advice do you have for people who'd like to work on game assets and cinematics?

A: Play games. Know what has been done before, try to duplicate it, and then *improve on it*. Go to a school to learn the tools and the craft. Land an internship and impress the company with your skills, or train with the tools at that company to improve your reel. Your reel—and the people you impress—are what will get you a job. Remember that creating a game is a team effort, so learn to work well with others. You don't need to be good at every facet of a 3D program—there are advantages to having a focus or specialty—but you do need to know the program well enough to function.

Q: Do you have any "dream project" that you'd like to work on?

A: I'm happy as long as I'm animating, and that my work amuses my audience and myself.

Q: Where would you like to be in five years?

A: Retired and doing animation—but as a hobby, instead of a job.

I'd like to thank Bob for taking the time to share his advice and experiences with us.

Low-Poly Modeling Tutorial

Topic covered:

Modeling a Flying Car

Modeling a Flying Car

In this tutorial, you'll use box-modeling techniques to create a very simple low-poly model of a flying car that you can add to your scene with the blimp. Because the model is low-poly, it will have to be positioned off in the distance, however.

This tutorial presumes that your 3D package allows you to manipulate vertices, edges, faces, and polygons (collections of faces on the same plane). If your package does not offer all these modes, you can still construct the model using only vertex and face-level editing. It also presumes that the world coordinate system in your package uses left-to-right as X, up and down as Y, and in and out as Z.

Although this model is based loosely on the Spinner cars from *Blade Runner*, the design has been changed somewhat to avoid any copyright issues. You are welcome to get reference from the film and make your own model as close as you want to the original, or head off in the opposite direction and create an entirely different design.

1. Start up a new scene in your 3D package. If your package offers a pre-view mode that highlights the edges of polygons, turn it on. Turn on 2D Snap and create a box with these dimensions: Width 60, Height 20, Depth 80 units. If necessary, convert the box to editable (polygonal) mesh.

   The box is the starting point for the body of the car. You'll use face extrusion to add additional form to the box. The next step is to make the wraparound cockpit windshield.

2. Turn off 2D Snap and go into polygon editing mode. Select the poly on top of the box and Face Extrude it 10.7 units. Perform a non-uniform scale to reduce the width of the poly to 68%. Finally, set constraints to the Z-axis, go into edge editing mode, select the edge at the bottom of the top viewport, and then move it up along the Z-axis 41 units. Examine the results in the perspective viewport (see Figure 5.6a).

3. Go into polygon editing mode, select the poly at the front of the body, and then Face Extrude it 6.8 units. Go to Vertex editing mode and from the Left viewport, select the two vertices at the top of the new section; move them down the Y-axis until they fall along the same line as the slope of the windshield (see Figure 5.6b).

4. Select the two large rectangular polygons on either side of the car and Face Extrude them 4.5 units. From the Left viewport, Non-Uniform Scale them down 65% along the Y-axis. Examine the results in the Perspective viewport (see Figure 5.6c).

5. Go into Vertex editing mode and turn on 3D Snap. Set your Snaps configuration to include vertices, so the mouse will now snap to vertices. In the Perspective viewport, select one of the vertices you just created with the extrusion and move it on top of the vertex from which it was extruded. Select the two vertices that now reside in the same spot and collapse them; the two vertices are collapsed (welded) into one (see Figure 5.6d). Repeat the same process for the remaining three vertices toward the front of the car, collapsing each of them into the vertex from which they were extruded.

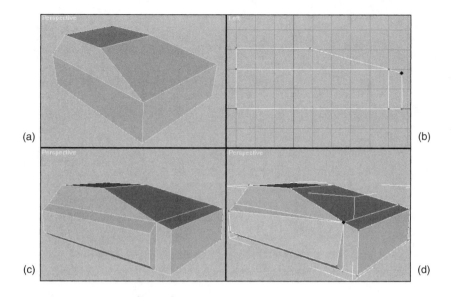

FIGURE 5.6

Constructing the main body of the car. (a) Create a box and extrude the upper part into a cockpit windshield. (b) Extrude the front of the car and move the upper vertices down to maintain the slope of the windshield. (c) Extrude the sides of the car out. (d) Move and collapse the vertices at the front of the new sections back into their original positions.

6. Orbit the view in the Perspective viewport so that you can see the back of the car. Go into polygon editing mode and select the four polys that make up the rear of the car, and then Face Extrude them 8.3 units (see Figure 5.7a).

7. Deselect the two smaller polys and Face Extrude the remaining two 28.7 units (see Figure 5.7b).

8. Go into vertex editing mode. In the Left viewport, select the upper two vertices of the new section and move them down along the Y-axis 7.5 units. Select the middle two vertices directly below them and move them down the Y-axis 6 units (see Figure 5.7c). Examine the results in the Perspective viewport (see Figure 5.7d).

You may notice that you can see two slightly differently shaded triangular polygons attached to the vertices you just moved. If so, this is a good indicator that the quad has become non-planar. If you orbit around the car in the Perspective viewport and look at the quad on-edge, you can confirm that this is the case. Although this may or may not be an issue for your 3D package, it can cause problems if the model were exported to a real-time 3D engine. Let's just assume this will be the case; so at this point, you have two choices: Either adjust the vertices to make the quad planar again, or break it into tris. I use the latter choice for this exercise.

FIGURE 5.7

Creating the rear section of the car. (a) Extrude the polys at the rear of the car. (b) Deselect the outer polys and extrude the rest again. (c) Move the vertices at the back of the car down to create a sloped rear end. (d) Differences in shade hint that the quad polygon has become nonplanar.

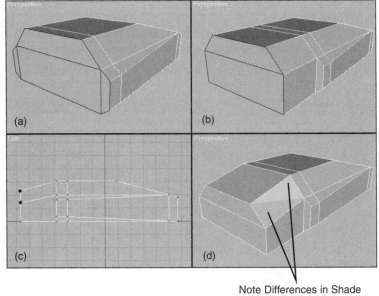

(a) (b)

(c) (d)

Note Differences in Shade
(Exaggerated for Clarity)

9. Go into edge editing mode and select the invisible edges running diagonally through the quads on either side of the car, and then set them to be visible. Examine the results in the Top viewport (see Figure 5.8a).

Both newly visible edges will probably be running parallel to each other. This is common and is not usually a problem with hi-res modeling, but it can be an issue with low-poly work because the two sides of the vehicle catch the light differently, and the fact that the faces aren't symmetrical may cause problems with mapping as well. In any case, this is an easy problem to correct.

10. Select the diagonal edge on the passenger side of the car and apply a Turn command to it. It rotates around so that it is situated between the other two pairs of vertices making up the quad (see Figure 5.8b). Now both sides of the car are symmetrical again.

11. Go into polygon editing mode, select the two polys at the rear of the car, and then Face Extrude them 6.3 units (see Figure 5.8c).

12. Select the lower polygon on the rear of the car and Extrude it 2.9 units, and then Bevel or scale it down -2.2 units so that it is about 93% of its original size (see Figure 5.8d).

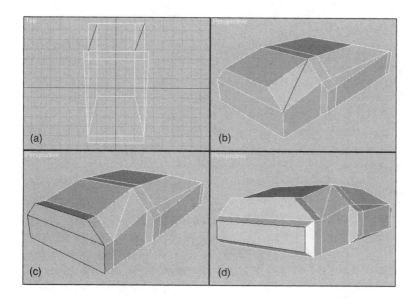

FIGURE 5.8

Refining the back end of the car. (a) The edges running through the center of the quads are parallel, making the two sides of the car asymmetrical. (b) Turning one of the edges orients it more appropriately and makes the car symmetrical. (c) Extrude the rear end once more. (d) Extrude and Bevel the lower polygon to create the rear bumper.

13. Select the upper polygon on the rear end and Face Extrude it .00001 units (so that you create the new faces, but they remain almost exactly in the same place as the originals); then Bevel or scale it down -1.5 units (see Figure 5.9a). Face Extrude it inward -2.5 units (see Figure 5.9b). This forms the exhaust nozzle for the engine.

14. Select the long polygon on the top of the car and Extrude it upward 5.5 units (see Figure 5.9c). This can be used as a light bar, like the one on top of a police car.

15. Create a box with the following dimensions: Width 7, Height 14, Depth 12 units. Position it 3.5 units behind the light bar, with the bottom front of the box just slightly above the sloping rear deck of the car (see fig. 5.9d). If necessary, convert it to editable mesh. This will form a pylon on the top of the car.

FIGURE 5.9

Finishing the back end
of the car. (a) Extrude
and Bevel the upper rear
polygon to start to form
an exhaust port.
(b) Extrude the poly
inward to finish the port.
(c) Extrude the poly on
top of the car to form a
light bar. (d) Create a
new box and position it
just above the rear
sloping part of the car.

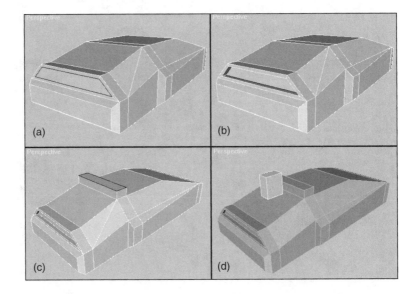

16. Go into polygon editing mode, select the poly on the underside of
    the box, and then delete it. The mesh will be positioned so close to
    the car that no one will be able to tell it is missing, and it reduces the
    poly count slightly.

17. Go into vertex editing mode and in the Top viewport, select the four
    vertices on the front side of the box. Set constraints to X and do a
    Non-Uniform Scale down to 55% (see Figure 5.10a).

18. In the Left viewport, select the bottom rear pair of vertices on the box
    and set constraints to Y. Move the vertices down along the Y-axis until
    they are just above the sloping rear deck of the car (see Figure 5.10b).

FIGURE 5.10

Finishing the pylon.
(a) Select the vertices on
the front of the box and
scale them toward each
other. (b) Move the ver-
tices at the rear of the
box downward to con-
form to the shape of the
rear deck.

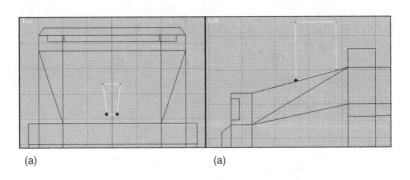

19. Create a 12-sided cylinder 12 units in diameter and 8 units deep with a single segment. Position it so that it fits completely within the rear section of the car, except for protruding out the bottom of the car by 5 units (see Figure 5.11a). This will be used for the rear wheel.

20. Create a box with the following dimensions: Width 28, Height 22, Depth 10 units. Position it over the top of that part of the cylinder that is inside the car, but allow the bottom of the box to drop slightly below the bottom edge of the car (see Figure 5.11b).

21. Perform a Boolean subtraction on the cylinder, using the box as a cutting tool. This should Boolean away all the cylinder that lies within the body of the car (see Figure 5.11c).

22. Go into polygon editing mode, select the poly on top of the rear wheel, and delete it. In the Top viewport, set constraints to X and copy the wheel; then move the copy to the opposite side of the car. Examine the results in the Perspective viewport (see Figure 5.11d).

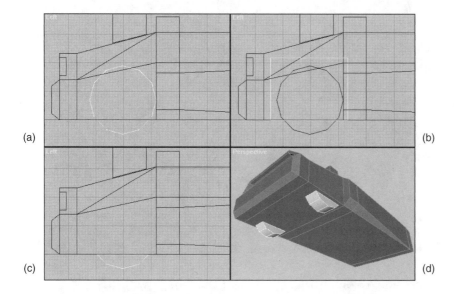

(a)
(b)
(c)
(d)

FIGURE 5.11

Adding the rear wheels. (a) Create a cylinder to be used as a rear wheel. (b) Create an overlapping box that will be used to cut off the parts of the wheel that are inside the car. (c) Use the box to Boolean off the upper part of the wheel. (d) Clone the wheel and position the copy on the opposite side of the car.

23. In the Left viewport, create a 12-sided hemisphere with a radius of 14 units, and position it 15.5 units away from the front of the car body (see Figure 5.12a). If necessary, convert it to editable mesh. This will become the front wheel.

24. In the Front viewport, position the bottom of the hemisphere 5 units below the bottom of the car, and position it to be roughly in line with the rear driver's side tire (see Figure 5.12b).

If you have trouble with the next step—step 25—it could be that the vertices in the center of the flat section of the hemisphere need to be collapsed together.

25. Go into polygon editing mode, select the polygons making up the flat part of the hemisphere, and then Face Extrude them 3.9 units and Bevel or scale them -6.2 units (see Figure 5.12c). Do another Face Extrude, this time 2.9 units, and then Bevel them -1 units (see Figure 5.12d). You may need to apply a normals smoothing operation to the wheel if it appears faceted when rendered.

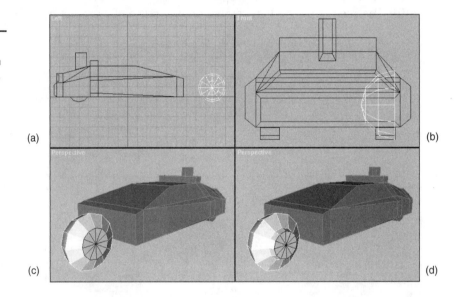

(a)

(b)

(c)

(d)

26. Next, make some struts to connect the wheels with the body. In the Left viewport, select the two outermost polygons facing toward the car body and Face Extrude them until they nearly touch the car body (see Figure 5.13a). Delete the polygons because they will not be visible in the finished model.

27. Go into vertex editing mode. In the Top viewport, move the vertices until they are very close to the car body and positioned roughly as shown (see Figure 5.13b).

28. You may notice that some of the quads in this extruded section have become non-planar. Make subtle adjustments to the vertices (particularly the three where the extrude section begins) to reduce or eliminate the planarity problems (see Figure 5.13c–d).

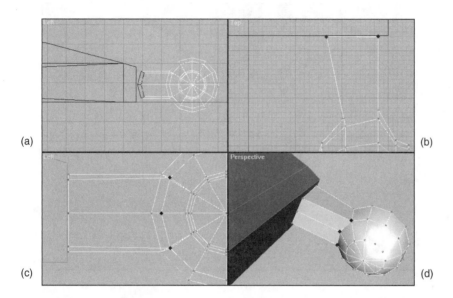

(a)

(b)

(c)

(d)

FIGURE 5.13

Creating the front wheel struts. (a) Extrude the polygons on the outmost edge of the front wheel. (b) Move the vertices until they are very close to the car body. (c–d) Take care of any non-planar polygons by carefully adjusting vertices.

Take a good look at the way the front wheel is constructed. Do you see some areas where triangles could be converted to quads for greater savings? Yes, the two center points on the wheel where a bunch of triangular polygons meet. By changing the tris into quads, you can reduce the model's poly count.

29. Go into edge editing mode. In the Perspective viewport, select every other edge that touches the center vertex on the flat part of the front wheel (see Figure 5.14a). Set the selected edges to be invisible, creating quads (see Figure 5.14b). Repeat this process on the other side of the front wheel.

30. In the Front viewport, copy the front wheel and rotate the copy 180°, and then move the copy to the opposite side of the car (see Figure 5.14c).

Mirror-copy might seem like the easier way to accomplish this step, but remember that some 3D engines may have problems with mirrored mesh. By using a copy-and-rotate approach, the problem is avoided.

31. Examine the car in the Perspective viewport and look for any problem areas (see Figure 5.14d).

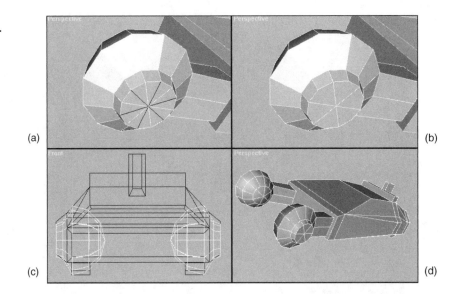

(a)   (b)   (c)   (d)

32. Render the car from a couple different angles (see Figure 5.15a–b). When you're satisfied with the model, you can leave it as-is until you texture-map it on your own, or you can Attach all the pieces together into a single object and name it FlyingCar01.

33. Save your work as FlyingCar.xxx and close the file. This concludes the Chapter 5 tutorial.

If you decide to include the flying car in your blimp animation, I'd suggest keeping it in the background and moving several of them across the sky in random directions or as part of a traffic stream.

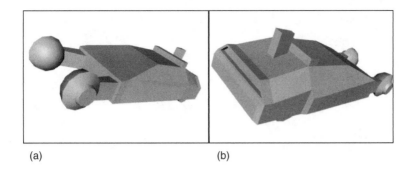

FIGURE 5.15

Render the car model. (a–b) Render different views of the model as a final check for problems.

(a)   (b)

Summary

In this chapter, you took a look at the growing use of real-time 3D models and animation for games as well as the web. You examined some of the technical issues and special techniques involved in low-poly modeling and mapping, including poly counts, levels of detail, texture budgets, and so on. In addition, you heard from three low-poly artists about the sorts of issues that can come up in actual projects—things you should watch out for when doing your own low-poly work.

In the next chapter, you'll see how mapping can be used to enhance the realism of mesh objects by giving them color and texture. You will also look at how mapping can be used in place of mesh for creating the illusion of detail without bogging things down.

CHAPTER 6

Texture Mapping

This image, created in Animation Master, features a unique blending of mesh dragon and textured mapped tattoo that creates one of the key points of interest in the work.
Image ©2002 Den Beauvais.

*T*he student worked carefully, adjusting the stone texture on his castle model until the blocks were neither too large nor too small. At last, the pattern tiled properly. The student leaned back to admire his work. "Perfect!"

"Perfect indeed," commented the Master, who walked up to examine the scene. "Mayhaps too perfect…"

"Say what?" The lad shot his teacher a confused look.

"Oh, you've done a fine job, lad. The structure is properly proportioned, all your textures are in place…but it's somehow lacking, don't you think?"

The student studied the scene intensely, mulling over the Master's critique. "Too perfect…" he muttered to himself. "I don't get it."

"Here, look at the path that leads to your castle gate," the Master said. "You have made it a brownish gray, like earth, and even given it some grittiness. But it's still too perfect. It looks artificial."

"But, it is artificial!" shot back the student.

"Ah, but it needn't look that way. Come, look out the window." The lad got up and joined the Master, looking down at the path that lead to his own keep. "See there, how the path is rutted with the tracks from wagons? There are patches of grass, hoof prints, and, uh, horse droppings as well."

"Oh, I see," said the student. "And there are pools of water in the ruts and tracks that reflect the sky. Those would look interesting in my model as well."

"Now you have it," the Master laughed, putting his hand on the lad's shoulder. "Say, perhaps you should go down there and have a closer look. Observe the variations in the stone walls and the grass patterns as well. Oh, and clean up those road apples while you're at it, hmmm?"

Mapping Defined

The key to stunning 3D scenes is practice—practice to be *imperfect*. Modeling perfectly rectangular and pristine brick is easier than shaping a more realistic, rough-edged one. The same is true of texture mapping. In many ways, mapping is just as important as modeling. A scene's textures have a major impact on its final appearance. Think about brick: A wall of nicely modeled bricks that have only flat red surfaces would actually look less realistic than a simpler model with a really good texture map. This chapter looks at the basics of texture mapping, and explores tips and techniques to make your texture work stand out from the pack.

Texture mapping is one of many areas in the 3D field that use a lot of confusing and contradictory terms, depending on which software package (or book) you happen to be using. Therefore, this section starts off with a few basic definitions:

Mapping (or *texture mapping*) is the process of developing and assigning material attributes to an object. Before textures are applied, all objects in a 3D package have a default plastic appearance, either gray or some range of colors. Mapping enables the user to give the object a specific color, adjust whether it's shiny or matte, apply a pattern, and so forth.

Material is the encompassing term for all the different attribute settings that are assigned to an object's surface. A material might be identified by a name, like "Shiny Red Plastic," "Tarnished Silver," or "Rosewood."

Surface attributes refers to the basic material settings, such as Color, Shininess, Transparency, and so forth. These generally affect all parts of an object equally.

Texture is often used interchangeably with *mapping* and *material*, but for the most part will be used here as a means of referring to a bitmapped image, either scanned or painted, that gives a material unique qualities that aren't available by simply varying surface attributes. Sample textures might include a scan of a block of wood that captures its grain patterns, a painting of rusty metal, or a 2D logo imported from a drawing program. Textures also can be used to vary the surface roughness, transparency, and color of an object.

Procedural is a type of texture that is mathematically defined. It can simulate wood, marble, and other materials, but usually doesn't look as realistic as scanned textures.

To sum up, then, mapping is the process of making and using materials consisting of surface attributes and/or textures that enable an object to appear as something other than default plastic. For example, the object could be mapped to appear as though it were made of glass, metal, stone, fabric, or wood, to name a few (see Figure 6.1).

Sample Textures

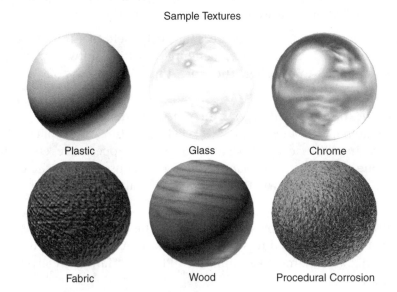

Plastic   Glass   Chrome

Fabric   Wood   Procedural Corrosion

Light and Color

When you look at an object rendered in a 3D program at Phong level (discussed in the next section) or better, you see the effects of three potentially different color sources: Ambient, Diffuse, and Specular (see Figure 6.2).

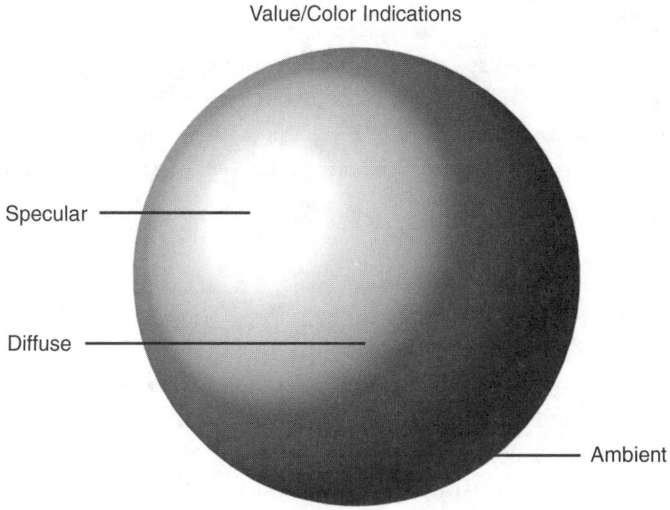

Value/Color Indications

Specular

Diffuse

Ambient

FIGURE 6.2

An object's rendered appearance is influenced by three different sources of color and value. Ambient is the color of the object in shadow; Diffuse is the color of the object's material; and Specular is the color of the highlights.

Ambient color is the hue an object reflects if it's not directly illuminated by a light source (that is, its color when in shadow). This is rarely black, because the ambient light in the scene usually guarantees at least some illumination on every surface. Generally, the ambient color is a very dark shade of the diffuse color, but it can be set to whatever the user desires. Ambient color may be set in the material editing section of your software, or in some cases it may be a global setting.

Diffuse color is the hue assigned to the object. This is the color that's reflected when the object is directly illuminated by a lighting source. Diffuse color is set in the material editing section of your software, where it may simply be referred to as Color.

Specular color is the hue of any highlights that appear on the object (at Phong rendering levels or higher). Specular color is also set in the material editing section of the package.

Note that Ambient, Diffuse, and Specular colors are affected by the color of any light sources. See Chapter 7, "Lighting," for more details.

Render Limits

Chapter 2, "Delving into Cyberspace," discussed the effects of rendering at different quality levels: Flat, Gouraud, Phong, Ray Traced, and so forth. Many programs enable you to assign *render limits* to a material as well, so that despite the final output settings you've selected for a scene, any objects with that material render to only their preset quality level (see Figure 6.3).

FIGURE 6.3

Materials can have render limits assigned to them that aren't exceeded even if the scene is rendered at a higher quality level. This scene was rendered at Metal level, but most of the materials on the objects were set to lower render limits.

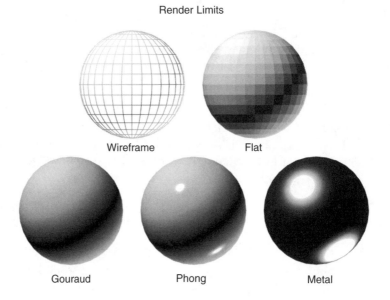

Render Limits

Wireframe   Flat

Gouraud   Phong   Metal

For example, say you set material A to have no render limit, but you set material B to have a limit of Flat. If you assign them both to objects in the same scene and render the scene at Phong level, the object with material A renders at Phong level, but the object with material B looks as though it was rendered at Flat level.

Render limits are often used when creating a scene in which most objects are rendered normally, but you want some objects to appear in wireframe. They are also useful for speeding things up in certain test render situations where you need to have multiple objects in the scene, but only some of them need to be rendered at maximum quality levels.

Surface Attributes

Surface attributes can be considered the most basic type of material settings, supported by virtually every 3D program. Most of these attributes are set with sliding controls or type-in boxes in the material editing section of the software (see Figure 6.4). Often, the material editor offers a preview feature, which enables the user to see what the material looks like before it is applied to the object. Many different attributes can be modified to alter an object's appearance, including Color, Shininess, Specularity, Transparency, Falloff, Index of Refraction, and Luminosity.

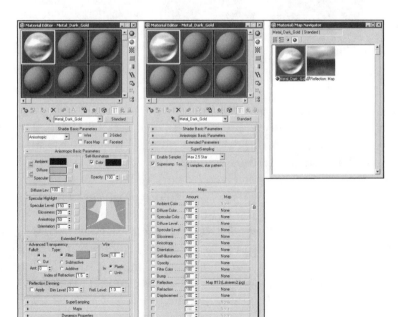

FIGURE 6.4

The Material Editor in Discreet 3ds max 4.2 offers a dizzying array of options for controlling the look of a material. The controls enable the user to set surface attributes, assign image maps and procedural shaders, and see a preview of the material before it is applied to the object.

Color

Color is the combination of three elements: Hue, Saturation, and Value. The *Hue* (or *Chroma*) of an object is generally what you think of when you hear the term color—it's determined by the frequency of the light coming from the object, be it up in the red range, or down in the violet. *Saturation* (or *Intensity*) is the measure of how concentrated a color is, a way to measure whether a red, for example, is as rich and full as it can be, or is somewhat weak and grayish. Finally, *Value* is the lightness or darkness of a color, and gauges whether a red is a tinted pink pastel or some dark wine-like shade.

Most software offers a full 24-bit range of color choices, or over 16.7 million different colors, including 256 gray values (see Figure 6.5). Color is usually set using *RGB* (Red-Green-Blue) or *HSV* (Hue-Saturation-Value) slider-type controls. In general, these controls also allow numeric input, using values ranging from 0 (none) to 255 (maximum) for each of the RGB settings.

Grayscale Values

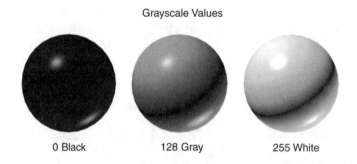

0 Black   128 Gray   255 White

It's a good thing to remember that not *all* colors can be duplicated by the RGB or HSV models, despite the millions of colors available. This may make it difficult to match the color of a physical object, with strong yellows in particular being hard to achieve. The root of the trouble is that most real-world objects are perceived by our eye based on the spectrum of light their surfaces reflect, whereas the colors of objects on a computer screen are created by projecting light directly at the eye. Technically, this means that non-illuminating real-world objects such as people, photographs, and furniture conform to the *subtractive color model* in which red, yellow, and blue are the primary colors, and mixing the three together results in a muddy brown. Computer monitors, colored spotlights, televisions, and other types of illuminating objects use the *additive color model*, in which red, green, and blue are the core colors, and mixing them together creates white! As a result, the *gamut* (color ranges) of these two color models are not identical, and although they do overlap to a large degree, certain colors available in one gamut are impossible to achieve in the other.

Another reason that computer colors can be tough to match to real objects is that with computer displays, everything on screen has a self-illuminated appearance, like looking at a projection of a color transparency.

Shininess

Shininess is the overall reflective nature of the object—in other words, its "glossiness." Shininess has an effect on the size of the *specular highlight* (the bright reflections of light seen on glossy objects), with matte objects having larger highlights and shiny objects having smaller ones (see Figure 6.6). Shininess, like most other surface attributes, is usually set with a slider control in the material editing section of the software.

Shininess

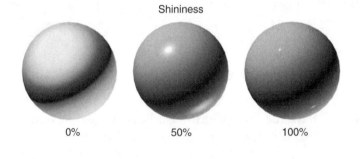

| 0% | 50% | 100% |

FIGURE 6.6

Shininess is a measure of an object's surface gloss. At 0%, the material is matte, and 100% is maximum glossiness. Note how the specular highlight shrinks as the object is made glossier. (Specularity was set to 50% for all spheres).

Shininess works together with Specularity to give the viewer information about the surface reflectivity and characteristics of the material, so pay close attention to how the two affect a material's appearance.

Specularity

Specularity adjusts the intensity of the object's highlight, if it has one (see Figure 6.7). Specular highlights are the bright reflections of light seen on glossy objects in Phong-level rendering or above. Remember that the *size* of a specular highlight is related to the Shininess of the object. Specularity is often set with a slider control or type-in percentage.

Specularity

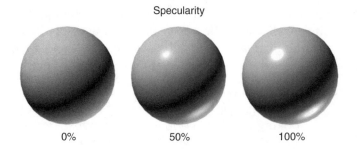

0%   50%   100%

FIGURE 6.7

Specularity sets the intensity of a material's highlight. Specularity and Shininess work together to define an object's glossiness. It also plays a major role in simulating metallic and plastic materials. (Shininess was set to 50% for all spheres).

> Don't underestimate the value of getting the Shininess and Specularity settings as close as possible to the material you're trying to represent. The behavior of reflections can have a big impact on the believability of an object or scene. Try to avoid completely matte or glossy settings for objects, because most materials are somewhere in between.

Anisotropic Highlights

The specular highlights you've seen so far have been *isotropic highlights*, meaning they have the same width regardless of the direction from which they are measured (in other words, *round*). *Anisotropic highlights* are elliptical, directional types of specular highlights that you see in materials such as velvet, brushed metal, the data side of a CD, and hair (see Figure 6.8). This kind of effect is usually caused by "micro structures" on the surface of real-world material that tend to be aligned in a certain way. The light reflects off these micro-structures very differently than it does off a smooth surface; as a result, the highlights are not round, but often highly elliptical. Their position and shape on the surface also varies greatly—with a CD, for example, the highlight seems to form two roughly triangular clusters radiating out from the middle. On a Christmas ornament covered in satin, the highlight may appear like a ring or crescent shape.

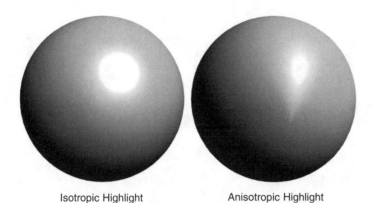

Isotropic Highlight   Anisotropic Highlight

FIGURE 6.8

Most objects with smooth surfaces produce circular highlights. Objects with tiny directional scratches or structures on their surfaces produce elliptical or ring-like anisotropic highlights.

At least two controls are added to materials with anisotropic characteristics: *anisotropy level* and *anisotropy direction*. The anisotropy level controls the relationship between the highlight's length and its width. If the level is low, the highlight appears circular; when its set high, the highlight becomes extremely elliptical—even "line-like." Anisotropy direction controls the direction in which the elliptical highlights point, rotating them around as the value is changed.

Transparency (Opacity)

Transparency and *Opacity* are opposite terms that both refer to the same thing—they control the amount of light that can pass through an object. If Transparency is set to 100% (or Opacity to 0%), the object is virtually invisible. If Transparency is set to 0% (or Opacity to 100%), the object is completely opaque. Any other setting makes the object more or less translucent (see Figure 6.9).

Bear in mind that unless your program supports ray tracing, some transparent objects may not look very realistic because the material doesn't refract light the way a real object would. See the next section, "Refraction," for more information.

FIGURE 6.9

Transparency controls the amount of background imagery that can be seen through an object. A 100% transparent object is nearly invisible, except for any specular highlights.

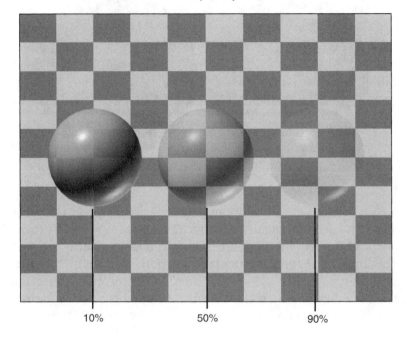

10%   50%   90%

Some additional settings for transparency have an impact on a material's behavior. First, you can set a material to be filtered, additive, or subtractive (see Figure 6.10). *Filtered materials* multiply the colors behind the translucent surface by the user-defined filter color. Depending on the relationship between the filter color and the color of the pixel behind the translucent surface, this setting either has no effect or tints and/or darkens the background pixel. This is the most common type of transparency setting.

Additive materials lighten the RGB value of whatever is seen though the object's translucent portions by adding the object's diffuse color to colors behind the translucent surface. Using the additive setting for transparent objects yields a more realistic effect, because the object appears to be picking up light sources.

Transparency Types

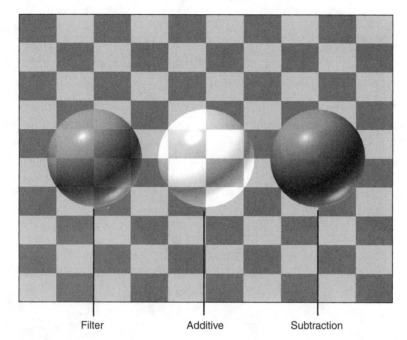

Filter   Additive   Subtraction

FIGURE 6.10

Materials seen through translucent portions of an object are affected by Additive or Subtractive settings. Subtractive darkens the RGB values of the filtered background pixels, whereas Additive increases them.

Subtractive materials darken the values by subtracting the filter color from the colors behind the translucent surface.

Another important setting for translucent objects is *one-sided* or *two-sided*, which tells the renderer whether to ignore faces on the opposite side of the object. The default setting is one-sided because it speeds up rendering, and you can't see the back faces on an opaque object anyway. However, because you *can* see the opposite side of a translucent object in real life, use the two-sided setting.

Falloff is another setting used in conjunction with transparency to refine how transparent an object is at its edges. Falloff uses the angle of a face's normal to determine the amount of variation from the overall transparency setting to apply. Faces that are perpendicular to the viewer are unaffected, whereas faces that are edge-on to the viewer have the maximum amount of change applied. This is also called the Fresnel (pronounced Fre-nel) effect. The classic example is looking down into a swimming pool full of water; if you look down at it from overhead, you can see the bottom, but if you peer at it from a low angle, it reflects the scene in the distance instead.

There are two types of falloff settings: Inward and Outward (see Figure 6.11). *Inward Falloff* reduces the amount of transparency as the faces become edge-on. This simulates materials that are denser at the edges, like blown glass objects. *Outward Falloff* reduces the amount of transparency as the faces become perpendicular to the viewer. This simulates materials that are denser in the center, like a container of murky liquid.

FIGURE 6.11

Falloff controls how much more or less transparent an object is at its center as opposed to its edges. Falloff can be either Inward or Outward.

Falloff

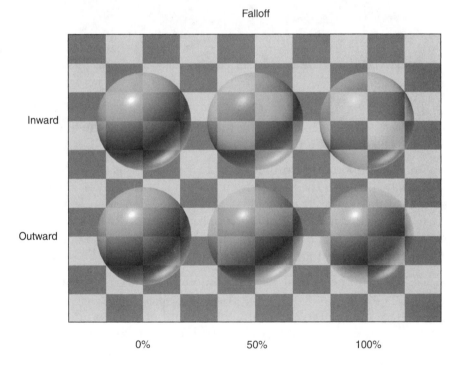

Refraction

Refraction controls the degree to which light is bent when it passes through a translucent object. This simulates the realistic bending of light in nature when it passes through different materials (see Figure 6.12). Refraction is supported only in programs that do ray tracing, but it can be simulated in other products by using refraction mapping (see the following section on map channels).

Refraction

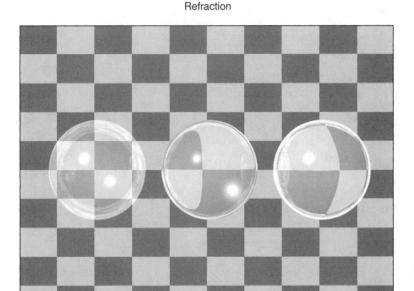

1.0   1.5   2.0

FIGURE 6.12

The Refraction setting adjusts the amount that light is bent when it passes through a translucent object. A setting of 1.0 means that no refraction occurs; higher numbers increase the amount of bending.

The use of translucent objects and refraction can make for some beautiful ray traced scenes using only simple forms, when they are carefully lit and arranged. Because refraction is based on physical laws, you can make lenses that really magnify and add them to your scene.

The amount of refraction is set by a scale called the *index of refraction*, in which a setting of 1.0 means that no refraction occurs. The proper index of refraction settings for different materials can be found in reference texts, such as CRC's *Handbook of Chemistry and Physics*. The following are some common material examples (rounded off to two decimal places).

Diamond:	2.42
Emerald:	1.57
Glass:	1.5-1.9, depending on composition
Ice:	1.3
Opal:	1.45
Quartz:	1.5
Ruby:	1.77
Water:	1.33

Luminosity (Self-Illumination)

Luminosity or *Self-Illumination* adjusts how much an object *appears* to be lit from within (it doesn't actually cast any light, however). As the percentage of luminance is increased, it flattens out the effects of the ambient and diffuse light sources, until the object appears to be one solid value (see Figure 6.13). Luminosity has no effect on specular highlights, however. Note that self-illumination is not to be confused with glow, which is an effect that extends outward from the object's edges (see Chapter 10, "Rendering and Output").

Luminosity

FIGURE 6.13

The Luminosity setting adjusts how much an object appears to be lit from within. 0% is completely unlit, while 100% is totally self-illuminated.

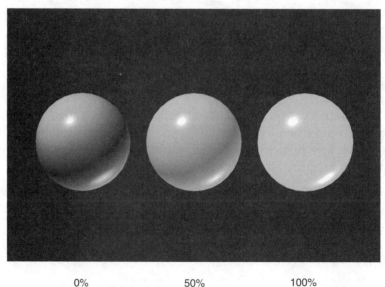

0%   50%   100%

Map Channels

Despite the range of settings that surface attributes provide, objects with materials that use only these settings tend to have an unrealistic, perfectly even, computer-generated look. Textures or procedurals are needed to bring more realism to the scene.

Textures (also called maps) can be derived from scanned images, 2D paint work, mathematical processes, and just about any other method that can be used to generate an image or pattern. Depending on your program, these images can be used to affect different aspects of the material's appearance, giving it a realistic visual pattern (such as wood grain or marble) or varying the roughness of the surface, its reflectiveness, transparency, and so on. The surface attributes of the material that can accept an image are called *map channels*.

Map channels fall into four basic categories: Diffuse, Bump, Reflection, and Opacity. Some programs also offer Shininess, Specularity, Luminosity, Refraction, and Displacement channels as well (see Figure 6.14). Note that some channels take into account only an image's grayscale values, regardless of whether the image is in color or not.

Map Channels

FIGURE 6.14

A wide array of material characteristics can be altered by using bitmaps in different map channels. Only displacement mapping alters the object's mesh, however.

As with the surface attributes, map channels usually have sliders or percentage values to adjust the amount of effect these maps have on the object. These sliders prevent the map from having any effect when set to 0%, or completely override the base attribute for that channel (or set the channel to its maximum value) when set to 100%. At other percentage levels, the channel's effect is reduced from maximum, and the result is a blend between the map and the base material.

Note that in addition to each of the map channels contributing to the overall look of a material, some programs allow more than one map to be placed in a channel. In fact, some programs allow an unlimited number of maps (subject only to the amount of RAM in the system). This enables the user to blend different maps together without having to composite them in a paint program first. Some software may also allow mathematical or masking operations to be performed on the maps, such as multiplying the images together, subtracting one from another, and so forth. The result is a much greater range of effects and patterns without having to leave the 3D package and do the work in a 2D paint program.

Diffuse Maps

Diffuse maps are generally in color and are used to alter the object's color away from that defined by the Color setting into a pattern or image. The amount of change from the base color of the object toward the map is set with a slider or percentage control. This enables the user to create a mixture of base color and map. However, in the case of diffuse maps, the map is usually set to 100%, completely overriding the base color.

To simulate a wood material on an object, for example, the diffuse map would be a scan or painting of wood grain set to 100%.

Bump Maps

Bump maps vary the surface roughness by manipulating the object's normals according to a grayscale image. Note that bump maps don't actually distort the mesh—they just adjust the normals' vector angle—so the effect may be lost at the edges of a rounded object. These maps use the value (lightness or darkness) of the map to determine whether a given section is protruding, flush, or indented. In some programs, for example, black portions of the image would cause an indentation, whereas white portions would appear to protrude. The overall effect a bump map has on an object is also determined by the slider or percentage value for this channel.

In the wood material example, the bump map would probably just be a grayscale version of the diffuse map, because grain tends to be darker than the rest of the wood already. This would cause the grain to appear indented.

Reflection Maps

Reflection maps are used to provide an "environment" for an object to reflect, thereby roughly simulating the effects of ray tracing in programs that don't offer it. In fact, reflection mapping is sometimes referred to as *environment mapping*. It works by overlaying (according to the percentage value or slider) a secondary diffuse map over the existing material, giving the impression that the object is reflecting the scene contained in the image. To simulate chrome trim on an outdoor surface, for example, it's common to apply a reflection map that looks like a landscape photo. Some programs offer automatic reflection mapping, which generates an image by rendering a panoramic view around the object and using it as the map.

One word of caution about using reflection maps: They can sometimes appear to be self-illuminated, which can be a big problem if the objects they're applied to are supposed to be in darkness. Check your program's material editing options for controls that will darken the reflection map if it is not lit by a light source in the scene.

You could use a reflection map on the wood example to make it appear freshly polished. The percentage of reflection mapping employed should be kept fairly low in this case, however. With chrome and other mirror-like surfaces, the reflection map is often set to 100%, and most of the material's characteristics come from the reflection map's settings and appearance.

Opacity Maps

Opacity maps are grayscale images that override the material's transparency settings and allow an object to vary from opaque to transparent. Like bump and reflection maps, they use grayscale values, and the slider or percentage value of the channel is used to set the transparency limits.

Opacity mapping would be useful in a situation where you're mapping dirty panes of glass that have been wiped clean in the middle. You also can use them as a way to "put holes" in objects without resorting to mesh changes. For example, say you wanted to create a chain link fence. One option would be to construct it with lots of thin cylindrical objects in a crisscross pattern, but an easier and more efficient route would be to use an opacity map. The crisscross material would simply be a flat panel with a metallic material and a crisscross opacity map applied. See the tutorials at the end of this chapter for more information on using opacity mapping.

Shininess Maps

Shininess maps adjust the reflectivity of the surface to which they are applied, overriding (depending on the slider or percentage setting) any Shininess settings in the surface attributes with their grayscale values. Shininess maps are useful for accurately portraying materials that have a range of shininess, such as metal with rusty spots, fingerprinted glass, or varnished wood.

Returning to the wood grain example, the same grayscale image used for the bump map could be employed in this channel as well, to vary the shininess of the surface. This makes sense because even when varnished, grain is often less reflective than the rest of the wood's surface. In the case of painted metal with rust spots, the shininess map would be dark (have low shininess) in the rusty areas and be light (have high shininess) in the relatively shiny painted areas.

Specularity Maps

Specularity maps vary the color and intensity of the specular highlights of the surface, depending on the image used and the percentage or slider value for the channel. They can be used to simulate various materials, like metals or metallic paints that reflect light in a spectrum of colors and intensities.

For example, if you wanted to create an object that looked like it was made of tricolor gold, you would create a specularity map that consisted of speckles of the appropriate colors. When applied to the specularity channel, the map would add these colors to the specular highlights, without affecting other parts of the object.

Specularity maps can also be used to create the appearance of tiny nicks and scratches on a surface.

Anisotropic Maps

Anisotropic maps vary the anisotropy level of the surface; they are controlled by the slider level and the characteristics of the grayscale image used. Such maps can be used to vary the level of anisotropy on the surface from full to nonexistent. In addition, by using varying shades of gray in the anisotropic map, you can produce interesting effects that help you refine the look of objects that have anisotropic characteristics.

Self-Illumination Maps

Self-illumination maps are grayscale images that create the impression that some portions of the object brighten as if they are lit from within; however, this is just an illusion—the affected areas don't actually cast any light. Like many of the other map channels, self-illumination uses a slider or percentage setting in conjunction with the grayscale values in the image to control the effect.

Self-illumination mapping would be useful for mapping a stained glass lampshade made from a single 3D object. The map would be set to make the glass panels appear to be lit, while leaving the lead that holds them together unaffected.

Refraction Maps

Refraction maps are a means of simulating the effects of light refraction in programs that don't offer ray tracing. The amount of simulated refraction is based on the grayscale values in the image and the slider or percentage control. Some programs may feature automatic refraction mapping that takes the shape of the object into account.

Displacement Maps

Displacement maps aren't surface embellishments as the rest of the material attributes are. As you may recall from Chapter 4, "Modeling: Beyond the Basics," the grayscale values of the displacement map and the percentage of strength applied actually affect the mesh, extending it outward or inward. Displacement mapping is often used to create terrain or organic models based on grayscale imagery. Even a simple radial gradient can be useful as a displacement map—you can use it to add a bulge or depression to an extruded object, like a gear. Just make sure you cap an object like that with a grid or tessellate the affected faces so that it has sufficient mesh resolution.

Procedural Textures

Although texture maps have the capacity to make materials much more realistic, they suffer from three main drawbacks. First, they consume memory, and scenes with numerous or very large maps may slow the rendering process to a crawl unless the system is equipped with a great deal of RAM. Second, if the object is going to be very large in the scene or will be seen close-up, a high-resolution texture map may be required so that the surface doesn't appear fuzzy or pixilated when rendered. Finally, they require mapping coordinates on the objects, and as you will see in the Mapping Coordinates section later in this chapter, it may be difficult to apply these properly after the object is built.

One way to get around the restrictions of using texture maps, but still retain some of their realism, is to use procedural textures. As was mentioned earlier, procedurals are mathematically defined textures that can be made to simulate such things as wood grain and marble (see Figure 6.15). In addition, they are useful for creating randomized or fractal patterns as well, and do a good job of creating realistic snow, rock, and gaseous nebulae.

FIGURE 6.15

Procedural textures require no mapping coordinates, and much less memory than bitmapped textures. However, the results are generally not very realistic unless you use very sophisticated procedurals. Procedural noise can be used to add realistic variation to any type of texture, or be applied as a bump map.

Procedural Textures

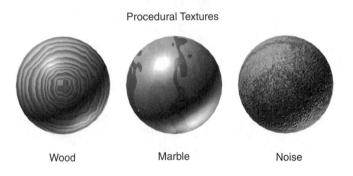

Wood   Marble   Noise

Procedurals have several advantages over bitmapped textures. The most obvious advantages are that they consume much less memory than bitmapped textures and require no special application of mapping coordinates. Unlike textures, which affect only the surface of an object, procedurals are three-dimensional; this means that Booleans and other cutting operations done to an object will reveal a properly formed interior texture. In addition, procedurals are easily animated, which makes it possible for them to change over time. This capability allows them to simulate all kinds of natural effects, such as fire, smoke, mist, water, or wind blowing across grass, plus some interesting special effects as well. Sometimes the animation can be looped, making procedurals useful for creating wave effects and other short, repeating animation.

A smoke procedural was used to great effect in *The Daedalus Encounter* to create a weird animated bump map for the alien ship's propulsion system. By applying the animated texture to the translucent intake and exhaust mesh on the ship, the craft seemed to come alive, driven by some unfathomable energy source.

One of the most useful functions available in procedural mapping is *noise*, which is mathematically generated "static." The amount of noise can be varied or calculated in different ways, and can be used to create a natural variation in the coloration of surfaces (or any one of the other map channels) without resorting to a grayscale image. For example, using fractal noise for bump and specularity mapping is a good way to turn a flat surface into a carpeted one.

Animated Textures

Procedurals aren't the only texture that can be animated. *Animated textures* use video or animation files rather than still images, which causes an object's texture to change over time when the scene is rendered. This could be useful for showing such effects as a landscape changing from spring to fall, or a 3D model of a television with a moving image on its screen. Animated textures are discussed in more detail in the "Incorporating Video into Materials" section later on.

It's important to note that if the sequence you are rendering is longer than the animation or video file used for a texture, the animation or video will probably loop, starting over again from the first frame. If this would not create a smooth transition, you can either use a longer source animation or video, or use a video-editing program to cross-fade and smooth out the differences between the last few frames of the sequence and the first few frames at the beginning.

Tiling

Tiling is a method of repeating one image over a large area, something like using individual floor tiles to cover a large kitchen. Tiled images use less memory, because the image is stored in memory only once, but they suffer from some drawbacks. First, they tend to look too uniform, with tiled stone or grass ending up looking like indoor-outdoor carpeting instead. Also, the tiles have a tendency to show seams or patterns because the images are all lined up in neat rows—like on your kitchen floor.

Your software may offer several tiling settings that can help reduce patterns by mirroring pairs of tiles. Also, see the "Mastering Maps" section later in this chapter for more information about creating custom seamlessly tiling textures (see Figure 6.16).

FIGURE 6.16

A seamlessly tiling texture uses a single small bitmap that can be repeated without showing unexpected seams. This saves a great deal of memory over using a full-sized bitmap without tiling.

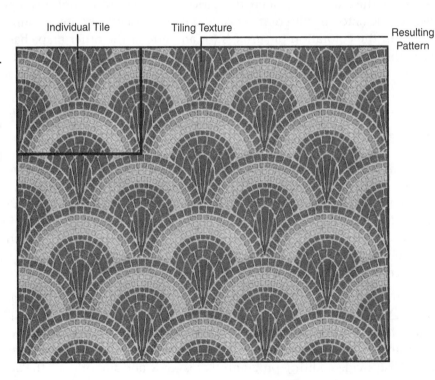

Individual Tile Tiling Texture Resulting Pattern

Use tiled maps with caution; a badly tiled surface is one of the most common mistakes that plagues novice work. Unless the surface is obviously intended to be tiled, take pains to make sure that the map is large and seamless enough so that it doesn't *appear* to tiled.

Face Mapping

Face mapping ignores any mapping coordinates applied to the object and instead tries to conform the image to pairs of faces that share an invisible edge (see Figure 6.17). The material editor in your software probably has a check box or setting that turns the material into a face-mapped type. Mapping is assigned by simply selecting the desired faces in the object and applying the face-mapped material to them. Note that the method by which objects are created or modified may have a dramatic effect on the way the faces are formed, so some planning or face-by-face manipulation of the mesh may be necessary to use this technique.

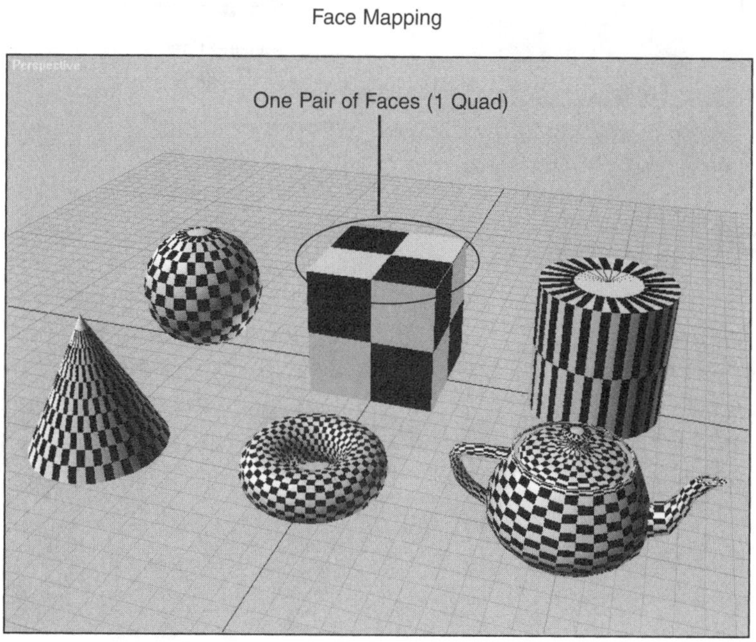

Face Mapping

One Pair of Faces (1 Quad)

Perspective

FIGURE 6.17

Face mapping causes the bitmap image to conform to each face on the object individually. No mapping coordinates are required, but the bitmap may be deformed depending on the size and shape of the faces.

Face mapping does conform nicely to many objects, especially ones with a fairly even size and distribution of faces, like a cube. However, as with any tiled material, you may see some problems if you aren't using a texture that can be seamlessly tiled in a range of sizes (see Figure 6.18).

Mapping Comparison

FIGURE 6.18

A comparison of mapping coordinates to tiled or face mapping. With the same (non-seamless) texture applied to both objects, tiling is evident on the face-mapped teapot in the foreground, whereas the mapping coordinates on the other teapot stretch the texture over the entire object.

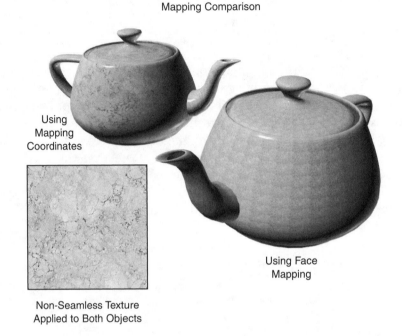

Using Mapping Coordinates

Non-Seamless Texture Applied to Both Objects

Using Face Mapping

Decals

Decals are images that can be applied to an object independently of any other texture mapping. They are great for adding small bitmapped details to an object that could otherwise make do with a procedural texture. They also can be used to precisely position image elements on a complex shape that would otherwise take a lot of trial-and-error image or mapping coordinate adjustments to achieve (see Figure 6.19).

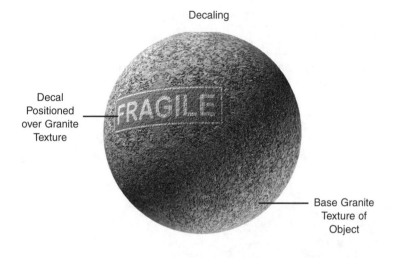

Decaling

Decal
Positioned
over Granite
Texture

FRAGILE

Base Granite
Texture of
Object

FIGURE 6.19

Decals are bitmaps
that can be independ-
ently positioned over
an object's base mate-
rial. They can some-
times be set to allow
some of the base mate-
rial attributes to show
through, as with the
bump map in this
example.

Texture Tools

Before you can employ real-world textures in your material development,
you obviously have to be able to get them into your computer system. You
have several options, some of which use the hardware discussed in
Appendix E, "Hardware and Software," on the CD-ROM.

Scanners

Scanners provide a way to duplicate a texture or logo easily, and can provide raw material for creating custom maps as well. You can even scan real
materials, as long as they have one flat side. Wood or paper samples scan
well, but reflective materials tend to cause some undesirable color shifting.
If a material is too shiny, too heavy, rounded, rough, or otherwise inappropriate for a scanner, take a photo instead.

Be wary when scanning printed images, because they can cause problems
to pop up in your scans. The most common problem is a *moiré* effect,
which is a pattern that appears when the scanning resolution doesn't
match the printing resolution perfectly (see Figure 6.20). In other words, a
135-dpi image scanned at 135 dpi should not have a moiré problem. There
are inexpensive "screen finder" tools available at graphics arts supply stores
that help determine the number of dpi or lpi (lines per inch) that were used

in the printing process, but these are tricky to use and not very accurate. Some scanning software may offer *de-screening* options that process the image and reduce or eliminate *moiré*, but you may have to try a few settings to find one that works best for the particular resolution you're scanning at.

FIGURE 6.20

Printed images are made up of a pattern of tiny dots. Scanning an image (like this one of the Twist modifier from the first edition of the book) can cause the patterns to become very noticeable, resulting in a blocky moiré pattern.

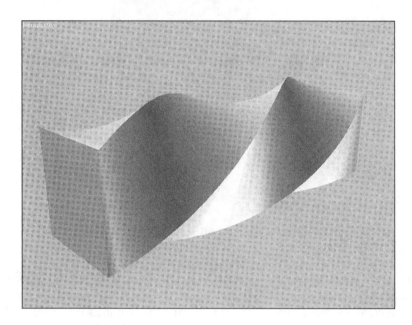

If your software doesn't offer de-screening, or you can't seem to get satisfactory results, you can try this "brute force" method that requires scanning at high resolution:

1. Scan the image into Photoshop at 200% and 135 dpi. For an 8.5"× 11.0" image, this makes a large 20MB+ file at about 2K resolution.

2. Rotate the image if necessary to straighten it up. Often it needs to be adjusted by only about 0.5–1.0 degrees. That sounds small, but can make a big difference, especially on a tiled pattern. To determine the amount of rotation needed, you can line up the measure tool in Photoshop along the edge of a portion of the image that you want to be vertical or horizontal. The angle of the measure tool will automatically be loaded into the Rotate Canvas:Arbitrary... dialog box.

3. Crop the image, removing any unwanted areas.

4. Choose Filter:Despeckle to blend together all the fine dots of color that make up a printed image. You also may use Median if you need more control over the results.

5. Reduce the size of the image to fit your needs.

6. Use Filter:Sharpen or Filter:Unsharp Mask to sharpen things up. Typical settings are: Amount 50-100%, Radius 1.0, Threshold 0.

7. If the image seems a bit washed out, try Image:Adjust:Levels and move the B and W pointers in a little to make sure the image has a full range of tones from black to white.

8. Using the printed image as a reference, adjust color and saturation with Image:Adjust:Hue/Saturation. Settings will vary by scanner. In some cases, you may have to select one of the color ranges on the left side of the dialog box and adjust it separately.

9. Use the Burn tool to darken any areas where the outside light has bled in and washed out the image. This often happens along the spine edge of a book.

Remember that nearly all material found in books and magazines is protected by copyright, so you're limited to images you can legally use. Because of the difficulty in finding license-free source material, and because the process of scanning it in and making corrections is time-consuming, you will probably want to rely on royalty-free image libraries for most of your common mapping needs.

Photography

Because you own the copyright to your own photographs, this is a safe and popular alternative to scanning book and magazine images. As mentioned in the preceding scanner section, using photography is a good alternative to scanning reflective or awkward objects, as well.

In the few years since writing the first edition of this book, photography has undergone its first real change in decades with the availability of reasonably priced high-resolution digital cameras. The fact that you can quickly take a photo of anything you want and get it into the computer within a few minutes makes digital cameras a great choice for expanding your texture library.

For best results, you should use a high-quality camera, preferably one with a macro lens for doing close-ups of materials. Because textures typically need to be sharp, use a tripod or copy stand when photographing objects. You will probably want to turn off the built-in flash on your camera, because it is likely to cause glare on the surface. Photograph the object with lighting set at an angle or diffused with a white card or umbrella.

Good texture subjects are easy to find—just take a long walk in the city or go for a drive in the country and snap away at walls, streets, signs, dirt, foliage, mountains, and the like. Early mornings or late afternoons are good times because they avoid the harsh midday sun. Shooting on an overcast day can help you avoid heavy shadows.

If you plan to shoot with film indoors, you need to use either tungsten slide film with incandescent lighting, or a strobe (flash) or other light that produces a daylight spectrum. If you try to use normal daylight film with incandescent or fluorescent lights, you get a severe color shift toward blue or yellow. Of course, you could try to correct this later in Photoshop, but some color fidelity may be lost.

If you plan to get some tungsten slide film, don't bother going to your drug store's camera department for it, because the clerk will just give you a blank look. Go to a *real* photography store and ask for Kodak Ektachrome 64T or something similar.

After you've shot the roll, you have to get it processed. Larger prints are better, of course, because you get more detail when you scan them in. Alternately, consider using a slide scanner (which also works for negatives) or getting the roll processed onto PhotoCD.

PhotoCD processing can be done to undeveloped rolls or existing slides and negatives, and involves taking or sending the images to a film processing outfit that offers the service. They put the images onto a multi-session CD-ROM that can be used with all but the oldest CD-ROM drives. The images are archived in five resolutions, ranging from 128×192 thumbnails to 2048×3072 high res, and more images can be added to the same disc later. For most textures, 128×128 or a multiple of that is ideal, because of the way that most programs allocate memory for maps or re-scale them to one of these multiples. Few texture maps will exceed 640×480, unless extremely high detail is needed over a very large object.

Be aware that PhotoCD processing quality seems to vary widely, so it would pay you to try a company's service with a test roll before you commit all your film into their hands. Otherwise, you may find yourself doing a lot of color and level correction work. Try asking at a good photography store for a recommendation.

Image Libraries

Image libraries are usually collections of royalty-free images available for download or on CD-ROM, professionally photographed and scanned. Some of them feature seamlessly tiling textures in addition to images of rock, wood, metal, tile, and so on. Many 3D packages come with image libraries already, but having *too many* textures to choose from is seldom a problem. CD-ROM texture libraries include Artbeats, ImageCELs, and Texture World (see Figure 6.21).

FIGURE 6.21

Sample textures from Artbeats' "Leather & Fabric" and "Marble & Granite" image library CD-ROMs. Royalty-free image collections such as these make excellent source images for your own materials.

Note that although some artists use these images straight off the CD-ROM or as starting points for custom maps, others feel that they're too recognizable (or overused) and prefer to modify them or create the textures from scratch. That's where 2D paint software comes in.

2D Paint Programs

Among paint programs, Abobe Photoshop is legendary, and generally regarded as a must-have application for artists. Although it lacks some of the texture tools and custom brushes that Corel Painter offers, it has a solid and easy-to-use interface that can be used with little training (see Figure 6.22). For those who want to explore its depths, Photoshop has a long list of powerful editing, compositing, and filter capabilities. In addition, adding plug-in extensions such as Alien Skin's Eye Candy, Kai's Power Tools (KPT), and others is a good way to add even more texture-generation possibilities.

FIGURE 6.22

Adobe Photoshop is one of the most popular programs for creating and manipulating object textures. It enables you to rasterize EPS files, create gradients and seamless tiles, and create opacity maps and other multichannel images.

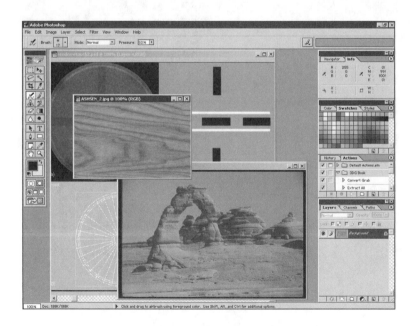

Corel Painter (formerly Fractal Painter) has some excellent brushes and features, and uses tools based on natural media such as chalk, oil paint, watercolors, and so forth. Like Photoshop, it too can be augmented by plug-ins.

3D Paint Programs

3D paint programs are a cross between 2D paint systems and 3D packages, and enable the user to paint "directly" on a 3D model. These applications range from the high-end *StudioPaint 3D* and *Amazon Paint* programs for the SGI, to *Deep Paint 3D* and low-cost *Mesh Paint*, which support most of the major packages. Overall, 3D paint is a very powerful, relatively new application that has the potential to solve a number of problems with precise positioning of maps, coordinate application, and most of all, the painful paint-render-repaint cycle that regular mapping with 2D paint images demands. Beyond even the capability to paint on a 3D object are some packages' capabilities to apply displacement mapping, turning a pressure-sensitive tablet and stylus into a virtual chisel for chipping away and deforming mesh.

On the downside, the system requirements for doing 3D paint work can be steep, and even when satisfied, the process can be rather slow and a bit unpredictable when it comes to detail work. Even if the performance of the package makes it difficult to use for all your paint work, it can still be employed as a way to rough out the texture and create alignment markers so that your map will line up properly with certain features in the mesh.

Other Tools

Terrazzo is a Xaos Tools product designed to create tiled textures or backgrounds from portions of other images. It works something like a "digital kaleidoscope," and can produce some surprising tileable textures when used with ordinary photographs.

A Wacom or other make of pressure-sensitive tablet and stylus are *de rigor* for texture mapping, enabling the user to work in a natural way while increasing subtlety and control of the virtual paint immensely.

Mapping Coordinates

For your masterfully created textures to appear on an object, you usually need to apply mapping coordinates (unless you are doing face mapping). *Mapping coordinates* are a set of coordinates that specify the location, orientation, and scale of any textures applied to an object. Without mapping coordinates, the software doesn't know where to apply any textures in the material.

Before delving into mapping coordinate systems and types, however, it would be good to understand image coordinates, because they also affect a map's orientation on an object.

Image (XY) Coordinates

When an image is used as a texture map, it's assigned a set of *XY coordinates*. At the top left corner (in some programs at least) is 0,0, which is also called the origin point (see Figure 6.23). The other three corners are also assigned coordinates. Although the image is generally left in the default position shown, the material editing section of your software might enable you to offset the XY coordinates for each texture image. This enables the image to be shifted so that it can line up with elements in the mesh.

Image (XY) Coordinates

X

FIGURE 6.23

The XY coordinate system is used to define points on a bitmapped image. Offsetting the coordinates shifts the map around on the object.

For example, say you applied a tiled map to the floor in a 3D model of a kitchen. You notice that the floor tile pattern looks a little odd because only a tiny sliver of one row of the tiles can be seen along a freestanding wall (in other words, the wall covers most of that row of the tiles). By adjusting the XY coordinates, you can shift the tiling pattern to make more of the tiles visible, or shift them so the seam is even with the wall.

Image Gallery

Figure I.1

"Ordinatographe." Created with Maya.
Image ©2001 Laurent Antoine.

Figure I.2

"Hyleyn." Created with Maya Unlimited.
Image ©2000 Marco Patrito/Virtual Views.

Figure I.3
"Darcron." Created with 3ds max, Maya
Unlimited, and Photoshop. Image ©2000 Marco
Patrito/Virtual Views.

Figure I.4
"Rocket Pants." Created with 3D Studio
Max. Image by Andy Murdock,
©2000 Mondo Media.

Figure I.5

"Street Scene" Created with TrueSpace.
Image ©2000 Terry Halladay.

Figure I.6

"3310" Created with LightWave 6.5b, textures created
in Photoshop 5. Image ©2001 Jussi Kemppainen.

Figure I.7
"Planto." Created with 3D Studio R4 (DOS), MetaBalls and BonesPro.
Image ©1995 Vadim Pietrzynski.

Figure I.8
"Untitled." Created with Animation Master. Image
courtesy of Momentum Animation Studios.

Figure I.9

"Asylum Catwalks from Zork:Nemesis." Image by
Mark Giambruno and Laura Hainke/Mondo Media
©1996 Activision.

Figure I.10

"Top_04." Created with 3ds max
4.2 SP1 and finalRender Stage-0.
Image ©2002 Akira Iketani.

Figure I.11

"Gone Bad" Created with 3ds max. Image by Britnell Anderson,
Marco Bertoldo, Kelly Kleider, Art Matsuura, Andy Murdock, and
"Goose" Ramirez. ©2001 Mondo Media.

Figure I.12

"Autumn Flirts with Winter." Created with
Poser, Ray Dream Studio, Painter and
Bryce. Image ©1998 Martin Murphy.

Figure I.13
"Zen." Created with Animation Master. Image ©2001 Jared Lim.

Figure I.14
"MEGA001209." Created
with Animation Master.
Image ©2000 ZINK.

Figure I.15

"Alkali." Created with Animation Master. Image ©2001 Brian Prince.

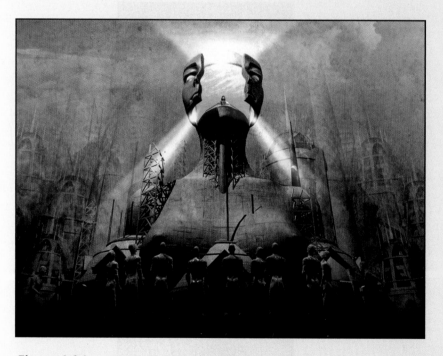

Figure I.16

"Lady of the Grey Tower." Created with 3D Studio Max, Poser and Photoshop. Image ©2002 Kenn Brown.

Figure I.17
"The Jester: Evil Served with a Smile."
Created with Animation Master.
Image ©2001 Frank A. Rivera.

Figure I.18
"Rainbow." Image ©1996 Eric Chadwick.

Figure I.19
"Cube Farm." Created with Animation Master.
Image ©2001 Darrin Mossor.

Figure I.20
"Daylight." Created with Cinema 4D.
Image ©2002 Carles Piles

Figure I.21
"Swing 2." Created with Animation Master.
Image ©2001 Masaru Kakiyama.

Figure I.22
"Alliance." Created with Maya. Image ©2002 Richard Mans.

Figure I.23

"Ballroom from Zork:Nemesis." Image by Andy Murdock, with elements by Mat Smiley and Mark Giambruno/Mondo Media ©1996 Activision.

Figure I.24

"Window." Created with Animation Master.
Image ©2000 Brian Prince.

Figure I.25

"CZ-75 Compact." Created with 3ds max. Image by Mike
Jones and Andy Murdock/Mondo Media ©1998 Pulse
Interactive.

Figure I.26

"Artbot." Created with 3ds max. Image ©1996 Richard
Green/Artbot.

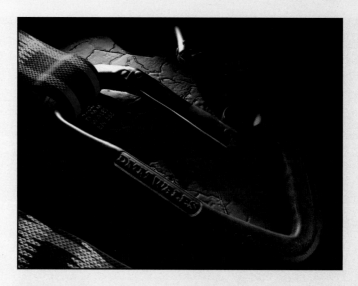

Figure I.27

"DMM." Created with Animation Master.
Image ©1999 Adrian Skilling.

Figure I.28

"Dragon." Created with 3D Studio
R4 (DOS) and MetaBalls.
Image ©1996 Vadim Pietrzynski.

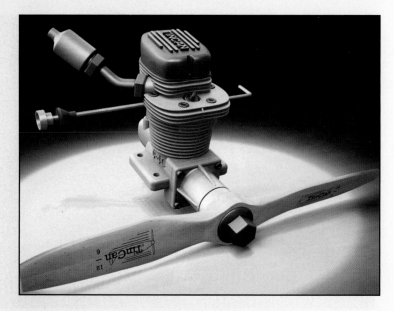

Figure I.29

"ENYA 90." Created with Animation Master and Darktree Textures. Image ©2001 Jeff Cantin.

Figure I.30

"Boiler Room from Zork:Nemesis." Image by "Goose" Ramirez and Mark Giambruno from a design by Cody Chancellor/Mondo Media ©1996 Activision.

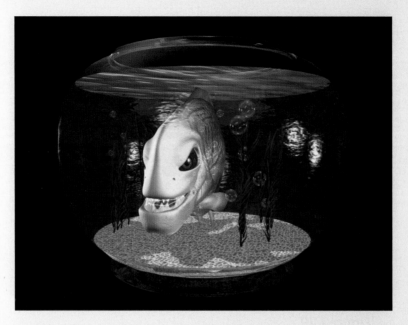

Figure I.31

"Niho Nui the Piranha." Created with Maya for the film *Tongan Ninja*. Image by Sheldon Whittaker/2d Post © 2002 Midnight Film LTD.

Figure I.32

"Mercury One." Created with LightWave. Image ©2002 Stefan M. Schmidt.

Mapping (UVW) Coordinates

The mesh itself also has a coordinate system for mapping, but it is the *UV coordinate system* (or *UVW coordinate system*). Why UVW? Because those are the three letters immediately preceding XYZ, and the two coordinate systems have a lot in common. The U axis is horizontal, like X, the V axis is vertical, like Y, and the W axis runs perpendicular to the two, just like Z.

Although UVW coordinates look similar to the XY image system, when applied they conform to the mesh no matter how it twists, bends, or stretches (see Figure 6.24). Note that the orientation of the UV or UVW coordinates may vary by product.

Texture (UVW) Coordinates

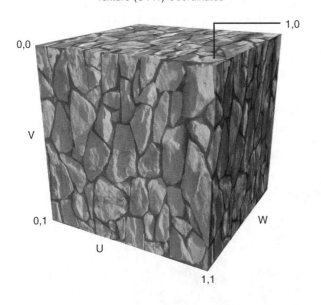

FIGURE 6.24

UVW coordinates are used for mesh objects, and shifting them allows very precise repositioning of maps on an object.

UVW coordinates can be offset just like the XY coordinates, but provide much more accurate positioning. In fact, a particular pixel in the image can be made to line up with a given vertex in the mesh! UVW coordinates are used in pairs, such as UV, UW, or VW, to adjust the orientation of the map. For example, offsetting the U coordinate in by a positive number shifts the map to the right, and offsetting the V by a positive shifts the map upwards. Offsetting W in a positive direction causes the map to rotate clockwise.

There are four common mapping coordinate types or *mapping projections*: Planar, Cylindrical, Spherical, and Cubic. In addition, some programs offer

Loft or Parametric coordinates as well, which are automatically applied (with differing levels of success) when you create the object.

> If you apply a material that contains texture maps to an object, but the texture doesn't show up when you render the scene, you've probably forgotten to apply mapping coordinates. Also, check to make sure that the texture is active and turned up to a visible level in the material editor.

Planar Coordinates

Planar coordinates are flat, like a sheet of paper (see Figure 6.25). Planar maps act as though they're pushing the map through the mesh, which may cause streaks along the side of the object. This is a common 3D *faux paus*, and can be avoided by using a different coordinate system or by mapping the affected faces separately (we'll get into this later).

Planar Mapping

FIGURE 6.25

Planar mapping applies a single, flat set of mapping coordinates to the object. This often results in streaking along the sides of the object, however.

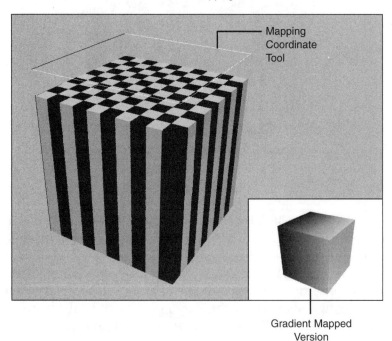

Mapping Coordinate Tool

Gradient Mapped Version

Planar coordinates are useful for mapping flat objects, such as walls and doors. However, you might want to use them in other cases as well, because they're very useful for precise positioning of texture map elements onto a mesh object, and they don't distort the texture maps like some of the other coordinate types do. For example, if you built a 3D model of a book, you would want to use a planar map for applying the cover texture and title.

Cylindrical Coordinates

Cylindrical coordinates wrap the image around one of the object's axes until it meets itself (see Figure 6.26). This may result in a seam, so consult the seamless tiling section of this chapter for information about correcting this situation. Also, like planar coordinates, cylindrical projections tend to create streaks across the top and bottom of the cylinder, so the end caps may need to be mapped separately. Some programs offer an option for planar mapping the end caps automatically.

Cylindrical Mapping

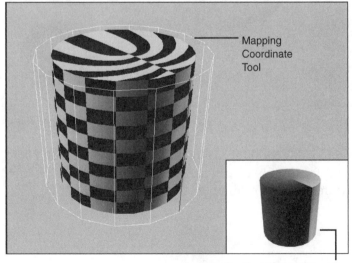

Seam in Gradient Mapped Version

FIGURE 6.26

Cylindrical mapping wraps the map around the object, but usually causes odd results on the end caps. A seam also may also appear where the ends of the bitmap meet.

Cylindrical coordinates are obviously ideal for roughly cylindrical object shapes, such as applying a label to a 3D bottle, or to apply a wood texture to a post.

Spherical Coordinates

Spherical coordinates wrap the image around the object in a cylindrical manner, and then pinch the top and bottom closed to surround it (see Figure 6.27). The pinching often results in a undesirable distortion of the image, so some additional tweaking may be needed on the image. Also, just as with the cylindrical coordinate system, a vertical seam may show up where the two ends of the image meet.

Spherical Mapping

FIGURE 6.27

Spherical mapping surrounds the object, pinching the top and bottom of the bitmap together to enclose it. This may result in a distorted, streaked appearance to the texture at these points.

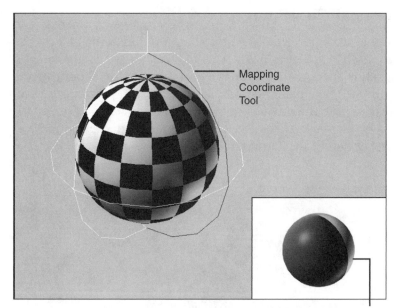

Mapping Coordinate Tool

Seam in Gradient Mapped Version

In addition to being ideal for mapping spherical objects, this coordinate system is useful for just about any irregular form that will be taking a generic sort of texture, like rust or marble.

Cubic Coordinates

Cubic coordinates apply the image from six different directions, and are also known as *box coordinates*. Obviously, they're ideal for mapping box-like objects, because they apply the image in planar form to each side of the object, preventing streaks (see Figure 6.28).

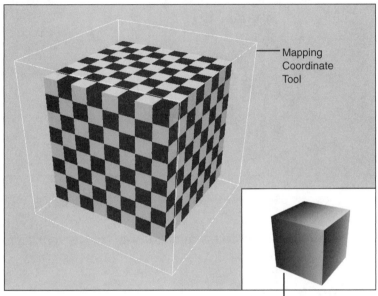

Gradient Mapped Version

FIGURE 6.28

Cubic mapping applies the bitmap to six sides of the object.

Wrap Coordinates

Wrap coordinates (or *shrink wrap coordinates*) try to smoothly surround an object while reducing undesirable pinching or streaking (see Figure 6.29).

FIGURE 6.29

Shrink wrapped mapping attempts to conform the coordinates to the object by stretching the coordinates in a more or less uniform manner until they fit.

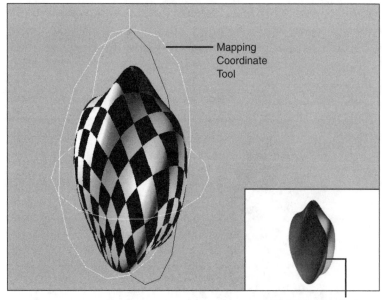

Mapping
Coordinate
Tool

Seam in Gradient
Mapped Version

When mapping a freeform object, you might want to try wrap coordinates as an alternative to spherical.

Lofting Coordinates

Lofting coordinates are applied to objects during the extrusion, sweeping, or skinning process. By applying coordinates during these mesh operations, the coordinates can follow a winding path much more faithfully than if you attempted to apply them later. Therefore, it's highly recommended that you make sure to use this option whenever you're creating a complex, winding form (see Figure 6.30).

The construction of a coiled 3D snake would be a perfect opportunity to use lofting coordinates, because the scaly texture would be evenly applied along the critter's winding length.

Loft Mapping

FIGURE 6.30

Lofting coordinates are
applied at the time an
object is extruded, or
swept, and allow the
texture to follow the
form of the resulting
object closely.

Seam in Gradient
Mapped Version

Mastering Maps

Mapping is an art in and of itself; it's a painterly discipline very unlike the
construction and sculpting skills that aid a 3D modeler. Although strong 2D
paint skills can be incredibly helpful in creating standout texture mapping,
you can get along pretty well as long as you can use the tools properly.

This section looks at how to go about the process of creating and applying
texture maps that will transform a plastic-looking model into a rich and
realistic object.

Using Maps Effectively

A common piece of advice about modeling is to use maps rather than mesh
whenever possible. This often cuts down on rendering time and also makes

it easier to work on your scene. However, here's another piece of advice to bear in mind as well:

Don't be too stingy with the mesh.

Maps can be very effective, but there are times when just a little more mesh, even if it's just some simple boxes or other primitives tacked on to break up the surface or the outline, will make the difference between being efficient and looking amateur.

The other thing to remember is that bitmapped textures consume memory, and too many high-resolution maps can bog down the rendering process unless you have a lot of RAM. Note that mapping a number of different objects with the same image has far less impact on memory consumption than using different images to map each object.

Breaking Apart Mesh

As you may have realized during the discussion of mapping coordinate types, cylindrical, spherical, and planar mapping coordinates all have limitations and drawbacks, and there is no single system that works well for all types of objects. One solution to this dilemma is to "break apart" a given object into simpler collections of faces that do lend themselves better to accepting one of these coordinate systems. If you detach the faces, each group is temporarily turned into a new object. After the coordinates are assigned to each piece, they can then be reattached and welded back together into one object, and each set of faces retains the particular set of coordinates assigned to it.

With some modelers, you don't actually have to "break apart" an object in this way—you just deal with it in sections by using sub-object selections of faces. You can then apply different coordinates and material attributes to each section.

One Artist's Approach

Sometimes the best way to learn, as our medieval student knows, is to watch a master at work. Take a look at how one artist approaches the task of doing highly detailed map work for 3D environments.

As you know if you read the interviews in the last section, Laura Hainke was once a senior graphic artist with Mondo Media/Mechadeus, where she earned her in-house nickname "The Texture Goddess" as result of her impressive 3D mapping work on both *Critical Path* and *The Daedalus Encounter*. The techniques described in this section are based on her process at that time, which was geared toward bitmapped texturing of polygonal objects. These days, she's usually dealing with NURBS models and uses sophisticated procedural shaders instead.

Because the development process at Mondo Media/Mechadeus used to separate modeling and mapping in order to maintain consistency, most of the mesh that Laura received had little or no mapping applied. It often didn't have mapping coordinates either, which meant she had to apply her own. This was often very difficult when complex objects were involved, so in many cases, she would detach faces to break an object down into multiple pieces, then map each element individually.

Laura applied basic materials to the objects first, and then rendered the scene to get a feel for the space, the lighting, and what the most important elements in the shot would be. This enabled her to home in on the key objects in the shot and make sure that the time spent on mapping them would be budgeted accordingly. It also enabled her to determine an overall color scheme and feel for the room to have. She usually started with either the walls or the most difficult objects first, painting the patterns and textures on one machine while rendering the 3D scene on another. (This was almost a necessity because we were using the DOS version of 3D Studio at the time, and it was difficult to get Photoshop, running under Windows, and 3DS going simultaneously on the same machine.) To save time and unify the design, she often reused textures from key pieces on other objects in the room.

When creating textures for walls, she rendered an elevation view (no perspective) of the wall and the objects attached to it, using it as the basis for a planar map. She would also think about the objects mounted to the wall and how they would be affected by age, moisture, and use. For example, if there were pipes coming out of the wall, she would paint stains running down beneath them. For oil lamps, she would airbrush smoky smudges onto the wall above them, and so forth. When she finished a detail, she applied the map to the object and rendered the scene to see how it looked in 3D.

Dirt and wear add a lot of character and realism to your objects. Laura tried to imagine the way a room would be used by its virtual occupants, then dirtied it up accordingly. For example, she may have picked out a "favorite spot" on a couch and applied extra stains and fraying to that cushion.

When working with spherical or cylindrical maps, Laura sometimes turned to Mesh Paint, a 3D paint program for 3D Studio, as a way to outline the perimeter of a map and mark key locations on it. She then liked to work on the map with her usual 2D paint programs, because Mesh Paint's tool set was not as fast or powerful. Another way she could approach the problem of getting a map aligned to the mesh was to apply a numbered grid texture to the object, then use a render of it as reference while painting on top of the same grid in a 2D paint package.

Like many other artists, Laura liked using Photoshop for its speed and control, often starting a map in Photoshop, then switching to Fractal Painter to make use of its superior brush selection. Case in point: To create a brick surface, she painted the bricks in Photoshop, making sure that the map would tile properly. Switching to Painter, she created the brick's grittiness by adjusting the image luminance, turning Shininess off, setting up a light to reveal the media's grain, then fading it down to about 20%. She then switched back to Photoshop again to apply the finishing touches, and used that diffuse map as the basis for the grayscale bump and specularity maps.

Laura enjoyed using Fractal Painter's watercolor tool for staining things. A small spattering brush "dipped" in burnt sienna made good mold spots on cardboard or paper. After applying the spatters, she grayed out the color and enlarged the brush, then squiggled it around the perimeter of the stains to create the fuzzy white mold.

She also made use of specular maps to vary the shininess of a surface, adjusting it where the object had been damaged or stained. For example, a shiny leather briefcase shouldn't be shiny where it is scuffed or scratched, so she would modify the bump map and use it as a specularity map.

Laura also relied on procedural maps, which can be very fast and powerful. They also can be real time-savers when you're dealing with an object that the camera gets very close to in an animation, because they don't become pixellated or "break down" the way bitmapped textures can. In addition, they don't require that mapping coordinates be applied to an object (which can be a real lifesaver with a complex organic object, or one you need to map quickly).

Scanned (laser digitized) mesh offers some special challenges. For a model of a 3D character named Chavo, a physical sculpture was created by a local artist, then scanned by CyberWare in Monterey, CA. The sculpture was scanned in pieces, which had to be reassembled after the objects were put into digital form. The pulling and stretching of the mesh during reassembly caused some loss of information in the joint areas. There were no mapping coordinates, so the model had to be separated into multiple pieces again so that they could be made to work with the planar mapping scheme. Laura used Mesh Paint to apply reference marks to the map, letting her identify which areas on the planar map correlated with mesh details such as the eyes, nose, mouth, and other key features.

Using the Render/Retouch Method

The *"render/retouch"* approach Laura often uses for creating custom maps is a popular technique that makes a big difference in the quality and believability of your work. It makes it possible to add properly positioned details, stains, graffiti, or what-have-you to an object. Here are the basic steps:

1. Construct the mesh and apply mapping coordinates (see Figure 6.31a).

2. Apply materials to the objects in your scene, adjusting them until the overall color scheme and look fits your needs. Using the non-perspective (orthogonal) viewports, render a close-up of the object on which you want to do additional mapping work and save the image to disk (see Figure 6.31b).

3. Load the render into a paint program and crop it, removing any portions of the image that you don't plan to re-apply to an object. Make the desired alterations and enhancements to the image, such as adding wear, stains, graffiti, text, additional details, altering the color balance, and so forth, and then save the file for use as a new map (see Figure 6.31c).

4. Back in the 3D program, add the enhanced image to a copy of the original material and apply it to the object. Use the modified map as the base for creating any bump, shininess, opacity, or other maps required, and include them in the material as well.

5. If necessary, break the object up by detaching faces, and use planar mapping to so that the enhanced image will fit the object perfectly. Render the scene, and make any corrections to the map until you're satisfied with the results (see Figure 6.31d).

FIGURE 6.31

Using the render/retouch method: (a) Build the objects and apply mapping coordinates to them. (b) Apply basic materials and render an orthogonal view. (c) Crop out anything not needed for the new map, and use a paint program to add additional details. (d) Remap the object (detaching faces if necessary) with the enhanced map.

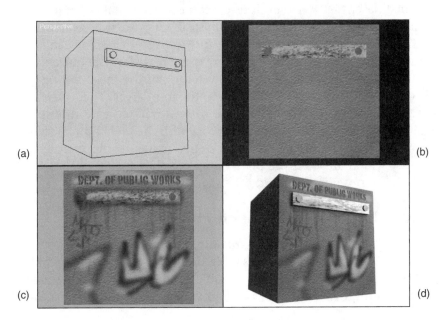

(a) (b) (c) (d)

Seamless Tiling

Earlier in the chapter, you saw how small bitmaps can be repeated to create large, tiled textures. Although many texture libraries offer seamlessly tileable bitmaps, you will probably need to create your own in many cases. Tiled textures are frequently used for mapping large objects that are made out of a material like brick or steel plates (see Figure 6.32).

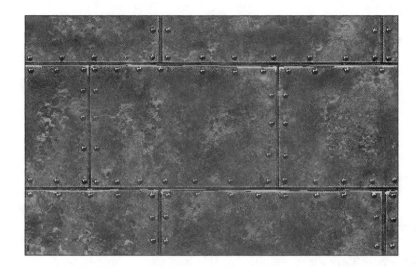

FIGURE 6.32

A custom-painted boilerplate texture map from Critical Path. It was designed to be seamlessly tiled over the surface of a huge furnace.

The main problem with creating a tiled texture is that telltale color and value patterns usually show up when a bitmap is tiled. These patterns or seams are often difficult to anticipate when working on a single tile, so you usually have to either repeat the pattern in the paint program, or apply the texture in the 3D package and render to spot them.

The simplest way to make a seamless tiling texture is by using your paint program to mirror an image horizontally, then mirror the new image vertically. At that point, you can paint extra details and variation in the image, but stay clear of the pixels at the edges. However, you will probably still notice unwanted patterns.

Another method to create seamless tiles in Photoshop is to use Filter>Other>Offset with Wrap Around Edges turned on in order to shift the image by 50% vertically and horizontally (see Figure 6.33). This places what was the corner of the image in the center, and wraps the edges of the image around to meet each other. This enables you to see what the edges of the texture will look like when tiled, and do any retouching necessary to get rid of the seams. When it looks good, just hit Cmd- or Ctrl-F to do the Offset again, which sets things back to their original positions.

FIGURE 6.33

Using the Offset filter
in Photoshop is a good
way to locate potential
seams and fix them
without having to
apply the texture in
a 3D program.

Original Image   Image Offset by 50%

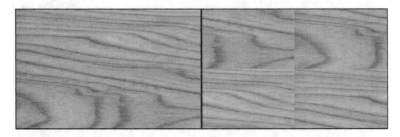

Keep in mind that another method of creating some incredible tiled textures is with Xaos Tools' Terrazzo, a plug-in for Photoshop that performs automatic tiling on selected portions of existing bitmaps.

Flat Poly Tricks

Simple 2D polygons (sometimes called *billboards*) can be used for many objects and effects in a scene, although their very lack of mesh can make it tough to spot and select them at times. (This is a situation where being able to select objects by name is a big advantage.)

In addition to using flat polygons for walls and floors where there is no need to see any depth to the surface, they are also great for creating the illusion of being much more complex mesh. By mapping a polygon with an image of a person, tree, or distant structure, you turn it into a sort of "cardboard cut-out" that can populate your scene with lots of detail, but almost no increase in mesh. The polygon can either be made in the same shape as the image you plan to map on it, or you can use an opacity map to render the unmapped portions of a rectangular polygon transparent.

Note that many programs take a relatively long time to render objects with transparency, so you should try a test to see whether you would be better off having the polygon follow the shape of the object rather than using opacity mapping. Remember that you may be able to create a polygon shape quickly by turning the image into a silhouette in a paint program and then using a draw program's auto-outlining feature to create a polygon or spline outline of it. The outline can be imported into your 3D program as a shape, and then mapped with the image.

Billboard tricks can even be used if you're moving the camera around in a scene. Just animate the flat polys so that they're always perpendicular to the camera. This can sometimes be accomplished automatically if your program offers certain kinds of animation behaviors (see Chapter 9, "Animation").

Of course, the effect will look odd if the camera moves a great deal, because the orientation of the objects always remains the same, like the creatures in the old *DOOM* games.

Incorporating Video into Materials

Using animated files or video as a texture enables you to integrate live action or previously animated elements into your materials. One obvious application is in rendering a scene that has control panels filled with flashing lights and video monitors. Animated files also are very useful for special effects such as explosions, fire, smoke, and so forth.

Blazing CDs

The *Pyromania!* series of CD-ROMs from movie effects house VCE, Inc., contain footage of numerous explosions, fire, and smoke effects. All the footage was photographed against a black background, then digitized and reduced to 640×480 resolution and saved as a series of sequential files on the CD-ROMs. Also included are downsized versions of the files converted to QuickTime movies for quick viewing of the effect.

One way to apply a *Pyromania* effects sequence to your work is to use a digital editing program such as Premiere, After Effects, or Composer to add the effect in post-production. Another method is to convert the files into a format that can be directly used by your 3D animation program and then incorporate the effect as an animated texture on a flat polygon or object of any shape. This is the preferred method for several reasons, but is practically a must if the camera is moving during the effect.

Mapping the effect onto a flat or curved polygon requires the creation of an opacity map, because most of the files don't come with
an alpha channel. How this is done will vary with the requirements
of your 3D animation system. In some cases, you can simply use the
same files or movie in the opacity channel and tweak the controls
until the black background becomes transparent. In other cases, the
use of a digital editing program, a paint program such as Photoshop
with batch capability, or the batch processing feature of a graphic
file converter such as DeBabelizer may be used to generate an alpha
channel or to palletize the images and replace the black background
with your program's "transparent" color. The *Pyromania* CD-ROMs
include some information on using Photoshop's Curves feature to
remove the background, as well as information on other controls
that can smooth out the matte lines.

Video Faces on 3D Mesh

You may find a technique we used in *The Daedalus Encounter* to place the
actor's faces inside 3D spacesuits useful for mixing live video elements into
your 3D scenes.

At one point in the game, the story calls for Ari (Tia Carrere) and Zack
(Christian Bocher) to don spacesuits and cross over to an alien ship. After
our costumer conducted an extensive but unsuccessful search for believable rental suits, we went with my backup plan, which was to create the
suits in 3D and use animated texture maps for the character's faces.

Using 3D models had some big advantages anyway, in that we could fly the
characters around without having to employ expensive and dangerous flying rigs on the actual bluescreen set. It also enabled us to design the suits
any way we wanted, so they would have a look that matched the other
Terran Alliance technology.

Scott Baker designed and built the suits using Alias Animator running on
our Silicon Graphics Indigo 2 Extreme system, which has an excellent
modeler for this type of work. I took photos of the actors' heads during the
shoot and Scott adjusted NURBS head models that came with Alias so the
models matched the sizes and shapes of Tia's and Christian's heads.

On the set, we had the actors sit down in the cockpit chairs and put pads
behind their heads to brace them. The idea was to have the actors say their
lines without moving their heads, and then map this live-action video

onto the animated 3D heads. It was very difficult for Tia and Christian to remain completely still, as actors instinctively want to move when acting.

When the time came to animate these sequences, the video was cut down to the exact length of the shot and turned into an Autodesk Animator file (called a .FLC file) that 3D Studio could use. The animator had to not only move the arms and legs of the suit, but also turn the 3D heads inside the suits in concert with where the actors were looking at the moment as well as with what they were saying.

Overall, the effect worked very well, and the only downside to our 3D approach was that we couldn't show the real actors taking off the suits without a great deal of very tricky animation that wouldn't be worth the effort. That scene worked around the problem by using live action close-ups and other editing tricks.

General Mapping Tips

The following are some miscellaneous suggestions to help you make professional maps:

♦ Complex objects can be very difficult to map with the usual planar, cylindrical, or spherical mapping systems. If possible, apply the mapping coordinates when you're skinning or lofting the object.

♦ Use dirt and wear to give your objects realism and a "history." Even a clean surface looks more realistic if it has some subtle mottling (after all, no surface is perfect). And remember to vary the specularity maps as well.

♦ Separating (or duplicating and offsetting) the faces on a section of an object enables you to apply custom details to that area while giving the illusion that it's just part of the rest of the surface. This is particularly useful if all your map layers are used up or your program doesn't have adequate decal support.

♦ If you can't duplicate faces and need to apply another map layer when none is available, try making a simple polygon and positioning it close to the other mesh. Apply the texture to the polygon and use an opacity map to make the unneeded portions transparent.

♦ Give yourself enough time for mapping. It often takes equal amounts of time to model and map objects.

◆ Use a map whenever possible, rather than building geometry. It speeds up your renders and will save you time in the modeling stage.

◆ Do test renders at the point where the camera gets closest to the mesh to make sure the resolution of the maps is adequate.

◆ Rendering a scene from a plan or elevation view makes a good starting point for mapping. You also can use a render of a mapped object as a guide for mapping another object to ensure that the maps line up properly.

◆ If you're doing low-polygon-count modeling, you may want to construct your model and map at a higher resolution first, then render it to create the maps for the low-res version. The subtle shading added to the maps will help make them look smoother on the low poly model.

◆ Be careful that your mapping coordinates are applied relative to the front surface of the object; otherwise, the indentations in your bump map will appear to protrude instead of recede.

◆ Projector lights are a good way to add decal-like textures to a procedurally mapped object, or one that has used up the map channels.

◆ The images you create will vary from system to system, mostly because of the differences between monitors. Check your work on a monitor similar to the one the end user is likely to have (usually a low- to mid-range unit). Note that scenes created on Macs often appear darker when ported to PCs because of differences in the monitors' gamma (see Chapter 10, "Rendering and Output," for more information).

Mapping Tutorials

Topics covered:

Using Base Materials

Using Procedural Materials

Using Decals

Applying Mapping Coordinates

Modifying Library Materials

Using the Render/Retouch Technique

Using Opacity Maps

Using Animated Maps

Now that you've constructed most of the blimp, it's time to apply some color and texture to it. This is an excellent opportunity to experiment, so feel free to make your blimp's materials totally different from the ones outlined here.

> Like 3D modeling commands, the material editing terminology and features vary from product to product. If the options or settings given in the tutorials are not available in your software, use your manuals and some experimentation to achieve a similar effect.

Using Base Materials

Most of the blimp model uses either mapped or procedural materials, but a few objects use only the basic surface attribute settings. These objects are the visible searchlight beams, the running lights, and the gondola window.

1. In the material editing section of your software, create a material called RunLite with the following settings: RGB Color: 255, 255, 191. Self-Illumination 100%. Opacity 100%. Additive Transparency. No Falloff. Select all the Run*Xxxnn* objects and apply this material. Do a test render to see whether the running lights are now self-illuminated, slightly yellowish objects (see Figure 6.34).

> The next step involves creating a visible searchlight beam using material settings. Note that some programs offer volumetric lighting (see Chapter 7, "Lighting," for more details) that can be used in place of this technique.

2. Create a material called SrcBeam and use these settings: Color: 255, 255, 255. Self-Illumination 100%. Opacity 40%. Additive Transparency. Falloff Outward 100%. 2-sided. Select the SrcBea01 object and apply this material. Do a test render to see whether the searchlight is now self-illuminated, and seems brighter in the center.

3. Copy the SrcBeam material and rename the copy Window. Change the Color to 255, 255, 191, and the Opacity to 60%. Select the window in the gondola and apply it. Do a test render to see whether the window is now self-illuminated.

FIGURE 6.34

Apply self-illuminated base materials to the running lights, search-light beam, and gondola window.

Using Procedural Materials

For ease and reduced rendering times, procedurals will be used for mapping the skin of the ship and most of the other mesh, including the gondola, catwalks, and so forth. Two different procedural materials are needed: a mottled green-gray rubber-like skin for the gas bag, and a procedural rust for most of the metal objects. First, the gas bag material:

1. Create a procedural texture map (using noise or fractals) with the colors 40, 58, 46 and 103, 108, 106 or whatever you like. Set Shininess between 10 and 30. Name the material BagTextr, and apply the material to the GasBag object. Because it is a procedural, no mapping coordinates are required. Render the results, and adjust the noise size to achieve mottling similar to the figure (see Figure 6.35).

2. Create another procedural texture with the colors 89, 51, 42 and 143, 121, 110 or similar. Set Shininess to 0. Add some noise to the Bump channel as well, to make the material look pitted. Name the material

Rust, and apply the material to the gondola, except the window. Render the results, and adjust the noise size to achieve mottling similar to the figure.

3. When you're satisfied with the look of the Rust material, apply it to the other metal surfaces on the model, except the thrusters and objects that already have textures applied.

FIGURE 6.35

Apply procedural textures to the blimp skin and metal portions of the model. Procedurals don't require mapping coordinates, which saves a lot of time.

Using Decals

Next, use decals to add some banners and signs on the blimp's skin.

If your program doesn't offer decals or the ability to apply multiple diffuse maps, there's an alternative. You could select a group of faces on the side of the GasBag object and use Detach Faces to turn them into separate objects, which you could map individually.

1. Using Photoshop or similar paint program, create a couple of small (128×128 pixels or less) signs for your blimp project. Consider using your name or company name, helping to underscore it when a prospective employer looks at your work. You can also use scanned

images if desired. In keeping with the overall worn and scruffy feel of the blimp, you may want to fade the colors somewhat and even add some dirt to them (see Figure 6.36).

FIGURE 6.36

Create signs and banners in Photoshop to advertise your services, reflect your interests, or just to look interesting. Weather the signs by reducing their saturation and working them over with an airbrush.

2. Following the decal methodology outlined in your software manuals, place the decals on the right side of the ship. Two are shown here, but many more are recommended. Unless your software offers interactive positioning, render the GasBag object and adjust the decal parameters to reduce stretching and tweak the positions (see Figure 6.37).

FIGURE 6.37

Add signs and banners to the GasBag object using the decal methods outlined in your manuals. Many programs allow 16 or more decals per object.

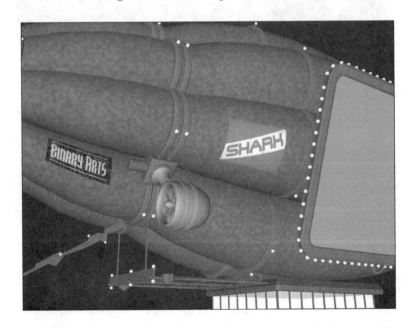

Applying Mapping Coordinates

Objects that use mapped materials require mapping coordinates. This tutorial covers three of the common ones: planar, cylindrical, and spherical. Make sure you apply appropriate coordinates to other objects that require image maps.

Normally, you want to apply mapping coordinates as you create each piece of mesh, so that when you duplicate them, all the copies are ready for mapping as well. Because it was impractical to introduce mapping coordinates during the modeling tutorials, we'll add them now to a few objects. In the future, however, make the mapping coordinate application part of your modeling process.

1. Select the object MonPnl01 from the Right viewport. Depending on your program, you may have to rotate it into a vertical position to make the application of coordinates easier (see Figure 6.38a).

2. Apply planar mapping coordinates, using Fit if available. The mapping coordinate tool should conform to the sides of the MonPnl01 object. Make sure that the planar map is right-side-up and that the coordinates are properly oriented so that the left side of the map will appear on the left side of the object. Usually there is some kind of indicator that shows this (see Figure 6.38b). Return the object to its original position.

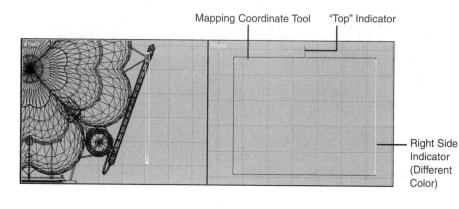

Mapping Coordinate Tool   "Top" Indicator

Right Side
Indicator
(Different
Color)

FIGURE 6.38

Apply planar coordinates to the monitor panel so that an image-mapped material can be applied. The mapping coordinate tools may have indicators to show the map's orientation.

It isn't necessary to rotate objects to a horizontal or vertical position when applying mapping coordinates, but it can make it easier. You can also rotate the mapping coordinate tool (as you'll do to map the thruster strut), or use an option offered by some programs that aligns to the surface normals.

3.   Select the object ThrStr01 (see Figure 6.39a).

4.   Try to apply cylindrical mapping coordinates. Note that the coordinate tool may not be in the correct position (see Figure 6.39b).

5.   Rotate the mapping coordinate tool and center it on the strut (see Figure 6.39c).

6.   Scale the coordinate tool to conform to the strut, and apply the coordinates to the object (see Figure 6.39d).

FIGURE 6.39

Applying cylindrical coordinates: (a) Select the strut object. (b) Activate cylindrical mapping. (c) Rotate the tool to match the angle of the strut. (d) Scale the tool to enclose the strut and apply the coordinates.

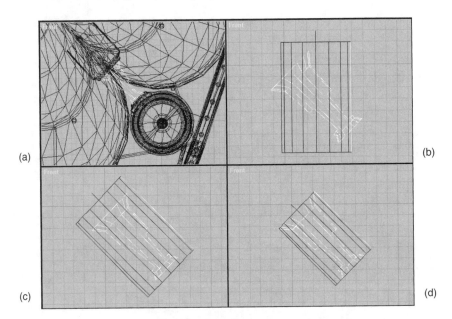

Use spherical mapping coordinates to map individual objects or groups of objects that will have textures applied that do not have to be oriented in any particular manner, such as Aluminum.

Some programs may not allow you to apply a single type of mapping coordinates to a group of objects. In this case, and in general, the best approach is to apply the most appropriate type of coordinate to each object individually, depending on its shape.

7. Select the rest of the lower portion of the thruster assembly. It will have coordinates applied as a group (see Figure 6.40a).

8. Activate the spherical mapping tool and Fit it to the selected objects. Apply the mapping coordinates to the selected objects as a whole (see Figure 6.40b).

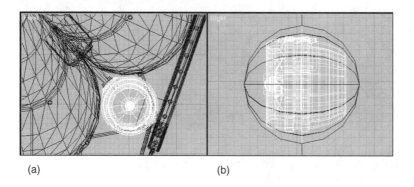

(a)   (b)

FIGURE 6.40

Applying spherical coordinates to the thruster: (a) Select the lower thruster assembly. (b) Position the spherical mapping tool in the center of the selected objects and apply the coordinates to all selected objects at once.

Modifying Library Materials

Often, you will find a material in your software's material library that will work as-is for an object. In other cases, you may be able to make slight modifications to turn one material into another. For this example, you'll create a dirty aluminum finish for the lower thruster nose assembly.

1. Check your material library for a reflective material, such as chrome, that you can use as the starting point. If one is not available, start with a default material and load REFMAP.GIF from the CD-ROM as a reflection map at 100%. Adjust the material type to Metal shading and set the Shininess to between 70–90; crank up the Specularity as well. Apply the material to the strut and lower thruster assemblies you just put coordinates on, and render the results (see Figure 6.41a).

2. To make the highly reflective chrome into a dull aluminum, make the diffuse color a medium gray, then reduce the reflection map setting to about 40%, allowing the gray to show through. Reduce the Shininess

and Specularity of the material to about 40 or until it has a dull metallic look. You may want to add some noise to the Bump channel to make the metal look pitted. Reapply the material to the thruster assembly (if required) and render the results (see Figure 6.41b). Keep tweaking the material until you are happy with it.

3. You may want to create variations on the dull aluminum, making it darker or lighter, or create some completely different materials (brushed bronze, copper, galvanized steel, and so on) and apply them to individual components of the lower thruster assembly. By using a greater variety of materials, the results are more interesting and realistic.

FIGURE 6.41

Modifying a library material: (a) Apply a library chrome texture to the strut and lower thruster assembly. (b) Adjust the surface attributes of the material to create dull, dirty aluminum look.

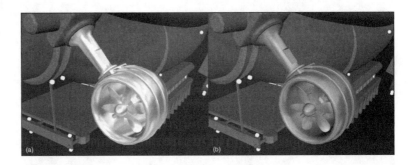

Using the Render/Retouch Technique

Next you'll use a variation on the render/retouch technique to create a custom bump map for the nose cone, adding additional interest to the object without doing more mesh work.

1. Select the nose cone object and any other mesh you used to enhance it (see Figure 6.42a). Hide everything else in the scene, including the flagpole-like docking assembly and the running lights on the nose cone.

2. Render the nose cone from the Front viewport as a close-up, making sure the image will be at least 480 pixels high. Save the render to the hard drive as an image file called NoseConeRetouch.psd (see Figure 6.42b).

3. Using Photoshop, load up the render and crop the image down to the edges of the object outline. Be sure not to leave any black background pixels on any of the four sides of the object (see Figure 6.42c).

4. Create a new layer called Stains, and set it to Multiply and Opacity to 85%. With the airbrush tool and some 0, 0, 0 black, paint some stains and dribbles (mostly on the lower half), using the render on the layer below for reference (see Figure 6.42d).

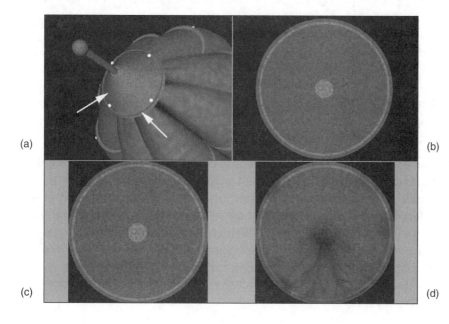

(a)

(b)

(c)

(d)

FIGURE 6.42

The render/retouch technique: (a) Select the nose cone objects and hide everything else. (b) Render the nose cone from the Front viewport. (c) Tightly crop the image in Photoshop. (d) With the airbrush tool, paint stains in a new Multiply layer over the top of the render in the background layer.

5. Create a new layer called Dark Shapes, and set it to Multiply and Opacity to 25%. Draw some rectangles with the marquee tool and fill them with black, again using the render of the object as a guide to where they will fall when mapped onto the strut. Save the file in .PSD form, then save a copy of the file as NoseConeRetouch.tif, which is to be used as the diffuse map (see Figure 6.43a).

6. Create a new layer called Bump Background and fill it with a 128, 128, 128 gray. Make a copy of the Dark Shapes layer called Bump Dark and move the copy on top of the Bump Background layer, then set it to Normal and Opacity to 100%. Create a new layer called Bump Light and add some 255, 255, 255 white rectangles to it. If you need to refer to the render on the bottom layer, just click the visibility (eye) icon for the Bump Background layer. When you're finished, save the file in .PSD form, then save a copy of the file as NoseConeRetouchBMP.tif, which is to be used as the bump map (see Figure 6.43b).

A screen grab of the layers in Photoshop is provided here as reference if you're having trouble (see Figure 6.43c). Because both diffuse and bump images are contained within the same .PSD file, you can manipulate either or both while using the other for reference. By turning the appropriate layers on or off, you can save off finished versions of either the bump or the diffuse map to another file.

8. Back in your 3D program, apply planar coordinates to the nose cone object from the Front viewport, making sure that the mapping gizmo is upright (see Figure 6.43d).

9. Make a copy of the Rust material and call it Rust_NoseCone. Replace the Noise in the Diffuse channel with the NoseConeRetouch.tif bitmap. Make the Bump channel into a composite (if your program offers that option), leaving the noise as half the composite material, and assign NoseConeRetouchBMP.tif as the second map. If your program doesn't offer a composite option, just replace the noise with the bitmap. Crank up the bump channel level and apply the material to the nose cone object. Unhide all the mesh and render the image (see Figure 6.43e).

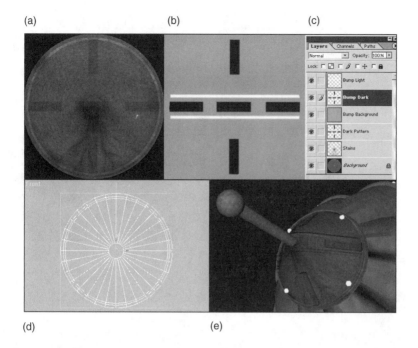

(a)　　　　　　(b)　　　　　　(c)

(d)　　　　　　　　(e)

FIGURE 6.43

Finalizing the
render/retouch process:
(a) The finished diffuse
map. (b) The finished
bump map. (c) The lay-
ers in Photoshop should
be arranged in this
manner. (d) Apply
planar coordinates to
the nose cone object.
(e) Apply the material
and render the results.

Consider using the render/retouch technique to do custom mapping on the gondola. To do this, render the gondola from different orthogonal views and paint on
top of the rust texture, but leave it mostly intact. Crop the images down and remap them onto the gondola objects (you may have to detach groups of faces to
do this).

Using Opacity Maps

Use opacity mapping to turn the flat panel on top of the catwalk into a
metal grid.

1. From the Bottom viewport, apply planar mapping coordinates to the
   large, flat boxlike platform sitting on top of the network of pipes in
   the catwalk area.

2. Copy the Rust material and name the duplicate RustGrid.

3. Create a tileable black-and-white cross-hatched map to use as an
   opacity map, or load the map CROSHTC2.TGA from the CD-ROM
   into the material's opacity channel and set it to 100% (see Figure
   6.44a).

4. Apply the RustGrid material to the platform object.

5. Render the object and adjust the UV tiling settings until the results are similar to the figure (see Figure 6.44b).

FIGURE 6.44

Using opacity mapping:
(a) Create a black-and-white tileable crosshatch.
(b) Modify a copy of the Rust material with the opacity map and apply it to the flat panel above the catwalk. The opacity mapping makes the panel look like a wire mesh.

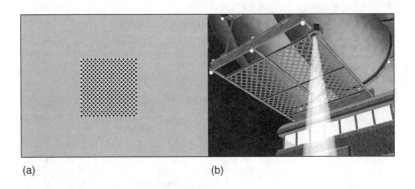

(a)   (b)

Using Animated Maps

To bring the monitor to life, use an animated map. This could be an earlier render of yours saved as a set of sequentially numbered .TGA files, an .FLC animation, or an AVI or QuickTime file or a clip of digitized video. You may also want to use Premiere to cut together a series of images and animations with wipes and effects for a true advertisement-like feel. Remember that your animation will loop if it is shorter than the animation you are rendering, so make sure that the looping will be seamless if this is the case.

1. Create a material using one of your own animated works (or use the OFF_WORLD.AVI file on the CD-ROM) as the diffusion map. Make the material matte by setting its shininess and specularity very low if you don't want the image to get washed out when light strikes it in a certain way.

2. Apply the material to the object MonPnl01.

3. Render a still of the scene to check whether the mapping coordinates were properly applied. They can sometimes be reversed when dealing with planar mapping (see Figure 6.45).

4. To see the full effect, render an animation with the same number of frames as your animated map.

FIGURE 6.45

Using an animation file for the monitor panel map adds extra movement and life to the scene, even if the blimp is sitting still at the moment.

At this point, all objects in the scene should be mapped. If any were missed, select the objects and apply the appropriate material to them.

Summary

In some ways, 3D is becoming more and more like desktop publishing was back in the early nineties, with the technology coming into everyone's grasp. Now *everyone* is using it. Setting your work apart in this increasingly competitive field will depend not only on your modeling skills, but also on your ability to create or modify textures that make your mesh sing. To aid you in this task, this chapter took a look at the basics of material creation, then went on to explore mapping coordinate systems and various techniques for obtaining and creating custom maps, including the important render/retouch method.

The next chapter explores the basics of lighting, and how it can be used to add drama and interesting effects to your 3D objects and scenes.

Lighting

Careful attention to lighting adds drama to an image and can help make it appear more realistic.
Image ©2000 Brian Prince.

*T*he storm raged around the keep, assaulting the stonework with pounding sheets of rain as the student labored within on his miniature version of the castle. The modeling was complete, and now he was intent on conjuring up the lighting. Unfortunately, the scene looked very flat, and the student wished he'd asked some questions of the Master before the old man had retired for the evening.

As if on cue, a shadow fell across the student and his work, and the lad looked up with a smile. "Master, I…" At that moment, a bolt of lighting stuck just outside the keep, silhouetting the standing figure in a blinding blue-white aura. The craggy face of the Master gazed down at the student, dramatically underlit by the candle clutched in his aged hands. The old man's eyes were ablaze with orange fire.

"Gaaa!" cried the student, falling backwards in his chair and landing in a heap on the floor.

The old man chuckled. "Sorry for the dramatic entrance, lad." The Master set the candle aside. "But it appears your project could do with a little drama."

"That's for sure." The student dusted himself off and settled in again. "Everything looks so…flat!"

"I'm afraid your choice of the weather conditions and time of day is to blame for that," the old man said. "You've lit the scene with what appears to be hazy mid-morning sun, which is common enough, but none too interesting. Here, let's clear the atmosphere a bit and set the lighting to around sunset." The student nodded as he watched the shadows in the scene darken and grow long. The castle took on a reddish tint from the sunlight peeking over the hilly virtual terrain.

"Ah, what a difference," the young man observed, "just from changing the light."

"Indeed," replied the Master. "Light is as much a tool as the virtual forms themselves. Now, to make the scene even more dramatic, we'll get rid of the sun altogether." With that, the sun set completely on the scene, and the castle model was plunged into darkness. "Hmmm. Seems your castle is not a very lively place in the evening, lad."

"I see… I guess I'll make some torches, and light the castle with those. That will be a lot more interesting, with all the different shadows that will be cast."

"Now you've got it." The old man grasped the candle and prepared to rise. "Make sure you make the firelight flicker like this candle, and you might want to add a touch of moonlight to show off the rest of the model. I think you'll find the mixture of warm and cool colors that result quite pleasing." The old man got up and ambled toward the door.

"Thanks, Master," the lad called after him. "That was very illuminating."

The elder groaned as he padded away.

Principles of Light

The none-too-subtle moral of this medieval yarn is that lighting has a big impact on the appearance of your final renderings. Flat, shadowless lighting is dull and lifeless, whereas multi-source, shadowy lighting is generally more realistic and much more dramatic. Before you can make lighting work for you, however, you must understand how light itself works.

As you no doubt remember from high-school science class, visible light is composed of a spectrum of colors running from red to violet. When light rays strike an object, some of these colors are absorbed by the material, whereas others are reflected. The amount and color of the light reflected from objects enable us to see them as red, yellow, lime green, or "that disgusting tooth-grinding purple."

Computer displays generally produce light rather than reflect it, so they create images using the additive color model. The additive color model is the one in which white light consists of equal amounts of red, green, and blue. If the level of any one of these three colors drops slightly below the others, the result is an off-white.

Color temperature is a scale used to differentiate between these near-white shades of light. Color temperature is measured in degrees Kelvin, which refers to what temperatures a black object must be heated to in order for it to radiate that particular spectrum of colors. This has nothing to do with the operating temperature of light sources, however—it's just a scientific scale of reference.

What color temperature does from a practical standpoint is indicate the "warmth" or "coolness" of the light in terms of color. The temperature scale is counter-intuitive, however; for example, cool (meaning bluish) fluorescent lights are rated at 4000K, whereas typical warm (yellowish) incandescent lamps are only 2900K. Quantifying color temperature can be helpful at times when you want maximum color accuracy because our eyes tend to consider the main source of illumination to be *white* regardless of whether it comes from noon sunlight (5000K) or a halogen desk lamp (3300K). However, when the image is output, the color differences may become more noticeable.

Another important element of light is *intensity,* the brightness of the source or reflection. As a light source becomes more intense, it can flood the object with light, and the specular highlights can become quite large and brilliant. This is sometimes referred to as "blowing out the highlights."

The angle at which a light ray strikes a surface and is reflected into our eyes (called the *angle of incidence*) has an effect on how brightly the object appears to be illuminated from our perspective. For example, if you hold a flashlight in front of your face and point it away from yourself along your line of sight at a *very* smooth, flat surface, most of the light is reflected back into your eyes, and the surface seems brightly lit. If, however, you left the flashlight where it was and stood at a 45-degree angle to the surface, light would not appear to illuminate the surface as well, because much of the light would be reflected away from your new position (see Figure 7.1).

FIGURE 7.1

The effect of angle of incidence on apparent brightness: (a) A surface lit and viewed at a 90° (perpendicular) angle. (b) The same surface lit from the same position but viewed at 45° angle.

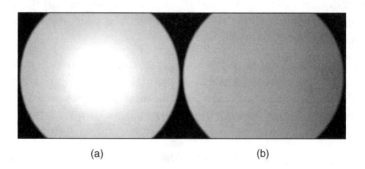

(a)   (b)

What this means from a practical sense is that the more off-angle the lighting, the more you have to increase its intensity to maintain the same apparent level of illumination. This is particularly true if you're trying to achieve an edge-lit effect.

In the real world, light reflecting off an object goes on to illuminate other objects as well—an effect called *radiosity*. The cumulative effect of all the light bouncing off all the objects in an area is called *ambient light*. This ambient light has no discernible source or direction, but acts to illuminate everything in the scene more or less equally.

Another property of light is that it becomes weaker with distance—a phenomenon known as *attenuation*. It occurs because the atmosphere is full of tiny dust and smoke particles that block and reflect light rays. Because of these obstructions, fewer and fewer light waves can continue along their original course as they pass through the atmosphere. Larger particles, such as those in smoke and fog, dramatically increase the effect, whereas attenuation occurs to a much lesser extent in space, because there are far fewer particles to block the light rays.

In some 3D programs, you can set light to be attenuated not only the farther it gets from the source, but the closer it gets as well. Although this violates physical laws, it enables the user to control the level of the light to a much greater degree, preventing objects that are close to the source from being over-illuminated.

3D Lighting Basics

3D programs seek to duplicate the behavior of light in the real world to make 3D scenes appear as natural and realistic as possible. This also helps to make lighting somewhat instinctive, especially if you have any experience with setting up lights for photography work.

Key, Fill, Backlight, and Ambient Lighting

There are three main sources of lighting in a classic photography setup—key, fill, and backlight—and the principles used to light scenes in studios or Hollywood sets carry over into 3D programs as well (see Figure 7.2). To help you understand these lighting types in 3D terms, imagine that you have modeled a scene of your computer desk.

FIGURE 7.2

Typical lighting setup.
(a) Key light, the primary
light source. (b) Fill light,
for illuminating darkened
areas. (c) Backlight, to
make the subject stand
out from the background.
(d) All light sources combined. Ambient light sur-
rounds and illuminates
the entire object.

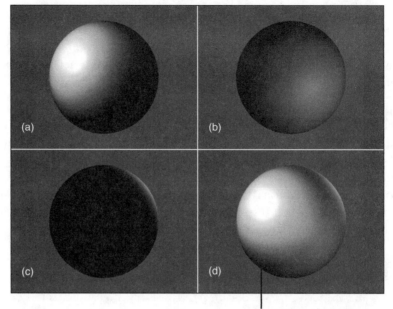

Ambient light from surroundings
illuminates otherwise unlit areas.

The *key light* is the main source of illumination in the scene and casts the most apparent shadows. In an outdoor scene, the key light is the sun. Indoors, it's the primary light source, which might be sunlight coming through a window, a nearby lamp, or a flash on a camera.

In your imaginary desk scene, you can think of the key light as your bright halogen desk lamp, washing across the keyboard and casting sharp shadows.

The *fill light*, as the name implies, fills in the dark shadows cast by the key light. Fill light in an outdoor scene often has to be created artificially, using reflective panels to reflect the sunlight. Indoors, it comes from a secondary source of illumination, like distant windows or light fixtures.

In the desk example, think of the fill light as the big floor lamp sitting on the opposite side of the room, throwing a soft, even illumination out in all directions. This fill light softens the shadows cast by the desk lamp and illuminates the other objects on the desk in a fairly even (but still directional) manner.

The *backlight* is the third major source of light in a scene. It is positioned more or less behind the subject and adjusted to create an edge-lit effect. This helps to separate the foreground subject from the background and make it more three-dimensional. Note that although backlights are commonly used when photographing people, they aren't always necessary, and in many situations a key light and fill light alone will do the job.

In your imaginary example, the backlight comes from a window on the opposite side of the desk from where you're sitting.

Ambient light is not really a light source per se, but is actually the illumination from the key, fill, and backlights bouncing off of walls and other objects and dimly illuminating other objects in a scene. However, unless you are using a 3D product that actually uses computationally intensive radiosity rendering, ambient light is probably simulated in your package; it does this by simply lightening all the objects in the scene by about 10% or so.

In the desk scene, illumination from the key, fill, and backlights would bounce off everything in the room, casting illumination on all objects to some degree, and ensuring that the shadows aren't completely black.

You may recall an ambient setting in the material discussed in Chapter 6, "Texture Mapping." That setting provides a way to create variations on a scene's general ambient light setting on a material-by-material basis.

3D Light Sources

To mimic these three types of lighting, 3D programs offer several light-generating objects or sources. The four main light sources in 3D programs are omni-directional (point) lights, directional (distant) lights, spotlights, and the global ambient light (see Figure 7.3).

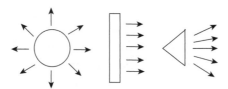

FIGURE 7.3

3D light sources: An omni or point light casts light in all directions, a directional light casts parallel light along a single axis, and a spotlight casts a cone or pyramid of light.

An *omnidirectional light* (or simply *omni light*) casts light in all directions, and is also known as a *point light*. This type of light is generally ideal for simulating any kind of "non-directional" light source, from a bare bulb fixture hanging in an attic to a sun in an outer space scene (see Figure 7.4).

FIGURE 7.4

Omnidirectional light source characteristics: An omni light source positioned in the center of a scene casts light in all directions. Note that some programs' omni light sources may not cast shadows.

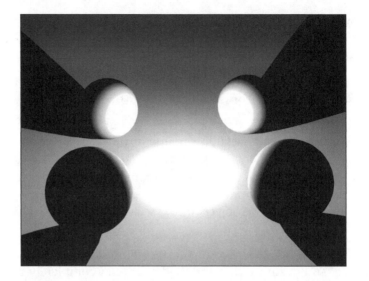

Depending on the program, omni sources may not be capable of casting shadows, which might make them undesirable for use as key lights. In some cases, the light from non-shadow-casting omnis may even pass *through* objects to light their interiors or illuminate other objects behind them. If this is the case, you may want to limit their use to fill light sources, adjusting them to take the edge off the dark areas in the scene. However, one advantage to this capability is that you can place the light inside a completely enclosed object (a model of a light bulb, for example), and the mesh of the glass bulb won't interfere with the light reaching other objects.

Directional lights, also called *distant lights*, project light along one axis only, and all the beams are parallel, not unlike a very wide laser beam. Directional lights are good for simulating sources that are very far away, such as the sun in a terrestrial or space scene. Because the source is so distant, nearly all but the most direct light rays have spread out so much that they no longer fall on the scene. As a result, all the shadows cast by this kind of light are parallel as well (see Figure 7.5).

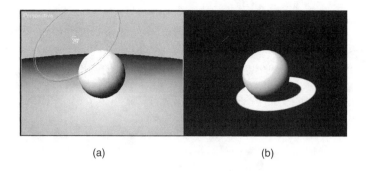

(a)   (b)

FIGURE 7.5

Directional light characteristics: (a) A directional light source, which casts parallel light rays, aimed down a sphere. (b) The resulting shadow from a directional light source.

Spotlights are directional as well, but they radiate light from a single point out into a cone or pyramid shape, the size of which the user can define. As a result, neither the light rays nor shadows are parallel, as they are with a directional light source (see Figure 7.6). Sometimes spotlights have a target connected to the source that indicates the direction in which the beam is pointed.

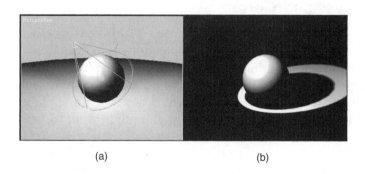

(a)   (b)

FIGURE 7.6

Spotlight characteristics: (a) A spotlight source projects a cone of light at a sphere. (b) Shadows created by a spotlight radiate away from the source.

"Spots" can be used in just about any lighting situation, and can even be used to simulate shadow-casting omnis in programs that don't offer them (see the Lighting Tips section later in the chapter). You can use them as substitutes for directional lights in 3D programs that lack those sources by setting them far from the objects in the scene. In addition, they're great for adding small highlights and accent lighting, as well as adding drama and realism to just about any scene.

Lighting Controls and Effects

Nearly all 3D software offers a standard set of controls for light sources, including intensity, color, and shadow settings. Some programs may provide additional controls as well, including include and exclude lists, attenuation, projection mapping, and so forth.

Brightness and Color

Intensity sets the brightness level of the source. Although some programs may limit a light's range of brightness settings from a 000 black to a 255 white, others allow nearly infinite settings by providing a *multiplier* setting to increase the *apparent* brightness past that point. Note that in an RGB image, you can't get any brighter than a 255 white; however, the application can use multiplier values to determine how a brighter light would affect the objects in the scene, and that result is what you'll see on the screen.

Cranking up the multiplier setting is a good way to "blow out" the highlights on an object, or give a scene the over-exposed appearance of being lit by a blinding light source.

As noted at the beginning of the chapter, *attenuation* is the natural reduction of light intensity over a distance. Your program may offer controls for 3D light sources that enable you to define the amount of attenuation and over what distance it occurs. This control can be very useful in scenes with multiple light sources because it enables you to limit light influence to the mesh in its vicinity only.

Some programs offer an *invert light* or *dark light* option, which makes the light source *absorb* light rather than emit it. This kind of light can be used to darken corners or other areas without making multiple adjustments to all other light sources.

You control the *color* of a light source with RGB or HSV sliders in much the same way that you can use them to select material colors. You can tweak the color of light source just a bit to match a natural source, like making it a little bit blue to simulate daylight, reddish to imply a sunset, or make it slightly yellow to give the impression of incandescent lighting. Pushing the saturation of the color up mimics the use of colored plastic *gels* over photography lights. The use of heavily colored lights can give a scene a theatrical flair, complementing the material colors and adding extra interest to lit surfaces. You can also create some interesting effects by blending different colored light sources together.

You'll find more information on using colored lighting in the "Color and Mood" section later in this chapter.

Using complementary colors can add an extra sense of dimension and a dramatic feel to objects, especially if they are somewhat side-lit from opposite angles, so that a shadow runs down the front of the object, keeping the colors separated.

Colored lighting doesn't have to be showy to be effective. By making subtle adjustments to the color balance of a light source, you can simulate the color temperature of an incandescent bulb, a fluorescent tube, or the sun on a hazy day.

definition

complementary colors
Colors that are opposite each other on the artist's (subtractive) color wheel, such as red and green.

Shadows

Two kinds of shadows are commonly available in 3D programs: shadow mapped and ray-traced (see Figure 7.7).

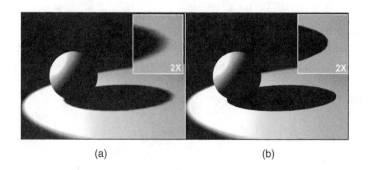

(a)   (b)

FIGURE 7.7

Shadow types:
(a) Shadow mapping produces natural-looking, soft-edged shadows. (b) Ray-traced shadows are sharper and more precise.

Shadow-Mapped Shadows

Shadow mapping is common in non-ray-traced (scanline) renderers. This technique works by creating a grayscale texture map based on the lighting and mesh in the scene, then applying it to the objects at render time. Mapped shadows are soft-edged and more natural than ray-traced ones, but may turn out blocky and inaccurate at times.

You can reduce the blockiness by increasing the *shadow map size* setting, which adjusts the amount of memory that the system can use to create the map. Increasing the size to 512K, 1MB, or more can go a long way toward creating smoother shadows, but this has an impact on render time and memory consumption as well, especially if there are a number of shadow maps that need this kind of resolution (see Figure 7.8).

FIGURE 7.8

Effects of shadow map size: (a) Blockiness and smearing with a 256K map size. (b) Increasing the map size to 1024K reduces the problem but increases render times.

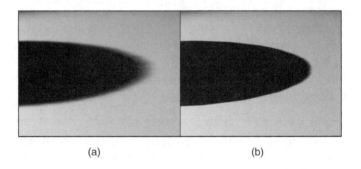

(a)   (b)

Another problem with shadow maps is that they may not be properly positioned in the scene. This most often occurs at the intersection of two objects, and the shadow of one is being cast on the other. In some cases, the shadow may be offset from the mesh intersection. Adjusting the *map bias* setting moves the shadow closer to or farther from the casting object, enabling you to correct this situation.

Finally, shadow maps generally don't take transparency into account; a shadow cast by a transparent or translucent object is usually just as dense as one cast by an opaque object. By the same token, the shadows don't take on the color cast of a translucent object, either. For dealing with these situations, ray-traced shadows are usually a better choice.

Ray-Traced Shadows

Ray-traced shadows are defined using ray-tracing renderer techniques, but can be found in some scanline renderer products. Unlike the results of the soft-edged shadow mapping technique, ray-traced shadows may have a hard edge (depending on your software), but are very accurate and precise. They're great for sharp, dramatic shadows, like those you would find in space or on airless worlds, such as the moon.

Although ray-traced shadows don't use maps, and therefore don't have blockiness problems, they may occasionally suffer from bias troubles like the shadow-mapped variety. Your program may have a *ray-trace bias* adjustment or something similar to adjust the offset of shadows from the casting object.

Generally speaking, you should resort to using ray-traced shadows only if you need the accuracy or are short on RAM. Shadow maps will always render faster than ray-traced shadows.

For an interesting look at how light and shadow are used to great effect in films, I recommended checking out a video called *Visions of Light: The Art of Cinematography* from Image Entertainment. Although many of the examples are from the black & white era, the principles and techniques are just as applicable to color work and 3D.

Hotspot and Falloff

Most spotlights and directional lights have controls that enable you to define the concentration of light in the beam they project. Usually, the adjustments are given in degrees and represented onscreen by two cones or pyramids that show how wide the beams are set (see Figure 7.9).

Spotlight Source   Hotspot Cone   Falloff Cone

FIGURE 7.9

Hotspot and Falloff
settings are often visu-
ally represented by
cones or pyramids.
This aids in positioning
and adjusting the lights
without doing a ton of
test renders.

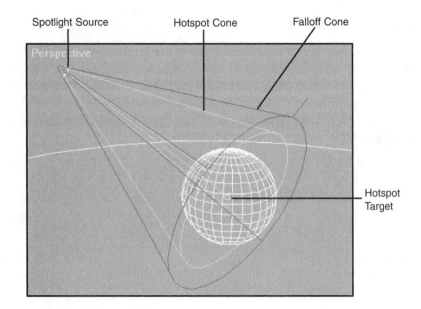

Hotspot
Target

The *Hotspot* adjustment defines the angle of the inner portion of the beam of light that is projected at the current intensity setting for that source. The *Falloff* adjustment sets the perimeter of the outer portion of the beam, indicating the boundary where the intensity has gradually dropped from the hotspot level all the way down to zero.

When the Hotspot and Falloff settings are within a few degrees of each other, the light appears to be sharply focused, with very little transition between full intensity and none at all. When the differences in angles are much larger, the beam looks softer, and tapers off gradually from the bright Hotspot to the edges of the beam (see Figure 7.10).

FIGURE 7.10

Effects of Hotspot and
Falloff sizes: (a) When
Hotspot and Falloff set-
tings are close together,
the beam appears
focused. (b) Widening
the difference between
settings makes the beam
softer and more diffuse-
looking.

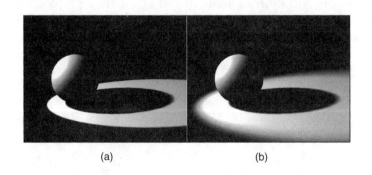

(a)   (b)

Hotspot and Falloff settings enable you to tailor the angle and concentration of the light beams to your needs, so that you can create the effect of a sharply focused flashlight or a more diffuse headlight or hanging warehouse-style light.

Some programs offer settings where a selected object either casts no shadows, receives no shadows, or both. This can be useful if you need to position a light inside an object and in other special circumstances.

Include and Exclude

Some programs enable you to set up lights that affect only certain objects that you identify. There are two ways to do this: *Include* enables you to pick a list of objects that the specified light affects, and *Exclude* is used when you want most of the objects in the scene to be affected, but you want to select a few that should be left out.

Include and Exclude are something of a cheat, because you can't control light that way in the real world. However, because lighting is such a time-consuming process, features like this are great for fine-tuning the look of your scene and achieving difficult effects more easily. Case in point: You've set up a spotlight that creates a perfect highlight on one of the objects in your scene. Unfortunately, the spill light from that spot is shining on many other objects that you don't want illuminated in that way. The solution is to add the desired object to the Include list for that light, so that only that object is affected. You can then light the other objects in the scene with additional lights, and Exclude the first object so it isn't washed out.

Another good example of when to use Include and Exclude is if you were lighting a spacecraft flying past a planet. In real life, the ship would be miniscule compared to the planet, so you would never see the shadow it might cast on the surface. In 3D, however, the scale and distance of the planet is much smaller for practical reasons, so if you lit both with a single light, you might see a large shadow passing over the surface. By excluding the planet from the light being used to illuminate the ship and vice-versa, you can avoid this problem.

Projection Mapping

Some 3D programs enable you to define a spotlight as a *projector*, meaning you can add a map to the light to change its shape or cause it to throw a pattern onto objects it illuminates.

The idea of controlling the shape of light goes back to photography and filmmaking, where steel cutouts called *gobos* are positioned in front of lights. The Bat Signal searchlight used by Gotham City is a good example of a gobo. Gobos also can be used to pattern the light in natural ways, giving the effect that a scene is being lit by dappled sunlight filtered through a tree or shaped by an offscreen window pane. In 3D terms, gobos are called *projection maps*. Unlike steel photographic gobos, however, these maps can be either grayscale patterns or full-color images (see Figure 7.11).

FIGURE 7.11

Projection map samples:
(a) Star-shaped gobo.
(b) Venetian blinds.
(c) Tree branches.
(d) Full-color or grayscale images can also be used.

For example, say you create a map consisting of broad horizontal bands of alternating black and white, and then apply that to a projector. When the projector is positioned to shine on an object, the map creates the illusion that the light source is being filtered through Venetian blinds (see Figure 7.12). If you were to use an imported stock image of a stained glass window as your projection map, the scene will appear to be illuminated like the interior of a church—without you having to go through the bother of creating a stained glass window object and mapping it, and then shining a light source through it.

FIGURE 7.12

A projector light with a gobo consisting of alternating black and white horizontal bands created the effect of sunlight peeking through Venetian blinds in this scene from *Under Cover*. Image by Mondo Media, ©1999 Pulse Interactive, Inc.

Projection maps can have some unusual applications, such as acting as another form of texture map. In *The Daedalus Encounter*, there was a scene where a small ship had smashed into a large alien vessel. We wanted to create skid marks on the alien ship where the craft had slid along the hull, but the procedural texture and the other mapping considerations made that difficult. The artists solved the problem by making a grayscale map of the skid marks and using a projection light source (set to inverted mode) to "shine" the damage onto the hull.

Lighting Strategies

Your lighting needs and procedures will vary depending on the scene you're working on, but there are a few guidelines that can help. In this section, I'll outline my own general approaches to lighting a scene and dissect an example from the Activision CD-ROM game *Zork: Nemesis*.

Default Lighting

Some programs automatically provide *default lighting* in an empty scene, which usually consists of two or three omni or directional lights (shadows off), distributed around the edges of the 3D universe. This enables you to start using shaded modeling modes and doing rendering without having to add a light source (see Figure 7.13). After you do add a light source to the scene, you may want to turn off the default lights. (With some programs, the default lighting is automatically turned off when the user defines a light source.)

FIGURE 7.13

Default lighting usually consists of two or three non-shadow-casting omni or directional lights arranged around the 3D universe.

For most of the modeling process, it's a good idea to stick with default lighting, or to set up 1–3 of your own shadowless omni or directional lights to illuminate the scene. At certain points, you may want to set up some shadow-casting lights to check your work, but in general, using a lot of lights at this phase just slows you down, especially if they have shadows turned on.

Lighting Arrangements

Before discussing adding finished lighting to a scene, this section looks at some common lighting arrangements and the effects they create on the mood of an image (see Figure 7.14).

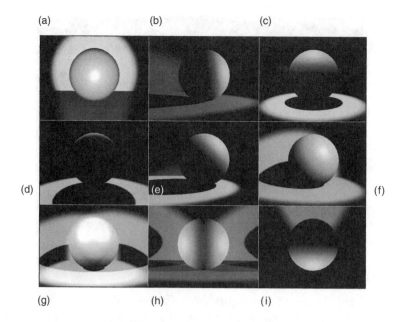

(a) (b) (c)
(d) (e) (f)
(g) (h) (i)

FIGURE 7.14

Sample lighting patterns:
(a) Frontal. (b) 90°
side. (c) Overhead.
(d) Backlight. (e) 45°
side. (f) 45° side/front.
(g) Twin 45° side/front.
(h) Twin 90° side.
(i) Underlight.

As you can see, the quantity and angle of the light has a great deal of impact, and can aid in giving character to an object. For example, *frontal lighting* (as in Figure 7.14a) gives the impression that the viewer is holding the source of light, such as a flashlight, and the unfortunate sphere has just been caught doing something unsavory. The *overhead lighting* in Figure 7.14c makes the sphere seem like an interrogation suspect. *Backlighting* an object, as in Figure 7.14d, makes the object appear mysterious and potentially dangerous. The *dual side lighting* in Figure 7.14h can be very creepy when applied to a face, and the old horror movie standard, *under lighting* (Figure 7.14i), is always sinister.

Lighting Methodology

This section covers the lighting of a very simple scene step-by-step. The scene consists of a few simple geometric primitives, a floor, and back wall, all with the same dull gray material (see Figure 7.15a). Despite the simplicity of this scene, the lighting principles used will be applicable to even the most complex models.

FIGURE 7.15

Even simple scenes benefit from dramatic lighting. (a) The sample scene with default lighting. (b) Add the key light to define the main source of light in the scene, as well as focus the viewer's attention. (c) Fill lights come next, revealing forms lost in shadow. (d) Accent lighting like the wall-washer in back add additional drama.

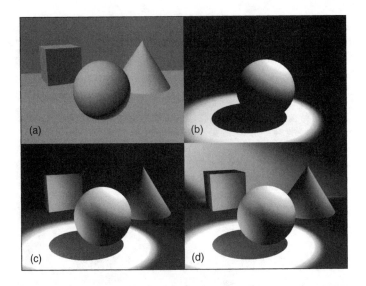

In general, try to use as few lights as possible to illuminate a scene. This makes it faster and easier to light the scene because you aren't dealing with a myriad of lights that are all interacting with each other. If you do need to have a lot of additional lights, make sure you get the core lighting scheme worked out completely first, then add the accent lights later on.

In general, ambient light is set to a very dark gray default and is usually left alone. However, if you're working on a space scene, you may find it beneficial to turn ambient light all the way off, and make the ambient setting in your materials black as well. This, along with ray-traced shadows from a single light source, will help to create the hard-edged lighting and deep shadows of realistic spacecraft.

Shadow-casting spotlights generally make the best key lights, and this is often the light that you set up first, adjusting it to kick up highlights on the object surface as well as create interesting, dramatic shadows. The key light should illuminate the main subject in the scene, or even the entire scene (if it's an exterior shot lit by the sun, for example). The key light is the single most important light source, and all the others should be adjusted to work with it, so take the time to get it just right. In the example scene, the key light is positioned above and to the right of the main subject, the sphere (see Figure 7.15b). The light intensity is set high to create a stage spotlight feeling.

The next step is to add fill light to areas that are too dark at this point, using additional spots or omni fill lights. Because fill lighting is often not represented in the scene by a recognizable light source, you may have to keep the fill light subtle, taking care that it's enhancing the appearance of the scene without drawing attention to itself. You can do this by keeping the intensity setting low, using attenuation to control the range of the lights, using Include/Exclude, and perhaps turning off shadow-casting features as well. That way, the key light shadows remain the primary ones in the scene. (Of course, if the fill light is supposed to be representative of another light source, like a lamp or window, leave the shadows on.) In the sample scene, two attenuated fill lights were added—one to the left of the sphere and one to the right of the cone (see Figure 7.15c). These fill lights illuminate all three objects in the scene, bringing out the form of the cube and cone while softening the dark side of the sphere. Fill light also can be used to backlight objects, giving them more dimension. As you can see in the example, a wall-washing spotlight was added to silhouette the objects against the background and bring out their forms even more clearly (see Figure 7.15d). The wall-washer was set to exclude all objects except the back wall and floor to avoid casting additional light on the cube and cone.

Creative lighting, like the "wall-washing" spotlight in the example, can add substantial kick to an image—don't be afraid to take some artistic license in the way you use them. In other words, don't worry too much about where a light is coming from; as long as it looks good, no one will question it. Lighting also can make good use of Include and Exclude to highlight an object without revealing that there's a light source at work at all, because the surrounding mesh is unaffected.

The final step in the lighting process is to add small accent lights as needed, to represent practical but minor light sources in the scene, such as indicator lamps on a control panel. (Note that it is sometimes possible to use a self-illuminated material rather than a light to keep the number of lights in a scene under control.)

Color and Mood

Careful use of colored lighting can have a powerful impact on the mood of an image. Whereas intense color can lend an almost theatrical effect, subtle color can help to unify a scene and push it gently toward either an energetic or languid feeling.

For example, cool colors such as blues and violets tend to evoke evening, stillness, and calm. Warm colors such as yellow, red, and orange are fiery and energetic, and generally make an image feel more intense and active.

You can combine warm and cool colors in a single scene to lead the viewer's eye and imbue the subjects illuminated by them with extra emotional punch. For example, imagine a scene in which a blacksmith is working at night near an open fire. The village around him is clad in a bluish mist, calm and relaxed. A few warm lights in the windows indicate activity in an otherwise quiet little town. The blacksmith himself, however, is bathed in the warm colors of the fire, which helps to underscore his power and vitality as he works with the hot metal. Because he's surrounded by cool colors, the warm colors illuminating him seem all that more intense.

As you work to develop your own lighting schemes, think about where color can be used to add additional impact. Be careful, though—even relatively subtle colors can really change the look of a material, and you may find the carefully crafted colors and textures of your subjects becoming muddied by colored lighting.

Lighting Case Study

While working on 3D models for Mondo Media's share of Activision's *Zork:Nemesis* artwork, I was given the task of building and lighting the Asylum Catwalk area. The Asylum is a roughly cylindrical structure more than 20 floors high, with an elevator running up along the open central core (see Figure 7.16). Because the Asylum was the location where all kinds of sinister research and experiments were conducted, the structure was to have a cold, hard, oppressive feeling.

FIGURE 7.16

The Asylum Catwalk area from *Zork:Nemesis*. Image by Mark Giambruno and Laura Hainke/Mondo Media ©1996 Activision.

For speed and ease of modification, I built the mesh in a modular fashion, with each of the three modules consisting of a wall section and a floor section. There were three kinds of walls: a plain one, one with a door, and one with an elevator shaft. All the floor sections were the same except for the one with the elevator, and included the circular railing. Each module also had one physical floor-to-ceiling light fixture.

All the lighting was worked out with only these three modules in the scene, and much of it was refined using only one module to keep test rendering times low. After the lighting design was completed, the modules and lights were duplicated and positioned as instanced objects.

My first concern in lighting the scene was to enhance the overall sinister mood of the place by using underlighting. I positioned a large spotlight, pointing up, in the center of the open area below the floor. I adjusted it to cast interesting shadows from the railing onto the walls, which helped break up the otherwise plain mesh. Because ray-traced shadows were too overpowering and hard-edged for the scene, I used shadow mapping. I made the map size fairly large, between 1–2MB, to keep the shadows from being too blocky.

The next step was to set up the lighting for the practical light fixtures that lined the walls. To give the impression that the fixtures were glowing, I placed omni lights with limited ranges just in front of the white tubes to wash out the edges of the fixtures and throw some light on the walls. To complete the effect, I set up spotlights above the railing and pointed them *toward the fixtures* to create a halo of light around the practical lights, including the ceiling and floor. Next, I used omni lights to illuminate the areas around the small elevator light fixtures.

The final step in lighting the scene was to set an omni light in the center of the open area, just above the floating sphere. I adjusted this to provide fill light to illuminate the dark portions of the scene so that some detail could be seen.

After completing the mapping, Laura Hainke instanced the mesh and lights from the three modules, so that the scene would appear to be of an enclosed, multi-floor structure.

The catwalk scene is a good example of how you can take liberties in designing your lighting. There is no way the practical lights in the scene would create the shadows on the walls the way the key spotlighting does, but because the result looks good, no one worries about that.

Lighting Tips and Tricks

The following sections offer a few suggestions for achieving certain effects, or working around limitations in your software.

Shadowless Omni Workarounds

The problem is as follows: You have a scene that's supposed to be lit by one or more omnidirectional lights. You want dramatic shadows in the scene, but your program doesn't offer them for point light sources. The solution is this: Arrange two or more shadow-casting spotlights in the same position where the omni would be located, but facing in opposite directions.

Use pyramids rather than cones to minimize overlapping, and keep the difference between the Hotspot and Falloff as small as possible for maximum evenness in the light distribution. Remember that the shadows may start to look strange if the Hotspots are set too wide, so you may need to use several lights to simulate an omni, not just two.

Faking Radiosity

Radiosity—the coloring and illumination of objects by light reflecting off of other objects—can be simulated to some extent by careful use of attenuated lights set to affect only certain objects. For example, say you have a bright red cube next to a white wall. In a radiosity render, some of the light striking the red cube would fall on the wall, creating a pink cast in the vicinity of the cube. You could fake this effect in a regular scanline renderer by adding an attenuated red or pink light that affected only the wall, and adjust it to get a similar casting effect.

Visible Lights

Although light source objects are generally invisible in the finished renders, there are times when you may want the light to *appear* to be visible.

For example, if you were doing a render of a room lit by a bare bulb, you would want the bulb to appear to be glowing. Although making the bulb object itself self-illuminated and placing the light source near it (or even inside it) will help, it still may not create the desired effect. To accomplish that, you can take one of three courses of action: First, apply a post-production glow effect to the bulb object (discussed in more detail in Chapter 10, "Rendering and Output"). Second, retouch the finished render by using an airbrush tool to spray white (or the appropriate color) over the vicinity of the bulb, making it appear to glow. Third, you could use volumetric lighting (if your program offers it).

As the name implies, *volumetric lights* have an adjustable 3D volume associated with them that can be made to simulate the behavior of natural light in an atmosphere. In other words, volumetric lights act as though the enclosed volume were filled with a mist or fog, and diffuse the light inside accordingly. Volumetric lights can be used to create the look of shafts of light in a dusty attic, or the headlights of a car in the fog (see Figure 7.17).

FIGURE 7.17

Volumetric lights have an adjustable 3D volume that can simulate the effect of the beam shining through mist or smoke.

Some programs offer visible light cones for spotlights that simulate volumetric lights. In addition, you can simulate visible cones by using translucent mesh. Simply make a cone of the proper diameter to fit the light fixture, and then widen it to the desired diameter at the far end. The following are the material setting suggestions:

Color: Adjust to approximate the color of the source

Self-Illumination: Maximum

Transparency Level: 75 95%

Transparency Type: Additive

Transparency Falloff: Inward

If possible, have the cone extend beyond any mesh in the room, so you never see the far end of it. If this isn't feasible, make the cone the maximum desired length and use a opacity map to make it fade out at the far end. This technique was used for the spotlights on the generic version of the tutorial blimp in Chapter 6, "Texture Mapping."

Lighting Tutorials

Topics covered:

Using Directional Lights

Using Spotlights

Using Point Lights

So far, we've been using default lighting or work lights for the modeling and mapping processes. Although these are good for general illumination, they lack the drama needed for a strong portfolio piece (see Figure 7.18).

FIGURE 7.18

Default lighting works well for construction purposes, but lacks the drama that can be achieved with shadow-casting lights.

Using Directional Lights

Because this is a night scene, it makes sense to make the key light in the scene shine up from the ground, as though it were coming from floodlights or a city.

1. Create a large, shadow-casting directional light with a radius of about 1600 units or more to encompass the blimp. Make the color a 255, 255, 255 white with a multiplier of 1. The hotspot limits should be as close as possible to the falloff perimeter (see Figure 7.19a).

2. Move the light under the blimp and rotate it to shine upward at a 15-degree angle, setting it off to the side of the blimp to illuminate more of the subject (see Figure 7.19b).

3. Mirror the light as an instance, moving the copy to the opposite side of the blimp (see Figure 7.19c).

4. Render the scene and adjust the lighting parameters to achieve a satisfactory level of illumination (see Figure 7.19d). Note how the suspended mesh casts interesting shadows on the skin of the blimp.

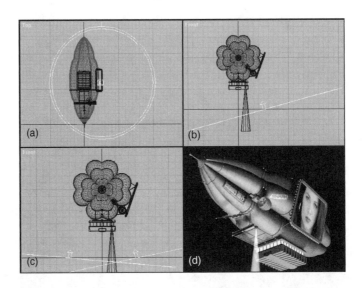

Using Spotlights

Next, we'll create some rotating beacons (like the ones on police cars) to add some additional light and motion to the ship.

1. Create a simple "bubble gum machine" beacon with a cylinder for the base and a hemisphere for the glass portion, located under one of the BagRng objects to which the thruster assembly is attached. Use face extrusion to stretch the flat part of the hemisphere to meet the cylindrical base. Set both objects to be non-shadow casting in the object properties section of your software (see Figure 7.20a–b).

2. Apply the Rust material to the base, and create a new material called YellowLite for the glass part. Make it a 255, 255, 0 bright yellow with Self-Illumination at 100%.

3. Create a free spotlight in the center of the light fixture suspended under the blimp. If your software doesn't offer free spotlights, use a targeted spot with the target a short distance from the source. Adjust

the beam to be shadow-casting, and have a hotspot of 65° and a falloff of 80°. Make the beam a 255, 255, 0 bright yellow, with a brightness multiplier of 2. Mirror-instance the spotlight and position the duplicate to face the opposite direction (see Figure 7.20c).

4.   Render the area around the light and check the results. You may need to experiment a bit to get the results you want (see Figure 7.20d).

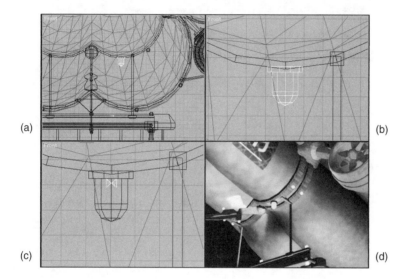

(a)

(b)

(c)

(d)

FIGURE 7.20

Creating the rotating beacons: (a–b) Build and position the beacon mesh. (c) Create two spotlights facing in opposite directions. (d) Render the result.

Using Point Lights

Although either point lights or spotlights could be used for this application, we'll use a point light with attenuation just so you can try it out.

1.   Copy the mesh from the beacon you just built (but not the lights) and position it on the end of the gondola. You may want to scale it up a bit (see Figure 7.21a–b). Create a new material called RedLite with a color of 255, 0, 0 and a Self-illumination of 100. Apply it to the beacon dome portion of the fixture.

2.   Create a point light in the center of the light fixture. Adjust the light to have a bright red 255, 0, 0 color, with a multiplier of 2. Enable attenuation and set the ranges to 70 units for the hotspot and 160 units for the falloff (see Figure 7.21c).

3.   Render the result (see Figure 7.21d).

FIGURE 7.21

Using an attenuated
point light: (a–b) Copy
the beacon mesh and
place it on the gondola.
(c) Add an attenuated
point light to cast a controlled pool of light
around the beacon.
(d) Render the results.

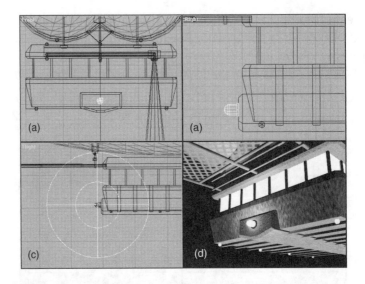

If your software has non-shadow casting omnis (like 3D Studio R4 DOS), you might see illumination on objects where the light shouldn't be shining, such as the fins under the gondola. In this case, you can use Exclude so that the light doesn't affect those objects.

Summary

In the course of this chapter, you've looked at the principles of light in the real world and how they apply to the 3D environment. You've examined the kinds of light sources and controls available in the virtual world, and seen some of the differences (and even advantages) that 3D light sources have, such as Include and Exclude. You also saw the different sorts of shadow creation methods and how to adjust them, went over lighting approaches, and got some tips on creating certain effects or simulating real-world lighting as well.

In the next chapter, you will see how the camera's position and focal length settings can further increase the drama in a 3D scene. You'll also see how to use the camera for storytelling purposes, based on the principles developed by filmmakers over many decades.

CHAPTER 8

The Camera

Proper positioning of the camera is essential for creating an interesting composition as well as bringing out detail. Image ©2002 Stefan M. Schmidt.

*T*he old man settled in heavily next to the student, who had been working diligently all afternoon. "You have something to show me?"

"Yes," the student replied. "I've been setting up recording lenses around the castle model to show off the work. Here, take a look at these."

The Master watched as a series of images appeared above the Glowing Pool, showing the model from different locations. After the tenth slide, the old man cleared his throat and spoke. "Lad, all these views seem to be facing dead center on the subject, and are set so far back that I can see the whole castle."

"Well, yes. I want the viewer to be able to see the whole castle, and I positioned the lenses so they wouldn't cause too much distortion."

"That might be fine if you were taking real estate photos," sighed the conjurer. "But in drama, lad, distortion is an ally."

"Huh?"

"Here, allow me to demonstrate." The Master selected a view that faced the front of the castle. "Lowbahl Spiekamm," he muttered, and the eerily floating lens shot down to just above ground level and raced toward the castle drawbridge, coming to a halt near the heavy chain that raises it. The Master tweaked the lens slightly, tilting it to face upward a bit.

"Wow," remarked the student, marveling at the way the lens angle made the castle seem to loom above them. "It looks so huge and imposing now."

"Aeroflot Fysheye," intoned the old man, sending the lens soaring high above the virtual landscape. He directed it downward and widened the field of view so that the castle seemed to reach up at them from a broad, peaceful valley.

"A dragon's-eye view..." the student said, "Hey, that gives me an idea."

"Good. I've made my point, then." The Master rose. "Don't be afraid to try unique angles, and it isn't necessary to show the whole subject, just what counts."

"Right!" said the lad. "I'm going to do the whole animation in super wide perspective, from really bizarre angles. It'll be so cool."

"Maylockx Alkiselltzer," groaned the old man, rubbing his stomach and heading for the medicine chest.

Camera Basics

It would seem that our student is either headed for a totally incomprehensible animation, or is laying the foundation for the first medieval music video. Either way, the camera represents the viewer's perspective on the virtual world, and is a key tool in the process of *visual storytelling*.

This chapter focuses on camera terminology and techniques, and looks at how the storytelling language developed by filmmakers relies on using the right camera locations to get the point across most effectively.

Chapter 2, "Delving into Cyberspace," discussed different viewpoints on the scene, and you've probably been using most of the common orthographic ones (front, back, left, right, top, bottom) for constructing your models. As you recall, these types of viewports are axonometric, meaning that all parallel lines remain parallel regardless of how the viewpoint changes. With camera views, however, the perspective tries to duplicate that of the natural world, where parallel lines eventually converge into vanishing points. The photographic term for the contents of a viewport (in other words, the visible portion of the scene) is the *frame*.

Virtual cameras duplicate the functions and controls of their real-world counterparts, while adding some special features of their own. One of the most common 3D camera controls with a direct relationship to real photo gear is the focal length setting.

Focal Length

In real cameras, *focal length* is the distance from the center of the lens to the image it forms of the subject on the film (or photo-electronic sensor in a digital camera). The normal focal length of a typical camera is around 50mm, which is similar to that of the human eye. This is why a 50mm lens is also referred to as a *normal lens*, because it sees the world more or less the way a typical human eye does.

There is a direct relationship between focal length and *field of view (FOV)*, which is the angle that encompasses everything that can be seen through a lens with a given focal length. The typical FOV for a 50mm lens is 40° (see Figure 8.1).

FIGURE 8.1

Focal length has a direct affect on the field of view. As the focal length is reduced, the FOV is widened.

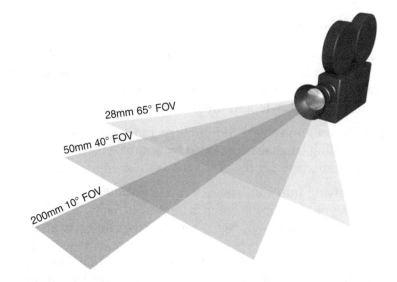

When the focal length of a lens is changed, the field of view changes by an inversely proportional amount. For example, if you reduce the focal length of a lens to 28mm, the FOV widens to 65°. This is why lenses from 20–35mm are commonly called *wide-angle lenses*. By the same token, if the focal length is increased to 200mm, the field of view drops to 10°. Lenses with 85mm and longer focal lengths are referred to as *long lenses* or *telephoto lenses*.

With all this discussion of real-world cameras and millimeters, bear in mind that film sizes, like 35mm, are a related but separate subject that has more to do with the final image output settings. This is discussed further in Chapter 10, "Rendering and Output."

At one time, photographers had to have many different lenses available for their cameras to properly shoot a variety of subjects, from a broad vista to a distant animal. As optics became more sophisticated, however, the *zoom lens* was developed, enabling photographers to adjust the lens over a broad range of focal lengths. These days, photographers can usually get by with just two lenses: a 35–80mm zoom and a 80–200mm zoom. These modern lenses often have a *macro lens* setting as well, which enables the user to take extreme close-ups, as though they were using a low-powered microscope.

In the virtual world, focal length is calculated by mathematical formulas, so users can define just about any focal length they want for a given camera. However, real-world cameras are still used as a reference, so many programs offer a standard array of focal lengths in addition to allowing you to type in your own settings (see Figure 8.2). Note that there is no need to include the equivalent of a macro setting, because virtual cameras can be placed very close to the subject to achieve that effect.

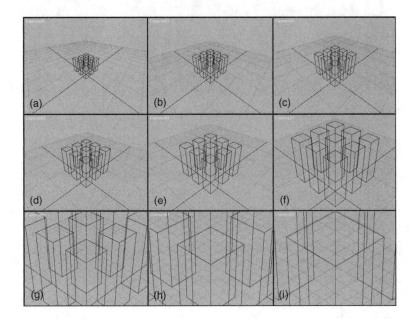

FIGURE 8.2

Sample focal lengths:
(a) 15mm (b) 20mm
(c) 24mm (d) 28mm
(e) 35mm (f) 50mm
(g) 85mm (h) 135mm
(i) 200mm.

As you can see, in addition to adjusting the size of the subject, the wide lens settings have a tendency to exaggerate the perspective in a scene, whereas the longer lenses reduce it. As a result, wide-angle lenses often impart a feeling of massiveness to a subject, whereas telephoto lenses are used to flatten scenes, compressing them so that distant objects seem like they're closer together.

Focus and Aperture

Of course, focal length isn't the only setting on a lens. In fact, the most commonly used control on manual cameras is the focus adjustment. *Focus* adjusts the optics in the camera so that the subject is sharp and clear. However, focus is not object-specific—it is a range, a set of near and far distance figures called *depth of field* (see Figure 8.3). Depending on the lens settings, the depth of field may be narrow, with only objects within a few inches of the focus point being clear, or wide (like many fixed-focus cameras), in which everything from a few feet away to infinity is sharp and clear.

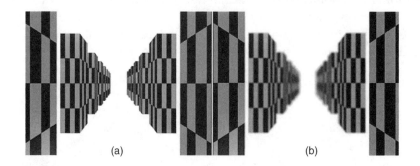

(a)   (b)

The *aperture* of the camera is a variable opening inside the lens that works like the iris in your own eye. When the aperture is wide open, the maximum amount of light is admitted. When it's closed to a pinpoint, very little light passes through. In camera terms, the different aperture settings are called *f-stops* and often range from around f1.2 (open) to f16 (nearly closed). Although controlling the amount of light reaching the film is one application of the aperture, an aperture also controls the depth of field by filtering out many of the more oblique light rays coming from the object. To demonstrate, try this simple experiment.

Close one eye; hold your left hand upright at arm's length from your face, and focus on it. Notice that everything beyond your hand is blurred, because the current depth of field of your eye is fairly narrow. Next, make a circle using the index finger and thumb of your right hand, tightening it so that only a pinpoint of light shines through (something like an overtorqued "OK" gesture). Focus again on your outstretched left hand, then place your circled finger and thumb directly in front of your eye so that you are looking through the "pinhole." Both your hand and the background should appear much more in focus, because you have done the equivalent of closing down the aperture in a camera.

In many 3D programs, there are no focus or depth of field controls, because everything in the scene is calculated mathematically and is equally sharp. Although this may be an advantage in many cases, it has the unfortunate side effect of making the imagery look unrealistic as well, because we *expect* certain things to be blurred; after all, that's how we ourselves perceive the world. Fortunately, more and more packages now have features that enable them to simulate depth of field either at render time or as a post-production effect, moving CG one step closer to photorealism.

Camera Movement

When it comes to movement, virtual cameras have a massive advantage over their real-world counterparts. In 3D space, cameras are free to move anywhere in the scene, even *inside* objects. In addition, multiple cameras can be defined, allowing the action to be viewed from several angles at the same time.

Clipping Planes and Targets

Another unique capability of virtual cameras is their *clipping plane*—the user-definable cut-off point that makes everything on the camera's side of it invisible during rendering. Although this isn't normally adjusted, there are instances where extending the clipping plane away from the camera can be useful. For example, manipulating the clipping plane enables you to create the illusion that objects are being carved away by an unseen force, revealing their interiors, as might be done with an anatomical animation.

Depending on your program, the virtual camera offered may come in *free* or *target* styles, just like lights. The target is a small cube or other indicator that enables you to see exactly where the camera is pointed from any other viewpoint, making it faster and easier to position. Cameras that don't have targets tend to provide smoother animation results in situations where the camera is being moved along a path.

Camera Moves

In addition to mimicking 35mm cameras, virtual cameras can imitate their motion picture and video counterparts as well. Although most of the following moves require a real camera to be mounted on a tripod or dolly (a wheeled platform), there are no such restrictions for virtual cameras, even though they can be moved in exactly the same manner.

Pan and Tilt

Two of the most common moves in filmmaking are pan and tilt. A *pan* is a horizontal rotation of the camera from right to left or vice-versa (see Figure 8.4). A pan is often used to move the camera from one subject to another or to see more of a landscape than will fit in the frame.

FIGURE 8.4

Pan and tilt camera movements: (a) A pan is a horizontal rotation of the camera. (b) A tilt is a vertical rotation of the camera.

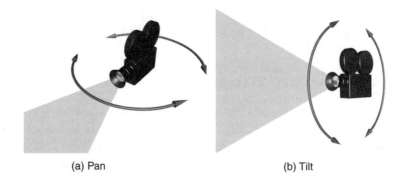

(a) Pan   (b) Tilt

In motion pictures, a *swish pan* is a type of pan that moves the camera so quickly that it blurs the scene completely. If you try this with the default settings in your 3D program, it probably won't work. You need to use the motion blur option in the software, and you may even need to do some additional post-production work with Photoshop's motion blur filter to duplicate the effect.

A *tilt* is the vertical equivalent of a pan, rotating the camera up or down. Tilts are often used to showcase tall objects, such as buildings, but also may be used on a character to give the impression that the viewer is sizing them up.

Tracking and Dollying

Dolly and track are two terms that seem to get confused or overlap, depending on which reference or program you use. I'll distinctly separate them in this text to avoid confusion.

A *dolly* is a wheeled platform on which a camera is mounted. The terms *dolly* or *truck* can also serve as verbs, and refer to moving the camera around on the floor during the shot to get closer or further from the action, or to view it from a different side (see figure 8.5). In 3D terms, the Dolly command usually moves the virtual camera toward, away from, or around the subject.

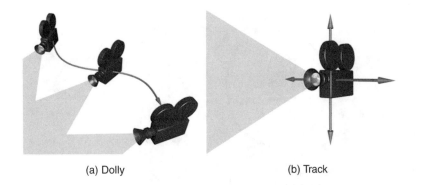

(a) Dolly   (b) Track

FIGURE 8.5

Dolly (truck) and track camera movements: (a) Dolly moves the camera around, usually on the same "floor plane" as the subject. (b) Track moves the camera horizontally or vertically.

Occasionally, you'll see an effect in which the room appears to close in around a character, usually to indicate that the character feels suddenly claustrophobic or in danger. This effect is created by dollying the camera away from the subject, while simultaneously zooming the lens to keep the subject the same size in the frame. This can be accomplished in 3D programs by using the same technique.

In filmmaking, a dolly is sometimes mounted onto a steel track, allowing the camera to move smoothly along a predefined path. Therefore, *track* usually refers to movement of the camera along a single axis, be it horizontal or vertical. The Track command in 3D programs normally keeps the camera the same distance from the subject, but moves it left or right (along the X-axis) or up and down (along the Y-axis).

Bank and Roll

In the real world, banks and rolls are difficult movements to do unless the camera is hand-held or mounted in a motion control rig; on the other hand, virtual cameras handle these moves with ease. *Roll* means to rotate the camera around its viewing axis, making the scene appear to spin (see Figure 8.6). *Bank* is simply an automatic roll that some programs do to the camera when it moves through a curve along a camera path. Creating the illusion that you're flying in a plane or tumbling out of control are two of the most popular uses for bank and roll.

FIGURE 8.6

Roll and bank camera movements: (a) Roll is the rotation of the camera around the viewing axis. (b) Bank is an automatic roll applied to cameras moving along a curved path.

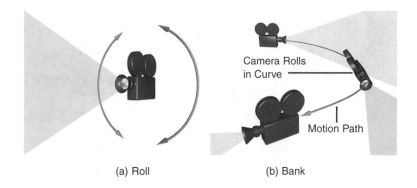

(a) Roll (b) Bank

Camera Rolls in Curve

Motion Path

There can be a problem when the camera and target become nearly aligned along a certain axis (usually Y), as when you are trying to set up an overhead view of an object. As the alignment comes closer to vertical, the camera may begin to roll dramatically, trying to position itself to be at the opposite angle after it crosses over the axis. This condition is called *gimbal lock*, and will be discussed in more detail in Chapter 9, "Animation." For now, one way around this problem is to simply avoid these situations by keeping your camera target offset from near-vertical.

Directing the Camera

In filmmaking, skillful use of the camera adds tremendously to a scene's composition and storytelling potential. Following some basic principles that were developed in the motion picture industry, you can add similar drama to your 3D animations. The ones noted here are just a start—Chapter 11, "The Reel," expands on these principles.

In the early days of filmmaking, movies looked more like a stage play—the camera was locked down, and the actors walked in and out of the frame. The camera was usually somewhat distant from the action, because directors wanted to be sure the actor's entire body was visible at all times. At the time, it was felt that if only an actor's head were shown, the audience would feel as though it had been chopped off. Tired of this staid look, pioneering director D. W. Griffith (*The Birth of a Nation, Intolerance*) reinvented storytelling for the new medium, providing the basis for the principles and techniques known as *film grammar*.

Viewpoints

One of the precepts of film grammar is that the camera should be treated as an observer—generally unseen—that is able to move to whatever angle best suits the message or image the director is trying to convey. Although the principles of good composition go back centuries (and are completely applicable to filmmaking), the variety of lenses and newness of the media encouraged more experimentation with viewpoints, resulting in unorthodox but effective results.

An example of this is the *bird's-eye view* or *high-angle view*, where the subject is seen from an elevated perspective. This type of shot is good for establishing the local environment, because it gives the viewer a commanding view of the surroundings (see Figure 8.7). A variation on this is the *overhead view*, where the viewer is directly above the subject. This can be useful in situations where the character feels like a rat trapped in a maze, or for creating the feeling that his every movement is being watched.

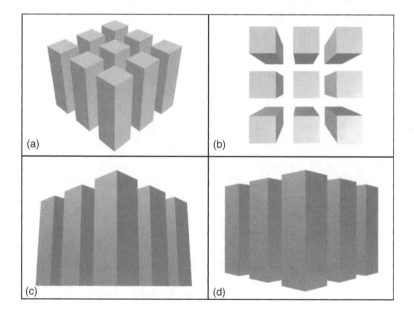

(a)

(b)

(c)

(d)

FIGURE 8.7

Camera viewpoint examples:
(a) Bird's-eye view.
(b) Overhead view.
(c) Worm's-eye view.
(d) Conventional view.

The *worm's-eye view* or *low-angle view*, in which the camera is positioned just above the ground plane, is popular for giving the subject mass and weight. It is often used to create a sense of foreboding about a location, or to make the subject look more intimidating.

Other angles popular for depicting people are the *head shot*, or *close-up*, where only the head and shoulders of the subject are in view; the *profile shot*, where the subject is shown from the side; the *waist shot*, where the subject is framed from the waist up; and the *knee shot*, where the subject is seen from the knees down, usually to disguise their identity or actions.

A *point-of-view (POV) shot* is one that is seen through the eyes of one of the characters in a film, and commonly used in horror films to convey the killer's actions without revealing the identity. A POV shot isn't limited to a human character, however. Any character can have a POV—even inanimate objects, especially if they've been established to be doing something active at the time (like a missile flying through the air, for example).

When two characters are together in the frame, it's called a *two-shot*. One popular framing for the two-shot is the *over-the-shoulder shot*, used when the director wants to focus on one of the subjects, but still have a shoulder or other portion of the other character in the frame. If using the shoulder is inconvenient, just about any shot that includes an identifiable portion of the second character's body will work.

Earlier in the chapter, you learned about focal length and its affect on the field of view. It's important to note that a wide shot means that you can see all of the subject(s) and a good part of the environment, but doesn't require the actual use of a *wide lens*.

One problem I've seen in a lot of student 3D animation is a failure to use the camera to provide drama, usually because it's improperly placed. When setting up the cameras for your work, take the time to experiment with positioning and focal length. Don't be afraid to try an unusual angle, or feel that you have to show the whole subject in every shot.

The Line of Action

This section examines another element of film grammar relating to scene continuity. During the course of making a film, where scenes may be shot many times from different angles to be edited together later, it's important to maintain *continuity*, so that the action doesn't suddenly appear to reverse from what the viewer expects to see. The *line of action* is an imaginary partition running though the scene, often following the path of the subject, or set up between two characters having an exchange (see Figure 8.8).

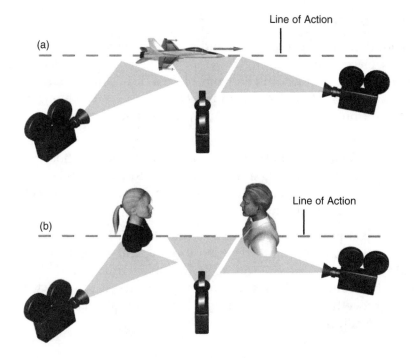

FIGURE 8.8

The line of action:
(a) The line may run
along a character's
path, or (b) connect
two characters having
an exchange.

The idea behind the line of action is that a character facing to the right in a scene should continue to face to the right, and not suddenly appear to be facing left because a shot from a camera on the opposite side is inserted. To prevent this sort of jarring switch, the camera should remain on one side of the line, except under certain circumstances.

But what if you need a cut from the other side of the line to show something that isn't visible from the current side, or to prevent a scene from appearing too monotonous? In general, if you want a camera to move over the line in anything other than a dolly move, you should bridge the line by having a shot where the camera is pointed in the same direction as the line, and is as close to crossing it as possible. At that point, you can then add shots from the opposite side of the line.

If you take continuity issues into consideration when setting up your cameras and doing the animation, it will help prevent problems in the editing process (see Chapter 11 for more information).

Tips and Tricks

Depending on how you position and use the camera, you create a mood for your piece, just as lighting does. For example, oddly angled close-ups with wide lens settings can give your piece a disturbing, paranoid sort of feeling. Smooth, elegant dolly and track shots give the impression of a Hollywood production, whereas shaky, rapid camera moves can create a documentary feeling.

Speaking of shaky camera shots, you can pull them off without too much extra keyframing by adding a noise controller to your camera and its target. You'll have to experiment a bit to get something that feels right. Turning on motion blur may also help the effect.

However you position your camera, always look for ways to add a bit of drama to the composition through positioning and movement. This helps to add additional interest and keep the shots fresh for the audience. Finally, be cautious of how you move the camera—it can affect how the shots cut together in the editing stage. Take a look at Chapter 11 for information on editing.

Many programs now have built-in or add-on motion tracking capabilities that enable you to add 3D elements to live action video sequences, just as ILM added 3D dinosaurs to match footage of the actors in *Jurrasic Park*. Generally, the tracking is accomplished by identifying some objects or markers in the live action footage and using them to calculate the position, angle, and FOV of a virtual camera that moves just like the original one. By using this motion-tracked camera to record 3D objects and animation, you can create new elements that can be composited on top of the live action footage.

Camera Tutorials

Topics covered:

Setting the Master Shot

Camera Positioning Tips

Continuing with the blimp project, this section provides guidance for setting up some cameras for still images and the animation to follow. Use the principles laid down in this chapter and your own sense of cinematic drama to find your own angle on the subject.

Setting the Master Shot

Here, the primary concern is to find dramatic angles and focal lengths to be used later for stills or animation. The first camera is set up to provide an overall perspective on the scene, also called a *master shot* in the filmmaking biz.

1. In the Top view, set up a 50mm camera to the right of the blimp, setting the camera target near the center of the ship (see Figure 8.9a).

2. In the Front or Right view, adjust the camera to be below the blimp (see Figure 8.9b–c).

3. In the Camera view, use the Dolly, Pan, and Track controls so that the blimp nearly touches the edges of the frame. It's fine for the searchlights to extend past, however (see Figure 8.9d).

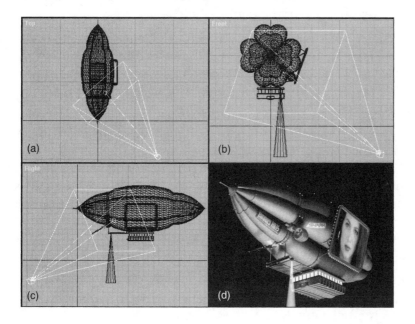

FIGURE 8.9

If you place the camera well below the blimp and use a normal (50mm) lens, the perspective and viewpoint resembles that of a person watching the aircraft from the ground.

Experimenting with Camera Positions

 This particular tutorial is more of a self-study module, and is intended as a jumping-off point for developing your own compositions with the blimp.

Camera positioning is an experimental process, and some surprising results can come from messing around and trying odd angles. In general, set up your camera in the Top or Side views to set the general location, then refine the angle and focal length in the Camera viewport, using the Dolly, Track, and Pan controls.

1. Set up a 50mm camera in front of and below the blimp (see Figure 8.10a). Although this position doesn't work that well for a still, it has potential for an animation, where the blimp would slide along very close to the camera. You can simulate the effect by dollying the camera along the side of the blimp.

2. Set up another camera with a 35mm focal length closer to the blimp, more focused on the gondola (see Figure 8.10b). This angle works for either a still or animation. The camera has a moderately wide field of view, and this position shows most of the elements on the underside of the blimp in a dramatic perspective.

3. Try another camera pointing up at the underside of the blimp, and positioned so that the nose is pointed toward the bottom of the screen (see Figure 8.10c). This one is a disaster, literally. It looks like the blimp is about to plummet into the ground, and the angle is much too orthogonal, because the camera is positioned almost directly under the blimp. This might still work for an animation, though, if the camera rolled a bit during the shot.

4. By changing the position of the last camera slightly, making the image roll around a bit, a good worm's-eye view of the blimp can be achieved (see Figure 8.10d). Now that the blimp is pointing upward, it feels more natural.

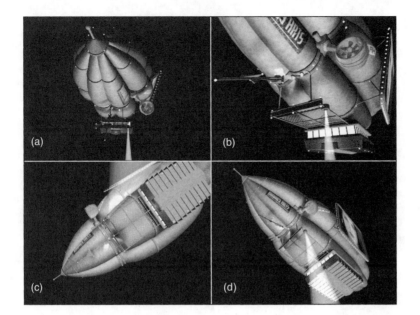

FIGURE 8.10

Four different angles on the blimp. (a) This shot could be dramatic, but much of the blimp is obscured. (b) A better angle for the approach. (c) *The Hindenburg*, Pt. II. (d) A better worm's-eye view of the craft.

Summary

This chapter began with a look at camera terminology, comparing virtual cameras to their real-world counterparts, then applied that analogy to camera movement as well. It also looked at how the camera influences the storytelling process through angles and continuity devices such as the line of action. Proper usage of the camera will help you create dramatic stills and set up the best viewpoints from which to render your animation.

The next chapter, "Animation," takes the storytelling process a big step forward by turning objects into performers. There, you'll see how the objects, lights, and cameras come together to create the visual message that you want to convey.

CHAPTER 9

Animation

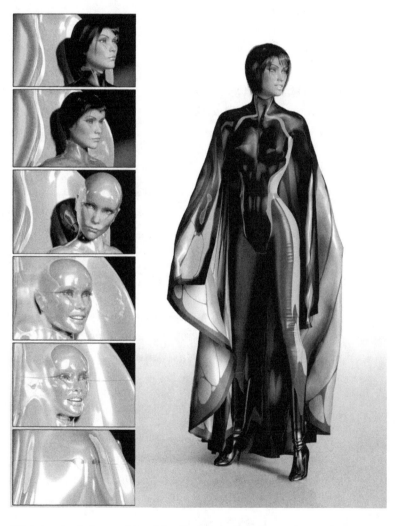

3D Animation is the art of breathing life into mesh and maps. Images from
Hyleyn by Marco Patrito/Virtual Views and *The Art of Sinkha* by Marco Patrito
(Vittorio Pavesio Productions) ©2001 Marco Patrito.

"*A*argh!! This is driving me insane!*"

"*Ehh? Wha…*" The Master was jarred out of the mid-day nap he had been enjoying. The old man straightened quickly and searched the room with bleary eyes, half-expecting to see the place overrun by Stone Trolls hunting for a human snack.

"*Oh, please forgive me, Master!*" the student was quick to say. "*I didn't mean to awaken you.*"

"*Well, I'm WIDE AWAKE now, so tell me what the trouble is.*" The old conjurer struggled out of his chair.

"*Well, it's this soldier. I'm trying to make him march along the ramparts, but his movement looks terrible.*"

"*Yes, well, let's see…*" the old man leaned across the Glowing Pool and peered at the animated figure.

"*Hmmm. He looks like a robot skating on ice,*" the Master not so tactfully noted. "*Lad, you have to realize that people and animals aren't mechanical. They move gracefully in arcs, not in rigid angles and straight lines.*"

"*That makes sense,*" replied the student, "*I guess I need to add more intermediate stages to each movement, then?*"

"*That would be a good approach.*" The old man nodded. "*As for the skating, summon some temporary objects to mark the positions of the feet. That will give you reference to mark his footfalls.*"

"*Great! Thanks for the advice, Master. I think it'll help a lot.*" The student paused and gazed at the old man quizzically. "*Just one thing, though. What's a 'ro-bot?'*"

"*Oh, I saw them whilst flipping channels on the crystal oracle last night,*" the old man replied. "*They're mechanical humans that will someday serve all of mankind's needs.*" He stroked his beard wistfully for a moment, then added, "*that is, until they decide to form a union.*"

Animation Basics

Technically speaking, *animation* is the modification of any kind of object, light, material, or camera over time. But, as the conveniently error-prone student discovered, animation is more than just moving things around. Animation is really about breathing life into an object or character—taking cold, mathematically defined mesh and giving it character and personality.

This chapter looks at the techniques of 3D animation, from basic keyframing to procedural motion. It also delves into the art of character animation, the most challenging (and for some, the most satisfying) part of the 3D experience.

Frame Rates

Although animation is a series of still images (called *frames*), human perception has a characteristic called *persistence of vision*, which is the tendency of the eye to continue seeing an image for a split second, even after the view has changed. Film and television take advantage of this characteristic to create the illusion of fluid motion. Even though film and television display a series of still images, our persistence of vision bridges the gap. The speed at which the images are displayed is called the *frame rate,* and is measured in *frames per second (fps).*

Generally, the minimum frame rate for acceptably fluid animation is about 15fps, which is slow enough for us to perceive the individual images as being separate (seen as a flickering effect), but is still "watchable." The 15fps rate was used extensively in the earlier days of digital video because the single-speed CD-ROM players and slower video cards had a hard time keeping up with anything faster.

A typical rate for high-quality animation is 30fps on the computer or 29.97fps for NTSC video because it is perceived with virtually no flicker. The best rate for European and some Asian television standards is 25fps. Most multimedia computers are capable of playing back 30fps animation and video these days, so consider it the standard for most of your work. If your animation is to be output to film, however, the rate is 24fps, which is the standard for film cameras and projectors.

Before beginning your animation, you must determine the frame rate at which it will be viewed. Frame rate is the basis of calculating the correct frame numbers to which to move an object over a given length of time. For example, if you decide to go with 15fps, and you want an object to be in motion for 2 seconds, you would start it on frame 1 and stop on frame 30 (30 frames divided by 15fps equals 2 seconds). On the other hand, if you choose to use 24fps, you would end the animation on frame 48 instead. Likewise, a 30fps frame rate would have you stopping the movement on frame 60.

3D programs usually have a simple timeline or VCR-control-like section of the interface that enables the user to select a particular frame, play back the animation in real time, change the fps settings, and so forth. For example, take a look at some of the animation controls for Max (see Figure 9.1).

Track View
Window

Motion
Panel

FIGURE 9.1

The basic animation controls for Discreet's 3ds max 4.2 are typical of 3D programs—they consist of a timeline and VCR-like playback controls. More sophisticated control over animation functions are provided in the Motion panel and the Track View window.

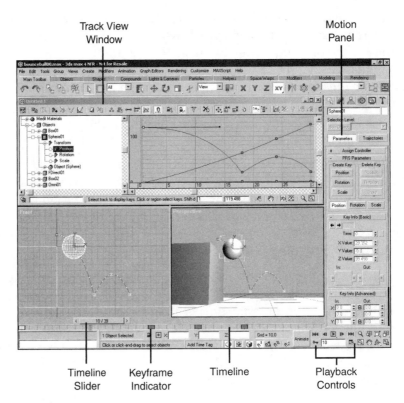

Timeline
Slider

Keyframe
Indicator

Timeline

Playback
Controls

Keyframing

To control animation, most programs use a method called *keyframing*, in which you pose your objects in key positions at specific frames (*keyframes*). Using a process called *tweening*, the computer then calculates the object's position for each of the intermediate frames, resulting in smooth motion from one position to the next.

For example, to animate a ball falling out of a box and bouncing on the floor, you would set a bare minimum of four keyframes (although in most cases, you would want to add additional keyframes to smooth and refine the animation). In the first keyframe, the ball would be teetering at the edge of the box; in the second, it would have struck the ground; in the third, it would be back in the air at mid-bounce; and in the fourth, it would have come to rest on the ground (see Figure 9.2).

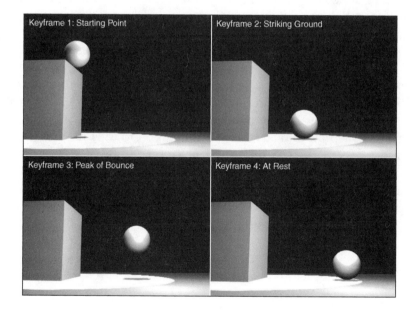

Keyframe 1: Starting Point

Keyframe 2: Striking Ground

Keyframe 3: Peak of Bounce

Keyframe 4: At Rest

FIGURE 9.2

Animating a ball falling out of a box requires a minimum of four keyframes to define the ball's movement. The software uses these keyframes to determine the timing and path for the ball to follow.

For the sake of clarity, I have generally limited the discussion of keyframes in this chapter to refer to movement. Generally, however, keyframing applies to any kind of animatable action, from scaling to rotating to changing light levels or material parameters.

Setting Keyframes

As mentioned earlier, the specific frame numbers for the actions in this ball example depend on the animation's frame rate and the duration of each action. To generate a keyframe, you select a frame number, and then move the object to the desired location. With some programs, that is all that's required, but others may require you to go into a special animation mode so that the program will record these movements, or confirm that you are actually setting a keyframe by hitting a particular button.

Let's take a step-by-step look at how the keyframing process works in 3D software. To animate the bouncing ball, you would first set up the model with the ball poised at the edge of the box. By default, with most programs, you are automatically working on the first frame of animation—in this case, frame 1 (see Figure 9.3a). Next, you would go to frame 18 and move the ball to the floor in about the center of the screen, and set a keyframe at that point (see Figure 9.3b). The line that connects the two positions is the *motion path*, or *trajectory*, which is a graphical representation of the object's movement. Third, you would advance to frame 24 and move the ball to the right and upward a bit, estimating the amount of rebound the ball would have, and set another keyframe (see Figure 9.3c). This position indicates the highest point the ball would reach before starting to fall again. Finally, you would advance the animation to the final frame—frame 30—and move the ball to its resting place on the floor, setting the final keyframe (see Figure 9.3d). You've now completed all the steps necessary to generate a very simple 30-frame animation.

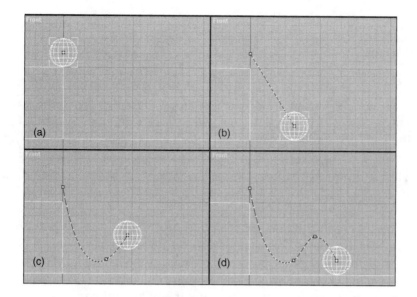

FIGURE 9.3

Keyframing: (a) At frame 1, the ball is positioned at the edge of the box. (b) At frame 18, the ball is moved to the floor near the center of the screen. Note the line showing the object's path. (c) At frame 24, the ball is moved again to simulate the rebound, and the path automatically changes to smooth out the movement. (d) The ball is placed in its stopping place at frame 30, and the path changes to reflect that.

When the animation is previewed by hitting the play button (or rendered to a file), the software makes sure the ball is displayed *exactly* where you placed in on frames 1, 18, 24, and 30. The software also figures out how to transition the ball between those frames in the smoothest manner possible, based on the *weighting* controls for each keyframe. Weighting affects the object's path, allowing the object to make a smooth transition into and out of the keyframe.

Note how the motion path is straight when the second keyframe is set at frame 18, moving the ball from the first keyframe to the second in a straight line, or linear fashion. When the third keyframe is set at frame 24, however, the preset weighting of the keyframes tries to smooth out the movement by adjusting the path from a straight line into a curve. Unfortunately, in this case the curve makes the ball *swoop* rather than *bounce*. You'll see how this weighting can be changed in the next section, changing the path so that the ball moves more naturally.

A useful capability in many 3D programs is the ability they give you to work *directly* with an object's motion path, which is a graphical representation of its movement, represented by a spline with small markers at each keyframe. You also may be able to edit the motion path directly, which can make it a lot easier to establish a complicated movement quickly and still yield very fluid results. If your program offers this capability, you can grab the spline at any keyframe point and move it around, with the path adjusting automatically to show you the revised movement. You also may be able to add, delete, and adjust the weighting of each keyframe with real-time feedback.

Keyframing is not the only means of controlling an object's path, however. Another approach is to draw a line with the program's spline creation tools, and then assign an object or objects to move along it. This type of *path animation* method can be used to make the object follow the contours of a model very precisely; just the thing if you are animating a set of roller coaster cars following a track, for example.

To manage the information about which objects are moved and when, most programs have adopted a *timeline animation interface* (see Figure 9.4). The horizontal axis is broken down into time units and/or frame numbers, and the vertical axis consists of a hierarchical list of objects and lights along with their animatable parameters. The markers placed on the line that extends out from the parameter's name indicate keyframes, and the timeline below it indicates their position on the appropriate frame number. This interface also enables you to add, delete, or move keyframes to adjust the time at which an animation event occurs. To move a keyframe, just slide it with the mouse.

Object Name

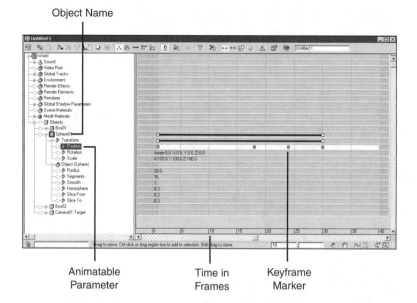

Animatable   Time in   Keyframe
Parameter   Frames   Marker

FIGURE 9.4

The animation timeline shows the animatable parameters for each object, with keyframes indicated by a marker placed according to the time (frame number) at which the keyframe was created. This timeline is a more sophisticated version of the basic timeline in the main interface.

In addition to displaying the time in frame numbers, most programs have an option to display it in the *SMPTE (Society of Motion Picture and Television Engineers)* format of hours, minutes, seconds, and frames, which is used extensively in video and film production. For example, a point in the animation designated 01:57:31:15 would mean 1 hour, 57 minutes, 31 seconds, and 15 frames (15 frames being 1/2 second at 30fps).

Keyframe Weighting

You can alter the keyframe weighting to affect the behavior of the object's motion path near the keyframe. Depending on your program, you may have one or more different keyframe weighting schemes (also called *animation controllers*) to choose from.

The most basic type is a point-to-point *linear weighting*, where the object transitions from keyframe to keyframe in a straight line, with no curvature at all. This is good for mechanical motion but little else.

A *TCB (Tension/Continuity/Bias) controller* is one of the most commonly used keyframe weighting systems. Some programs use a graphical method of representing how the settings will affect the motion path and speed of the object as it enters and leaves the keyframe (see Figure 9.5).

FIGURE 9.5

TCB weighting is
sometimes controlled
by a graphical preview
dialog, like the one
shown here. The graph-
ics show changes to
the motion curve and
object speed depend-
ing on the TCB settings
below them.

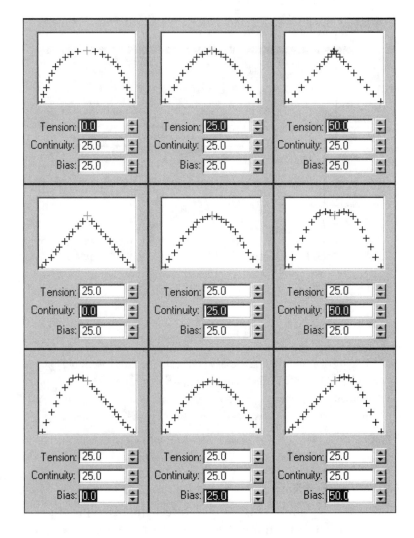

TCB Tension varies the amount of curvature that the keyframe allows
in the path before and after the keyframe. The default in this max
example is 25, which makes the motion fairly smooth, except that
the object tends to slow down a bit right around the keyframe. If the
tension is set low, the path can be very loose and curved going in
and out of the keyframe, and the object's speed becomes more even.
If it's set high, the path becomes totally linear between keyframes but
slows down dramatically at those points.

TCB Continuity adjusts how tangent the path is to the control point. The default setting of 25 results in a smooth curve, whereas a low continuity setting makes the path more linear and the distance the object travels per second very steady. If the continuity is set high, the path overshoots the keyframe position on both sides, and the object tends to slow down a lot near the keyframe. If the continuity were set high on the bouncing ball, it would appear to hit mud rather than a hard floor, sinking in a bit before bobbing up to hit the keyframe point. Then, it would sink once more before popping up into the air.

TCB Bias adjusts the maximum extreme point, or peak, of the curve. When it's in the default position, the peak occurs at the keyframe (unless the continuity is set too high). Low bias causes the curve to peak before the keyframe, and high bias causes it to peak afterward. A high bias setting on the ball at ground zero would cause the ball to pass through the keyframe point and plow into the floor like a meteor, burrow underground, and then pop back out for the bounce.

Ease To and *Ease From* control the acceleration of the object into and out of the keyframe. In the default position, there's a certain amount of deceleration coming into the keyframe, and some acceleration coming out, just as you might slow down a bit as you drove your car into a curve, then accelerate as the road straightened out again. By adjusting Ease To, you can vary the amount of acceleration or deceleration prior to the keyframe, whereas Ease From does the same thing to the far side of the keyframe. Ease controls could have some strange effects in the falling ball example. If the ball's impact keyframe was adjusted to have a high Ease To setting, the ball would slow down as it got closer to the ground, almost as if it were trying to avoid the impact.

Although weighting is often represented in separate dialogs when the user clicks on a keyframe, the best feedback and control is provided by those systems that enable you to see and edit both the keyframe position and weighting on a function curve, or on the object's path in the 3D space.

A *function curve* is a graphical way of displaying object transformations. It often consists of three differently colored splines, each representing a different axis (see Figure 9.6). If the splines are flat, it means no activity is occurring on that axis. If they curve, however, the amount they are displaced and their position indicates the degree of change on that axis and at what points in time those changes occur.

FIGURE 9.6

Function curves represent the movement of the bouncing ball along each axis. The horizontal (X-axis) movement is fairly linear, and the vertical (Y-axis) curve is very similar to the motion path of the ball. The Z-axis curve is flat because there is no movement along that axis in this example.

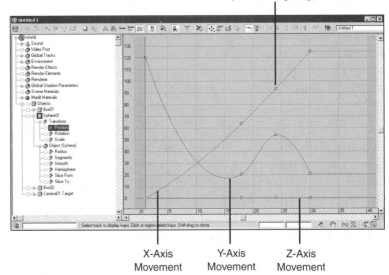

Keyframe Markers
(Linear Weighting)

X-Axis
Movement

Y-Axis
Movement

Z-Axis
Movement

If you change the type of weighting from the default linear to Bezier style, it is possible to graphically control the object's behavior as it passes through the selected keyframe positions. Such *Bezier spline weighting* adjustments work in much the same way as the 2D spline editing you may have done in drawing programs or in modeling 3D objects. The handles on the control point are capable of controlling the same sorts of parameters that TCB controls do, but in a more intuitive manner. For example, to vary the tension, you shorten the handles, reducing their effect on the spline. To adjust continuity and bias, position the handles to tweak the curve passing through the keyframe.

For the bouncing ball example, if you change the keyframe weighting to Bezier and then adjust the handles, the function curves can be adjusted to make the ball move properly. On the first keyframe of the Y-axis, the handle has been stretched out horizontally so that the path of the ball "rolls" off the box rather than slices down into it like before (see Figure 9.7). Also, the second keyframe of the same Y-axis function curve has been changed so that the ball plunges down and then pops right back up, "bouncing" rather than "swooping." The third keyframe is left with its original linear weighting, because the extra control offered with Bezier weighting is not required here. With a bit of tweaking to the fourth keyframe, the Y-axis function curve—and therefore the motion path of the ball—becomes more natural.

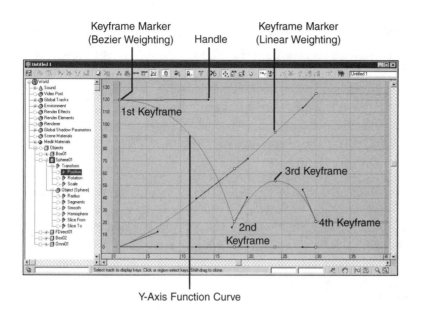

Keyframe Marker (Bezier Weighting)   Handle   Keyframe Marker (Linear Weighting)

1st Keyframe

3rd Keyframe

2nd Keyframe

4th Keyframe

Y-Axis Function Curve

FIGURE 9.7

By switching the keyframe weighting type on the bouncing ball to Bezier, then adjusting the Bezier handles, the function curves can be made to move the ball in a more natural manner.

Pivot Points and Axes

In animation, an object may be transformed around one of several axes or pivot points (centers of rotation). The pivot point is often located in the center of the object, which may not be appropriate depending on how you plan to animate the object. In the case of a jointed character, for example, the pivot point for the lower arm would need to be relocated to the elbow region, at the upper end of the arm. You also may need to relocate the pivot point to have objects spin around a non-local axis, located on another object or out in 3D space (see the Nulls section later in this chapter for more tips on this).

In most cases, the pivot point for an object can be relocated by choosing a Pivot Point command, Center of Rotation command, or something similar, and selecting the new location for it by clicking in one or more viewports. The axis of rotation is often set by the General Axes Constraints setting or by using a hotkey or mouse click to choose the desired axis. It should be noted, however, that some programs do not allow the repositioning of the pivot point once the object has been animated. Therefore, it is usually best to define pivot points for objects before the animation process is started.

Preview

At some point in the animation process, you will want to see a representation of how things are moving. In most cases, there is some kind of *preview mode* that either displays a simplified version of the scene in real time or outputs a fast-rendering version as an animation. Be aware, however, that such previews can be misleading, and you have to rely on properly rendered tests to be sure everything is working properly.

If you need more accuracy, or the program's real-time preview can't keep up with the complexity of the scene, you can usually render a low-resolution flat or Gouraud shaded animation with mapping and shadows turned off in a fairly short amount of time. Hide unnecessary objects to speed things up even more.

Links and Chains

To create jointed characters, machines, or other objects that have multiple parts that move each other, you have to establish connections between the component objects. This is accomplished through the use of links. A *link* is a connection between two objects, so that animation affecting one also influences the other. When a link is established, the first object is called the *parent*, and movement applied to it is transferred to the second object, the *child*.

When you get into animating objects that have been linked together, you might encounter situations where the object refuses to rotate past a certain point or might suddenly snap into a particular position. This condition is called *gimbal lock* and is due to the mathematical limits and rotation orders of certain animation controllers. Consult your program's documentation for workarounds if you run into a situation like this.

A *chain* is a series of linked objects; it uses the same parent-child relationship, but extends it by additional generations to grandchild, great-grandchild, and so forth. So if the parent object is moved, the child is moved, and because the child object is the parent of the grandchild, the grandchild object is moved as well.

If it weren't for links and chains, jointed objects would come apart as soon as you started to animate them. By joining objects together with linking, you create a *hierarchical tree* in which moving the trunk (parent) affects all the branches (offspring), and moving a single large branch affects the smaller branches (later-generation offspring) attached to it (see Figure 9.8). In fact, the tree model is often used to display the link relationship between objects when working with the animation.

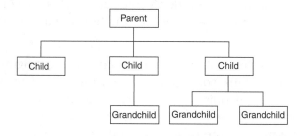

FIGURE 9.8

Graphical representation of the hierarchical tree structure of potential links. This information is often presented in text outline format in 3D software.

Linking objects is not necessarily like welding the objects together, however. There are different kinds of links that can be established that affect the chain's behavior. One link, sometimes called a *ball joint*, is similar to a human shoulder joint in that it has a wide range of motion (see Figure 9.9). If you don't want the link to be that free, you can set up *constraints* by turning off some of the axes of rotation. The amount of rotation also can be constrained by angle limits, so that the joint can't bend in certain directions or fold back on itself.

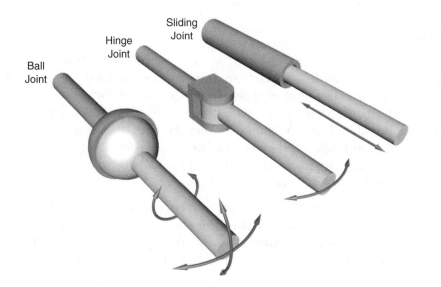

FIGURE 9.9

A physical representation of some of the types of links and constraints available in a typical 3D program.

A hinge-style link, which is not unlike a human knee joint, allows rotation around only one axis, and is often used for doors, levers, and other mechanical devices (or body parts) that move that way.

Other links may not enable rotation at all, but set up a sliding relationship between the objects, as in segments of a collapsing telescope. In this case, the link is constrained to a single axis of movement running along the length of the two objects. The allowable distance of movement also can be constrained, so that the sections don't come apart. This type of joint would be useful for constraining the motion of the button part of a doorbell, for example.

Methods of establishing links and chains vary among programs, but generally you select the Link command or icon, then select the child object followed by the parent object or vice-versa. At that point, you can add additional links or edit the link to add constraints. You can test the link's performance by moving the objects around in the interactive animation environment. Naturally, you also can *unlink* an object from the chain, removing it from the influence of other objects.

In programs that have separate modeling and editing modes (such as 3D Studio R4 DOS), establishing links in the animation module may generate strange results if the objects are edited later in the modeling mode. In cases like this, you should unlink the objects before you edit them, and then re-link them later on.

Nulls

Nulls or *dummy objects* can be used as invisible components of a chain or group, or as invisible objects that provide a pivot point to orbit other objects around. They usually appear as cubes or other simple objects when you're editing the animation, but do not render, which is why they are considered invisible. Nulls or dummies may be part of the standard set of object creation tools, but they're more likely to be found in the animation toolbox instead. Other than that, they can usually be scaled, rotated, and moved like any other 3D object.

Nulls are frequently made large enough to enclose a complex linked object, and then assigned as the parent to the enclosed objects so that you can more easily move them around as a unit. This makes it less likely that you will accidentally select a child object when you try to select the parent of the chain instead. For example, helicopter rotors have a lot of small parts clustered around the drive shafts, making it difficult to select a drive shaft with the mouse (see Figure 9.10). By adding a null object and making it the parent of the drive shaft, you can simply rotate the null, and the propeller drive shaft will rotate as well, turning the props and other components with it.

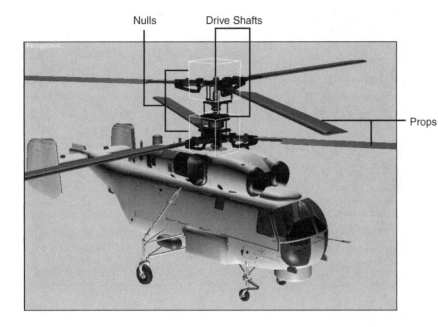

Nulls   Drive Shafts

Props

FIGURE 9.10

Establishing a null or dummy object as the parent in a complex chain makes it easier to select and transform the objects linked to it. This Kamov KA-27 helicopter requires two null objects—one to control the rotation of each of its two sets of counter-rotating blades.

Another use for nulls is to establish a rotational axis some distance from an object, because it can be hard to accurately select the correct spot in open 3D space. In this case, the null serves as a visual marker containing the correct center of rotation. On top of that, it can move so that the center of rotation can change over time.

Nulls are also good for marking waypoints or providing other reference marks for animation. In the opening story, the Master suggested using temporary objects to mark the soldier's footprints. Null objects are perfect for this.

Bone Deformation

Bone deformation is the technique of animating an object (usually a character) by defining and animating an internal skeleton that automatically deforms the surrounding mesh. In the case of humanoid characters, the *skeleton* is a much-simplified version of our own, with *bones* for the arms, hands, fingers, legs, spine, and so forth. You can animate the bones of the skeleton, and the predefined areas of the surrounding mesh—the "skin"— are then smoothly animated along with it (see figure 9.11).

FIGURE 9.11

A seamless mesh of a baby attached to a bone deformation skeleton. By moving the bones, the mesh will move as well.

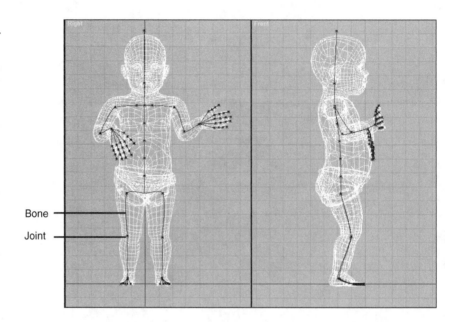

Bone

Joint

Not only is bone deformation one of the best ways to animate the broad motions of an non-jointed (seamless) mesh character, but the bones also can create subtle distortions of the mesh as well, allowing muscles to bulge, the chest to heave, and so on. Even facial expressions can be created with bone deformation.

In a production environment, the process of setting up or *rigging* a character with bones is often left to a technical director called a *Character T.D.*, who specializes in this sort of work. Character rigging is usually a lengthy process that requires a lot of fine adjustments to get it right. Improper rigging results in the mesh being stretched in unnatural-looking ways during the animation phase.

If bone deformation is not part of your standard 3D package, there's a good chance that someone offers it as an add-on. Naturally, bone deformation processes vary from product to product, but here's a general outline of the procedure:

1. Create the mesh skin by using standard modeling techniques or by using a digitized character. It's generally set in a neutral pose, preferably with any body joints at least partially open.

2. Create a skeleton, either by defining bones one by one, or by using a standardized skeleton and adjusting it to fit. The skeleton should be completely enclosed within the mesh.

3. Define those areas of the mesh that fall under the influence of a given bone. Although the mesh around most of the bone will probably be automatically included, there will probably be some fine tuning required in the joint areas (such as the shoulder) to prevent, say, a portion of the rib cage being affected by the upper arm bone.

4. Reassign portions of the mesh. Testing the effects of the bone deformations will probably result in creases showing at various undesirable points. Further refinement of the mesh assignments may be needed, or you may need to add additional elements to correct this. In some cases, you may be able to define *tendons* that pull on certain areas of the mesh according to other deformations in the skin.

5. Define the subtle stretching and bulging of the skin when a joint or bone is moved in a certain way. This may be controlled by a path deformation technique similar to those used in sweeping an object, or you may have to do it manually to the mesh.

Character Setup: An Interview with Eric Ronay

Eric Ronay was born in Pasadena, California during the "Summer of Love," 1969. He grew up fascinated by movie special effects, and as far back as he can remember, loved to watch stop-motion monsters, dinosaurs, creatures, and just about anything that was animated. Anything and everything fantastical riveted his attention.

He dabbled in art while he was growing up, but never quite got the hang of working in traditional 2D media. He had a particularly difficult time dealing with perspective and foreshortening. As a result, he shied away from doing art until 1996, when he started taking 3D classes at the Computer Arts Institute in San Francisco. 3D software offered him a way around some of his traditional media woes, and he found that working in 3D was the ideal way to finally release his creative frustrations. After graduation, he went to work at Visionary Media on a game for Microprose called *Star Trek: First Contact.* He worked there for two years, but unfortunately, the game contract was ultimately cancelled. He then started doing contract work for Mondo Media, and later, Treanor Brothers Animation (www.tbanimation.com). In 2001, he was hired full-time at Treanor Brothers.

I met Eric when I was searching for people to work on the original *Mechwarrior 3* cinematics. He came in for an interview and showed off some of the great work he'd done on *Star Trek: First Contact.* He had good modeling and animation skills as well as technical directing ability, so he was perfect for the team. I hired him on, and we worked together on both *Mech* and *Under Cover.*

Q: What made you want to get into 3D?

A: Seeing *Tron,* and the realization that you could do *anything* in 3D. I was immediately fascinated by the fact that you could build and create these rich, virtual worlds directly from your imagination.

Q: How did you learn to do 3D modeling and animation?

A: I learned 3D Studio R4 back in 1996, when it was still a DOS program. I worked at a small private CG school called Computer Arts Institute in exchange for being able to take classes free. I was exposed to all the good desktop graphics programs, but I mostly concentrated on what I thought were the "big three": 3D Studio, Photoshop, and Premiere. Those three programs provided most of the tools necessary to build, map, animate, and edit whatever I wanted.

Going to CAI really helped me with the basics. I really learned the most about the technology and the tools of the trade while working on projects, especially when working with people more skilled than myself. I find it very difficult to learn things just working on my own. I learn much better by first reading everything I can, and then listening and talking with people who are more experienced than me.

Q: What 3D software do you use, and why?

A: I use discreet 3ds max 4. I've been using max for years and feel comfortable that it will enable me to accomplish whatever I need to do without too much trouble. It's powerful, but fairly easy to use as 3D packages go.

Q: What projects have you worked on over the years? How big were the teams doing these projects?

A: I've worked on a great many projects over the years. Being a contractor and working with companies that do service work, I've had the pleasure of working in the worlds of *Star Trek*, *Mechwarrior*, *Barbie*, *The Land Before Time*, *X-Men*, *Army Men*, and *Tiger Woods Golf*. I've also worked on numerous other projects that aren't as well known. The teams usually consisted of between two and eight people.

Q: How did you get in with Treanor Brothers Animation, and what do you do there now?

A: I started contracting for Treanor Brothers Animation back in 2000 and was hired on full time at the beginning of April 2001. While I've been here, I've done a little bit of everything: modeling, texture mapping, character setup, animation, lighting, camera work, After Effects, editing, and even production organization. My specialties are technical direction and animation.

Q: Which models or animation have been the most interesting for you? Which have been the toughest, and why?

A: The most interesting are the original projects. Unfortunately, they're a little too few and far between. I like them best because you're able to create something that hasn't been seen before. The most difficult projects are models and animation for well-known properties like *Star Trek*, *Barbie*, or *X-Men*. They're fun because you're adding to their universes, but difficult because you have to match a well-established look. Sometimes you really have to bust your ass to get it to look the way it's *supposed* to.

Q: How do you approach setting up a character for animation?

A: Answering this question completely would take up a whole book! I can give you some advice in what to look out for in setting up your characters, though. If you want an in-depth explanation about rigging characters in 3ds max, I recommend checking out the book *3D Studio MAX 3 Professional Animation* by Angie Jones and Sean Bonney. I've found it to be an excellent resource for character setup in max. Hopefully there will be an updated version for 3ds max 4.

My down-and-dirty max character studio approach is this:

First, build your mesh low-res, and use a Mesh Smooth or Tessellate modifier in the stack to increase resolution. This way, you can turn the extra detail off in the viewport and not suffer a performance hit from all the extra polys.

Next, use Biped to create a skeleton about the same size as your character. While it's in figure mode, you can use move, rotate, and even nonlinear scale transforms to shape the bones of the skeleton to fit your character. You may want to turn on Show Links in the Biped display panel while positioning the skeleton; this gives you a better idea of exactly where Biped's joint pivots will be located. Try to make the bone structure—particularly the joint positions—of your character as close to real-life skeleton as possible.

Most bipedal characters, and even quadrupeds, such dogs and horses, can be set up using Biped. You can use Biped's extra bone structures—tails and ponytails—in creative ways, as jaws or extra limbs. If you want to set the skeleton up as a quadruped, you can bend it over at the waist and use the arms as forelegs.

Keep in mind that Biped isn't the ultimate animation plug-in by any means; it's a tool to be used in its proper place. Add to it as you wish, and make it bend to your will. If its built-in features aren't fulfilling your needs, add bones onto it to fit the needs of your character. There's a solution to every setup problem; it's all about getting the software to do it for you.

If you do end up adding extra bones to Biped, you'll want to maintain a zero keyframe for them so that you can get the skeleton back in the default pose. You'll want to work from the default pose to make any tweaks or additions to the skeleton. You may even want to save off the extra bones in their default positions to a separate file. That way, if you need to rebuild the skeletal system, you can create a biped, load your figure file, import the extra bones, link them, and you're ready to apply a Physique file. (Physique is character studio's tool for assigning mesh envelopes to a skeleton.)

Now, this is very important: If you have additional mesh structures attached to the character, like long hair or clothing and accessories that dangle down, you'll want to build a separate setup for them. For example, say you have a female character with long strands of hair that you want to be able to animate. Keep the hair a separate mesh object, and only use Biped for setting up her body. Then, build a separate skeleton system for her hair using boxes, dummies, or whatever you want. At the root of her hair skeleton, you'll want to swap its Transform: Position/Rotation/Scale controller with a Transform: Link Constraint controller. This can be done within max's Motion panel.

The Link Controller is a very powerful tool for character setup. By using a Link Controller, you avoid making a hierarchal link between the hair and body, which Physique would try to deal with when you bind your mesh to the skeleton. This way, you will have to worry only about the mesh envelopes that are affecting the body at this point. If you hierarchically attach a complex bone setup—like the hair skeleton—onto the Biped skeleton, you're going to add a mesh envelope link for all those extra bones, and you don't want that. It's extremely helpful to keep your setups as clean and organized as possible, so try to set them up to deal with one thing at a time, instead of the entire character and it's accessories at once.

The Link Controller can be used for anything extraneous that you want to attach to the Biped skeleton. I usually use it for hair, eyes, and anything the character will hold or directly manipulate. The best part is that the link is animatable, so you can even have your character pick up objects and set them down without having to create a direct hierarchical link between the objects and the character. This makes for a much more flexible and stable animation setup.

The third step is applying Physique to the character. I usually configure Physique so that Set to Link Length is on and Blending is set to N Links. I then go in and adjust the envelopes and vertex settings until I'm happy with the way the skeleton deforms the mesh when moved.

How you use Physique really depends on what part of the mesh you're applying it to and why. It never hurts to play around with the settings until you find out what works best. I also use an "exercise" animation (.BIP) file to test how well the mesh is holding up when deformed. The file should feature a lot of extreme movements so that you can immediately spot problem areas.

Also, it's very important to *cover your ass*. Understand your setup well enough to fix it, no matter how badly your team may screw it up. One of the most powerful attributes of Character Studio and Physique is the ability to save and load settings—Physique files, Biped information, and animation keys. Making backups and using these intelligently can save you a lot of trouble down the line. You never know when you may have to rebuild a file from something that's barely functional.

Finally, the Modifier Stack is your friend. The better you understand it, the better your characters will turn out. Use it creatively and intelligently.

Q: What sorts of things do you have to watch out for when setting up a character, and what general tips do you have for this process?

A: It sounds difficult, but what you want to keep in mind while setting up a character is that you are rigging it for flexibility and ease of use for the artists who are going to be working with it. Develop and maintain rigging standards that your animation team can be comfortable with and rely on to perform in an expected way. Make sure you're open to their suggestions, and that you continually refine your rigs accordingly.

Take your time polishing your model and mapping before starting animation setup. It's easier to set up a completed character than one that's still in flux.

Make sure the model is in the "da Vinci pose" with limbs, fingers, and toes spread apart; this makes it much easier to manipulate the mesh envelopes for every joint.

Also, it's good to do a lot of experimentation. It's always easier to try things on a small scale with simple, low-res objects before you try to implement the same techniques on a larger scale. By making some simple experiments first, you can discover what works and what doesn't in minutes instead of hours.

Q: What advice do you have for people who'd like to work on game assets and cinematics?

A: Practice, practice, *practice.* Learn, learn, *learn.* Don't ever let yourself get discouraged, and don't ever stop. People will immediately respect a work of quality. Quality comes only from love for what you're doing, and doing it as well as you possibly can.

Q: Do you have any "dream project" that you'd like to work on? (Either your own, or some book you think would make a great effects film...)

A: I would love to work on Marco Bertoldo's *Gone Bad* (www.gonebad.com). I'm a huge fan of the 3D work that was done on that project at Mondo Media, and I have also had the pleasure of reading a recent draft of the complete miniseries script. It would be an awesome and rewarding project to work on.

I would enjoy the challenge of translating Robert Jordan's *The Wheel of Time* books into a miniseries of some sort. It's an epic story, which if given some love, a tight script, and some sweet storyboarding, could be a *godlike* show.

Eli Libson, one of my coworkers at Treanor Brothers, is an excellent artist with an imagination as fertile and charming as Brian Froud's. He's fleshing out a wonderful story that would be an amazing and fun piece to make.

Eventually, as I refine my own artistic sensibilities and talents, I'd like to be able to make a living doing my own online 3D animated series. I figure that as the technology matures and refines itself, it will enable smaller groups of people—or even just individuals—to cost-effectively put out longer, more complex works. It would be wonderful to make a living by directly distributing your own imagination.

Q: Where would you like to be in five years?

A: Working on one of my dream projects!

I'd like to thank Eric for taking the time to share his knowledge and experiences with us in this interview. Eric's personal website can be found at `http://www.afriverse.com/~moonshdw/Index.html`.

Forward and Inverse Kinematics

Forward Kinematics (FK) is the default method of animating linked objects, in which the movement of the parent object affects all the offspring on down the chain. If you move the parent, the children move too. If you rotate the parent, you rotate the children, and so forth. Of course, because there's no backward link from the child to the parent, the child also can be moved independently, which can mean a break in the mesh if you move the child away.

This method of animation makes a lot of sense for mechanical devices, because they usually operate in a "this moves that" mode that forward kinematics duplicates. It's not so good for character animation such as walking, however, because it requires you to move the body first, and then adjust all the limbs to be in the proper places. This usually results in *skating*, a problem where the position of a character's feet slides around on the ground instead of remaining firmly planted. Forward kinematics is also a problem for controlling arm movement as well. For example, if you were animating an arm and wanted to touch the finger to an object, you would start by adjusting the root object (the upper arm), then the forearm, the wrist, and finally, the finger (see Figure 9.12). This is very laborious and inaccurate, and requires a number of corrections and fine adjustments.

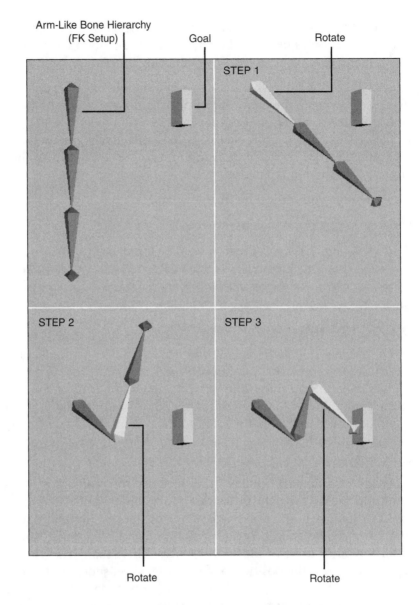

Inverse Kinematics (IK) is a method of controlling linked objects by moving
the very end of the chain and having the rest of it adjust to compensate, a
bit like the tail wagging the dog. With IK, you move the finger directly to
the object, and the wrist, arms (and even the rest of the body) bend and
adjust smoothly and automatically to make it work (see Figure 9.13).

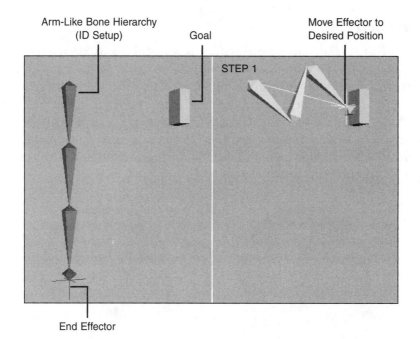

Arm-Like Bone Hierarchy (ID Setup)   Goal   Move Effector to Desired Position

STEP 1

End Effector

FIGURE 9.13

Inverse kinematics enables the user to move the end of the same arm-like bone hierarchy directly to the desired spot—the bones rotate automatically to keep the chain in one piece.

IK makes it much easier to animate characters, because you can concentrate on the final position of hands and feet, rather than on the full-body adjustments you have to make to ensure that the limbs can reach their targets. Also, because the movement of the limbs in response to the changes is fairly natural and tends to affect much of the body, you get a lot of "free" animation with IK, meaning that you don't have to go in and make as many adjustments to keep the form looking loose and natural. This is also one of the downsides to IK, because you don't have precise control over how the body responds to your demands. Therefore, you often have to use a combination of forward and inverse kinematics in your animation.

Inverse kinematics can be used with any sort of properly linked object, including jointed characters and skeletons (discussed in the next section). Generally, IK offers six degrees of freedom (translation and rotation times three axes), allowing full freedom of movement, but you should constrain some of the axes so that a character's joints move in a natural manner only (so the elbows don't bend backwards, for example).

Morphing

Morphing as it relates to 3D animation is a technique that enables you to make smooth changes to an object's shape by copying the base (original) mesh and modifying it into a different shape or *morph target*. Good examples of what morphing is capable of are the transformations of the liquid metal T-1000 in *Terminator 2: Judgement Day*. Morphs can turn just about any form into another, but they also can be used to animate organic forms realistically, such as a snake's slithering motion or a person's facial expressions and speech (see Figure 9.14).

FIGURE 9.14

Morph targets often consist of minor variations on a base character to create expressions. However, they can also be used to transform the character completely. (a) Base character. (b) Lip-sync morph target. (c) Facial expression morph target. (d) New character morph created by heavy manipulation of the base character mesh.

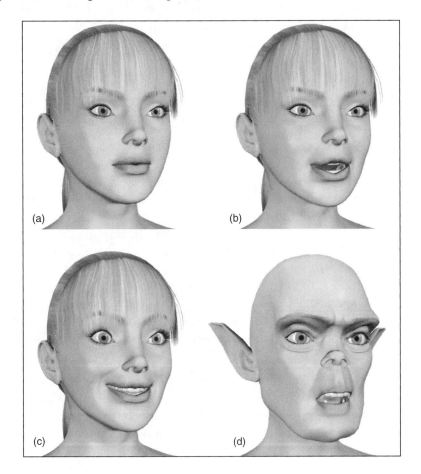

Before bone deformation became popular, morphing was one of the few ways to animate an un-jointed character. In some cases, it's still used for that purpose because it can be difficult to get precise results with bone deformation. Morphing still remains one of the only ways to transform one (non-parametric) polygonal object into another, but it's no small task.

In most software, the shapes you morph from and to (the morph targets) must have the same number and orientation of vertices, so that the program knows exactly where each vertex being animated starts and ends. Consider a cube with its eight vertices; move the four vertices on the top of the cube together and you have essentially morphed it into a pyramid.

This can be difficult to accomplish if you build the targets as two separate objects, so users often construct one of the target objects, then copy and transform it vertex by vertex into the next target. Also, because the software uses a straight-line approach to moving the vertices from their starting to ending positions, intermediate targets are often needed to prevent parts of the mesh from collapsing or distorting in some undesirable way during the animation.

After the targets are created, you set a keyframe for each form of the object, telling the animation program that it's supposed to transform the object completely by this time. The software then handles the movement of the vertices automatically, adjusting them frame by frame to make a smooth transition.

Deformation Grids

Deformation grids or *space warps* are used to define an area in 3D space that has an automatic effect on objects passing through its influence. Depending on the type of deformation selected, the object may respond to gravity effects, become wavelike, disintegrate, or change its path (see Figure 9.15).

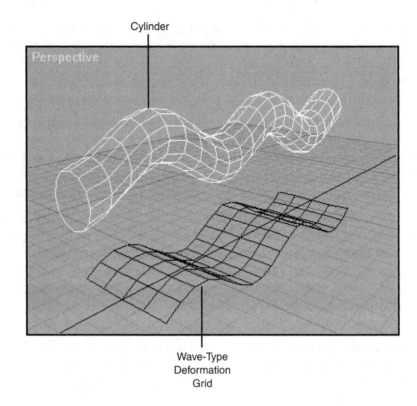

Cylinder

Perspective

Wave-Type
Deformation
Grid

FIGURE 9.15

Objects—like this cylinder—that pass within the field of a deformation grid are distorted or otherwise affected by the grid. Other deformation types can create different effects on the object, or modify its path.

Deformation grids make it easier to cause certain effects to occur on cue, such as having an object shatter as it strikes a floor, or to create motion that would be a chore to do entirely by hand, such as animating a boat on a storm-tossed sea.

Using deformation grids is pretty straightforward. Depending on the program, you usually just set the object in position and adjust its parameters to the desired settings. (You may have to set parameters on any objects you want to be influenced as well.) After that, any objects that move over or through the grid area are automatically deformed.

Particle Systems

Some software packages offer built-in or add-on particle systems. *Particle systems* are 3D animation modules that enable you to generate and control the behavior of a vast number of tiny objects, which can simulate such natural effects as water, fire, sparks, or bubbles. Particle systems can also be used to create a flocking effect for animating groups of birds, butterflies, or fish. The particles are linked to instanced models of these creatures, controlling their movement. In addition, you can use an unanimated particle system as a 3D star field that you can move a camera through.

A good example of particle systems at work is the solar flare and luminous gas cloud in the opening of *Star Trek: Voyager*. The individual particle objects usually are very simple, consisting of only a few faces each. When the proper material is applied to them and they are massed together, however, they act like the individual molecules making up a larger organism, taking on a form that belies their simplicity (see Figure 9.16).

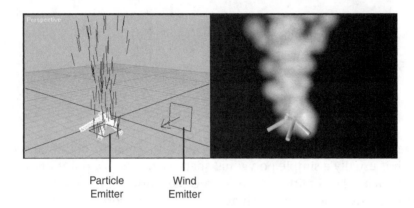

Particle   Wind
Emitter   Emitter

FIGURE 9.16

Particle systems can create controlled fluid or vaporous effects (in this case, smoke). The appearance of the particles depends on the type of material applied to them.

The value of particle systems is that they bring a natural vaporous or liquid element into the normally hard-edged and well-defined 3D environment. Unlike such post-production fire effects as VCE's Pyromania CD-ROM series offers, however, they can be animated as part of the rest of the scene and made to interact with other 3D objects. Real-world physics can be applied to the particles, causing them to bounce naturally off other objects. You also can apply user-defined levels of gravity, wind, and other forms of turbulence as well. For example, you could design a particle system to act like water and cascade automatically off 3D obstacles to make a virtual waterfall (see Figure 9.17).

FIGURE 9.17

A particle system
waterfall. Particle sys-
tems can interact with
mesh in the scene and
can be affected by
forces such as wind,
turbulence, or gravity.

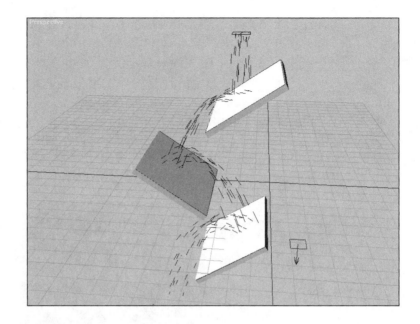

In general, particle systems work by enabling you to define an *emitter*, which is usually a simple polygonal shape that acts as a point of origin for the particles. The emitter is often scaleable, allowing the effect to be generated across a large area. There may be some sort of *boundary object*, perhaps part of the emitter itself, which limits the effect to its interior. The user defines the approximate number of particles to be active at any given time, and then applies a material to them. If wind, turbulence, or gravity effects are needed, those parameters are set next. Because rendering particle animation is time-consuming, some programs offer an interactive preview mode that enables the user to examine the general effect before rendering.

Procedural Motion

Because the actions of deformation grids and particle systems are set by formulas and parameters and not accomplished through direct user keyframing, the movement of particle systems is sometimes referred to as *procedural motion*, but other techniques carry this title as well. For example, a *noise controller* is a type of animation utility that uses randomly generated noise to vary the size or position of an object. This is useful if you want to portray a piece of equipment vibrating out of control. Another is the *audio controller*, which uses the amplitude of a digital audio file to control motion. This would be useful for synching actions to a prerecorded soundtrack, or possibly even doing some rough lip-synching.

An *expression controller* is another source of animation data—it uses formulas you input to control the action of objects in the scene. This can be very useful for accurate mechanical simulations, or to illustrate a scientific principle with 3D animation. Expressions can also be used for character animation, to keep a character's pelvis centered between its legs, or to prevent its feet from going through the floor.

Behaviors are object-level controllers (Look At, Bounce, Spin, and so on) that simplify certain animation work. You assign a behavior to a given object, and it does what you tell it automatically, freeing you to build on that action to make a more complex movement. For example, if you were animating a scene in which an eye watches a rolling ball, you could assign a *Look At* or *Point Toward* behavior to the eye and make the ball the target object. From then on, no matter how you move the eye or the ball, the eye would always be looking in the right direction.

Scripted Animation

Like procedural animation, scripted animation controls objects or parameters in the scene without hands-on attention from the animator. Instead, *scripted animation* is controlled by a text script written in a program-specific *scripting language*, such as MAXScript for 3ds max, LScript for LightWave, or MEL for Maya. In other words, you become a programmer of sorts, and write a program to control the animation. The script can be as simple as a single command that makes a primitive appear, or it can be a very complex programming algorithm.

Scripting enables an animator to create motion that is mathematically precise, or that would be very difficult and time-consuming to do by hand, such as animating a multi-legged creature over a rough surface. To do this task manually, you would have to move each leg forward one at a time, and make sure that the tip of the leg didn't end up floating above the ground or sticking down through it. With scripted animation, you could define a particular motion for one leg and then apply it to all the legs. You could also make the script check for contact between the tip of each leg and the ground, so that each leg was properly situated.

Character Animation

Character animation is the process of imbuing objects with movement that communicates a *personality*. Note that the last sentence said "objects," not "characters." That's because any 3D object—including a simple cube—can have personality, depending on how the animator makes it move. By the same token, even the most detailed and accurate human model can come off as being lifeless if its motions are dull or mechanical. The key to compelling characters is making them act naturally, and there are several techniques that can help you—from the low-tech "looking in the mirror" approach to using high-tech motion capture equipment.

Just as good reference is suggested when modeling objects, video and still image reference can be very useful for doing animation. Sports event footage, Muybridge's famous motion studies, and your own home videos are just a few examples of good resources. Taking dance, martial arts, and drama classes can greatly improve your awareness of human motion and timing as well.

Analyzing Movement

In order to be successful, nearly all animation requires some analysis of an object and how it might move in the real world. Even if the motion is intentionally exaggerated and cartoony, it is usually based on real world physics and motion that have been taken to extremes. Often, squash and stretch are employed to distort the character or props to exaggerate the motion even further.

Consider a baseball player practicing in front of a batting machine. In the real world, the player steps up to the plate and settles into position to hit the ball. He bends his legs, twists his torso a bit, and cocks the bat. Let's call this the *ready position*. As the ball approaches, he adjusts his position, twisting his body away from the ball even more and cocks the bat back further to give extra impact to the hit. In animation terms, this last-minute preparation for the primary motion—the bat being swung—is called the *antic*, short for *anticipation*. The antic is usually a slow movement in the opposite direction of the primary action that follows. An antic helps to hint at what action is about to take place.

Note that the amount of antic is proportional to the amount of force the character wants to apply; in other words, the antic would be small if the player were trying to hit a wiffle ball and big if he were swinging at a bowling ball.

The antic is an important but often overlooked part of computer animation. All too often, there is no "wind-up" in computer animation, and the action ends up looking very mechanical as a result.

Next, the player swings the bat forward, accelerating the swing in an attempt to strike the ball. We'll call this the *primary motion*.

Roughly halfway between the antic and position where the bat strikes the ball is the point traditional animators call the *breakdown* or *passing position*. In cel animation, the animators would continue subdividing the motion in half, adding additional breakdown poses until the motion is smooth. The point at which the bat actually strikes the ball would be called the *contact position*.

Let's look at another example for a moment. If you were animating a walk, there would be a contact position at the point where the character's right heel hits the ground. The next contact position would occur when the left heel hits the ground, and so on. The breakdown or passing position would occur in the center of these two key poses, at the point where the character's weight is firmly on the right foot, and the left leg is in mid-stride, about the time when both legs pass by each other.

Okay, let's get back to the baseball player. Shortly after reaching the contact position, the player stops exerting energy to swing and starts to let the bat slow down to prevent from losing his balance. He also lets go of the bat with one hand, letting it bleed off speed and energy during his follow-through. This phase is called the *accent* or *overshoot* by traditional animators.

Finally, the player settles down into a more relaxed, neutral position, usually to watch where the ball ended up going. In traditional animation, this position is appropriately called the *settle*.

As you can see, many changes occur during a motion, even one as seemingly straightforward as swinging a bat. Looking for and thinking about these phases of motion will help you decide where to set your keyframes and what kind of timing and weighting to use for them.

Body Language

If you're planning to be a character animator, you'd better become an avid people watcher as well. Consciously or not, humans and many animals use *body language* to communicate their states of mind. Folded arms or fidgeting, for example, may indicate boredom or impatience depending on the situation. When people are at ease, their posture relaxes, and if they're sitting down, they may seem to sprawl out a bit. This is just the opposite if the person is tense—he will be rigid and withdrawn.

Animators rely heavily on body language to communicate the emotional states of their characters, and to give them a natural and realistic feeling. This is a lot of work, because the default mode for objects in 3D graphics programs is utterly still and rigid. The use of body language is particularly important for characters that have no other way to communicate their emotions, such as the lamps in John Lasseter's *Light Entertainment* (also known as *Luxo Jr.)* animation. If you haven't seen this short, one of the lively lamps appears as part of the Pixar logo sequence in their feature film releases.

Generally, animators rely on their own body language instincts as a guide for moving their characters. In a sense, they become actors, portraying the roles of their virtual counterparts and noting their own actions and mannerisms, which they then re-create in the program. This isn't limited to human body language either—you can take on just about any role, from cautious mouse to city-trampling monster. Just make sure the door is closed when you start getting into your Godzilla suit; *people might talk.*

The way a character walks can speak volumes about who they are and how they feel about themselves. Although somewhat skewed toward traditional cel animation, Richard Williams' book *The Animator's Survival Kit* offers a wealth of information on walks and breathing life and personality into your characters.

When doing character animation, try to keep your subject standing or moving in an asymmetrical way. For example, people generally don't stand with their weight evenly on both feet, or their shoulders perfectly level all the time. They shift their weight, dip one shoulder or the other, put a hand in a pocket, and so on. Injecting such subtle shifts in position when a character is standing "still" keeps him natural-looking. Also, when doing speech or lip synching animation, remember that more than a person's mouth moves when she's talking—her eyebrows raise, her hands gesture, her whole body gets into the act.

> If you're doing character animation, it's a good idea to have both a full-length and hand-held mirror available. You can act out broad body motions in the full-length mirror, and use the hand-held one for facial expressions. You also can face away from the full mirror and use the hand-held mirror to see what your motions look like from the rear.

Timing also plays a role in conveying emotions. How long a character maintains a position, how long it pauses before reacting to something, and the speed at which it moves can speak volumes about its state of mind. Having an easy-to-reset stopwatch is a useful tool for timing these gestures as you act them out.

Facial Animation

Whereas body language conveys emotion in broad strokes, the expression on the character's face handles all the subtleties. Of all the features of the human face, the eyes are the most telling about a person's state of mind; the combination of the eyes and eyebrows alone can paint nearly the entire range of emotions. The mouth is the second most important feature, and helps to refine and reinforce the emotion being telegraphed by the eyes.

Although the ears and nose are rarely very communicative in humans because of their lack of articulation, they can, however, be very expressive in animal characters, especially stylized ones. Don't overlook the ears and nose when creating expressions for those kinds of characters.

As mentioned earlier in this chapter, facial animation usually is created using either morph targets of various facial expressions or bones used to manipulate the mesh in the face. Regardless of method, both tend to make use of a library of expressions and mouth positions through which the animator can pick and choose (see Figure 9.18). Controls also enable the user to adjust each individual feature, like raising or lowering an eyebrow, opening the mouth, and so on. In addition, the artist can create new morph targets manually by manipulating the mesh with deforms and vertex-level editing.

FIGURE 9.18

Poser characters—such as DAZ's Victoria 2.0—usually come with a library of predefined poses and expressions, and the artist can create and save new ones to the library. In addition, the thumbwheel-style facial animation controls control the influence of dozens of morph targets that deform the mesh in real time.

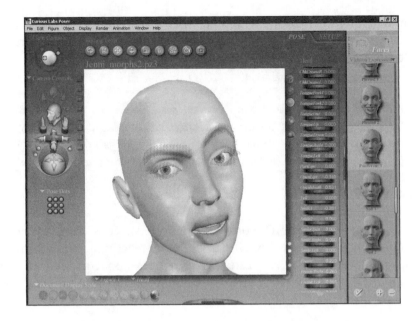

For characters that speak, lip-syncing the mouth to the soundtrack is one of the more labor-intensive facets of facial animation. To understand how to approach creating animated lip-sync, we need to take a look at the building blocks of speech—phonemes.

Generally speaking, *phonemes* are the set of sounds that are used to create speech. The American English language has about 35 phonemes; other languages and dialects may have a different number. What's important to animators, however, is the number of *mouth shapes* that are required to make a character look like it is enunciating these 35 phonemes. Sound out the vowels *A, E, I, O, U (ah, eh, ee, oh, ew)* and notice how your mouth changes to a very specific shape to make each sound. Now sound out *vi* and *fi*—notice that your mouth shape is very similar for both, even though the sound produced is different. The same may be true of entire words, like *buy, my* and *pie*. What this means is that you can get away with about half as many mouth shapes to represent the full range of phonemes (see Figure 9.19).

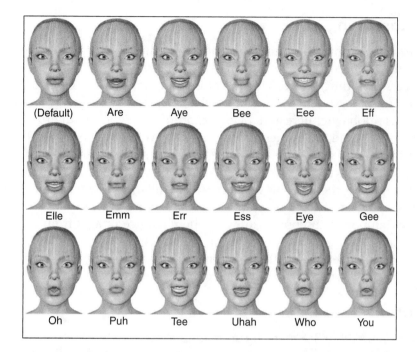

FIGURE 9.19

Because the same mouth shape may be used to create several different phonemes, you don't need 35 different ones to create realistic lip-synced animation. DAZ's Millennium Girls characters come with a set of 18 predefined mouth shape morphs.

To animate lip-synced speech, animators generally import a sound file of the character speaking its lines into their 3D package. By adding the sound file into the animation timeline at the appropriate frame, you can work with the dialogue in small bits, figuring out which phonemes and mouth shapes you need to plug in to make the character appear to talk. Getting the animation to look right usually takes a fair amount of time, and fine adjustments usually need to be made, pushing a phoneme keyframe forward or backward a frame or two and previewing the animation with sound to see whether it looks as if the sync is correct.

To make lip-syncing a moving character easier, place a camera close to the character's face and link it to the head, so that it moves with the character. This will give you a "locked down" view of the character's face despite whatever acrobatic maneuvers it may be performing.

Rotoscoping

If you need more character animation help than a mirror can offer, roto-scoping enables you to copy from—or embellish—reality. *Rotoscoping* is the process of adding film or video to animation, either as a finished element or for use as a reference for the animated characters. Using a video program such as Adobe Premiere and a video capture card, you can digitize moving images and load the frames into the background of a 3D package. This provides you with a very accurate frame-by-frame reference of a motion. If you position the model beside or over the top of the background images, you can duplicate the activity very accurately. In this way, you can think of rotoscoping as the "poor man's motion capture system." Most 3D programs support rotoscoping, drawing the reference images from a series of numbered still images, or from an animation or digital video file. The image sequence is set to begin at a given frame number, and automatically changes whenever you advance to a different frame.

Motion Capture

The popularity of 3D character animation for games, television, and movies is partially the result of advances in generating economical yet realistic motion. *Motion capture* is any one of several processes that enable a performer's actions to be digitized and used to drive 3D characters. There are several types of motion capture technologies, each with its pros and cons.

One motion capture method uses a battery of wired RF (radio frequency) transmitters that are strapped onto the performer's body near the main joints. They emit radio signals to a central receiver, and the software calculates the positions of the transmitters relative to the receiver, in essence capturing the figure's position at any given moment. Completely wireless motion capture systems have been introduced, which give the performer much more freedom of movement (see Figure 9.20).

FIGURE 9.20

Ascension's MotionStar
Wireless is a real-time
motion-capture product
without bulky trailing
cables. Image courtesy of
Ascension Technologies.

Another popular motion-capture system uses *optical tracking*, where the performer is covered with little targets (usually reflective discs or balls), and one or more video cameras are used to digitize their actions. Here, the software tracks the positions of the targets and uses that to determine the figure's positions. Prior to the introduction of wireless radio systems, optical motion capture was the only way to record high-action sequences over a large area.

Optical or mechanical tracking is also used for *facial motion capture*, so that a character can speak and have expressions on top of its overall body movement. This is still done separately from the body motion capture, but at some point, a reliable integrated solution will probably be developed.

The use of motion capture enables you to create vast amounts of character animation that would take far longer to create with keyframe methods, but it does have its drawbacks. First of all, it's still a fairly expensive proposition, although service bureaus are popping up, so you can satisfy your needs without having to purchase the gear. Second, the capture methods are still far from perfect, so animators often have to do cleanup work, adjusting the movement manually to take out glitches, or add motion that wasn't properly captured.

Motion Libraries

With a custom motion capture session being uneconomical for many projects, companies such as Viewpoint have started to offer motion libraries for sale, just as they offer libraries of mesh. In addition to things such as walk and run cycles, *motion libraries* offer action such as reaching, bending, stretching, eating, dancing, and so forth. There are also martial arts moves and sports motions such as swinging a baseball bat or throwing a football.

Although it's unlikely that you would be able to do an entire animation using only these canned sequences, they do give you a head start on creating custom animation that includes libraries as a component. They're also useful for adding motion quickly to background subjects to inject more activity into a scene without a lot of extra work.

The motion library data is used just like any motion capture information—you apply it to the bones of your character. Of course, the motions are all derived from humans, so if you're applying them to a character that has additional joints or some other alien characteristics, some modification is bound to be needed.

Character Animation: An Interview with Gustavo "Goose" Ramirez

Gustavo "Goose" Ramirez was born in Guadalajara, Mexico, but grew up in the small Northern California town of Woodland, just north of Sacramento. Like most kids, he was into comics and cartoons. Growing up, he spent a lot of time drawing cartoons for fun, but later became more focused on art as a serious pursuit. As soon as he graduated from high school, he left the town he refers to as "Woodpile" and went on to college. In both high school and college he tried to find a good balance between practical industrial technologies and art, both of which interested him. This eventually led him to computer animation.

I met Goose while putting a team together to work on the 3D graphics for *The Daedalus Encounter*. One of the artists we'd hired, Bill Niemeyer, was the cofounder of the company where Goose was working and told him we were looking for animators. Goose came in for an interview, and I hired him. Goose did a lot of the animation of the main character flying around and interacting with the live actors. He also did the very challenging work of animating the Seti alien queen at the end of the game. Over the years, we worked together on other projects, including *Zork: Nemesis*, *Blade Runner*, and *Under Cover*. During his time at Mondo, Goose became one of the company's best animators and eventually went on to become a mentor and management representative of the art team.

Q: What made you want to get into 3D?

A: I was originally studying to get into traditional film special effects—model building, creature make-up, stop-motion animation, and post-production 2D effects animation. While I was in college, the tools and processes of the special effects trade became more and more computer-oriented, so I started learning about computer animation as well. Now, just about every special effect in film is wholly or partially computer generated.

Q: How did you learn to do 2D animation? What about 3D animation?

A: I took classes in 2D animation at San Francisco State University as part of my film effects studies, but it's a great form of filmmaking in and of itself. I grew to really appreciate the amount of talent and hard work that goes into creating really great 2D, stop-motion, and ultimately 3D animation. Slowly but surely, I started sharpening my animation skills in 3D by working at various animation studios.

Q: How did you get in with Treanor Brothers Animation, and what do you do there now?

A: I knew Todd Treanor from working with him at Mondo Media. His company, Treanor Brothers Animation, is a small studio focused on creating 3D computer game cinematics. I came here after Mondo stopped doing high-resolution 3D game work and focused on Flash animation for the web instead. I'm currently the studio's animation director.

Q: What projects have you worked on over the years, and what were your roles?

A: I've worked on a number of games, including *The Daedalus Encounter*, *Rebel Assault 2*, *The DIG*, *Blade Runner*, *Interstate 76*, *Under Cover*, *X-Men 2* and *X-Men 3*, among others. I've also worked on animation for a few television shows and station ID spots.

Q: Which animation projects have been the most interesting for you? Which have been the toughest, and why?

A: I always enjoy working on projects where I learn something while I create the artwork. Two projects that I really enjoyed were an animated feature about Aztec Mythology called *The Fifth Sun*, and a miniseries on microbes, *Intimate Strangers*. Coincidentally, they both aired on PBS. The projects I enjoy the *least*, as far as animation goes, are the ones where there is not enough money in the budget to make the work look really good. In those situations, the team usually ends up putting in overtime hours of their own accord, due to that nagging "artistic integrity" thing.

Q: How do you approach animating a character?

A: There are basically two parts to almost all character animation: first, defining the character and the motives of their actions; and second, making the character perform those actions in a believable manner. If I understand not just *what* a character is doing, but *why* a character is doing it, then I can figure out *how* the character is going to do it. This may sound like it relates more to acting than to animating, but they're both based on the same principles.

After the *what*, *why*, and *how* questions are answered, I try to figure out the timing, acting, and poses on paper first—even for 3D animation—because it's easier to create, refine, or throw out ideas quickly and solve problems before it's too late. Sketching poses also helps to establish action lines and motion arcs.

I use a stopwatch and either act out the motion myself or visualize it in my head to figure out the timing. I usually do two or three run-throughs to get a good read on the timing, and then start in on the drawings. I sketch poses on 3"×5" cards to help me visualize the action or posture. It's important to figure out the anatomical mechanics of how the character moves, as well as understand the effects of physical forces, like gravity and inertia, and take them into account; this will make the motion from pose to pose look and feel natural and believable. After that, it's just a matter of translating the ideas and motions from paper to 3D animation form on the computer.

Q: What recommendations do you have for people who want to improve their 3D animation skills?

A: Understand the big picture, and pay attention to the details. Get some reference that illustrates what you're trying to create. Most of the people I know who are working in 3D got into it because they grew up watching cartoons, movies, and reading comics, so we all have some common references in our heads.

No matter what area of 3D work someone gets into—modeling, texturing, lighting, staging, or animation—you need to really understand in detail what you're trying to achieve. 3D work is a study in verisimilitude—that's my dollar word for the day—or making something look believable. This doesn't necessarily mean *realistic*, although that can be part of it. For example, no one has ever seen a real dragon, but if you're going to build one in 3D, you'll probably want to get some good lizard or iguana reference. For animation, video or film footage is always handy to have around. You want the audience to believe in what they are seeing, not just look at pretty renderings.

Q: You've looked at a lot of demo reels over the years. What sorts of things made some stand out? What things made you shut some of them off partway through?

A: I enjoy watching work that feels *crafted*—works where the creator really put some heart into it and made the effort to polish his ideas. Although I may not appreciate, agree with, or even understand the idea, if the quality is there, I'll still enjoy watching it. I would rather watch a well-crafted two-minute piece than a half-baked twelve-minute piece anytime. When it comes to demo reels, I strongly believe that *quality* reigns over *quantity*. So if a person has a ton of work, it's best to edit it down to a nice, short reel containing only the highest quality pieces.

Q: Do you have any "dream project" that you'd like to work on?

A: I think the time has come for low-budget, independent, animated feature filmmaking, and I hope to be leading an animation team on one of them someday. I have some ideas for both short and long format films that I hope to see in production at some point. One project of this caliber would be *Gone Bad*, for which we've already created a few minutes of animation.

Frankly, being able to work with other talented people over the years has been a dream in and of itself.

Q: Where would you like to be in five years?

A: Didn't I just answer that?

I'd like to thank Goose for taking the time and effort to share his experiences and advice.

Visual Effects

Visual effects include all kinds of special effects: smoke, fire, sparks, explosions, floods, lightning, weapons discharges—all the stuff you expect to see in an action film. Like character animation, special effects animation is almost a field unto itself. This section focuses on explosion, fire, and smoke effects. Many of the principles discussed here can be applied to all kinds of different effects.

> Much of the information in this section comes from my article "Cry Havoc!" for *InterActivity Magazine*, and is used with permission.

One of the most challenging parts of an effects shot is the *result* of the stunt—the explosion, debris, fire, and smoke that ensue. There are two reasons for this: First, traditional 3D modeling and animation tools are too clumsy and ill-suited for creating these effects; and second, we're all very familiar with what these natural phenomena look and feel like, so we spot errors easily. In some ways, the complexity and accuracy required when creating these effects offers much the same challenge to the animator as, say, duplicating human movement.

There are three common approaches to creating these effects. One relies on traditional 3D tools and using skillful mapping and animation techniques to create an acceptable (if a bit stylized) result. The second is the use of real effects that have been filmed and digitized and are then composited into the scene. The third is the use of particle systems and specialized plug-ins as an enhancement to the standard 3D toolset. Often, all these techniques are combined in a single effect.

Before trying to design or animate any effects, try watching some action movie sequences to get a sense of scope and timing. The *Terminator* or *Die Hard* series are good bets. Study the effects frame by frame.

Effects CD-ROMs

Pyromania CD-ROMs are from movie effects house VCE, Inc., and contain footage of numerous explosions, fire, and smoke effects. All the footage was photographed against a black background and then digitized and reduced to 640×480 resolution and saved as a series of sequential files on the CD-ROMs. Also included are downsized versions of the files converted to QuickTime movies for quick viewing of the effect.

One way to apply a Pyromania effects sequence to your work is to use a digital editing program (Premiere, After Effects, Composer, and so on) to add the effect in post. Another method is to convert the files into a format that can be used directly by your 3D animation program and incorporate the effect as a mapped polygon. This is the preferred method for several reasons, but is practically a must if the camera is moving during the effect.

Mapping the effect onto a flat or curved polygon requires the creation of an opacity matte because most of the files don't come with an alpha channel. How this is done varies with the requirements of your 3D animation system. In some cases, you can simply use the same files or movie in the opacity channel and tweak the controls until the black background becomes transparent. In other cases, you might use a digital editing program or a graphic file converter's batch processing feature to generate an alpha channel or to palletize the images and replace the black background with your program's "transparent" color.

Explosions

A lone tank rumbles across the charred battlefield, seeking prey. From a distant stand of trees, an Apache helicopter releases its deadly payload, a television-guided Maverick missile. Too late, the tank commander realizes his peril as the missile slams into the tank, shattering it into…a couple hundred triangular polygons?!

All too often, this is the anticlimactic result of a polygonal 3D explosion effect. The target object is destroyed with all the gut-wrenching power of a Christmas ornament shattering on a hardwood floor. The problem results from the fact that most 3D models are hollow—like an empty eggshell—and the only material available to these "shatter" effects is the skin of the object itself.

Part of the solution is creating some innards for the model. These do not have to be very detailed, just make sure the *volume* of stuff inside seems reasonable, say about 30-60% of the object volume that would be in the model if it were complete and undamaged. Most of the mesh should be burnt, bent, and broken. One way to get this mesh assembled quickly is to use old models and mesh libraries as your source. Grab some objects, jumble them around, and apply a map that makes them look suitably pitted and charred. If the objects are mapped already, you may want to alter the existing maps, adding burn marks and gouges, or add a second "damage" map to the material.

Another important part of the process is breaking up the exterior of the model into chunks that you can animate flying outward instead of relying on a polygonal shatter effect. Boolean tools work well for this, especially if you create a "damage tool." This would be a jagged, bent piece of mesh that could be used to Boolean your existing model into numerous chunks of debris. With some programs, if the damage tool is properly mapped, it will automatically apply the damage material to the places where it cuts the original model, saving you some time. Be sure to save your damage tool before using it if your program deletes the original objects as part of the Boolean operation.

Effects Lighting

Lighting is a key element in explosions and goes a long way in heightening the realism. Multiple, bright, shadow-casting lights arranged near the blast centers and animated in concert with the mesh exploding throw illumination onto the debris and surrounding objects. You can also add projection maps to some of the lights that make the effect more apparent if the lighting alone is not enough. These maps could be still images or animations and consist of a radial gradient from white in the center to yellow/orange midway to black at the edges. They may also have bright spikes radiating outward.

Refer to your action movie library to get a sense of timing for the blast. I find that most animated explosions start off too slowly or end too quickly. An explosion is fast and violent at the beginning, then slows as the energy is dissipated over a larger area. The more slowly the fireball moves toward the end of the explosion, the larger the explosion appears.

Here are some other tips to keep in mind when animating an explosion:

◆ Shake the camera around a little bit, especially a few frames after the start of the blast, when you would expect the shock wave to hit the camera's position.

◆ Have some small objects skitter along the ground near the camera when the shock wave strikes.

◆ Adding a single white frame in the animation or in post at the instant the explosion becomes visible can be very effective. You may also want to brighten the frames before and after the white one in post.

◆ Put some additional touches, such as lens flares, hand-drawn debris, or blast damage, into some of the frames in post. Adding stuff this way may be faster then rendering and re-rendering the animation until it is just right.

◆ Use smooth arcs to define the path of the debris.

◆ Make the projectiles move quickly at first, then slow them down gradually.

◆ Make your debris rotate as it flies through the air. Small objects should be spinning quickly, whereas large objects may turn only a few degrees.

◆ Have some of your hi-res debris appear to strike the camera or pass close to it.

◆ Consider applying some of the Pyromania effects or other animated maps to the debris. This can give the appearance that the debris is burning as it flies through the air.

There are a couple ways to create the explosion's fireball. One is to add a Pyromania-like effect by creating a polygon near the center of the blast area and mapping fire footage or an animated map onto it. Take care that the timing and length of the footage matches your lighting and mesh animation or vice-versa. Another method involves making a bright, fiery sphere that gradually fades out as it expands, or model an object that has numerous spikes all around and use it in the same way, allowing it to follow some of the debris and consume other portions.

So, what usually follows an explosion? Fire, of course...

Fire Effects

Whereas explosions typically have a beginning and end that tend to be close together, fire and smoke tend to go on for long periods of time. In fact, if the scene is a long one, and you're using filmed effects, the effect may need to be looped. To loop a live effect, you can use anything from a simple cross-fade to a fancy, time-consuming morph.

Much of the advice on mesh in the preceding explosions section also holds true for building fire and smoke effects. Crumbled walls, blackened pipes, and I-beams jutting out add realism to the scene. Having a few smoldering pieces of debris in the foreground helps, too.

Have a significant amount of your illumination coming from animated lights in the center of the conflagration. The lights should be set up to vary in illumination fairly quickly, casting a flickering effect on the surrounding area. You may want to make an animated projection map from a close-up of a flame loop and cast that over the area as well.

Consider using several polygons mapped with the flame and/or smoke effect so that they can be positioned in front of and behind various pieces of mesh. This gives the fire more depth and realism. Scaling the polygons also creates the illusion of a mixture of large and small blazes. Be sure to offset the start points of the loops so that all the fires are not burning in sync.

If you need a quick and dirty fire or smoke effect, create a few maps of the effect in slightly different positions in Photoshop. Apply the first map to a flat polygon, with opacity mapping dropping out everything but the fire or smoke itself. Duplicate, then rotate the polygon on its vertical axis about 5-10° and then apply the second map to the new polygon. Repeat this, varying the maps, until you have something that looks like a cylinder made up of radially arranged, flat polygons. Light the assembly from below and rotate it during the animation. The effect works something like a flip-book, with the rotating polygons revealing slightly different maps as they spin. To cut back on rendering time or improve the effect, you may want to save this sequence off as an animation with an alpha channel, then modify it with a paint or 2D animation program and apply it to a single polygon in your project. The effect is not as good as using filmed effects, but will work in a clutch, or for a very brief shot.

Smoke Effects

Using your program's particle effects system is one of the best ways to create quality smoke effects. With the particle system, use opacity-mapped flat polys for the particles. The opacity should be greatest (but far from opaque) in the center of the polygon, and then fade out to completely transparent at the edges. The resulting particles may not look like much individually, but when combined together and animated, the effect is pretty good for light smoke effects. For thick, volumetric smoke, you'll probably need to use a specialized plug-in, such as Afterburn for 3ds max.

Animation Tutorials

Topics covered:

Creating Nulls and Links

Duplicating the Mesh with Links

Creating Looping Rotation

Creating Blinking Lights

Adjusting Motion Paths and Controls

Using Inverse Kinematics

Creating Nulls and Links

This tutorial will create nulls and links for the thrusters to ensure that the props and thrusters move properly when they're animated.

1. Create a null object in the center of the thruster, extending beyond the shroud to make it easier to select. Name it ThrNUL01. Use Align

to center the null around the shroud, and then rotate it 45° (see Figure 9.21a).

2. Use Axis Move to slide the null's local axis forward until it is in the center of the mounting bracket. This ensures that the thruster will pivot around the mounting bracket, not the center of the shroud (see Figure 9.21b).

3. Link the blades and other parts of the prop to the thruster nose cone, ThrNos. Try rotating the nose around its central axis to see whether the blades spin properly (see Figure 9.21c).

4. Link all the thruster components, including the strut, to the null object ThrNUL01. Try rotating the null around the local axis that points toward the center of the mounting bracket to see whether it turns properly, and then return it to its original position (see Figure 9.21d).

FIGURE 9.21

Linking thruster components: (a) Positioning the null object.
(b) Adjusting the local axis of the null for proper rotation. (c) Linking the blades to the nose cone.
(d) Testing the links by rotating the null object.

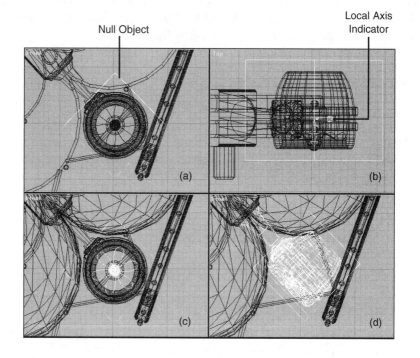

Use the same techniques to link the mirrored spotlights for the rotating beacon to a null object.

1. Create a null object in the center of BeaGls01, extending beyond the glass to make it easier to select. Name it BeaNUL01. Use Align to center the null around the glass (see Figure 9.22)

2. Link the two spotlights (and their targets, if any) to the null object. Try rotating the null around the beacon's central axis to see whether the lights spin properly.

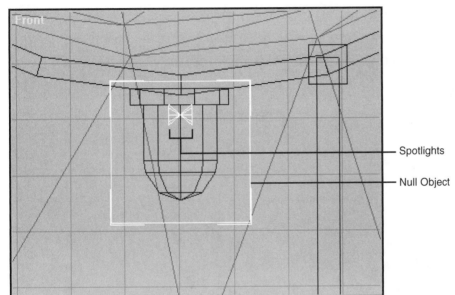

Spotlights

Null Object

FIGURE 9.22

Prepare the beacon for animation by creating a null object centered over the beacon and linking the spotlights to it.

Creating Looping Rotation

Looping rotation can be achieved in a couple of ways, depending on the software's capabilities. For example, you may be able to assign a behavior that does it automatically. Here, you create a keyframed loop that can be varied in length and number of rotations. The steps describe the process for the blimp thruster, but you should create a similar movement for the rotating beacons as well.

Note that in this generic tutorial, frame 0 is used as the first frame of the animation.

1. Activate the animation module or mode for your software. Go to frame 30 (see Figure 9.23).

2. Rotate ThrNos01 around its central axis a full 360°, making the linked blades rotate. Move the animation slider back and forth from frame 0 to frame 30 to make sure the rotation is working properly. You may need to assign a linear rotation controller to the motion, or adjust the continuity on the TCB controller for both keyframes to 0 to eliminate variations in speed or direction.

Current
Frame
Indicator

Frame 30
Keyframe
Marker

Time
(in Frames)

FIGURE 9.23

Creating a rotational loop: Activate animation mode, then go to frame 30 and rotate the thruster nose cone 360°; this will create a rotational keyframe. The blades will rotate as well because they're linked to the nose cone.

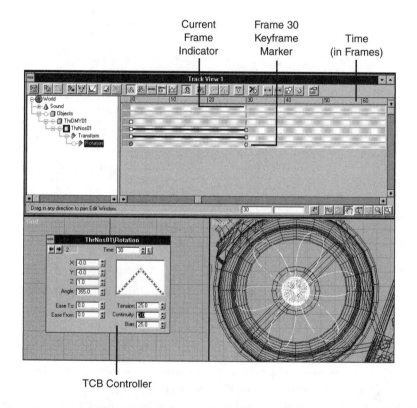

TCB Controller

At this point, if you were to render frames 0–29 and play them back in a continuous loop, the propeller would rotate smoothly. The reason you would not include frame 30 is because then you would have two frames (30 and 0) that were identical, and the loop would have a momentary hitch in it at that point.

3. Use the same technique to rotate the dummy object attached to the rotating beacon light. Have it spin at the same rate—360° over the course of 30 frames.

If you want this rotation to repeat over a longer period, either use a rotation behavior or use the following method instead.

1. Determine the total length of the animation, and calculate the number of times the blades would have to rotate for that period of time.

2. With the first keyframe at frame 0, activate animation mode and go to the last frame of the animation, based on your calculations. Rotate the ThrNos01 around its central axis the appropriate number of times.

Note that some 3D packages ignore rotations of more than 360° between keyframes. For example, if you rotate an object 380°, the program may only consider it to have been rotated 20°, ignoring the full rotation completely. In these cases, there may be special settings you can use (see your manual) or you may have to set a series of keyframes, rotating the object 360° or less each time.

Creating Blinking Lights

To create the effect of a blinking strobe light, you can animate the brightness setting of the point light on the end of the gondola.

1. Activate the animation module or mode for your software. Select the point light next to the gondola (see Figure 9.24a).

2. The light's color was set to 255, 0, 0 red when it was created, and this information is held in frame 0. Consider this keyframe as the ON keyframe. Go to frame 1 and set the light's output level to 0, or its color to 0, 0, 0 black. Consider this one as the OFF keyframe (see Figure 9.24b).

3. Copy the ON keyframe in frame 0 to frame 5. If you were to render the animation now, the light would be on in frame 0, off in frame 1, and gradually increase in intensity from frames 2 to 5 (see Figure 9.24c).

4. Although some programs offer controllers that simply turn things on or off, we'll assume that this feature is unavailable. Therefore, copy the OFF keyframe for the light from frame 1 to frames 4 and 6. The light remains off between frames 1 and 4 because both keyframes are OFF types (see Figure 9.24d).

5. Render frames 0–6 as an animation. The light should blink twice, once at frame 0, and again at frame 5. You can then copy frames 4–6 as needed to continue the blinking sequence.

6. Use a similar process to animate the color of the beacon object itself, from a bright red material to a very dark red to reflect the changes in the light levels.

FIGURE 9.24

Creating a blinking light: (a) Select the point light next to the gondola. (b) Frame 0 is already ON, because the light was set to a bright red. Go to frame 1 and change the color of the light to black, turning it OFF. (c) Copy the ON keyframe to frame 5. (d) Copy the OFF keyframe to frames 4 and 6.

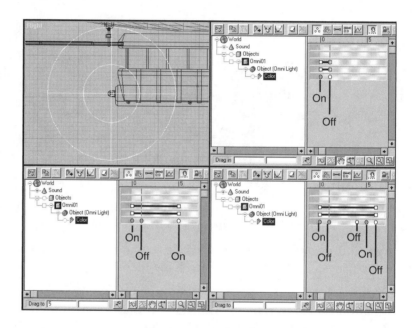

Duplicating the Mesh with Links

The last step in the general modeling process is the mirroring of those portions of the mesh that have links and materials applied to fill out the rest of the model.

1. Select the spire assembly and Rotate-copy it around the center of the GasBag, so that there are four of them at 90° angles (see Figure 9.25a).

2. Copy the beacons, searchlights, and other elements that need to be duplicated on the other side of the blimp into position. Rotate the copied beacon 90° so that the beams from the two beacons won't be pointed at each other. Place a second copy of the searchlight assembly near the front of the blimp, facing forward to act as a headlight. The monitor assembly doesn't need to be duplicated, because it won't be seen in the shots you are doing (see Figure 9.25b).

3. Select the thruster assembly, including the strut and base objects. Mirror-copy them and move the copies into position on the opposite side of the blimp (see Figure 9.25c).

4. Hide or Freeze the GasBag, monitor, and gondola assemblies, front searchlight, and the ball and cylinder extending from the nose cone of the blimp. Use Mirror-copy to create a reversed copy, and position the mesh, using the GasBag as a reference (see Figure 9.25d).

5. Create a large null object in the center of the GasBag, extending out a comfortable distance. Name it BmpNUL01. Unhide and/or Unfreeze all objects and link them to the null object.

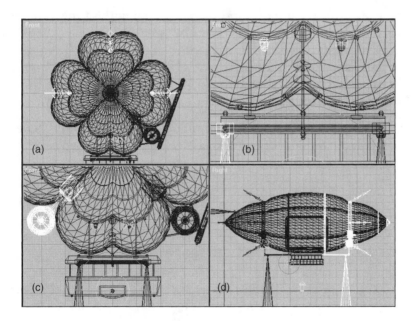

FIGURE 9.25

Finishing off the mesh: (a) Duplicating the spires. (b) Mirroring the thruster assembly. (c) Copying the search-light and beacon. (d) Mirroring most of the mesh on the front half of the blimp.

Adjusting Motion Paths and Controls

At this point, it's time to move the airship around a little. The basic plan is to have the blimp come into the frame, slow down, and stop. On your own, you can have it dock at this point with a tower that you'll be using in the next tutorial. Because the cameras and lights are already set up, you'll make the current position of the blimp the ending point for the animation, and move backward. This is actually a pretty common practice in animating, because it enables you to set things up precisely in the modeling phase.

1. Activate the main camera view that was set up in the Chapter 8 tutorials. The blimp was linked to the large null object earlier, so you'll move the blimp by moving the BmpNUL01 null object (see Figure 9.26a).

2. To speed things up during animation and test renders, turn off all mesh except for the GasBag object and null. If your software offers a fast viewport mode, switch to it so that the screen updates even faster (see Figure 9.26b).

3. Activate animation mode and set the total length of the animation to 121 frames (meaning that it ends on frame 120, because there is a frame 0). This is much too short for the move you are going to do, but is more practical for this type of tutorial. You can extend the overall length of the animation later. In the top view, note the present position of the blimp (see Figure 9.26c).

4. Go to frame 120 and rotate the null object 90° clockwise. Move the null diagonally until the GasBag object is just off the edge of the Camera view (see Figure 9.26d).

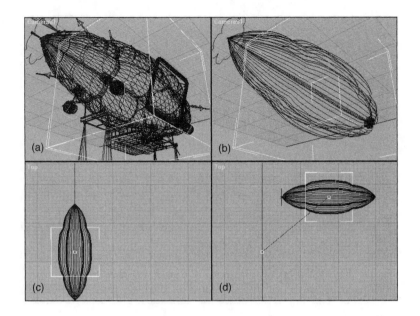

FIGURE 9.26

Moving the blimp:
(a) Select the camera viewport. (b) Hide unnecessary
mesh. (c) Switch to the Top
view and activate anima-
tion mode. (d) Rotate the
null to which the blimp is
linked and move it diago-
nally until it disappears
from the camera viewport.

5. Select the movement (translation) keyframe at frame 0 and examine
    the TCB controller. The blimp should settle into or out of position,
    rather than start or stop abruptly, so set the Ease From control to
    about 35 (see Figure 9.27a).

6. The move is too linear right now, so go to frame 60 and move the
    null object to create a little curvature to the path (see Figure 9.27b).

7. Keep an eye on the animation timeline to make sure that the
    keyframes are properly located, and that other object parameters
    haven't been inadvertently altered (see Figure 9.27c).

8. Make a preview or quick render of the move from the camera view-
    port and make any adjustments to the path or controller settings.
    Try to avoid extreme settings, because they tend to cause trouble in
    adjacent keyframes as well.

FIGURE 9.27

Completing the blimp
move: (a) Set the TCB
controller for the start-
ing frame to Ease From
frame 0. (b) Add a
keyframe in the middle
of the path to make it
curve a bit. (c) Check
your work in the ani-
mation timeline periodi-
cally, and use it for
any time or weighting
adjustment of
keyframes.

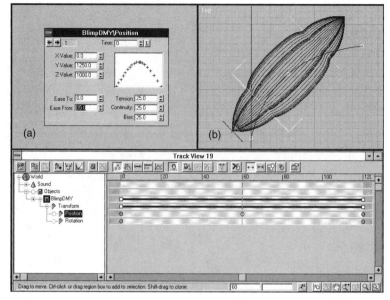

(a)

(b)

(c)

This is just the beginning of setting up a animation move like this. After the movement is solid, go in and add additional elements, such as subtle rocking, drifting,
and elevation changes, as if a breeze were affecting the blimp. You can also rotate
the thrusters and have the blimp's attitude change in response. Don't forget to
continue the looping animation of the lights and props throughout the length of
the animation.

Using Inverse Kinematics

Located on the CD-ROM is an additional model of a docking structure constructed by the previous edition's Technical Editor, Simon Knights. You may either
import the model when needed, or build a docking tower of your own design as
another component of your exercises. Because the tower and blimp are both
large projects that could bog down your system if loaded simultaneously, only the
key portions of the tower and blimp are used in this tutorial.

In this tutorial, set up movement constraints on the pre-built tower, then experiment with inverse kinematics to see how the tower equipment can be moved to grab hold of the blimp's docking point.

1. Load the exercise file IKTUT.3DS or IKTUT.DXF from the CD-ROM. This file contains portions of the tower and blimp project (see Figure 9.28a).

2. The key portions of the tower relating to IK are the gear-like platform and the docking machinery mounted on it (see Figure 9.28b).

   The purpose of the exercise is to link and constrain the docking equipment (see Figure 9.28c), so that it can swing around and latch onto the end of the blimp nose cone (see Figure 9.28d).

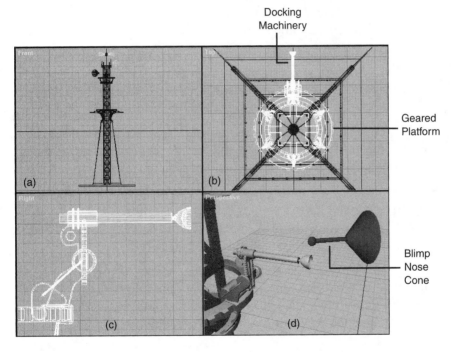

Docking Machinery

Geared Platform

Blimp Nose Cone

FIGURE 9.28

Components of the IK exercise: (a) The tower assembly. (b) The platform and docking machinery. (c) Side view of the docking machinery. (d) The object is to set up IK constraints and connect the docking machinery to the end of the blimp nose cone.

3. Identify the components of the base assembly that will rotate around the geared platform. These components will be linked to the Base object, which will have constraints applied to it (see Figure 9.29a).

4. It's nearly always best to adjust the pivot point of objects before linking. Make sure that the Base object's pivot is at the center of the geared platform.

5. When linking, make sure that you understand the order in which your software asks you to link objects. Start at the Base object, making this the parent of the base assembly objects above it. When all the base assembly objects are linked, continue the process by linking the Rack object to the chain. Continue on, linking the other members of the rack assembly to the Rack object. Finally, link the Rod object, and then the plunger, onto the chain. At this point, you should have linked everything between the Base object and the plunger at the end of the rod assembly.

6. To confirm that you have linked everything correctly, rotate the Base object around the pivot point, which you already set to the center of the geared platform. All the pieces should move with the Base object as it circles the platform. Many software packages also have a Show Hierarchy or Show Tree command that enables you to visually check that the links in the model are correct.

7. Next, all the joints of the mechanism have to be defined. This involves choosing whether a joint rotates or slides, then determining in what ways it needs to be constrained.

8. Using the method described by your manuals, set the Base object to be a rotational joint constrained to rotate around the vertical axis, so that it can freely traverse the perimeter of the geared platform, but cannot rotate in any other direction (see Figure 9.29b).

9. Set the rack to be a sliding joint, and constrain it so that it can move up and down along the vertical axis only. Set the constraints so that it will not smash down into the base assembly when lowered, or come apart from it when raised (see Figure 9.29c).

10. The plunger-like rod assembly also needs sliding constraints, so that it can extend outward and retract while remaining inside the sleeve at the top of the rack assembly. As with the last step, make sure it doesn't slide too far in or out (see Figure 9.29d).

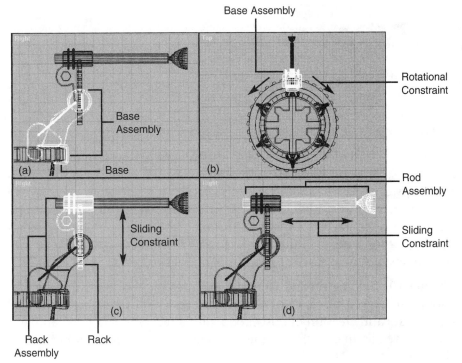

Base Assembly

Base
Assembly

(a) Base

(b)

Rotational
Constraint

Sliding
Constraint

(c)

Rack
Assembly

Rack

Rod
Assembly

Sliding
Constraint

(d)

FIGURE 9.29

Setting the constraints:
(a) Link the various
components of the
docking machinery
from the Base object to
the plunger at the end
of the rod assembly.
(b) Constrain the base
to rotate around the
platform only. (c) Set
the rack assembly to
slide up and down.
(d) Set the rod assem-
bly to slide back and
forth.

11. After all the constraints are set, make sure that IK is active and pre-
    pare to test the docking machinery movement (see Figure 9.30a).

12. Select the end of the plunger and move it to the nose cone. If every-
    thing is set properly, the docking machinery will rotate and slide as
    needed to make the two objects meet (see Figure 9.30b).

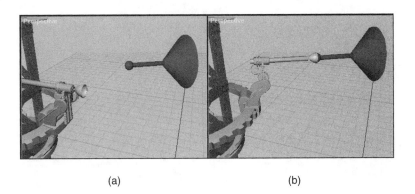

(a)   (b)

FIGURE 9.30

Test the constraints by
selecting the end of the
plunger and moving it
to the nose cone. If
everything is set prop-
erly, the docking
machinery will rotate
and slide as needed.

You are encouraged to experiment with a lot of additional animation, moving the blimp in other ways and doing moving camera shots as well. You may want to read up through Chapter 11, "The Reel," which can help you decide how to tell a story through these different shots.

Summary

This chapter started out with a look at basic animation terminology and techniques, from the timeline to motion paths, and discussed the differences between forward and inverse kinematics. It described how bones can be added to mesh to animate and distort it, and touched on the tools and techniques of character animation. Although books can provide an understanding of the basic techniques of animation, you have to build your skill and understanding of the subject through practice and experimentation.

Chapter 10, "Rendering and Output," explores render-time issues such as resolution, aspect ratios, color depth, palettes, and atmosphere. You will see the uses and creation of post-production effects such as glows and lens flares, as well as an overview of the different types of output, from slides to videotape.

Rendering and Output

Images and animation often require the use of compositing and other image-processing techniques to achieve the final result. Image ©2002 Kenn Brown.

*T*he Master rose slowly from his chair and stretched. "I'm thinking of retiring early, lad," he said to the student, who was mulling over a scene floating above his Glowing Pool.

The youth shook himself out of his reverie. "Oh, can I ask a couple quick questions before you leave?"

"Certainly. Let's see what you have." The Master walked over to consider the student's scene, set near a pond with the castle a short distance away. Tiny fireflies circled the pond, zipping into and out of the image. "Nice job on the lighting," the old man said, "and the composition is good, too. Needs a little atmosphere, though."

"That was my first question!" chirped the student. "How do I summon a bit of mist?"

"Fawghorne Vaeporrub," intoned the Master, causing a gentle vapor to rise from the pond. The fog made the castle in the background seem to become more integrated into the environment, making the scene much more realistic.

"That's great," commented the lad. "Now, about the fireflies—right now they just look like little white dots floating around."

"Indeglow Luciferase," replied the old man, causing the white specks to generate tiny halos of light. "You see, they just needed a bit of a glow to them, like the real thing."

"Wonderful!" exclaimed the student. "But there's still something funny about the way they move."

"Hmmm." The old man settled into a chair to rest his weary bones. He studied the movement of the fireflies for a short while, then said, "Yes, you see the ones that zip in and out of the image, close to our viewpoint? They're too sharp."

"Too sharp?" asked the lad.

"Yes, they should blur a bit when they move, like so. Dizipaace Shinkansen," the Master chanted, making a swirling gesture with his hand. Now, the fast-moving fireflies left short and subtle but realistic trails of light as they darted about.

"Excellent! That did it!" cried the lad.

The Master smiled and got halfway up before the student bade him to wait. "Just one more thing, Master..."

"Yes?"

"How would I make the fireflies swarm together and transform into a faerie princess in a swirl of color and light?"

The old man groaned and fell heavily into his chair once more. It was going to be a late night.

Rendering

As the beleaguered Master demonstrated to his student, some effects can be applied to 3D imagery at rendering time to take the "hard edge" off and make your scene appear more natural and realistic. Before you're ready to attempt these digital sleights of hand, however, you should review some render-time basics, including resolution, alpha channels, palettes, and so on.

Resolution

After you decide on the type of rendering to use—Flat, Phong, Ray Tracing, or any of the others detailed in Chapter 2, "Delving into Cyberspace"—you must tackle the question of resolution. As you no doubt recall, resolution refers to the number of horizontal and vertical pixels in an image. Resolution is defined by a set of two numbers, such as 640×480, which means that the image is 640 pixels wide (horizontal), and 480 pixels high (vertical).

The relationship between the width and height of the image is called the *aspect ratio*, and is calculated by dividing the horizontal resolution by the vertical resolution. In the 640×480 example, the aspect ratio would be 640 divided by 480, which equals 1.33:1 (or 4:3). This is a common aspect ratio for television and computer monitors. However, if you were doing film special effects work, the aspect ratio would be between 1.33:1 and 2.35:1, depending on the type of film and projection system, because movie screens are generally much wider than television screens in relation to their height.

The following is a list of common resolutions and aspect ratios:

720×486, 1.48:1—NTSC D1 Video*

720×576, 1.25:1—PAL/SECAM D1 Video*

*You may be wondering why the standard video aspect ratios don't match the 1.33:1 (4:3) aspect ratio you would expect from measuring a TV screen. The reason is that part of the image is lost to overscan, and televisions also squeeze the image 10-11% horizontally.

1080×1980, 16:9—HDTV Video

720×1280, 16:9—HDTV Video

640×480, 1.33:1—Base-level computer monitor resolution

800×600, 1.33:1—Moderate-level computer monitor resolution

1024×768, 1.33:1—Moderate-level computer monitor resolution, low print resolution

1280×960, 1.33:1—High-level computer monitor resolution, low print resolution

1600×1200, 1.33:1—High-level computer monitor resolution, moderate print resolution

2048×1536, 1.33:1—Moderate print resolution

4096×3072, 1.33:1—High print resolution

3072×2048, 1.5:1—High 35mm slide/film resolution*

6144×2048, 3:2—70mm film resolution*

*Note that in films, there are many additional aspect ratios (2.35:1, 1.85:1, 1.66:1) and resolutions because not all the available image area may be used, and CG output to film doesn't usually take advantage of the maximum resolution available to control rendering times.

QuickTime VR and similar formats enable the user to navigate around a 360° still image view of a space or object (see Chapter 1, "The Virtual Path"). To create this kind of "surround" rendering, you can set up a camera to rotate a total of 360° over a space of 120 frames. Render your images at the vertical resolution desired, but make them only three pixels wide. When the rendering is done, assemble the first 190 three-pixel-wide renderings into a single panoramic image. A Photoshop macro can be created to do the assembly chore automatically.

Another measurement related to resolution may be more familiar to you as a printer specification: *dots per inch* (*dpi*). This dpi measurement means exactly what it says—the number of dots that the medium can display (or print) in one inch. With computer monitors, a dot is a pixel, and the setting varies according to the monitor's size and the video card's resolution. However, you can usually adjust the monitor to yield 72–75 dpi, which translates to a 1024×768 resolution on a 17" monitor. This dpi setting works out nicely for desktop publishing work, because common printer resolutions are usually a multiple of 75, such as 150, 300, 600, or 1200 dpi.

To see how pixels and dpi interrelate when printing, consider a 640×480 image as an example. If you print the image at a low-quality 75 dpi, the resulting image is 8.53"×6.4". To calculate this, you simply divide the resolution by the dpi value (640 pixels divided by 75 dpi equals 8.53). At a moderate 150 dpi, the image would print out at 4.27"×3.2". At 300 dpi (the typical laser printer maximum), it would be only 2.13"×1.6", and so forth. By the same token, suppose you wanted to create an image that would print at 8.0"×10.5" and 150 dpi. By multiplying the size of the final image by the desired dpi, you get a required image resolution of 1200×1575.

Color Depth

The *color depth* of an image is how many colors each pixel is capable of displaying. The value is usually expressed in terms of how many bits (a computerese term for a single binary number) an image contains. In an 8-bit image (such as a .GIF file), for example, each pixel is represented by 8 bits (called a *byte*), which allows the pixel to be any one of 256 different colors. To understand how the 8 turns into 256, you must take a side trip into some binary math.

As you know, computers use binary numbers, a system also called Base 2. A single binary number (a bit) can be only one of two things: either 0 or 1. Therefore, to represent larger numbers, a series of bits are strung together, like 1011. The position of each binary number within the series (from right to left) becomes an exponent of 2, and then they are added together. For example, binary 0001 = 1, binary 0010 = 2, binary 0100 = 4, and so on. In this way, 8 bits = binary $11111111 = 2^7+2^6+2^5+2^4+2^3+2^2+2^1+2^0 = 128+64+32+16+8+4+2+1 = 255$. Because zero counts as a number, a total of 256 numbers can be represented.

By the same token, a 4-bit image has a maximum of 16 color possibilities (8+4+2+1 = 16, when 0 is counted), a 16-bit image has 65,536 potential colors per pixel, and a 24-bit image has a whopping 16,777,216 color options. The latter palette is nearly the full range of colors that are visible to humans, and enables you to work with smooth, accurate color images.

In 24-bit color images, the total number of bits per pixel is divided by three, and assigned to each of the three primary colors that make up light: red, green, and blue. In other words, a single pixel in a 24-bit image contains 8 bits of red information, 8 bits of green, and 8 bits of blue. Each R, G, or B *channel*, being 8-bit, can display that color in any one of 256 levels of brightness, with 0 being no brightness and 255 being full brightness. That's why RGB colors are specified by three sets of numbers, such as 0,0,0 (black), 255,255,255 (white), 255,0,0 (red), 255,0,255 (violet), and so forth.

Who said math was boring?

It's worth noting that although 24-bit color is the most common depth in use for computer displays right now, video cards, scanners, and other devices may use even higher color depths for doing internal calculations and for high-end output. These color depths include 32-, 48-, or 64-bit color, and even high-precision floating point formats. By making more colors available, these new standards help to reduce banding as well as other errors that can creep in when image data is processed or filtered.

Alpha Channel

Just when you think you've got bit counts figured out, along come alpha channels. An *alpha channel* is an optional layer of image data that provides an additional 8 bits of information about transparency. This information is simply tacked onto the RGB data that defines the image, so a 24-bit image with an alpha channel becomes a 32-bit image. The alpha channel, like each of the R, G, or B channels, is capable of 256 levels of intensity, but instead of being interpreted as a color, the information is used to vary the transparency of the associated image against a background (see Figure 10.1). In this way, the alpha channel functions as a *mask* or *matte*, allowing portions of an image to be seen, while the rest is replaced with the background image.

(a) (b) (c) (d)

FIGURE 10.1

Alpha channel example: (a) Foreground image with opaque and translucent objects. (b) Alpha channel from foreground image. (c) Background image. (d) Composite of foreground image over background image using alpha channel to control transparency.

In most programs, 0 (black) is fully transparent, so pixels of that color in the alpha channel do allow the foreground image pixel in the same position to show up at all, meaning that the background pixel color behind it is unaffected. A 255 (white) pixel is completely opaque, so that the foreground image pixel completely obscures the background pixel. All other levels of gray would blend the foreground and background pixel colors to some degree.

Because alpha channels allow for transparency effects, multiple images with alpha channels can be composited together into a single image. Using alpha channels is a convenient method for compositing 3D images over still photographs or video, because you can render the model with the alpha channel setting activated, and any objects that appear automatically mask out the background image, enabling you to combine the images in a paint or editing program.

Alpha channels are also convenient when you are working entirely in 3D, because render-intensive scenes can be broken into layers and rendered with alpha channels, then composited together later. This is particularly useful when you are dealing with elements that can be used in multiple scenes, because you have to render them only once, then can combine them with other elements later on. This also gives you the opportunity to use image processing on the layers to adjust contrast, change the color balance, or add effects. In addition, you can insert digital video into 3D scenes by filming the subjects against a blue or green background, then dropping the solid color background out by converting it to an alpha channel.

Finally, compositing enables those with less-powerful systems to create very complex scenes by rendering only as many objects as the computer can comfortably handle, and then rendering out additional batches and compositing them all together.

> The multi-layer 3D approach was used extensively in the Artemis cockpit scenes of *The Daedalus Encounter*. The scenes consisted of five layers, starting with a looping render showing POV movement through a starfield. Next came a still image of the ship's hull, which was repositioned to make more of the stars visible. On top of that was the interior of the cockpit, with control panels and displays. Next came the actors in their chairs, the only live element in the composite. Finally, the foreground layer was a console that was located between the two actors.

In most programs, activating the alpha channel is easy. It's usually located in the render options dialog, and is either on or off. Compositing can then be done in the 3D program's video post system (if it has one) or in Photoshop or a digital video editing program such as Premiere.

Palettes

In 16-bit and higher color images, each pixel specifies the actual RGB color, like 127,64,198. Images with lower color depths use a different method. In *indexed color images*, the pixels point to an index of color registers (think of them as "paint pots") which contain the necessary RGB values (see Figure 10.2). This index method is used because it allows an image to be defined with less data; instead of each pixel containing a set of three numbers to define the RGB values, it contains only one number—the color register number. In an 8-bit image, there can be up to 256 of these color registers or "paint pots," but each pot can hold any one of the over sixteen million colors available.

The colors in the color registers define the *palette* for the image; that is, they specify the entire list of specific colors that are available for use in the image. In fact, another term for color register is *palette position*.

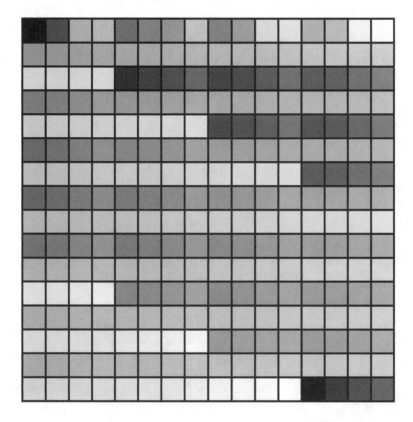

FIGURE 10.2

A 256 color (okay, grayscale in this book) palette. Each individual color location is called a color register.

Not so long ago, palette management was a major consideration in the multimedia and games industry, because most computers had video cards that could display a maximum of only 256 simultaneous colors. Presentation designs had to be carefully planned to ensure that all the graphics would work with a single palette, or that the switching of palettes was carefully disguised. Still, despite all the planning, the last few hours before the deadline were often devoted to tracking down *palette flashes,* the bizarre color shifts that can occur when a palette is changed.

Now, with even fairly low-end computer systems offering 16–24-bit color, the painful memories of having to deal with 256 color graphics have faded. Still, some situations still demand the speed or other special capabilities of 8-bit graphics, particularly the web, some games and products or presentations designed for the broadest possible market.

When developing a product or application to be used with an 8-bit graphics display, you will probably have to force the image to a predefined palette to avoid flashes. If you have to do this, there is a lot to be said for using the native palette of the target system (the Windows or Apple *system palettes*). Because these palettes are already pre-loaded, and all the desktop graphics and most other applications use them, the problem of the screen flashing is eliminated, because you never switch to a custom palette. Unfortunately, the system palettes are ill-suited to most photographic images and usually result in smooth gradients becoming banded or the appearance of other strange patches of color.

If your 24-bit image needs to be reduced to 8-bit or less, you can use the 3D program or Photoshop to generate an *optimized palette* for the image, one that includes the best combination of colors to keep it as faithful as possible to the original. Unfortunately, the palette that works best for one image rarely works well for another, unless they have a very similar color scheme. If you have multiple images that need a single palette, try grouping them all together into a single image and extracting a palette from that.

There was an article in *Morph's Outpost* years ago in which someone came up with a universal palette (if I recall correctly) based on a study of how the human eye perceives color. I tried to locate some additional information about this palette and its creator on the web, but couldn't find any mention of it. However, it is included on the CD-ROM as UNIVPAL.GIF so that you can give it a try.

Using the *dither* setting can help a lot as well, because it enables the program to break gradients up into patterns of variously colored pixels to simulate a wider range of colors. The best type of pattern to use for most images is a *diffusion dither*, because the positions of the pixels are randomized, and look more natural and unobtrusive.

One interesting offshoot of the 8-bit palette is the ability to perform color cycling animation. This type of animation works not by altering the image itself, but by changing the colors in it through direct manipulation of the *color registers* (the individual "paint pots" in the palette). This method was often used to create the illusion of water flowing in 8-bit games.

The most impressive application of palette animation I ever saw was in a daily organizer product called *Seize the Day*, created by one of LucasArts' animators. It featured 12 fantasy landscape scenes with effects such as rippling water and reflections. Interestingly, the scene would change in keeping with the actual time of day, so that the lighting and colors would change as the sun rose and set. On random days, even the weather would change, at times appearing to be foggy or overcast, or even raining.

Anti-aliasing

Because digital images are basically made up of a matrix of dots, lines that aren't perfectly horizontal or vertical take abrupt "drops" when they enter a new row or column of dots (an effect called *stairstepping*). The resulting lines look jagged, which is why images containing them are described as "having the *jaggies*" (see Figure 10.3).

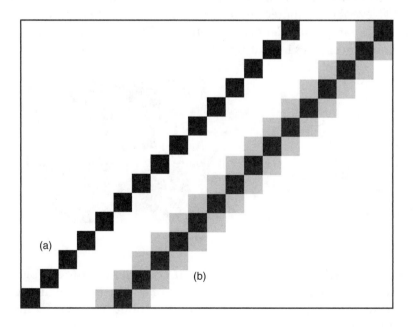

(a)

(b)

FIGURE 10.3

Line types: (a) Non-anti-aliased line show-ing stairstepping effect. (b) Anti-aliasing inserts middle tones that blend the line into the back-ground, reducing the jaggies.

Anti-aliasing is a method of reducing jagginess by filling in pixels at the stairstepping points with colors that are midway between the line color and the background color. The result softens the stairstepping and makes the line look smoother.

Most programs enable you to adjust the amount of anti-aliasing in an image or at least turn it on and off. Because anti-aliasing does increase render times, you may want to leave it off for most of your test renders, then turn it back on for final testing and output.

Atmosphere

Adding *atmosphere* settings to a model causes it to render with a user-defined level of diffusion, creating the effect of objects being seen from great distances or through a mist. Some programs may also include fire and volumetric lighting in their atmospheric effects.

Fog is the most common atmospheric effect, and is just what it sounds like—a mist effect. It can, however, have colors assigned to it, so it's really more like evenly distributed smoke (see Figure 10.4). Fog is usually defined with a set of ranges that delineate where the effect begins and ends, as well as a pair of percentages indicating minimum and maximum concentration.

FIGURE 10.4

Atmosphere samples: (a) Fog effect using white for the atmosphere color. (b) Depth cueing created by using black for the atmosphere color.

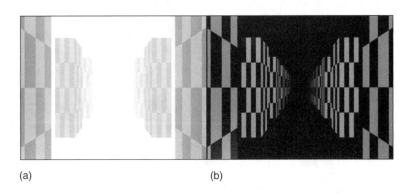

(a)   (b)

If the fog color is a light gray, you get an effect similar to real fog. If the color is black, distant objects become dark or totally black, which can be convenient for downplaying a background without having to fiddle with the lighting too much.

It's a good idea to use fog for most exterior scenes. Keep the color on the blue side and the concentration low for "clear days" so that distant objects have a realistic haze to them.

Some programs have the capability to use bitmaps to define fog color, or even volumetric fog, which is similar to the volumetric lighting discussed in Chapter 7, "Lighting." *Volumetric fog* can often be animated, so that realistic variations in the mist concentration drift through the scene.

Geometry Channel

Although a rare feature, the Geometry Channel is an interesting item that bears mentioning. *G-buffer* or *geometry channel* support means that the program is capable of outputting additional image channels that use grayscale images to describe the *geometry* in the model. G-buffer channels include: Distance, Normals, XYZ position, UV coordinates, and others.

With the right kind of image editing or post-processing software, this feature enables you to do such seemingly impossible things as replacing the texture map on an object *after the image is rendered*. This would be particularly useful in applications where the structure of something has been decided upon, but the material is still under consideration. One use would be in the kitchen cabinet design business, where a 3D model of the kitchen with the new cabinets has been built, but the clients want to look through different wood types and finishes without waiting for the scene to be re-rendered.

Alternative Renderers

Many programs now can export to specialty rendering software, or use alternative rendering plug-ins. These specialty renderers can be used to create a range of looks from extreme photorealism to total cartoonish.

If photorealism is what you're after, renderers that use *global illumination (GI)* rendering techniques such as radiosity create the kind of lighting interactions and realistic shadows that you see in the real world. The results are best seen large and in full color, so check out sites such as www.lightwave3d.com for examples created with LightWave's built-in GI and caustics capabilities. Also take a look at www.splutterfish.com for a gallery of samples created with the Brazil rendering system.

You can fake radiosity to some degree through clever use of lighting. For example, if you have a large red sphere sitting inside a white box, you could put a low-intensity, distance-attenuated red light inside the sphere. As a result, the white walls of the box will take on a reddish cast, just as they would in a radiosity-rendered scene.

To create a look similar to hand-drawn traditional animation, *cel shaders* render surfaces as broad washes of solid color, and then add ink-lines to finish the effect (see Figure 10.5).

FIGURE 10.5

Terrence Walker used LightWave 3D's cartoon rendering capabilities to create *Understanding Chaos*, a short film he would like to see expanded into a major motion picture. Image ©2000 Terrence Walker/Studio ArtFX.

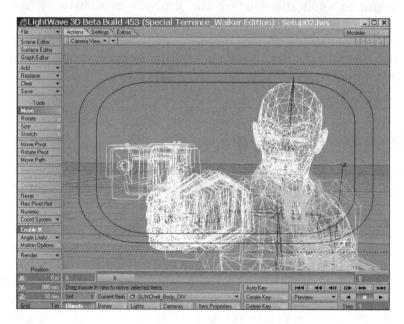

Cartoon shaders have been used in films like *The Princess Mononoke* and *The Iron Giant* to blend 3D elements as seamlessly as possible into 2D animation.

Note

Even if your program doesn't offer built-in or add-on cartoon shading effects, you can probably come up with a way to simulate the solid-color look by using a combination of high-contrast lighting and bright colors in the ambient and specular channels of the materials. To create the ink lines, render out the image at two to three times the desired resolution and put two copies of it on different layers in Photoshop. Run a Find Edges filter on the upper layer and set it to Multiply; then shrink the whole image back down to the desired size.

Post-Production Effects

Some effects are difficult to achieve in the animation or rendering phases of production, so some 3D products offer built-in *post-production effects*, which include transitions, color manipulation, and a host of special effects. If your program doesn't offer this capability, you can probably use paint programs or digital video editing software for most of the effects mentioned in this section.

One of the most common capabilities of built-in post-production effects are images and animation compositing features using alpha channels or chroma keys. Other popular features include lens flares, glows, and motion blur.

Lens Flares

A *lens flare* is the pattern of bright circles and rays that is seen when you point a camera lens toward the sun or other bright light source (see Figure 10.6). Lens flares add realism to scenes with bright lights, helping to create the illusion that a real camera was used for the shot. Interestingly, although the human eye never experiences this kind of effect, we're so used to seeing it in films and television that it "looks right" to us.

FIGURE 10.6

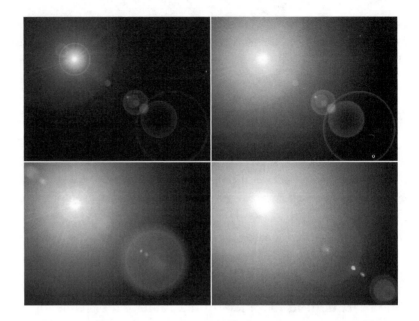

Lens flares are caused
by bright sources of
light interacting with
camera lens elements.
Their appearance
varies significantly,
depending on the lens
type and brightness of
the light source.

Depending on the program, the Lens Flare control may be built in, or added on as a plug-in. Controls range from a basic brightness control to extensive choices of real-world lens effects. Some products, such as LightWave, can use any light object to generate a lens flare. Other programs may have invisible "generator objects" or emitters that are the focus of the effect. In this case, you would place the generator near the apparent light source.

Lens flares are particularly dynamic and effective when either the camera or the light source causing the flare are in motion. Another nice touch is to have the subject block the light source momentarily as it moves across the screen. Take care not to use lens flares at every opportunity, however—they've become a bit cliché.

Glows

Chapter 7 talked about ways to add a realistic halo of light, or *glow,* to an exposed light source (such as a bare bulb). The glow effect is a commonly needed one for 3D graphics, and many products incorporate this capability (see Figure 10.7).

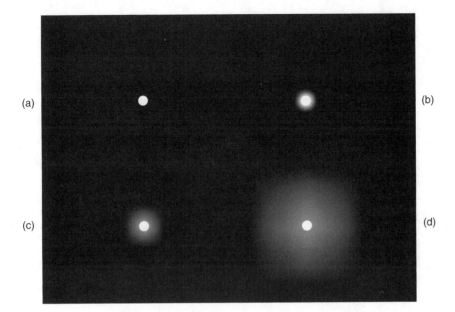

FIGURE 10.7

Glow effect samples:
(a) Self-illuminated
sphere without glow.
(b–d) Various amounts
of glow applied to the
sphere.

In most cases, the software applies the glow as a 2D post effect after the image is rendered. Glows are usually either assigned to objects (using a G-buffer), a particular color in the scene, or a material. Using a particular color to trigger the glow effect can be troublesome, because there may be other objects in the scene that are of a similar color, but aren't intended to glow.

Another problem is that glows may not work if there is a translucent object between the glowing material and the camera. This might occur if you build a typical clear light bulb where the tungsten filament is contained inside an airtight glass "bottle." If you apply the glow effect to the filament object, the glow may not appear because the transparent glass is between the filament and the camera. One workaround for this is to render the glowing filament without the glass, and then render the glass separately against an alpha channel and composite the images together.

Motion Blur

Motion blur is the smearing that occurs in an image when the subject or camera is in motion (see Figure 10.8). Motion blur is a natural occurrence, and fast-moving objects in an animation look unnaturally sharp if the effect isn't present. It also works well in still images to convey a sense of movement and speed.

FIGURE 10.8

Motion Blur effects:
(a) Unaffected object.
(b) 20-pixel Motion Blur
applied with Photoshop.
(c) 5-step motion blur
created by 3D renderer.

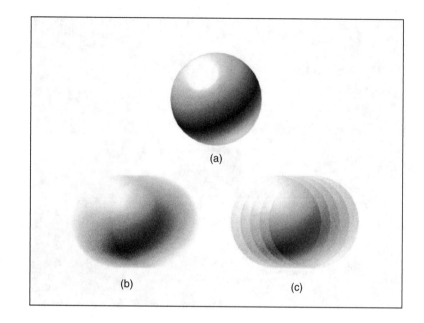

Motion blur occurs in film and still photography because the shutter on the camera is open long enough for a significant movement to occur. Because virtual cameras have no shutter and freeze all action perfectly, this effect has to be added through special rendering techniques or post-production image processing.

One of the common techniques programs use to create motion blur is rendering the scene a number of times while advancing the animation slightly. The multiple images are then composited together into a single, motion-blurred image. Of course, this means a 4–5 fold increase in rendering time. Another way to create the effect is by applying a directional blurring filter in postproduction using either a plug-in or paint program. This type of blur is generally more realistic, and renders faster as well.

Post-Processing with 2D Programs

Photoshop, Premiere, After Effects, and other 2D programs that can deal with sequential images can all be used to create certain post-production effects. You can either use the built-in filters these products offer, or create 2D paint or vector elements and composite them on top of your 3D renders.

Despite the capabilities of built-in video post features or digital video editing products such as Premiere, there may be times when you need even more control or capabilities to pull off an effect. For this kind of work, you can turn to your good old 2D paint program, or one that features "video painting" capabilities (the ability to paint on a digital video file, either frame by frame or over a series of frames). These methods, although they might be more time consuming, enable you to do compositing, create lens flares, and apply glows and motion blurs with a great deal of control over the final result.

If you opt to do motion blurs with a 2D paint program, you can reduce your workload by rendering the object to be blurred against an alpha channel and by restricting the blur effect to objects that pass close to the camera. The motion blur is most pronounced when the object is close by.

If you're a Photoshop user, familiarize yourself with the Actions (macros) and Batch processing features. Photoshop can be used to create some really unusual effects in your work if you apply sequences of filters and adjustments to a series of rendered images. For example, Andy Murdock likes to add a cool blurring effect to some of his work. The effect can be created with just about any paint program, Premiere, or After Effects (see Figure 10.9). You may also be able to create a similar effect without postprocessing by finding a plug-in that does blooming effects.

(a)   (b)

FIGURE 10.9

Using a combination of Screen layers and Gaussian Blur can create an interesting nostalgic look for your renders. (a) Straight render of finished blimp. (b) Results of postprocessing in Photoshop.

To create the Photoshop effect shown in Figure 10.9, follow these steps on an 800×600 render of the finished blimp:

1. Load up your image, then choose Image>Adjust>Levels. Set the middle slider to .6 and click OK. The image darkens significantly.

2. Duplicate the background layer twice and rename the duplicates Overlay01 and Overlay02, arranged so that Overlay02 is the top layer, followed by Overlay01, then the Background layer. Set both Overlay layers to be Screen layers.

3. Select Overlay01 and choose Filter>Blur>Gaussian Blur. Set the Radius to 5 pixels. Now select Overlay02 and apply a Gaussian to it as well, but with a Radius of 10 pixels.

4. Flatten the image to combine all the layers, then choose Filter>Sharpen>Unsharp Mask. Use settings of Amount: 60%, Radius: 1, and Threshold: 0 to bring back some of the detail.

The result should be a soft blurred image with blown-out highlights that may remind you of the look of an old film. If you were to create a Photoshop Action to perform the same process automatically, the look could be applied to an entire animation. If you try to apply this technique to other images, keep in mind that that the Photoshop settings will vary depending on the resolution of the image as well as its content.

Fractal Painter has frame painting controls built in, enabling you to preview your work much more easily than you can with Photoshop. Fractal also offers a wide range of interesting effects brushes and filters. The downside is that many artists find Fractal's interface clumsy, and lacking in the solid, basic brush controls that are Photoshop's strength.

We made good use of both Premiere and Photoshop post effects in *Daedalus*. Premiere allowed us to composite the bluescreen video over the 3D backgrounds, adjust color balance to get rid of the bluish cast, create complex multilayer mattes and composites, and do some easy but effective static and video roll effects. Photoshop was used to add sparks and debris coming off two colliding ships, as well as to cause some real spherical props held by the actors to be absorbed and disintegrated into a receptacle created with 3D graphics. For details on how these effects were accomplished, see *The Official Guide to the Daedalus Encounter* and the July 1996 issue of *InterActivity* magazine.

Output

After you've decided what to render and how to render it, you just have to decide in *which format* to render it. This section discusses the various output destinations, examines common file formats and compression methods, and explains the special requirements of videotape.

Output Options

Typical destination media for 3D images and animation includes computer files, photographic slides, and videotape. Take a look at what each of these has to offer.

Files

The primary destination for your rendering is most likely a file or files stored on the hard drive, even if your project will ultimately be output to 35mm slides or videotape. Because outputting to a file is an integral part of your 3D software, there's not a lot to be said about it, short of considering the file formats and compression methods available, which are discussed later in this chapter.

Of course, an important part of the disk output process is file naming and management. For information on these subjects, and how to develop a file naming convention, refer to Appendix G, "Planning and Organization," on the CD-ROM. Information on mass storage options to hold all those files can be found in Appendix E, "Hardware and Software," also on the CD.

The biggest problem you're likely to experience with disk output is running out of hard drive space—unless you have several hundred megabytes of free space. Remember that rendering often consumes a great deal of virtual memory provided by the hard drive, so the amount available when you start the render may drop by tens of megabytes or more later in the process. Also, the total size of image files can add up when you're rendering a large animation, so multiply the number of frames you're rendering by the typical file size for each image and leave plenty of room beyond that.

Videotape

Before desktop video became so popular, animation was often rendered to a frame buffer and output directly to videotape via expensive single-frame VCRs. In some cases, special interface gear also was required, such as VTR (Video Tape Recorder) controllers that would sense when the frame was rendered and activate the VCR. Besides being expensive, frame-by-frame animation took a heavy toll on the video recorder and forced you to put a great deal of trust into a single $30.00 tape cassette.

With mass storage being so fast and reasonably priced, almost everyone saves the files to disk first, then lays the animation off to tape with desktop digital video gear, a commercial *framestore* (high speed digital playback system), or off-line frame-by-frame recording. There are, however, a number of restrictions related to video output, which are discussed in more depth later in this section.

Slides

35mm slides are another popular output destination for still imagery. Although just about any resolution will work for slides, for the best results, create high-resolution images at around 3072×2048 pixels or higher, keeping the aspect ratio at 1.5:1 (3:2). You can have the slides made by a service bureau (unless you have a film recorder).

Prints

Print is also a popular destination format, but the subject of matching the image onscreen to the final press result could fill a book by itself. The main thing to keep in mind is that the screen and print color gamut are quite different, so a lot of RGB colors you can have in your rendering don't reproduce properly in a CMYK print. *CMYK (Cyan Magenta Yellow blacK)* refers to the different colors of ink in the 4-color process that are applied as tiny dot patterns to form the gamut of printing colors. Photoshop has many features that are geared toward making the transition from digital file to print output, including a CMYK viewing mode as well as filters and alerts that flag or correct unprintable colors.

Calibration

Computer monitors suffer from several big drawbacks. First, they're very nonstandard, varying tremendously from manufacturer to manufacturer and model to model. Second, their brightness and contrast settings are easy to change. As a result, if you look at the same image on different monitors, you will almost certainly see differences in hue, saturation, and brightness.

This lack of standardization is an endless source of wasted time and frustration in computer graphics. Different artists working on different systems see different results, and make corrections based on false information. As a result, when scenes from these artists are assembled into one project, the inconsistencies can become glaringly obvious.

The best way to correct this problem is to use a quality monitor and to adjust it regularly with a *color calibrator*, a device that is held up to the screen and adjusts the monitor using a special reference image that is displayed at the time. Unfortunately, these devices are still fairly uncommon outside of companies that work with digital imagery bound for print.

One adjustment that you can easily make is *gamma*, which refers to the overall brightness of the screen. Photoshop has a built-in gamma adjustment, as do some 3D programs. This gives you an onscreen pattern of dots that you can use as a guide to adjust the screen gamma. Gamma varies by display, platform, and output type, so adjusting it in this manner enables you to see how your monitor image (gamma 1.6–2.0) will look when output to a CMYK print (gamma 1.8) or on videotape (gamma 2.2).

Some programs may offer several gamma adjustments: one for the screen, one for file output, and perhaps one for file input as well. Leave the file gamma settings at the default setting unless you're certain that you need to change them. Altering the output gamma can cause big problems if your work is being integrated with other work that has a different gamma setting.

If you're creating a project for video, you really need to have a television monitor hooked up to your computer in addition to your regular monitor. Video tends to do a lot of unpleasant things to computer imagery, so a television monitor will enable you to see what your output looks like in its destination format so that you can make adjustments.

Compression

To reduce image and animation or digital video file sizes, various methods have been devised to compress the data in the file. Compression falls into two general categories: lossless and lossy.

Lossless compression reduces file size without impacting the image quality. One method by which it does this is by finding strings of identical information and using an algorithm to encode the color and location of repeated data. For example, if you were compressing a file that had a 100-pixel-long block of solid white, the compression software would use a shorthand method such as "255×100" rather than repeat the number 255 one hundred times in the file. Because the data isn't really lost, just recorded in a more efficient way, the image quality remains unchanged. Lossless compression capability is built into many of the image formats, including .GIF, .TGA, .TIF, and others.

Lossy compression reduces file sizes by changing the data or throwing some of it away. The most popular types of lossy compression are ones that reduce the color depth or use compression algorithms to eliminate small differences in pixel colors, or discard colors based on human perception. Although lossy compression usually has a negative impact on the image quality, you can reduce the degradation by generating a custom palette for the image, or using only a moderate amount of compression.

Digital video file formats such as .AVI and QuickTime are designed to accept plug-in compression methods called *codecs (COmpressor/DECompressorS)*. Some of the popular ones are MS Video, Indeo, and Cinepak. Each has its own strengths and weaknesses, and the correct selection depends on the application, target platform, and storage medium. MPEG compression seems to be the current winner for picture quality and compression, but may require special hardware support for best results during compression and/or playback.

File Formats

Quite a number of image formats are in use, ranging from proprietary formats used by only one or two programs or platforms to those that span virtually all systems. Unless otherwise noted, all the following are 24-bit or 32-bit formats that can handle lower bit depths as well:

◆ *AVI (Audio Video Interlaced)* was developed by Microsoft as the digital video standard for PCs. It can accept many different types of compression methods.

◆ *BMP (BitMaP)* was developed by Microsoft as the native format for icons and images in the Windows environment. It is interchangeable with *DIB (Device-Independent Bitmap)*.

◆ *FLC (FLiCk)* is an 8-bit animation format developed for Autodesk multimedia products. It features lossless compression in several resolutions. An older format, *FLI*, was limited to a 320×200 maximum resolution.

◆ *GIF (Graphics Interchange Format)* is an 8-bit lossless compression format owned by CompuServe but used extensively by commercial and shareware products. Recently, the popularity of animation on the Web has led to the use of GIF-89a as an animation format, a capability it always had, but one that was rarely used.

◆ *IFF (Interchange File Format)* is popular on the Amiga system, and has made its way onto other platforms through products such as LightWave.

◆ *JPG, JPEG (Joint Photographic Experts Group)* was developed as a lossy way to radically compress photographic images by eliminating minor differences in pixel colors. This method achieves one of the highest compression rates, but can cause undesirable artifacting if pushed too far, or if the image is compressed more than once. If you use this method, it's a good idea to have a lossless version saved as well. JPEG also can be used to compress digital video files.

◆ *LBM (interLeaved BitMap)* is an 8-bit format popularized by Deluxe Paint, a rather old program that's still in use for creating some game graphics and other 256-color imagery.

◆ *MPG, MPEG (Motion Picture Experts Group)* is a lossy video compression method that's considered to be the best currently available. There are two implementations: MPEG 1, which is currently in use for Video CDs (VCDs), and MPEG 2, which DVD players use.

◆ *PCT, PICT (PICTure)* is the native still image format popular on the Macintosh. A unique feature of this format is that it can contain both bitmap and vector information (from a drawing program). A variation on this format, *PICS or PICTS (PICTure Sequence)* is used for storing animation.

- *PCX (PC eXchange?)* is an 8-bit format used mostly on the PC platform. It originated with Z-Soft's PC Painter software.

- *PNG (Portable Network Graphic)* is a lossless format with a lot of flexibility and good compression. PNG was developed as a response to the patent holders of part of the GIF image specification deciding to charge licensing fees.

- *QT (QuickTime)* was developed by Apple as the first commercial digital video format for the Macintosh. It can be applied to both still and video files, and can accept a variety of different compression methods. A version called *QuickTime for Windows* was developed for the PC and uses the extension .MOV.

- *TGA (TarGA)* is a still image format developed by Truevision (now Pinnacle Systems) for use with their Targa line of videographics boards, designed for capturing video and outputting computer graphics or digital video to tape. It features lossless compression.

- *TIF, TIFF (Tagged Image File Format)* is a still image format that has slightly different implementations depending on whether you're using a PC or Macintosh, but many programs are now equipped to accept either variation. TIFF has several different lossless compression options.

The question of which format is most appropriate to use will depend on the type of image and your application. For images with a limited number of flat, solid colors, any of the 8-bit formats (GIF, PCX, TIFF) work fine, although if your destination is the web, GIF or JPG are probably your best choices because of browser compatibility. Images with smooth gradations or photographs are better off with the 24-bit formats (TGA, TIFF). If file size is a concern, your best bet is JPEG. For video files, AVI or QuickTime are normally used, although QuickTime generally looks better and is cross-platform. If you have the gear and software and it will work for your application, MPEG compression can deliver terrific quality.

If you run across an unfamiliar file extension, here's a good website that lists information on a huge number of them: http://www.webdesk.com/ filename-extensions/.

Video Considerations

If you plan to record your animation for playback with video equipment, there are some restrictions you need to take into consideration.

Video Standards

First of all, there are three video standards in common use around the world. Each of these standards uses its own set of signal configuration, frame rate, and resolution standards:

NTSC (National Television Standards Committee) is used in the Americas and Japan. It is characterized by 525 scan lines at 60Hz.

PAL (Phase Alternating Line) is used throughout most of Western Europe. It uses 625 scan lines at 50Hz.

SECAM (Systeme Electronique Couleur Avec Memoire) is used by France, Russia, and other Eastern European nations. Like PAL, it uses 625 scan lines at 50Hz, but other aspects about the signal make them incompatible with each other.

NTSC televisions have 525 *scan lines*, meaning that the electron beam paints the image with a total of 525 horizontal passes every 1/30th of a second (called a *frame*). However, the lines aren't scanned in sequence, because the beam scans only every other line during the first 1/60th of a second (called a *field*), then goes back and paints the ones it skipped the first time (a process called *interlacing*). It then starts all over for the next image in the sequence.

The reason these time periods are in 60ths of a second is related to the American household power system, which is 120 volts AC (Alternating Current) at 60Hz (60 cycles per second). That's why other countries have 50Hz television standards—because they use 50Hz power systems. In any case, the method used to display television signals has two impacts on computer graphics.

First, horizontal lines only one pixel high tend to flicker, because they're being painted only once per frame, instead of twice like the rest of the image *appears* to be. This is very distracting and undesirable, so make sure that your horizontal lines are at least two pixels high, or post-process the image with a de-interlace filter.

The second consideration is that movement should occur every 1/60th of a second to be as smooth as possible. If you render your animation normally (*frame rendering*), it will be updated only every 1/30th of a second, or after a full frame has been displayed. To get the best quality, you need to use the *field rendering* option of your 3D software, which causes it to render the images in the same way the television displays them: as two images—one set with every odd scan line rendered, and the other with every even line rendered. Using this method may take a bit longer, but it makes fast-moving objects look much smoother because the image is being altered just as fast as the television can display it.

It's important to note that there is no standard as to which field should be rendered first—the even scan lines or the odd ones (sometimes referred to as the upper scan lines and the lower scan lines). The order in which they should be rendered is dependent on the video editing hardware you're using. Make sure you check into that specification before rendering a project for video.

If you're doing field rendering on multiple computers, ensure that the field rendering settings for all the systems are identical. Otherwise, one computer may be generating the even lines first, while the other is doing the odd lines. This must be kept consistent, or your video will appear to shake up and down at times.

In addition, if you plan to have your work viewable in countries that use standards other than your own, check your software to see whether it has options for outputting that type of signal (remember you still need a recorder capable of handling that format). If not, you can save the video in the local standard format and have the tapes converted at a video post facility. The other possibility is that some companies abroad may have multi-format VCRs that can accept any VHS tape.

Visible Area

One problem common to all video formats is that much of the recorded image is never seen, because part of the television screen is covered up by the case and the bezel holding the tube in place. This condition, where the picture tube does not reveal the entire image, is called *overscan*. To make matters worse, the amount of overscan on a television varies from model to model, and even from set to set. To take this into account when video-taping subjects, the television industry established two guidelines: video safe and title safe. These are actually boxes displayed on the monitors of broadcast video cameras, which graphically delineate the portions of the image that are likely to show up on any television. The outer guideline, called *video safe*, is considered the edge of the typical television set's screen, so anything outside of that may not be visible (see Figure 10.10). The inner guideline, *title safe*, is the reliable limit for any text that will be displayed on the screen, such as titles or credits.

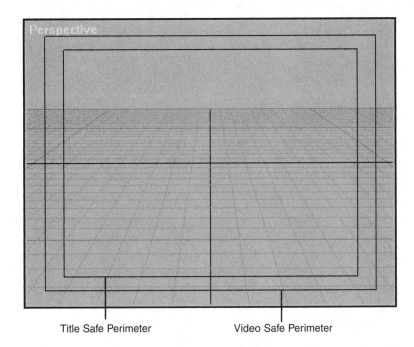

Title Safe Perimeter   Video Safe Perimeter

FIGURE 10.10

Title safe and video safe perimeter limits in a viewport enable the user to determine what portions of the image will appear when displayed on a television.

Your 3D program also may offer video safe and title safe guidelines, possibly as one of the options for a viewport (particularly a camera viewport). If you plan to output to video, use these guidelines in framing your subject to ensure that your work will be seen on any television.

Color Smear and Moiré

Another consideration with video is that certain colors will smear on a television screen. This is a particular problem with reds, but can happen with any saturated color. To avoid this, you must stay within the gamut called *video safe colors.* Some programs may offer color limiting filters or alerts that automatically keep all the colors video safe, or warn you when a material or background color falls outside this range. If yours doesn't offer such a feature, then keep your luminance levels below 80% of maximum, and do a video test to check for smearing.

The FCC (Federal Communications Commission) strictly prohibits the broadcast of colors outside the NTSC standards because they may cause color bleed or distortion on viewers' TV sets. If your animation is intended for broadcast, you should have someone use video test equipment such as a waveform monitor and vectorscope to check your work. Otherwise, the broadcasters will crank down the signal until everything meets standards, which may result in much of the image being illegibly dark.

Keep in mind that your work will rarely look as good on a television as it does on the computer screen. Some level of smearing, bleeding, and color shift will almost always occur, at least with the television technologies in general use today.

As if this isn't enough to worry about, patterns in the materials applied to your 3D objects can cause moiré patterns when recorded to video. This is very common with black-and-white striped patterns, but can show up with just about any sort of non-solid-color texture. Your program may offer map filtering controls to reduce or eliminate this problem.

Render Settings

One of the other funky things about rendering for video applications is the fact that the pixels are not square, as they are on a computer monitor; instead, they're taller than they are wide. This means that if you don't set the pixel aspect ratio properly, your image will probably appear squashed when displayed on a television.

Many programs will offer preset rendering specs for video, but in case yours doesn't, here's a checklist:

◆ Set output resolution to 720×486.

◆ Set pixel aspect ratio to 0.9.

- Set rendering to field (instead of frame).

- Set field order to Odd/Lower or Even/Upper, depending on how your video editing system expects it.

- Turn on video color checking.

- Set output gamma to 2.2 (usually, but not always).

- For best quality, output sequential images (BMP, TGA, or TIFF) with lossless compression. If drive space is an issue, outputting JPGs with very low compression will probably work fine.

After the computer cranks out a couple seconds worth of frames, confirm that the files are rendering properly by loading them up in your video-editing gear. If there's a problem, track it down now rather than after the whole project has been rendered.

Well, that's it for the theory. On to the tutorials!

Rendering and Output Tutorials

Topics covered:

Adding Glow Effects

Creating Fog

Alpha Channel Compositing

Rendering Animation

The rendering and output phase of a project gives you the opportunity to add special effects or produce multi-layered composites from different animations. For the blimp tutorial, the focus is on glow and fog effects, as well as using an alpha channel to composite a still image.

Adding Glow Effects

Adding effects such as glows to the running lights makes the lights much more realistic. In some programs this is a post-production effect, whereas others can create it as part of the rendering process, so the instructions here are very general.

1. The glow effect may be triggered by a setting assigned to the light objects themselves, or in the material applied to the object. Determine the correct parameters and set them so that all the spherical running lights on the ship will glow.

2. In some programs, you may have to set up a post-production effects task list to create the effect. Consult your manual on how to accomplish this.

3. Render the image as a straight still or through your software's video post module, depending on the requirements of the glow effect (see Figure 10.11).

FIGURE 10.11

Glow effect applied to the point light material. Glows are often added as post-rendering effects or as part of the rendering if volumetric lighting is used.

If your program doesn't offer glow effects, consider creating the glows with translucent spheres that enclose the point lights. Use material settings similar to those on the visible searchlights to create the illusion of a glow.

Creating Fog

By adding atmosphere effects to the scene, the ship appears to come out of the fog. This adds an element of mystery and realism, but would require some lighting adjustments to simulate a daytime setting. Here, just try it out as an opportunity to play with the effect.

1. Depending on your program, set the render setup parameters or environment to allow Fog. Set the minimum level to 0% and the maximum to 100%, and the fog color to white.

2. Set the ranges on the camera to define the beginning and end of the fog effects. In Figure 10.12a, the circles surrounding the camera indicate the minimum and maximum ranges. Set the minimum range at the point where you want the blimp to be completely clear, and the far range to the point where you want the blimp completely occluded.

3. Render test stills to check the effect, and adjust the ranges as needed (see Figure 10.12b).

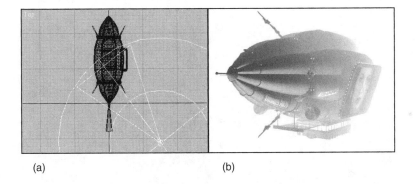

(a)   (b)

FIGURE 10.12

Controlling fog effects: (a) Set the ranges on the camera to delineate the distance or range over which the fog effects operate. (b) Render the result and adjust the ranges or density percentages to suit your needs.

Alpha Channel Compositing

This exercise composites a still image with an alpha channel against a background, and then uses retouching to add additional interest.

1. Select a background image for the blimp. It might be a cityscape or other landscape image, or something entirely abstract. A file called HONGKONG.JPG is provided on the CD-ROM if you don't have anything else available.

2. Set a camera at the proper location and the focal length to match the background. If your software supports it, loading the image into the background is helpful (see Figure 10.13a).

3. Although some products allow background images to be automatically composited during the rendering process, they would become a single image, making it difficult to adjust the foreground and background separately. Therefore, render the image with no background, but with the alpha channel turned on. Use an image resolution that is the same as the background image (see Figure 10.13b–c).

4. Load the background image into Photoshop. Load the blimp render with alpha channel in as a separate document. In the blimp document, choose the Select>Load Selection menu option, and set the dialog to use Alpha 1 as the new selection. Click OK and the blimp should appear with a selection lasso around it. Choose Edit>Copy to place the selection into the clipboard, and then choose the background document. Create a new layer, and then use Edit>Paste to paste the blimp into the new layer (see Figure 10.13d).

5. Make any desired adjustments to the color balance, levels, or positions of the two layers. You can also paint additional details onto the blimp, or add lens flare effects and airbrushed glows to the lighting, if desired.

FIGURE 10.13

Compositing an image:
(a) Load in the background image, and adjust the position and focal length of the camera to match the scene.
(b) Render the foreground with an alpha channel.
(c) The alpha channel, shown for reference.
(d) Composite the foreground and background in Photoshop or video post.

(a)

(b)

(c)

(d)

Rendering Animation

The final stage of the formal tutorials is to render the animation from the Chapter 9 tutorials off to AVI or QT files.

1. Check your hard drive for adequate space. You may want to defragment it first if the rendering will consume a lot of virtual memory.

2. Choose your camera viewpoint and set up the rendering parameters as follows: 640×480 resolution, using an animation or Cinepak-type codec, Alpha channels off (unless you plan to composite it over a background later), and frames set to the total length of the animation.

3. Render the animation. Make sure a couple of images have rendered properly before you leave the system alone to proceed. If your software doesn't have a render time estimator, use the time it takes a typical frame to render and multiply that by the number of frames in the animation.

> Chapter 11, "The Reel," discusses the techniques of editing different camera viewpoints together to tell the story in an interesting and effective manner. It is recommended that you use the information presented in that chapter to help cut together the different clips you can generate from this scene.

Summary

This chapter looked at the render-time issues you're likely to be faced with when outputting your animation. These considerations include resolution, aspect ratios, color depth, palettes, and atmosphere. Post-production effects and their creation were also examined, including glows, lens flares, motion blurs, and other custom effects that you can add with paint software or digital editing programs. Finally, it looked at common types of output, from digital files to 35mm slides to print output, as well as many of the problems involved in laying off animation to videotape.

Chapter 11 delves into the process of creating a reel, from brainstorming for ideas to scriptwriting and direction issues to doing the sound and editing. This is where your work moves from a collection of animation clips into a finished work.

The Reel

Reels with story-based samples tend to be more compelling and memorable. They also give you an opportunity to show off other filmmaking skills, like writing, directing and editing. Image by Andy Murdock, ©2000 Mondo Media.

"*G*ads, but you're up early," grumbled the Master as he stumbled into the workroom, half-asleep and clutching a steaming tankard of blackthorne tea. He padded slowly across the cold stone floor over to where the student was hard at work, poring over a table filled to overflowing with all manner of notes and sketches.

"I'm working on my demo," explained the young man, altogether too buoyant given the early hour. "Wanna see?" Taking the Master's bleary-eyed grunt as an enthusiastic yes, the student began to spin his tale.

"It opens with a young conjurer standing on the ramparts of a mighty keep at dawn. Gazing into the sky, he sees a small dragon soar down towards him. With a cry, it lights upon his shoulder, and he gives it a friendly pat. In a nearby tower, a princess smiles at the scene, her eyes full of wonder for the handsome and mysterious young man. Suddenly, the hills are blackened by hordes of approaching barbarians..."

About twenty minutes later, the lad concluded with, "...then, after the king and princess have been rescued from the dark tower of the evil sorcerer, and his barbarian hordes have been banished into oblivion, the powerful young conjurer calls forth the grown-up dragon to carry the princess and himself away, into the direction of the setting sun."

"So, what do you think?" asked the young man, beaming. The Master put down his now stone-cold tea and placed both hands on the lad's shoulder. He leaned close to the young man's face, gazing at him intently. The Master got so close, in fact, that the student could see every tiny crease in the old man's weathered skin, and could count the capillaries in the aged, bloodshot eyes.

"Is it your intention, lad, to look like me before you finish your project?" rumbled the Master.

"I...er...uhhh, well, n-no..."

"Well, then," whispered the old man, "you may just have to trim out a few scenes, then."

"S-sure," the student babbled out. "W-what should I cut?"

"Oh, just about everything from 'Suddenly, the hills were blackened by hordes of barbarian soldiers' onward should do it," growled the Master. He released the lad, then snatched up his chilly tankard. The only sound in the chamber was his bones creaking as he made his way back toward the door.

"I-I'm sorry, Master," said the student, realizing his folly.

"Ah, 'tis not your fault, and I'm the one to apologize for being upset," replied the old man, stopping to turn back and smile reassuringly. "I should have known better than to suggest you get some ideas by going to see that Dragonheart, Princess Bride, *and* Excalibur *triple-feature at the drive-in last night."*

> Much of the material in this chapter is adapted from a series of articles called "The Maltese Bolt," which I wrote for the Animata column of *InterActivity* magazine. My thanks to Miller-Freeman Publishing for granting permission to share this information with you.

The Hero's Journey

The idea of coming up with a story may seem daunting, but remember that we've all spun tales at one time or another (if only to explain why Mom's favorite lamp was broken). Remember that you aren't really starting from scratch—certain storyline structures and character types are well-established foundations in storytelling.

To see how storytelling principles are employed, take a look at one of the greatest success stories of all time: *Star Wars*. A few years back, LucasFilm revamped and re-released the *Star Wars* trilogy in theatres. Although some people thought it would be disastrous to try to bring back a 20-year-old film that had been on video and television many times and expect people to shell out $7.00 again, they did so in droves. Although some of its success lies in great special effects (and marketing), George Lucas attributes the core of its popularity to the principles of *mythic storytelling*. He sites Joseph Campbell's 1949 book, *The Hero with a Thousand Faces* as being instrumental in developing the characters and storyline for *Star Wars*.

In his book, Campbell states that all stories consist of some similar structural elements found in myths, fairy tales, dreams, and movies, which can be summed up as "The Hero's Journey." Because these principles and structures are universal to human beings, it explains why stories are enjoyed and understood by all, even when they come from distant lands and strange cultures.

The Hero's Journey can be broken into stages, which can be arranged according to the *three-act structure* that most stories employ. These three acts are basically the beginning, middle, and end sections of the story, which are also referred to as the setup, development, and resolution phases (more on this later). Here's one way in which the stages of the Hero's Journey fit into the acts, taken in part from Christopher Vogler's book *The Writer's Journey*, which reworks Campbell's ideas into a practical guide for storytellers and screenwriters.

ACT I

The Ordinary World: We see what "normal life" is like for the Hero. In Star Wars, this shows Luke doing mundane chores on the moisture farm, and the relationship between him and his relatives. He also reveals his desire to go off and fight the Empire.

Call to Adventure: The Herald appears, with a message for the Hero that beckons him or her away from the Ordinary World. R2D2 was a Herald, calling Luke to adventure with the message from Princess Leia.

Refusal of the Call: Oftentimes, the Hero resists the call to adventure because of the demands of the Ordinary World. Luke did this, saying to Obi-Wan that he had to worry about moisture converters, not some far-away rebellion.

Meeting with the Mentor: This meeting often provides the background information necessary for the audience and the Hero to see the quest being laid out. During his time with Obi-Wan, the old man provided Luke with information and a weapon with which to start his quest.

Crossing the First Threshold: This is the first great test for the Hero, one that often compels him or her to give in and take on the quest. The destruction of the farm and the death of his aunt and uncle was the turning point for Luke.

ACT II

Tests, Allies, Enemies: The heart of the story, where the Hero may face many Threshold Guardians, join with friends, and encounter his enemies. Luke was tested by his attempts to use the Force, and his battles with the enemy, Imperial Stormtroopers, and pilots. Han Solo, Princess Leia, and the droids became his allies.

Approach to the Inmost Cave: This is the entrance into the darkest place of the quest, the stronghold of the Shadow. In Star Wars, this event was the Falcon's forced landing inside the Death Star. To a degree, it occurs again during the Rebel attack on the Death Star.

Supreme Ordeal: This is the dark moment, when all seems lost, and the Hero seems doomed. One example would be the scene in the Trash Compactor where Luke is pulled under, and the walls start to close. The attack on the Death Star also contains these elements.

Reward (Seizing the Sword): As a result of surviving the Ordeal, the Heroes capture or retain something valuable. The escape from the Death Star with the plans intact was one reward. The space station's final destruction was another.

The Road Back: The forces of the Shadow are still potent, and pursue the Hero as he or she escapes the Inmost Cave. This was represented by the Tie Fighters pursuing the Falcon when it escaped from the Death Star. In some cases, this marks the return of the Hero to the Ordinary World (or a new one).

ACT III

Resurrection: Critical moments when a character appears doomed, but survives. While this happens many times in *Star Wars*, an example of an Act III Resurrection is the return of the repaired R2D2.

Return with the Elixir: The Hero must bring something back from his quest, but it isn't always an object. In the film, the Elixir was hope. Luke's destruction of the Death Star brought hope to the Alliance that the Empire really could be beaten.

At this point, I'd love to be able to say, "All right, you've established a basic understanding of the elements of storytelling. Just use this information to flesh out some ideas for your animation." Unfortunately, I can't do that. Storytelling is more than a chain of events strung together in an interesting manner. If that weren't the case, reading the synopsis of a film in

TV Guide would be almost as entertaining as watching it. No, what you need to consider before undertaking story development for your project are characters that give the story interest and involve the viewer in their fate.

Getting into Character

Another one of the principles from Campbell's book (based in part on the work of psychologist C. G. Jung) is that characters in stories are not just divided into "good guys and bad guys," but can be classified as one of several *archetypes* (prime examples of human nature). Because understanding these archetypes makes it easier to define and develop characters to suit our needs, let's examine some of the common ones.

Hero: The good guy (usually). This is the character at the center of the story, the one who the audience identifies with and often admires. The Hero is an active character, and usually undergoes some growth during the course of the story. There are many heroic figures in *Star Wars*, but the story really revolves around Luke Skywalker, making him the Hero. He grows from being a farm boy to a hero of the Rebel Alliance during the film.

Mentor: Often a parent, guardian, or senior to the Hero in years and status, the Mentor serves to guide the Hero down the right path, providing information and items needed to get the quest underway. In Star Wars, Obi-wan Kenobi was a brief but important Mentor to Luke, telling him the story of the rebellion and providing him with the lightsabre.

Threshold Guardian: This is a lesser obstruction to the Hero than the Shadow, and is often played by concerned family (Luke's aunt and uncle for example) or the forces of the Shadow (the Imperial Stormtroopers). Guardians serve to build up the Hero by allowing him or her to grow a little at a time through conflicts.

Herald: This character often makes only a brief appearance in the story. His or her function is to issue a challenge or "call to adventure" to the Hero or other characters. R2D2 was a Herald when it played the message from Leia, calling Luke away from his ordinary world.

Shape-Shifter: A character who changes personalities or forms depending on the situation. In the *Star Wars* saga, Darth Vader turned out to be a Shape-shifter character, changing from good to evil to good again. A perfect example of a physical Shape-shifter (as opposed to a psychological one) was Odo from *Star Trek: Deep Space Nine*.

Shadow: The bad guy. The character whose mission is at odds with the Hero—in other words, his greatest nemesis. Though *Star Wars* had lots of villains, Darth Vader was definitely the Shadow.

Trickster: A character that serves to knock other characters down to size, create lighthearted moments to relieve the tension, and generally bring a little chaos to the story. Tricksters are often relegated to being the Hero's sidekick, but they can play the lead as well. For example, Jim Carey's lead role in *The Mask* was a perfect example of a Trickster/Hero. In *Star Wars*, the Trickster was usually played by the mischievous R2D2.

Characters are the emotional touchstones that the audience needs to involve themselves with the events unfolding. Good characters inspire love, anger, fear, pity—the full range of feelings, in fact—that make the story gripping.

If you understand the characters that you create for the project and guide them according to the archetypes that you define them as possessing, determining their movement through the events in the plot becomes easier. In this way, developing a concept with both plot and character development in mind helps you overcome the "blocks" that occur in the writing process, when you can't decide what the characters should do next. In many cases, writers claim that their characters come to life at one point, taking the tale in directions that the author never imagined.

Now that you've looked at some of the mechanics behind storytelling, it's time to look at what it takes to come up with your own tales.

Telling Your Story

One of the first decisions you have to make about your demo reel is whether you will simply be showcasing your abilities or trying to tell a story. Although a showcase contains a number of different models, animation fragments, and so forth strung together in a visual collage, a story, even a simple one, is more likely to be memorable, and demonstrates skills other than your 3D talents.

Before actually launching into the development and production of a piece, I recommend you check out the "Managing an Animation Project" section on the companion CD-ROM in Appendix G, "Planning and Organization."

What it comes down to is this: If you have the time and resources only to compile your existing work (and perhaps add a few transitions to bridge the pieces together), that's fine, and most reels are just like that. However, if you want your work to stand out from the others, and particularly if you want to get into the character animation field, a good story-based reel can take you a long way.

Most people drawn to the animation field, be it traditional or CG, have a story they want to tell (or re-tell). These stories range from short, often humorous bits running only a few seconds to feature-length efforts of epic proportions, rather like the student's ambitious concept.

Whatever your tale, be it short or long, funny or poignant, complex or minimalistic, doing your reel is your opportunity to share your vision and talent with others. It's your opportunity to be a Steven Spielberg or a James Cameron, a Tim Burton or even an Ed Wood. On the other hand, because we're talking animation here, perhaps a better goal would be a Chuck Jones, a John Lasseter, or a Mamoru Oshii.

Although popular fiction, be it books or movies, is an excellent showcase of the creative powers of others and a great source of study, it's a good idea not to rely on it *too literally* when developing your own ideas. You want your concept to be fresh and original, not a rehash of some little chunk of *Star Wars*. For ideas, look to non-fiction and biographies as well; some of the things that happen to real people are even more incredible than fiction, and you can use such events as inspiration for your own fictional work.

Developing a Concept

Few things are more mysterious than the creative process. When you work on a project, sometimes the ideas seem to spring forth immediately, needing only the details worked out. Other times, you rack your brain for days or weeks. Help is available, however, when those dark moments strike.

Inspiration is everywhere—in films, books, museums, comics, music, conversations, and nature. All you have to do is look for it.

What If...

A good technique is to free yourself from everyday experience, and allow your mind to explore things from unique perspectives, without concern for whether they're accurate or even possible. For example: What would it be like to live in a drop of pond water? What if inanimate objects could talk? What if everything was made of ice? What if the world was inside out? What if *we* were inside out? *Ewww.*

The point is, 3D animation allows you the freedom to explore the impossible (or at least, the extremely unlikely), so you may want to take advantage of that.

Ideas based on personal experience can be very powerful, especially if you can imbue your 3D characters with the emotions that the experience brought forth. Creating an animation based on something that you feel strongly about may result in some very potent imagery or performance, and viewers who connect with your story will appreciate you for more than your ability to make a good-looking model or a nice camera move.

Academy Award-winning animator Nick Park gets the inspiration for some of his work from conversations with ordinary folks. For the short film *Creature Comforts*, Park recorded interviews with people, asking them what it was like to live in a big city. A typical response was something like, "It's too crowded, there isn't enough space, and it's too noisy. I was a lot happier where I was before." He then used the recordings as the dialogue for claymation animals being interviewed about life in a zoo.

How the Other Half Does It

For a fresh perspective, look at foreign films and books. You'll find a wealth of unfamiliar folklore, imagery, and concepts that may lead you in directions you would never have gone if you relied strictly on Western culture and ideas. The Japanese, for example, produce a vast amount of *anime* (animated films), television series, and OAVs. *OAVs (Original Animation Videos),* which are also called *OVAs (Original Video Animation)*, are animations that are produced for the direct-to-video market. Although much of this animation focuses on space battles, giant robots, and high school romance, there are a lot of unique and interesting story concepts, effects, and editing tricks from which to learn.

One of the most visually stunning examples of anime is Masamune Shirow's *Ghost in the Shell*, which is available on video. The film combines traditional cel animation with 3D graphics, and features some impressive mechanical designs and interesting ideas. Directed by Mamoru Oshii (*Urusei Yatsura, Patlabor*), the film may be a bit difficult to follow unless you're familiar with the original *manga* (Japanese term for comics).

Another route is to look through stock photo catalogs and art books. These two sources may work because they're filled with hundreds of widely varying images. I haven't seen it, but I've heard that the film *Koyaanisquatsi: Life out of Balance* is like looking at hundreds of stock video clips strung together.

The Software Route

Say you've puzzled and puzzed 'til your puzzler is sore, but you still haven't come up with anything that feels really *original*? Well, if you're *thoroughly* stuck or want an idea that's totally off the wall, you might consider an "idea generator" software program, such as IdeaFisher, which has been described as a "thesaurus on steroids." It contains not only synonyms, but metaphorically related terms as well.

Sometimes you can stumble across the seed of an idea just by opening a dictionary to a random page and blindly plunking your finger down on a word. It sounds kind of hokey, but it all comes down to what you would create out of a seeming jumble of words like: pizza, turtle, ninja, or martial arts, battery, matrix.

Group Brainstorming

Need a little help with your concept? Bouncing ideas off another person can pay off in a big way with unexpected and interesting ideas and perspectives. It's also a good way to do a reality check on what you have in mind, to make sure it doesn't get the dreaded, "That sounds just like that movie/animation/TV show I saw last week," response.

Brainstorming on the commercial projects I've been involved with usually included the entire art staff, the producers, programmers, and sometimes client representatives. The sessions produced a lot of ideas, but seldom a consensus. Most of the time, it fell upon the creative or project director to weed out all but two or three of the ideas for further development. Sometimes, two seemingly disparate ideas were combined to create a unique approach. In other cases, the brainstorming led to nothing at all, and the ultimate idea was inspired by an image from a film or magazine, or the stirrings of a half-asleep mind as its owner slapped the snooze bar for the third time.

I'm reminded of a time at Mondo Media after we had conducted a large-scale brainstorming for the launch of the first *portable* Compaq computer. We had come up with a number of good ideas, but nothing that really seemed to nail it. The owner of the company had to place a call to the client in a few minutes to pitch the ideas, and came over to ask me if I had any last-minute ideas. We started to bounce some things around, and one of the things he said was "detective." At the mention of that word, the whole thing seemed to gel. "That's it!" I said. "We could use a detective sneaking around, trying to find out information on the new line of computers. It's perfect!" Unfortunately, he didn't see the potential of his own suggestion, and had to run off and make the call before I could explain it. I listened as he pitched the client on the other ideas and could tell that none of them were sticking. "Detective!" I yelled over to him. "Tell them about the detective!" Finally, after all the other ideas had been mentioned, he said, "Oh yeah, we just had one other idea, but I don't know. It's about a detective..." The client reacted just like I did—they loved the concept, and the project was ours. This is yet another reason to talk about your ideas with others—they may spot something in a suggestion that you may not, or vice-versa.

One of the tough things about brainstorming is keeping in mind the limitations you're working under. After all, you may come up with a great idea, but if it's too big to pull off with the resources you've got, you're right back at square one.

Way back when I was first getting into CG as a profession, I started taking Crystal 3D/Topas classes at Computer Arts Institute. Our particular class was unusually small—only three people. So, when the time came to do our final class project—a group animation piece—we had to make sure that we took on something that was possible given our limited personnel. Classmate Kevin Byall and I kicked ideas around while we made the six-hour drive to Los Angeles to attend the NCGA show. The concept we came up with was *Meter Madness*, a cartoony look at what happens to a coin when it's deposited into a parking meter. By the time we reached LA, we had tons of different ideas for goofy things to happen to the penny, including laser scanning, a thorough washing, mug shots, and so on (see Figure 11.1). The story was also very scalable, allowing us to add and subtract scenes as needed to make sure we didn't run out of time before the piece was finished.

A couple years after finishing my classes at CAI, I visited the school to give a talk during their open house. While I was there, the head of the faculty told me that their videotape of *Meter Madness* had been so popular for demonstrations that it had completely worn out. I attribute its popularity to the fact that it told a simple story, making it more compelling than cool visuals alone.

Writing the Script

Unless you plan to make your work a "stream of consciousness" animation, you should put your ideas on paper and formulate a script. Although your story is likely to be a very short one, here are some guidelines for story design that can help.

The Three-Act Structure

Most stories can be broken down into what is called the *three-act structure*. Such stories have—not surprisingly—a beginning, a middle, and an end, which are also referred to as the setup, development, and resolution phases.

Setup

Act I, the story's setup phase, introduces the characters, the environment, and the situations. Keep this act fairly short, setting up a clear direction and style for the story. You don't want the viewer getting lost and wondering what's going on, instead of enjoying the piece. At the end of Act I, the viewer should have a clear idea of the characters, the key situations, and especially the *central question* of the story. Typical central questions are: Will the cop catch the bad guy? Will the aliens take over the Earth? Will the lovers be reunited? Act I often ends with a turning point in the story, an event that turns the story around or forces the main character to make a major decision, such as choosing to embark on a quest.

Development

In-depth story development occurs in Act II. The longest act, it contains the meat of the story and is the part when characters become more deeply involved with each other, new information comes to light, and previously unclear intentions start to become known. It is also one of the most difficult portions to figure out, because it can easily bog down and lose your viewer's attention. Act II also ends with a turning point, very often taking the form of a *dark moment*, during which all seems lost. This is usually followed by a change in the direction of the story, and an acceleration of the action.

Resolution

Usually the shortest and most exciting of the three, Act III is the resolution of the story. In Act III, the central question of the story, set down in Act I, is finally answered, in what is called the *climax*. Following the climax is usually a brief *aftermath* or *epilogue* that reassures the viewer that everything is okay again. In many films, the aftermath often sets the stage for a sequel as well.

Balls and Blocks

Don't worry that the three-act structure seems too complex and involved for your portfolio pieces. Even very brief and simple stories can follow this structure. For example, consider Alan Coulter's "Balls and Blocks," which was a short piece from one of the Animation Master demo reels.

During the introduction and title sequence voice-over, the artist's son asks his dad to look at something that he has set up. The kid's little demo turns out to be balls rolling down a makeshift ramp and onto a seesaw-like arrangement of toy alphabet blocks, which tumble into position forming the title of the piece. This introductory segment serves as both a title sequence and acknowledgment of his son as providing the inspiration for this piece.

The first act opens with a yellow Hot Wheels-like track arranged in roller coaster fashion, floating in the sky. The sounds of children playing can be heard, and then you see variously colored balls rolling along the track. They come off the biggest hill and roll through a stone arch that straddles the track at the bottom. Next, the main character is introduced, but he is a cube-shaped *block*, not a ball. He hesitates for a moment, then slides down the hill and smacks into the arch, blocking the way for all the other characters. He's too big to fit through the opening because he has corners, and there's no other way to get past the arch. A turning point in the story has been reached, and Act I closes.

At this point, you know the setting, and the main character. You also know the central question of the story—how will the block get through the arch, if at all? The core of this story could be considered "the odd man out" or "the fish out of water."

During the second act, a crowd of balls gathers at the top of the hill to taunt the outsider and watch as he strains to force himself through the opening. At one point, he tries to pound his own corners flat, rounding himself off, but he still can't fit through. It looks hopeless, and he gives up. This is the *dark moment*, and the second turning point that marks the end of Act II.

In the final act, one of the balls gets upset at the others, rolls down the hill to comfort the block, and offers to help push. Seeing that the good Samaritan ball and the block are trying their best, other balls join in to help, and the climax is reached when the pressure causes the upper part of the arch to fall away, allowing the block to get through. The aftermath shows both balls and blocks sliding through happily now that the obstruction is gone.

Of course, not all animations follow this structure, and some have been made famous through their rejection of it. Probably one of the best known is "Bambi Meets Godzilla," an old black-and-white hand-animated piece. Over half the animation is dedicated to the opening credits, showing a Disney-style deer peacefully grazing in a meadow. In the credits, creator Marv Newland fills every role, from Executive Producer to Writer, Director, Cameraman, you name it. The credits end, and a huge Godzilla foot crushes Bambi in an instant. Again, the lengthy and ludicrous credits roll. Godzilla's toes curl, and the scene fades to black.

At this point, I'll assume you have at least an inkling of what kind of story *you'd* like to tell, and that you need to get it down on paper.

Developing an Outline

When working out a story plot, try to keep things loose at first, putting ideas down in outline form, shuffling them around, and adding or deleting pieces until you're happy with the story as a whole. Getting too far along with one portion of the story without having the rest figured out leads to problems and wasted time.

Organization and brevity is crucial at this point, because it can be difficult to keep all the particulars and different ideas for a plot in a clear and accessible form that also lends itself to easy revision. One time-honored technique dating back to the days of the manual typewriter is the use of 3"×5" index cards and a cork bulletin board. The writer jots down scene ideas, settings, and character notes on the cards and then shuffles them around on the corkboard to experiment with the story sequence. Nowadays, the use of word processing software or simple databases makes it easier to make changes and shuffle elements around without resorting to Wite-Out and thumbtacks.

The Screenplay Format

After you've worked out the ideas for your story and put them in outline format, it's time to write a script or screenplay as a guide for modeling and animating the piece. Although you can create this in any way you like, you may want to follow the well-established screenplay format. Here's a familiar scene from my younger days:

INT. LIVING ROOM - DAY

PAUL, DAVE and MARK are three bored kids lounging around and trying to figure out what to do on a pleasant Sunday afternoon. MARK looks up from his doodle-covered sketchpad to look at PAUL.

    MARK:

    So, what do you want to do?

    PAUL:

    I dunno. What do you want to do?

They both look at DAVE.

    DAVE:

    Uhhh, why don't we go play mini-golf?

The three consider this for a moment.

    PAUL, DAVE, MARK:

    (In unison)

    Waste o' time, waste o' gas, waste o' money.

There is a long silence. Mark adds another goofy character sketch to his sketchpad, and then looks up at PAUL again.

    MARK:

    So, what do you want to do?

This tragic tale of youth begins with a notation that indicates the location where the action is taking place. It usually begins with an abbreviated INTerior or EXTerior note, followed by the location and time of day. Next follows a description of the action (or lack of it) in the scene. Character names are given in caps, probably to make it easy for actors to spot their staging and lines.

When a character speaks, its name is centered in the page. If the character is narrating a scene or is off-camera, the abbreviation for Voice-Over (V.O.) appears after the speaker's name. Dialogue appears immediately below, with the margins pulled in to create a compact text block. Notes about the delivery are sometimes noted in indented parenthesis.

To help you format a document in proper or modified screenplay format, shareware or public domain Word style sheets may be available. In addition, more sophisticated screenwriting Word add-ons, as well as dedicated programs such as Final Draft, are available.

Lots of screenwriting books are also available, dealing with everything from story issues to the latest trends in formatting. I recommend one called *Making a Good Script Great* by Linda Seger. Other books you may want to check out are *Screenwriting Tricks of the Trade, Fade In: The Screenwriting Process*, and *The Complete Guide to Standard Script Formats* (in case you decide to skip this whole 3D art thing and just go Hollywood).

Scriptwriting Tips

The following are some suggestions to help you organize your thoughts and generate a script for your animation:

◆ Make character notes and use them to help define the personalities and actions of your virtual actors. In some cases, you may find it helpful to create a little history for certain characters, using this to guide you in determining how they might respond to a situation.

◆ Even though you're using high-tech tools, rely on traditional techniques to tell your story. The grammar of filmmaking is well-established and accepted, so take advantage of it.

◆ Set the mood early in the story, possibly with an establishing shot that evokes an emotional response from the viewer. If it's a dark or sad tale, for example, opening with a rainstorm would be an obvious (albeit cliché) choice.

Designing the Look

After the script is written, it's time to move on to the production design phase. This is the point where you use sketches to put the various ideas laid down in your script into a visual form so that they can be further refined and adapted to suit your needs. Drawing enables you to explore the possibilities while it simultaneously forces you to make your inspiration concrete. Sketches are also vital when you're in a group development effort. When you talk about your concepts, you never know how others are envisioning them, but when you put a sketch on the table, everyone tunes to the same wavelength.

For *Under Cover*, a game for the Japanese version of *Dreamcast*, artist Leila Noorani created pre-production paintings of several of the key locations, both for client approval and to get everyone on the team to understand the kind of look we wanted to achieve for this piece. Leila would use simple objects to compose the scenes in a 3D program, then render out a high-res image and go to work on it in Photoshop, adding texture, details, and additional lighting (see Figure 11.2).

But, what if you can't draw? 3D attracts people from both artistic and technical backgrounds, so it's not that unusual to find a good 3D artist who can't push a pencil to save his life. The solution is to simply "go with what you know." If you're more comfortable developing ideas directly in 3D, that's fine; there are many artists who prefer to do rough 3D models to develop a design. Some people also like to use 2D drawing software rather than draw. Others prefer to use Photoshop to do rough paintings or photocompositions. You can use your own photos or existing artwork to develop a look that you can use as a basis for your 3D work.

Fleshing Out Your World

In the design process, both style and substance come to the fore. Should the project imagery be in a classical style? Contemporary? Retro, perhaps? Is the emotion you want the viewer to experience upon viewing this work awe, humor, or sadness? Of course, the execution of the work has just as much bearing on the viewer's reaction as the design does, so ensure that everyone understands the intent of your design.

Sometimes when you're doing design work, it's useful to go back to the script to flesh out a character, vehicle or location, filling in additional detail that may not come out in the story, but helps to guide your design decisions. For example, if you're designing a futuristic society, you might decide which technologies they have developed and which they are unaware of. For example, what are their power sources? Are they clean, compact, and environmentally friendly, or primitive, bulky, and toxic? Your decision would have a huge impact on the look and feel of your world—the cities, the vehicles, and perhaps even the characters themselves.

Speaking of characters, they should be sketched out in great detail if you can, because they're difficult to execute in 3D, and a little extra prep work results in a faster and more satisfying modeling experience (see Figure 11.3). It may also be worthwhile to create a model sheet, showing the character exhibiting a range of different expressions and body language. By knowing how you want to exaggerate the character's form in advance, you can more easily plan proper mesh density and bone locations in the model.

FIGURE 11.3

The Seti queen from *The Daedalus Encounter*. The original design sketch and resulting 3D model were created by Scott Baker. ©1995 Mechadeus.

Planning out anything but the simplest environment pays off as well. At the very least, you should have a map of where the main objects in the scene are located so that you can plan out the actions and camera angles. This also can help you determine which portions of the environment can be flat polys or other low-res objects, as well as which objects need to be executed in high resolution.

Finally, creating at least thumbnail-level sketches of key scenes will help you work out overall compositional issues and give you a head start on storyboarding.

> Every now and then, a sci-fi film or television show comes along that redefines visual effects and influences other filmmakers for years afterward. In 1966, the original *Star Trek* TV series pushed aside the rocket ships and flying saucers that dominated earlier sci-fi films in favor of sleek, sophisticated starships. Three years later, *2001: A Space Odyssey* used painstakingly accurate criteria for presenting a believable look at the near future. In 1977, *Star Wars* came along and broke away from the traditional clean and shiny sci-fi look with its dirty, careworn ships and environments. 1979 saw *Alien*, and H.R. Giger's biomechanical creature set a new standard for movie monsters. *Blade Runner* came out in 1982, presenting a dark, retrofitted future in a lushly designed super-metropolis. *Starship Troopers*, *The Fifth Element*, *The Phantom Menace*, and the *Final Fantasy* movie also come to mind as sci-fi films that had strong visual design, plus they pushed the limits of 3D graphics to new heights. One of the cool things about 3D is that it allows *you* to create imagery that either fits in with these well-known futures, or breaks the mold and is just as unique and groundbreaking as these films were.

Monstrous Design: An Interview with Derek Thompson

Derek Thompson is an artist and designer specializing in creatures. After graduating from Otis/Parsons with a BFA in Illustration, he got his start in comics working for Dark Horse, penciling and painting covers for several titles, including *MONSTER* and *Predator: Bad Blood*.

Later, he went to work for Rhythm and Hues, Inc. as an assistant designer on their first video game project, *Eggs of Steel*. This led to a position in 1995 as a concept and storyboard artist for Industrial Light and Magic (ILM), where he spent four and a half years working on numerous film projects.

Since leaving ILM, he's worked on several films, including *Unbreakable* and *13 Ghosts*. He is currently working on his personal website, www.derekmonster.com, and developing various fine art and media projects. One of his recent projects is a comic book called *Bindu*.

I met Derek while I was art directing *Spiral*, a Flash-based Mondo Mini Show for the web, and we hired him to conceptualize the alien landscape and structures of the planet Kaatu. The entire team was blown away by the quality and quantity of conceptual designs he came up with in only a few days. Eventually, his designs were realized in 3D and used as bitmapped backgrounds for the show.

Q: You've worked on a number of big film projects, including *The Mummy*, *The Mummy Returns*, *Unbreakable*, and the *Men in Black* films. How did you get involved in those projects, who did you work with to conceptualize it, what were the challenges, and how long did it all take?

A: I worked for several years in the Art Department at Industrial Light and Magic, so I got involved with the *Mummy* films and the *Men in Black* movies while they were still in pre-production; that was typical for our department. Usually, a project would either be awarded or not based on the strength of our conceptual work, and a lot of other things.

Fortunately, in the case of the *Mummy* films, the director was very excited, which in turn got Universal excited, and a lot of our work made it through to the final release. I was fortunate on those shows, because a lot of my creature designs ended up coming to fruition in post-production—specifically, the Pygmy mummies and the Scorpion King.

Because we were generally involved at the pre-production phase—so nothing had been shot yet—most of our work was done directly from the script, going through internal review and revision processes. We would then get feedback from the director and make additional changes. Most creature designs would go through this process a number of times, and things would get more and more fine-tuned as they went. Other considerations came into play too, such as feedback from the model-makers about how they needed to rig and animate the creatures. Other design refinements also were needed to streamline things for production.

Every project was different, though, and the approach would change from show to show, as would our interactions with different directors. Usually, we had to be on our toes and ready to adjust and tweak and refine at every turn.

Unbreakable came along after I left ILM, so I worked on it as a contractor. That was a completely different challenge, because the artwork I was doing was to be built as actual set pieces—props—for live filming. There were a number of pieces specified in the script, and I did sketches and variations of these and sent them along to the production designer and the director. After a few rounds, a final version was agreed upon and I would create the finished artwork. In some cases, it was actual artwork that was to be hung on the wall of a set, and other times it was artwork for a comic book prop. In those cases, they actually fabricated a little fake comic and put my artwork on the cover with some graphics. It ended up looking pretty convincing. I even did some artwork for a newspaper article that appeared near the end of the film, as well a lot of background gallery pieces.

Q: How do you approach doing production illustrations? What about storyboards?

A: I try to start everything with pencil and pen; I'm a bit of a traditionalist that way. I really try to get as much down as I can the old fashioned way. After that, depending on the nature of the piece, I'll either color it with markers or use Photoshop.

One thing I learned at ILM was that some directors have a hard time visualizing a concept or creature from a pencil sketch. I had to learn how to use Photoshop to give my drawings a more photographic feel, making it easier for the director to imagine the creature in a scene. Storyboards are almost always done with pencils.

Q: What suggestions do you have for newcomers to 3D who are trying to develop their own unique characters and environments?

A: Be fearless, be imaginative, and *have fun*. Always try to use inspirations and resources that are different and unusual. Read. Draw from life. Travel.

It's tough to give advice on this, just because everyone has a unique method and different sensibilities. What works for me may not work for the next guy. In any case, never give up, and always push yourself to improve.

My thanks go out to Derek for taking the time to share his thoughts and experiences on feature film design here.

Planning the Action

With the general look and feel of your world worked out, it's time to concentrate on planning out the cinematography and visualizing the *action* in your story. Two key processes for doing this are storyboarding and creating animatics.

Storyboarding

Storyboarding is the process of visualizing an animation by breaking it down into a sequence of sketches that illustrate the key points in the scene (see Figure 11.4). Usually, a description of the scene and dialogue or voice-over excerpts appears in a box below the image. Storyboards are also used to indicate camera movements (such as pans and tilts) in addition to the movement or actions of objects or characters in the frame. Such movement is usually represented by arrows drawn in perspective along the path of an action.

FIGURE 11.4

Storyboard frame showing a dead Vakkar alien from Daedalus. To the right is the finished frame from the sequence. The Vakkar was designed and modeled by Cody Chancellor. ©1995 Mechadeus.

Take a look on the CD-ROM for an example of a complete storyboard, animatic, and final animation for one of the *Under Cover* cut scenes.

Storyboarding requires you to interpret the script, transforming the words into a visual experience. Whether an action or visuals will be boring or dramatic often depends on the camera position and focal length of the lens. Where the script might say, "A group of Terran fighters fly LEFT across frame," the storyboard shows the size of the planet, the position of the ships, and the camera angle. Although they are seldom as dramatic as the finished sequence, storyboards serve as an excellent starting point for an artist setting up a shot. This is important, because the same action that looks terrific from one angle may be totally disorienting or dull if viewed from another.

Storyboards can be simple or elaborate, depending on your skill and the amount of time you can invest. The key point is that they should at least roughly define the composition, movement, and perhaps lighting in a scene. Good boards provide a valuable visual reference for yourself or other 3D artists who are modeling and animating the scene. Although the finished sequence rarely matches the storyboards precisely, it makes for a good starting point.

Although you can purchase storyboard pads that have ready-made image and text boxes in different sizes, I find that creating custom storyboard templates with a drawing program such as Canvas, CorelDraw, or Illustrator provides a lot more flexibility. You can customize the size and aspect ratio of the image and the text panels, define how many you want on a page, and so on.

One other advantage of using the drawing program method is that you can scan in the sketches and assemble them in the program, enabling you to label them with typed-in text and generate any number of quality originals. For maximum flexibility, you could even use graphics-enabled database software such as Access rather than a drawing program to manage the boards, allowing you to rearrange their order or find a given panel quickly. This does add significantly to the time it takes to storyboard, however.

Often, you can come up with modeling shortcuts during the design and storyboarding process. If you plan your action carefully, you may not need to build large portions of some models if they won't be seen. You also may be able to design certain models to be flat, mapped polygons by considering how close the camera gets to them and how long they will remain on screen. Filmmakers get away with all kinds of things because they know just how long they can show something on screen before the viewer realizes that it's fake.

Although you may choose to do so, it may be unnecessary to completely storyboard every single scene. Storyboarding is very effective when used to define scenes with a great deal of action going on, to make sure that they flow together smoothly and don't confuse the viewer. Storyboarding an animation is no small task, and it can be one of your greatest assets—or a complete waste of time—depending on the circumstances. If you're experienced with cinematography and are working on a short personal piece, you may already have visualized the action in every detail, or prefer to experiment in 3D to figure out the shots. In a larger project that involves several other animators—or if you have a client who has to sign off on the animation concept—you may not have a choice. On the other hand, if the concept or movements are fairly straightforward, or if the scene would be difficult to sketch out, you might be better off doing a 3D animatic instead.

Creating Animatics

Animatics or *story reels* are simple re-creations of a scene made with anything from paper cut-outs to toy action figures to 3D primitives. They serve a dual purpose in film productions, enabling the effects people to work out movement and timing issues, as well as providing stand-in footage until the real shots are completed.

In their simplest form, animatics are merely storyboard frames scanned into the computer and assembled into a slide show set to a temporary voice track in Premiere or some other video editing package. Most of the time, though, I find that adding some movement, effects, and music helps me to refine the timing and have a better idea of what the animation needs to be like before I move on to the 3D production phase. In these cases, the animatic also serves a place to insert 3D scenes as they progress so that you can see how they fit with the other shots.

Take a look at the files for this chapter on the companion CD-ROM. Among them you'll find the storyboard, animatic, and final animation for one of the interstitial cinematics I directed for the *Under Cover* game.

Depending on your project, you may do a 2D animatic based on the storyboards or thumbnail sketches, then proceed to the 3D animatic phase, or you may just jump directly into doing the 3D animation. *3D animatics* are basically very rough 3D animations, usually created with minimal stand-in mesh for the characters and environments. Using low-poly stand-ins with default lighting and simple colored materials means that these scenes can be tweaked with real-time playback, and that they render very quickly. All that means you can do a lot of experimentation, adjusting timing and composition until you get the results you want. 3D animatics not only enable you to produce a full-motion version of your animatic or story-board, but if done properly, can actually form the starting point for your final 3D animation. On *Mechwarrior 3*, for example, the animation setups were designed so that the low-poly models used for the animatics could be replaced with the high-res ones later on.

For more information on storyboarding techniques, I recommend getting books such as *Comps Storyboards and Animatics*. Another reference with many cinematic storyboard examples is *Film Directing: Shot by Shot*. Although this book deals mainly with conventional "live" cinematography, it's important to remember that the techniques work just as well with 3D animation. Remember, just because you have a virtual camera capable of flying anywhere in a continuous shot doesn't mean that you should always use it that way.

Producing the Animation

With the script completed and design sketches and storyboards in hand, it's time to launch into the production process. *Production* is the bulk of what you do as a 3D artist—the creation, mapping, animation, and rendering of scenes.

Because most of this book has focused on the production aspects of 3D, there isn't much more to be said here, except that when setting up your animations, be sure to over-render the scenes a bit. *Over-rendering* means that you render at least a few more frames of animation at the beginning and ending of a sequence than you think you'll need. Sometimes you should over-render as much as a second or two of extra footage. The extra frames will give you leeway in adjusting the length of the scene during the editing process.

Editing Your Scenes

Editing is one of the key elements in the post-production phase of the project. *Editing* is the process of assembling the various scenes created and rendered during production and turning them into a cohesive whole. To this end, good editing results in a well-paced, understandable, and enjoyable viewing experience. Bad editing results in confused, disoriented, or just plain *bored* viewers (the agonizingly long effects shots in *Star Trek: The Motion Picture* come to mind).

Editing is an art form in and of itself, and I can't hope to cover even a fraction of it in this short section. For more information and guidelines, get a good book, such as *Edward Dmytryk on Film: Editing*. Getting assistance from someone experienced in editing techniques can be a big help when you're working on a piece or assembling your reel.

Editing Definitions

Film editing has its own vocabulary. Most of the terms are applicable to animation editing, as well, so I've adapted the definitions to reflect this.

Cut (or *shot*): The smallest individual piece of animation. A cut or shot may be as short as a single frame, but it is usually a half-second to several seconds in length, and these shots are assembled together to tell the story. If you were animating a piece that included a car chase in a city, a shot might consist of a couple seconds of footage of the cars roaring past the camera. Note that a *cut* also refers to the edited version of the entire project.

Scene: A cut or collection of cuts that takes place at a single location. In the car chase example, there might be several shots from different angles of the cars avoiding a bus at a particular intersection; these shots would make up a scene.

Sequence: A segment of the story made up of a sequence or sequences. It is usually almost a mini-story in itself, and has a beginning, middle, and end. In the car chase example, the sequence would last from the time the chase started until it ended.

L-Cut: A cut during which the sound from Cut A overlaps the image from Cut B. This aids in making a smooth transition.

Insert: In filmmaking, a shot of an inanimate object, used to bridge sequences or establish a new location. Also known as "cutting to the kitchen sink."

Wipe: A visual transition in which the new scene is "painted over" the old one, usually from left to right. The *Star Wars* films use a lot of wipes, but most films stick with cuts.

Rough Cut: A version of the animation in which all the pieces are in place, but the timing hasn't been fine-tuned.

First Cut: The editor's first complete cut. In filmmaking, the director then reviews this cut.

Director's Cut: The result of the director's revisions to the First Cut.

Final Cut: Producers often retain the right to revise the film after the Director's Cut, so this is the release version of the film.

Editing Concepts

Editing uses some fairly straightforward precepts to determine where and when to make a cut. It is not, however, a formula-based process; it is just as much an art form as building a model or animating a character.

Probably the most important thing to bear in mind is that *you should never use a cut without a reason.* Just because something looks cool from a certain angle is no reason to throw it in (unless, of course, you're doing something like a music video, where the style is to use disjointed sequences).

Basically, a cut should always show the viewer one of three things:

◆ *What the viewer wants to see, whether he or she realizes it or not.* This means you may have to anticipate what the viewer expects to see, and when they expect to see it, and place the cut there. An example would be a scene where one character is revealing something important to another. Rather than focusing only on the speaker, there should be cuts to the listener when something critical is said, because the audience wants to see that person's reaction.

◆ *What the viewer should see, whether the viewer wants to or not.* This includes sequences that the viewer must be aware of to make sense of the story later on. An example might be a minor character revealing an important piece of information about the plot or one of the main characters. It could also show a character doing something that will cause a turning point in the plot shortly thereafter, like an assassin unpacking a rifle and peering over the edge of a building. This sets up a scene later on where the main character is fired upon from a rooftop at an unexpected moment.

◆ *What the director or editor manipulates the viewer into thinking that he or she wants to see.* This is where the filmmaker creates misleading impressions on viewers, allowing them to follow one train of thought while setting it up to be derailed later on. A good example of this would be the scenes recalling a very large and powerful-looking Keyser Soze killing his family in *The Usual Suspects*. This only reinforced the image that most people probably had in their minds based on what various characters had said about his "power."

Editing Tips

Although editing is three parts black arts for each part learned mechanics, here are some tips to help you "choose what to lose."

◆ Viewers should remain immersed in the story, rather than be allowed the opportunity to remember that they are watching an animation.

◆ Cuts should never draw attention to themselves. They should remain unnoticed and not disrupt the viewer's concentration.

◆ Never show the viewer something unimportant, unless you're using it as a short bridging device, such as an insert.

◆ After a cut has delivered its punch, don't linger on it.

◆ Never make a cut without a positive reason. In other words, never cut "just to change things."

◆ Whenever possible, cut *during* action. Don't have everything come to a complete stop before the cut. For example, if a character is leaving the screen, cut near the point his eyes leave the frame, instead of waiting for him to clear the frame completely.

◆ Viewers unconsciously notice rhythm changes, so if you were cutting between shots of a character walking, use the moment a character's foot hits the ground as the end of one shot and the beginning of the next. That way, the rhythm of the character's movement remains smooth.

◆ Except at the beginning or end of a sequence, always use the L-Cut, in which the audio from Cut A overlaps the image from Cut B. With animation, the entire soundtrack is often added after the picture is complete, so this principle can be applied at that stage.

◆ Make sure that your edits don't have the camera crossing the line of action in a scene. This should be avoided if the principles laid down in Chapter 8, "The Camera," are followed, but keep an eye out for it here as well.

- Don't try to use fancy transitions just because the program can do them. Most of your cuts should have no transition at all, but those at the beginning or end of a scene may use a fade or wipe.

- If you have to repeat the same shot during a scene for some reason, make sure the later cuts are kept brief, because the viewer is already familiar with the subject.

- If you need to linger on something, do it at the beginning of the cut, while the shot is still fresh to the viewer's eye.

- By using a loud sound, or forcing viewers to re-focus their attention, you may be able to mask a "problem" cut.

- POVs (such as an insert of a letter being read from the point of view of one of the characters) are difficult to time properly. Make sure you give the viewer plenty of time to read things.

Editing Tools

You can edit with either video recording gear or computers equipped with video editing hardware.

Video-based editing is best done with SVHS, Hi8, 3/4", or Beta SP decks so that the image degeneration inherent in the editing and duplication of videotape will go unnoticed in the final result. In addition to needing two of these video decks to make a master tape, you also may require an editing controller to synchronize and operate the decks. Some professional and *prosumer-* (professional consumer) level gear may have editing capabilities built into the deck's controls and remotes. When the editing is completed, the master tape is duplicated, usually onto VHS tape, for distribution.

Unless you have access to video editing gear, getting the work done can be an expensive proposition. Video editing suites are usually quite pricey, especially because many require that you pay an operator to run the equipment. Schools, cable companies, public TV stations, and filmmaking clubs may be able to point you toward facilities that are set up to enable students and other non-professionals low-cost access to video gear and editing suites.

For animators, the idea solution is to add high-quality *digital video editing* capabilities to your computer. This can set you back a fraction of the cost of even an SVHS or Hi8 editing setup. Many high-end Macs have good video-editing capabilities, and companies such as DPS and Pinnacle make quality systems for PCs. Quality, capabilities, and compression levels vary widely on these systems, so make sure the one you want can output clean, full-frame, 60-field-per-second animation with synced CD-quality audio to ensure that you can produce professional results. Hard drive space gets eaten up fast with digital editing, so make sure you have plenty of AV-compatible hard drive space. Some systems may require dedicated drives that are hooked directly to the video-editing card.

Probably the most popular editing software for desktop digital video is Adobe Premiere (see Figure 11.5). Software such as Premiere enables you to do *nonlinear editing*, which means you can do the editing in any sequence you want, as opposed to most tape-based systems, which require that you start at the beginning and work through until the end.

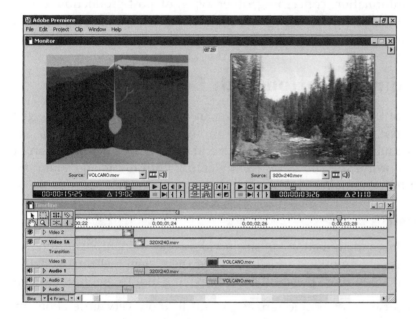

FIGURE 11.5

Adobe Premiere is a popular digital video software package that offers non-linear editing of image and sound. It can be readily used for animation editing and the addition of basic special effects as well.

Adding Post-Production Effects

Video editing software and systems often have a suite of basic *post-production effects* capabilities, including unusual transitions, color manipulation, color keying, and other special effects. In some cases, these effects would be difficult to achieve in the animation or rendering phases of production, so post-work gives you the opportunity to apply them as part of the editing process.

Video Effects

Although the basic video editing systems frequently offer transform effects such as seizing a frame of video and spinning it around, duplicating it, stretching it, and so forth (think cheesy used car commercials), the digital editing software provides more sophisticated possibilities. Products such as Premiere and Adobe After Effects can do all the basic transform effects, plus apply Photoshop-style filters such as Spherize distortions, Find Edges, Blurs, Emboss, and the like.

Post-production effects also enable you to combine live video and animation together, using alpha channels or chroma keys to drop out the background and enable you to composite the different elements together. After Effects in particular excels at such compositing effects.

For information concerning other types of post-production effects and techniques such as video painting, refer to Chapter 10, "Rendering and Output."

Adding Emotion with Sound

One of the most common mistakes in creating a first reel is to ignore or underrate the audio aspect, even though it is nothing short of amazing how much good music and sound add to a scene. The coolest animation in the world still comes off feeling empty until music and sound add the emotional undertones that bring the imagery to life.

Music

For films and animation, music provides a way to manipulate and reinforce the viewer's emotions, usually without them even realizing it. This makes a production more powerful and compelling, not to mention *memorable*.

Of course, most people (artists included) know very little about making music. What they *do* know is what sounds good to them, and this is a major consideration in selecting music to go with the visuals you have prepared.

Just as there are all kinds of animation styles and looks, there are all kinds of music to choose from. Although the high-tech feel of 3D animation often encourages a contemporary, techno sound to go with it, something funky or nostalgic can be used to great effect. Classical music is another popular choice, as it has a timeless quality that can be just as appropriate for a space battle as for a character animation piece. The most important thing is that the music you select should complement the piece and strengthen it without drawing the viewer's attention toward itself instead of the visuals. Although you may love thrash metal retro-punk at distortion levels, the people reviewing your reel may not.

Music Sources

Of course, the ideal source for your reel's music is a professional score composed especially for your work. Given most artists' limited budgets, this is probably not an option. However, you may find a local band that will license an original piece to you for a reasonable fee. You may even be able to work out a mutual trade where you can use the music and they can use your animation for a video or stage effects.

Another option is *buy-out music*, which is a little like getting an image from a stock photography outfit. You get a demo CD of different music, pick out the score you want, and pay a flat fee. Other CDs may enable you to use any of the music for the purchase price of the CD, more like the texture libraries discussed in Chapter 6. Unfortunately, you're unlikely to find anything really exciting on these CDs, because most are created with the multimedia presentation market in mind, and tend to be somewhat lifeless.

What if you want to use music from professional recording stars? Well, because the music is protected by copyright, legally you have to obtain permission from them to use it in your reel. Because there doesn't seem to be any easy or inexpensive way to do that, the use of unlicensed copyrighted music in demo reels is commonplace. Another point to consider with popular music or songs is that it may trigger thoughts or feelings about the musicians or singer, rather than the emotions you want to evoke with your animation. You don't want someone musing about Marilyn Manson's weirdness when they should be concentrating on your animation.

Sound Effects

Like music, sound effects add extra mood and impact to your visuals and help to make the action clearer. Using the right sounds can make your work seem more realistic, bizarre, or humorous. The trick is getting the *right* sound and putting it in the perfect spot. However, the ideal moment to insert a sound effect is not necessarily at the instant the picture would indicate. Experiment with the position of effects to see whether they work better when leading or trailing the visuals of the event. Also, remember that a sound effect that occurs just before a cut should usually extend into the next shot.

Royalty-free sound effects are generally a lot better and easier to come by than royalty-free music. *Sound effects CDs* can be found in any music store, and libraries of sounds can be found online for free or at minimal cost. These libraries contain hundreds of different sounds, from raindrops to explosions. You can use these sound effects as-is or modify them to suit your needs.

Most Hollywood film sound effects are created specifically for the movie, using custom libraries of natural sounds and what is called a foley stage. A *foley stage* is a soundproof room filled with all manner of different flooring types, tools, building materials, musical instruments, and even fresh vegetables. Sound designers use these materials to create the sound by pounding or stepping on them, rubbing them together, breaking them in half, and so on. Recording the sounds this way gives them much more control over the type and duration of the effect, and produces effects that don't sound "canned," the way effects CDs might.

You can create your own simple foley stage in a quiet room with a good microphone, tape recorder, and some typical household items. You also can record direct to your hard drive using your computer's sound card, but you may have trouble masking the sound of your computer's cooling fan. Whatever you do, don't block the airflow going into the machine or out of it trying to muffle the noise.

Keep in mind that the sounds don't have to be literal, meaning that you don't have to set off a firecracker to get a explosion sound. You may find that popcorn popping works very well when tweaked a bit. Also, breaking fresh celery or tearing apart a head of lettuce can produce some interesting effects. For mechanical sounds, try running thin objects like pencils or pens across rough surfaces. To create the sound of lava bubbling, use an immersion heater in a cup of milk, and so forth.

To further enhance your pre-recorded or foley sounds, use some audio manipulation software such as SoundEdit for the Mac or Cool Edit for the PC. Try dropping a steam locomotive sound by three octaves or slowing down tropical birdcalls to get an idea of how much sounds can be changed by this kind of software. Premiere also enables you to do some effects, in addition to providing fade controls and other basic audio editing capabilities.

Original 3D Works: Creator Interviews

To cap off our discussion of developing and producing original content for your reel, I'm pleased to present interviews with three creators—Marco Bertoldo, Andy Murdock, and Marco Patrito—each with unique and original visions that they have executed in 3D.

3D Characters Gone Bad: An Interview with Marco Bertoldo

Marco Bertoldo was born in Turin, Italy in 1967. He was always into making stuff, whether model airplanes or music. Although he was always following creative pursuits, he never attended an art institute. His father told him, "You can't make any money in the arts." His father would know; he went to a conservatory for nine years to study piano. Marco ended up going to accounting school, but says, "I really sucked at it. Numbers and I just don't get along."

I met Marco while acting as creative director on *The Daedalus Encounter*. We were looking for artists, and Andy Murdock told me he'd been working with Marco at Earwax studios and he would be good. He admitted that he didn't know 3D Studio and hadn't worked with PCs before, but Andy said he would help get Marco up to speed. I gave him the green light, and Marco came on board, bringing a bit of European flair to our motley American crew. He learned the software quickly and became an accomplished 3D artist and eventually a director. We ended up working on several projects together, including *Akuji the Heartless*, *Under Cover*, and the Mondo Media game demo reel.

Q: What made you want to get into 3D?

A: It was pure luck that I got involved with 3D. Back in 1993, I came to San Francisco to live with my girlfriend (we're married now), but I was pretty lost. Then I met someone at a dinner party who had a sound studio called Earwax, but they were also doing computer graphics. I'd used programs like CorelDRAW and such, but I didn't know anything about 3D.

When I went to visit the studio, I met Andy Murdock, and he showed me an animation he had done with the computer. My jaw just dropped; I couldn't believe the power that 3D animation could offer. It was love at first sight—not with Andy, although I like him a lot—but with the concept of 3D.

Q: How did you learn to do 3D modeling and animation?

A: I started going into the Earwax studio every day, for about six months, to intern. I was given the opportunity to use a computer—a Macintosh—and I started out learning Swivel 3D. Eventually, I worked my way up to StrataVision 3d and Electric Image. Having someone as talented as Andy to offer advice and give me inspiration was a huge help.

Q: What 3D software do you use, and why?

A: I use Discreet 3ds max. I started using it when I got hired at Mondo Media to work on *The Daedalus Encounter*, and I've been using it ever since. It's one of the best tools for working on videogames, and its fairly complete and intuitive.

Q: What projects have you worked on over the years, and what were your roles on them?

A: I've worked mostly on video game projects. After *Daedalus*, I worked as an artist on *Rebel Assault II*, *Spot goes to Hollywood*, *Zone Raiders*, and *Under Cover*. Later, I got an opportunity to direct cut scenes for *Interstate 76*, which had over 26 minutes of 3D animation. It was a great experience for me, and since then I've directed cinematics for a number of other games, including *Akuji the Heartless*, *Pandemonium II*, *Die Hard*, *High Heat Baseball*, *Gauntlet Legends*, *Alien vs. Predator*, and *Planet of the Apes*.

Q: Which projects have been the most interesting for you? Which have been the toughest, and why?

A: The most interesting project for me has been *Gone Bad*, mostly because I consider it "my baby." I have a lot of creative control over it. The toughest project has also been *Gone Bad*, for the same reasons.

Q: What are the most important things to remember when directing a 3D project?

A: One of the big challenges of doing a 3D project versus live action is that you don't have multiple takes and you don't have extra footage, because every second of animation costs a lot to make, and you can't afford to make anything you don't absolutely need. That means that priority one is having a very clear vision of what you want to say, and how you're going to say it.

Without a doubt, the most challenging thing is to make the characters come to life and seem believable. Overall, though, I'd say the most important thing is making sure you have a good story to tell, because without a good story, everything else falls apart.

Q: When you direct a project, what sorts of tasks do you take on yourself, and why?

A: I enjoy making the animatics during the pre-production phase, because I get immediate gratification and it gives me an idea of how well the piece is going to work. If there are problems, I fix them at that point, before the other artists come on board and start producing the scenes.

After production gets underway, I also tend to adjust and animate the cameras to get just the right angles and moves I want. I also animate some of the characters if I have time.

Q: How do you decide where to place the camera in a given shot?

A: It's pretty instinctive. I try to put the camera were it makes the most sense and still go for a composition that looks interesting. You want to tell a story that is clear to the audience the first time they see it, and the camera setup is very important in that regard.

Q: Do you try to move the camera whenever possible, or keep it locked off?

It varies from shot to shot. If you can get the effect you want from a locked-off shot, that's fine. Lots of times you need to move the camera to give the viewer a better idea of the layout of an environment, or to add some extra drama. You can also create a lot of mood by moving the camera in a way that it feels like it's being hand-held; putting in a bit of wobble and bounce instead of having a mathematically perfect move.

Q: What do you think are the most common mistakes people new to 3D make with their camerawork?

Some of them seem to put the camera in crazy places all the time, just for the hell of it. Others frame the scene too wide, or don't change camera positions often enough to hold the audience's interest.

Q: What tips or tricks—particularly about camera work—can you offer that could help someone trying to improve their work?

A: I think that watching a lot of films with an eye toward what the camera is doing can be really useful. You can learn a lot of interesting things by paying attention to the way a good director and cinematographer use the camera.

Q: You developed and directed *Gone Bad*, **a series of short, interlocking 3D films. Tell us a bit about it.**

A: *Gone Bad* got its start at Mondo Media, when we got into producing original content for the web. Being a fan of horror movies, I thought it would be fun to do a zombie film in the mood and style of the campy, even downright cheesy horror flicks produced in the seventies and eighties.

I contacted Niccolo Ammaniti, an Italian writer whose books I really enjoy. He was very excited about the chance to work on a 3D animation project and came to San Francisco. Over the course of two weeks, we came up with the story: a comedy/horror film with a "Spaghetti Western" flavor. We made two episodes that ran about five minutes each, and they both made it into the Sundance Online Film Festivals held in 2000 and 2001.

Q: Do you have any "dream project" that you'd like to work on?

A: At the moment, my dream project really is *Gone Bad*. It would be great to find a sponsor and be able to finish the entire series.

Q: Where would you like to be in five years?

A: Under a palm tree in the Virgin Islands, sipping a piña colada.

I'd like to thank Marco for taking the time and effort to share his thoughts and experiences here.

Robot Dreams: An Interview with Andy Murdock

Andy Murdock was born on an Air Force base in Michigan during a blizzard in 1965. His father was a member of a B-52 bomber crew who spent many of his off-hours oil painting. He told Andy at a very young age that he was going to be an artist, and the prediction seemed to stick. In high school, he took as many art classes as he possibly could. He also took one computer class, which he failed. The school had a Tandy TRS-80, whereas Andy had a Commodore PET at home, and no way to prove to the teacher that he was learning to use it instead. Andy moved to San Francisco in 1984 to study painting, filmmaking, and sound design at the San Francisco Art Institute. He graduated in 1987 and got a job as a recording engineer at Earwax Productions, doing records and demos for local bands.

I met Andy while Mondo was doing some work for Microsoft's Encarta CD-ROM. We didn't have enough in-house people for the job, and Andy's employer, Earwax Productions, was hired to do sound and some animation for the project. I enjoyed working with Andy, and when we started doing *The Daedalus Encounter*, he told me he'd like to work on it. I was thrilled to have him join the team, as I had always been impressed with the quality and broad range of his skills. We worked together on several other game projects over the years, including *Zork:Nemesis*, *Blade Runner*, and *Under Cover*.

Q: What made you want to get into 3D?

A: I was really inspired by Carl Sagan's *Cosmos* series on PBS. I can't remember if there was much in the way of CG going on in the show, but it came along at about the same time that I was learning to paint with an airbrush, program video games (with ASCII artwork) on our 4K Commodore PET, and listening to Pink Floyd. It all just seemed to fit together.

Q: How did you learn to do 3D modeling and animation?

A: Back when I was using a Mac II—the first color Macintosh—to do digital audio editing at a recording studio, a friend loaned me copies of Photoshop and Swivel 3D. After that, I stayed up all night for about a year learning all the graphic programs I could get my hands on. I started using Macromind 3D, StrataVision 3d, Electric Image, and Director to create interactive games and multimedia presentations. Then I met Mark Giambruno at Mondo Media where he got me a job making video game graphics and animation. Thanks, Mark!

Q: You're welcome! What advice do you have for people who'd like to get a job doing 3D graphics?

A: Try and study all aspects of your craft. If you specialize in one skill too much, you will definitely get stuck doing the same thing all the time, which is no fun.

Q: What 3D software do you use, and why?

A: I use 3ds max. I've been using the 3D Studio line since 1993, and I've watched it grow into a very powerful tool. Of all the 3D software tools, max alone gives me the power to create and render an entire animation all by myself, without the need for a team of programmers to deal with writing shaders. The renderer is fast and looks great. MAXscript gives me the ability to create my own, very powerful custom tools. It's also a package that's easy to learn. I tried Maya, but I found it just took way too long to do even the simplest things with it. I also bought LightWave for the Macintosh, but could never get it to work for more than a few minutes. The separate module paradigm just didn't work for me, either.

Q: What projects have you worked on over the years?

A: I worked on the film *The Peacemaker* and the PBS program *Intimate Strangers*. As far as games go, I worked on *The Daedalus Encounter*, *Zork:Nemesis*, *Blade Runner*, and *Tekken 2*, and have done little bits and technical assistance on dozens more. For the web, I did *Rocket Pants*, and right now I'm working on my own piece, *Lots of Robots (LOR)*.

Q: Which models or animation have been the most interesting for you? Which have been the toughest, and why?

A: Facial animation is both the most interesting and the most challenging form of animation for me. I find myself going back and forth between making facial animation systems that are overly complex and overly simple. Trying to find the right balance between simplicity and power is the key to making a facial animation system work well. You need to have a system that provides fast feedback for the animator, but is also loaded with features to help make the model come alive.

Q: Do you prefer a particular type of modeling?

A: Polygonal modeling with subdivision surfaces is the only way to go. I'll be happy to race anyone using another technique.

Q: You created some unique characters for *Rocket Pants* and *LOR*. Talk a bit about how you came up with them.

A: I built Cliff, the main character from *Rocket Pants*, as a toy for me to practice my character animation skills. I did a few test animations with him and just kept going, until I ended up with a whole piece. All of a sudden, I had a theme song and I'm taking him to the Sundance Online Film Festival.

LOR is a something of a creation myth—a Garden of Eden with robots. It's based on a real theory, believe it or not. Some people think some sort of intelligent being created life. This version of the myth has a scientist playing the part of the creator. The metal robots we see are the creator's design experiments—the prototypes for real animals made of flesh and bone.

As a story, *LOR* develops as I animate it. I have a rough idea of where it's going, but I don't really decide its coarse until I actually start animating the characters. I think if I had a script already set in stone, I might run out of steam, or feel conflicted when better ideas popped into my head. It's not that I don't have any idea of where the story is going—I have many well-developed ideas—I just don't make any final decisions until I sit down and do it. After that, I look at what I've made, and hopefully the story will guide me along.

Q: How did you approach modeling the robot centipede character in LOR?

A: It would probably help to look at the piece first; it can be found online at `http://www.lotsofrobots.com/LorMovieLaunch.htm`.

To me, each robot critter in LOR represents a particular characteristic of nature. The hummingbird represents grace and agility, the pelican is curiosity, and the centipede reminds me of how some very simple-minded creatures can have the most complex and beautiful physical bodies and motion. The centipede's cyclical motion is hypnotic when all the pods are moving together, whereas one set of legs moving by themselves would be rather dull. If each of our human traits were personified in animal form, then turned into a robot, you would basically see my world.

The animation for the centipede sequence was created using MAXscript. First, I built one of the segments (pods) of the centipede that included legs, and hand keyframed a walk cycle for it. Next, I analyzed the animation and measured the extents of the IK skeleton—that is, how far it moved in a single stride. Then I wrote a script that would place the pod's feet and body at the positions of a set of moving guide dummies (null objects) and looped the process every few frames until I had the pod walking wherever the guide dummies went. Even though the motion is scripted, it was still derived from the animation I did by hand, so it still had personality.

The next chore was to make the guide dummies follow and align themselves to an arbitrary mesh surface—in this case, the tree. I created a spine on the tree by using max's 3D Snap To Face feature, drawing it along the length of the tree. Next, I built a MAXscript gizmo that followed that line and watched for intersection at three parallel points on the surface of the tree. The intersection points were used to help generate three additional splines that would be used as paths for the guide dummies (body, left foot, and right foot). The guide dummies were assigned to the three paths, and yet another MAXscript was used to manage the rotational alignment of the dummies as they spiraled around the tree. Finally, I wrote another

MAXscript that merged and renamed multiple copies of the pod because I needed 24 of them to make up the centipede.

After I had all the "connecting hoses" set up between the body and the feet, I wrote a MAX script that walked all the pieces up the tree. The walking script has many variables that I can tweak: how fast it walks, how long the stride is, how many steps it takes, how high the legs lift, and so on. There are also starting steps and stopping steps, plus secondary motion functions for when the centipede comes to a halt. The really cool thing is, with all these tools and scripts, I can animate this critter again and again just by running the scripts on a new surface. That is, of coarse, if I can remember all the little details.

Q: In addition to LOR, do you have any other "dream projects" that you'd like to work on?

A: I'd really like to continue work on *Gone Bad*. It's a 3D spaghetti western zombie horror flick.

Q: Where would you like to be in five years?

A: Still alive, but in a better world.

I'd like to thank Andy for taking the time and effort to share his knowledge and experiences with us.

Building a New Universe in 3D: An Interview with Marco Patrito

Marco Patrito was born in 1952 in Turin, Italy, where he still lives today. His love for drawing developed at an early age. Later, he attended a high school specializing in artistic disciplines. He went on to university studies, but although he graduated with a degree in architecture, he never entered the profession. Instead, he remained lured by the beauty of imagery, becoming a painter, photographer, comic book author, and scriptwriter with many of his stories published throughout Europe. He is also an accomplished science fiction illustrator, with more than 160 published covers.

I first became aware of Marco Patrito and his company, Virtual Views, from the StrataVision 3D ads that featured his work on *Sinkha*. When the multimedia version of *Sinkha* came out, I bought a copy and was very impressed—I even devoted much of a column to it in *InterActivity* magazine. When I wrote the first edition of this book, I worked with the U.S. distributor of *Sinkha* to use images from the CD-ROM for the cover and gallery art. This time around, with extensive assistance from translator Maurizio Manzieri of Virtual Views, I was able to work with Marco to secure new imagery and an interview. Marco and Maurizio were a great pleasure to work with, and I'm sure you'll enjoy their contributions to the book.

Q: What made you want to get into 3D?

A: There came a time when I felt I was being limited by drawing two-dimensional worlds, and I wanted to move onto something that had "depth"—a new way of creating things that I would be able to explore from an infinite number of viewpoints. By that, I mean a drawing that you would have been able to admire from different angles. This is the great attraction of 3D graphics.

Q: How did you learn to do 3D modeling and animation?

A: Today, almost all of my friends in the art field have worked with modeling software, but back in the '80s my brother Fabio was the only one who was experimenting with 3D graphics. He was a true pioneer, with amazing skills. Later, the first interesting graphics programs appeared on the market, but often the developers didn't really have a clear idea about the potential of their products. There were no tutorials available, so I had to learn how to use them on my own.

Q: Talk a bit about *Sinkha*, and how your company, Virtual Views, came into being.

A: The *Sinkha* universe was born in 1991, as a response to a challenge of sorts—a few of my publishers stated that it was impossible to create acceptable illustrations with a computer! I strongly disagreed, and began to develop a fantastic universe that would be able to make the most of the computer graphics technology of the time. The final result had to appear much more spectacular than people would have thought possible. At the same time, I wanted to tell a story that would not be too restrained by the technical limitations of CG. It was a beautiful challenge! On top of all that, in order to create this universe, I would need a company able to manage and produce the project. Virtual Views was therefore born in order to create *Sinkha*.

Q: The visuals in *Sinkha* were incredible, yet the software tools of the time were relatively primitive. What processes did you go through to create them?

A: At that time, hardware and software were far short of their present capabilities, yet the rendering software I choose—StrataVision 3D—included material and mapping features that were very advanced. I relied a great deal upon those advanced texture-mapping features, which took advantage of my experience in drawing and painting.

If the modeling capabilities of Aldus Super 3D weren't up to the task, I used bump mapping to add the illusion of additional detail. I even used bump maps to create a bevel-like edge on the mesh to help smooth out hard edges.

Q: The multimedia CD-ROM version of *Sinkha* was quite unique, combining still images and animation with text, music, and sound effects. How did you come up with this concept?

A: I wanted to somehow combine the feeling of a story told through images—like a graphic novel—together with elements usually confined to the cinema, including animation, sound, and music. There were two interesting aspects to this formula. The first was linked to the charm of comics, where the narrative and still images illustrate dynamic events. The second was having the chance to tell a story more like the way a movie does, but with a very tiny budget and virtually no acting.

Q: How many people make up Virtual Views, and what are their roles?

A: It has varied substantially during the history of the company. I worked alone during nearly three-quarters of the development of the first *Sinkha*, and then ramped up substantially during production, when I had quite a lot of people working with me at Virtual Views.

We're much more efficiently organized now, and with the *Sinkha Universe* returning to full production, I've decided to step away from my managerial role for as long as possible and dedicate all my efforts to creative work. There are fewer collaborators, and almost all are freelancers dedicated mainly to support activities. I do nearly all the modeling and animation myself, but with a complex project like *Sinkha*, it's essential to have collaborators who specialize in the other aspects of production: writing, public relations, music, sound, marketing, and so on. For example, a Hollywood screenwriter will be polishing our script for the English version.

Q: You've recently published a sequel to *Sinkha* called *Hyleyn*, and a multimedia CD-ROM version of the new title is also in the works. Please tell us about them.

A: The *Sinkha* adventure is being re-launched. We've climbed onboard Darcron once again, heading off with renewed enthusiasm. The Sinkha

Project will present a series of adventures in both print and CD-ROM form, coming out about once a year. For the time being, we're planning to present the stories in three languages: English, French, and our native Italian. Both the print version and the multimedia version of the chapter titled *Hyleyn* will be available in the United States by the summer of 2002. By the way, the multimedia version of *Hyleyn* will include an interesting remake of the original *Sinkha*.

Q: How have your work processes changed since the *Sinkha* days?

A: Time goes by, and after so many years, 3D programs have completely changed. But I believe a big part of the difference is due to the hardware—back when I did *Sinkha*, computers were very expensive, and not very fast—factors that limited my creative options. The computers we're using now are within the reach of everyone, and hundreds of times faster!

Thanks to these advances, it's become possible to use powerful 3D software like Maya, a terrific program when it comes to character animation. Nonetheless, I've used many 3D programs over the course of my career, and the real difference comes down to the 3D artist himself.

Q: What advice do you have for people who'd like to create print or multimedia graphic novels of their own in 3D?

A: It's difficult to give out specific advice, because everyone develops his or her own peculiar style and has a different kind of story to tell. I will say that it's very important to be well organized before starting production. You have to make a lot of sketches and plan out all the details in advance.

Another important thing is to have clear ideas about what you're going to do in post-production. Know what things you need to create within the 3D scene, and what you can add later on with an excellent program like After Effects.

Q: Where can people purchase *Sinkha*, *Hyleyn*, and *The Art of Sinkha* book? Will other *Sinkha* goods be available soon?

A: At this time, only *The Art of Sinkha* book is currently available in English, and just last week we completely sold out the first press run. In the summer of 2002, it will be available worldwide, but I cannot say through which retailers at this time. It will probably be available through Amazon.com, though, because they're already selling *The Art of Sinkha*. We're also negotiating with the big bookselling chains. We'll also be opening a Sinkha Shop at our website, www.sinkha.com, which will showcase side productions such as a "making of" feature with a lot of interesting technical information.

Q: What's next for you and Virtual Views? What would you like to be doing five years from now?

A: The first *Sinkha* was a triumph, proving that the multimedia graphic novel concept was a winning idea; we were wrong not to continue along that path. Now we're planning an expansion of the Sinkha Universe based upon that formula, although updated and improved, hoping not to get distracted from games and movies.

We're confident this is the right path for us, the winning one...but obviously, we have to keep our options open in case something interesting and unexpected comes along!

I'd like to thank Marco for taking the time out from his busy schedule to share his thoughts and experiences with us. My thanks also to Virtual Views' Maurizio Manzieri for arranging this interview and providing the English translation.

Summary

This chapter began exploring the creative process a bit, and looked at some ways to generate and develop ideas. It discussed the value of adding story elements to a reel, and went through the pre-production processes of scriptwriting, designing, and storyboarding a piece. It also talked about post-production, and the editing, visual effects, and audio aspects of doing a reel. Your demo reel is vital ammunition in your most important battle: getting a job.

The next and final chapter explores the business aspects of 3D animation, discussing the pros and cons of being an employee or contractor, how to assemble a resume and portfolio, and how to secure the job you want.

Appendix A

Glossary of Terms

2D paint   Traditional computer paint systems and software such as Photoshop. These packages are primarily bitmap-oriented, but may include some vector and pseudo-3D features.

2.5D   "Two-and-a-half-D" imitates the look of 3D graphics by scaling and positioning tiled 2D graphics in such a way that they appear to have depth. This technique is the basis for the DOOM-style first-person shooters.

3D   Short for three-dimensional—something that has height, width, and depth. 3D software treats objects as though they were 3D, but generally present them as 2D-rendered images.

3D acceleration   Video hardware and software enhancements that dramatically speed up the manipulation and display of 3D information.

3D digitizer   A mechanical arm, with sensors, that determines the physical position of key points on an object and creates a 3D version based on that data.

3D object library   Stock 3D objects sold in a variety of different formats and resolutions as an alternative or adjunct to modeling.

3D paint software   A software program or plug-in that enables the user to paint texture maps directly on a 3D model.

3D scanner   A device that uses optical and/or laser technology to scan a physical object, to generate a wireframe mesh (and sometimes a full-color map) of the object. This technology is often used to create highly accurate models of complex objects or people.

A

additive blending   A texture blending method that uses the additive color model. The pixels of a base map and a light map are blended together to make a brighter texture.

additive color model   The way in which colors are created with light, as opposed to pigment. In the additive model, red, green, and blue are the primary colors, and mixing them together creates white.

additive transparency   The method of using the additive color model to calculate a background pixel's brightness when it is viewed through a transparent object.

ADO   Ampex Digital Opticals. Basic video effects named after a company that made the dedicated video gear to create them. ADO-style effects include changing the scale of a segment of video, stretching it, spinning it around, reversing it, and so forth.

aliasing   The tendency of diagonal lines and surfaces to look like stair steps because of the size of the pixels.

align   A command that brings object surfaces flush with each other or centers multiple objects along one or more axes.

alpha channel   An optional layer of image data that provides an additional 8 bits of information about transparency. The alpha channel is used as a mask for compositing one image over another.

ambient color   The hue an object reflects if it isn't directly illuminated by a light source. It is intended to be representative of the color of the light reflecting off the objects in a scene, but only radiosity rendering can truly accomplish this.

ambient light   In theory, the cumulative effect of all the light bouncing off all the objects in an area. Generally set as a global value that illuminates all objects in the scene equally.

angle of incidence   The angle at which a light ray strikes a surface and is reflected into the viewer's eyes.

animated texture   A video or animation file used instead of still images as a texture map, causing the texture on an object to change over time when the scene is rendered.

animatic   A rough animation intended to work out timing and composition issues. Often inserted in the working cut of a film as a placeholder for effects sequences that aren't yet completed.

animation controller Any of a number of different methods for creating or modifying animation keyframes or object behavior. Controllers include TCB, Bezier, audio, noise, and expression.

animation The creation of action or movement with inanimate objects. In 3D graphics, the modification of any object, light, material, or camera by moving it or changing its properties over time.

animator Mutant human who enjoys creating films frame-by-frame.

anime Japanese loan-word (word adapted from a foreign language) for animated films and television programs. The correct pronunciation is AH-KNEE-MAY.

anisotropic highlight The highly elliptical highlights caused by micro-structures on surfaces such as hair or brushed metal.

anti-aliasing A method of softening rough edges in an image by adding or modifying pixels near the stairstepping points. These create a blend between the object and background colors.

array A matrix or pattern of objects extrapolated from a single object or group of objects.

Common types include linear arrays (which follow a straight line) and radial arrays (which form all or part of a circular path).

art director Senior artist responsible for maintaining (and sometimes developing) the vision for the overall look of a project (subject to the desires of the director). The art director is involved in the day-to-day management of the production artists and reviews their work to ensure quality and consistency.

artifacting Corruption or degradation of image data that contributes to an overall loss of quality. An example would be the blockiness that occurs in an image when too much JPEG compression is applied.

aspect ratio The relationship between the height and width of an image or pixel, expressed as a decimal ratio. It is calculated by dividing width by height. For example, an image 4" wide and 3" high would have an aspect ratio of 1:1.333.

atmosphere A user-defined level of aerial occlusion (such as fog) applied to a scene, creating the effect of objects being seen from great distances or through a mist.

attach A command that enables two separate elements

to be joined into one object. The opposite of *detach*.

attenuation   The gradual reduction in the intensity of light as it gets farther from the source, which is caused by light being occluded by particles in the atmosphere. In 3D programs, attenuation is a light source option controlled by range settings.

average transparency   The method of calculating the brightness of a background pixel when it is viewed through a transparent object by averaging the background and translucent object pixel colors together.

axes   The plural form of axis, pronounced AXE-EASE.

axis   An imaginary line in 3D space that defines a direction. The standard axes used in 3D programs are called X, Y, and Z.

axis constraints   Controls that restrict the axes that are available for use when transforming an object. Using axis constraints helps to prevent an object from being transformed in the wrong direction. Also known as axis locks.

axonometric   A drafting representation in which the viewer's location is infinitely distant from the object, so that all lines along the same axis are parallel.

B

backfaces   Polygonal faces that are oriented away from the viewpoint.

backface culling   The process of ignoring or eliminating polygons facing away from the viewpoint. This speeds up 3D calculations because the program pays attention to only those polygons on the "front" of objects (facing the camera).

ball joint   A type of constrained link that enables two joined objects to have six degrees of freedom.

bank   The rotation (or *roll*) that an object or camera may perform when it moves through a curve in a path. This simulates the results of centrifugal force on a real-world object as it executes a turn.

batch rendering   Setting up a computer or network to automatically render scenes from multiple projects.

behavior   Object-level controller (Look At, Bounce, Spin, and so on) that simplifies some animation work by having the computer reorient the objects according to the set behavior.

bend   A transform that deforms an object by applying torsion around the selected axis.

bevel A flat transitional plane located between two other planes, usually set at an angle that is half the difference between the two. Also called a *chamfer*.

Bezier splines A type of spline in which the control points always reside on the resulting curve. Extending out from the control points are tangent points, which allow the curve to be modified without moving the control points.

bias In a TCB (Tension, Continuity, and Bias) animation controller, bias adjusts the location of maximum extreme point (or peak) of the motion path or control curve in relation to the keyframe.

billboard A 2D polygon with a texture map, used to create the illusion that a more complex 3D object occupies the same space.

birail A type of *sweep* that makes use of two guide curves and one cross-section. Popular for creating complex curved objects, like the fender on a sports car.

bit depth See *color depth*.

bitmap A 2D digital image.

bluescreen A blue background that serves as a stage for actors. The blue can be removed after filming and replaced with a different background. Costumes and props shot on a bluescreen stage cannot contain blue or purple pigments, because the compositing process causes any blue or purple elements to become transparent. An alternative is greenscreen, which allows blue and purple objects, but no green ones.

bone deformation A technique of animating an object (usually a character) by defining and animating an internal skeleton that automatically deforms the surrounding mesh.

Boolean operation A set of commands that adds or subtracts one object from another. Boolean operations are commonly used to re-shape or "drill holes" in objects based on how they intersect with other objects.

bounding box A stand-in in the shape of a box that has the same overall dimensions as the object. Bounding boxes replace mesh-intensive objects during movement or other translations, so that the system won't be bogged down redrawing a large amount of mesh.

box coordinates A type of mapping coordinate system well suited to rectangular objects. It applies the image coordinates from six different directions, one for each surface on the object. Also called cubic coordinates.

BSP Tree   In 3D engines, a BSP (Binary Space Partition) tree subdivides 3D space with 2D planes to help speed up sorting. It is also sometimes used for collision detection purposes.

B-spline   A type of spline that has control points with equal weights that adjust its shape. Control points rarely reside on the resulting curve in this type of spline.

bucket rendering   A rendering process that subdivides and renders an image in small blocks, rather than as *scanlines*. Buckets may offer some advantages in network rendering situations.

bump map   A grayscale image that varies the apparent surface roughness of an object by manipulating the normals.

buy-out music   Stock music that can be used commercially for a set fee and does not require payment of a royalty. The music samples are available on CD and work much the same way as stock photography purchases.

C

CAD/CAM   Computer Aided Design/Computer Aided Manufacturing. CAD is the use of the computer and a drawing program to design a wide range of industrial products, ranging from machine parts to homes. CAM uses CAD drawings to control the equipment that manufactures the final object.

camera target   A small cube or other object attached to a virtual camera that indicates the center of the camera's field of vision (in other words, where the camera is pointed).

Cartesian coordinates   The most common way of describing and delineating 2D and 3D space. Space is delineated by three vectors at right angles to each other, labeled by longtime convention as X, Y, and Z, and starting at a center point called the Origin. This coordinate system is based on the ideas of Rene Descartes, also known as Cartesius of "Cognito ergo sum (I think, therefore I am)" fame.

caustics   A rendering extension intended to more accurately simulate the behavior of light in a scene, particularly how it reacts to mirrored surfaces, transparent objects, and water.

CD-ROM drive   A removable media drive that can read data from CD-ROMs (Compact Disc Read-Only Memory) or music CDs.

CD-R/CD-RW drive   A CD-ROM drive that is also capable of creating new CDs using CD-R (Compact Disc Recordable) or CD-RW (Compact Disc Re-Writable) media. These recorders are used to "burn" CD-ROMs during the development process so the program can be checked from its destination format. They are also used to back up data and create custom music CDs.

cel animation   Animation that is hand-drawn or Xeroxed onto sheets of specially punched, transparent acetate. The sheets are called cels (short for celluloid), and these cels are then photographed one at a time onto film or video and projected to create the illusion of movement.

cel shader   A type of 3D renderer or process that attempts to mimic the look of hand-drawn cel animation.

chain   A series of linked objects, using the hierarchical parent-child relationship, but extending it by additional generations to grandchild, great-grandchild, and so forth.

chamfer   See *bevel*.

channel   An individual attribute of a material that can accept images or be set in such a way as to affect the appearance of the object to which the material is applied. Typical channels include diffuse, bump, opacity, shininess, and self-illumination.

character animation   The process of imbuing objects not only with movement, but with personality. Virtually any object can take on personality if character animation techniques are applied to it.

cheap mesh   A slang term for an object that has a low polygon count or is very efficient and quick to render.

child   An object linked to another that is closer to the beginning of the hierarchical tree (its parent).

chroma   The color of an object, determined by the frequency of the light emitted from or reflected by the object.

chroma key   A process that electronically or digitally removes a solid color (usually blue or green) and allows it to be replaced with another image. Often used to composite actors into virtual environments. In cases where chroma key is being done with analog video editing equipment, a "super black" signal is sometimes used rather than a visible color.

clipping plane   Also known as the *viewing plane*. A user-definable cut-off point that makes everything on the camera's side of it invisible during rendering.

clone   To copy or otherwise duplicate something, such as a 3D object.

closed shape   A shape that has an inside and an outside, separated from each other by an edge.

CMYK   Cyan Magenta Yellow blacK. The different colors of ink in the 4-color printing process that are applied as tiny dot patterns to form full-color images.

codec   COmpressor DECompressor. Any one of a number of different methods for compressing video and playing it back. Digital video file formats such as .AVI and QuickTime are designed to accept plug-in compression technologies in the form of codecs.

collapse   (1) To collapse vertices or faces means to merge a group of them into a single vertex or face. (2) To reduce a model and any modifiers it has

down to a basic polygonal mesh.

collision detection   A programming algorithm or process that checks to see whether two items are touching or overlapping each other. In 3D packages, collision detection might monitor whether a particle has struck a deflector or boundary object. If it has, the program may cause some kind of change to occur in the particle, like splitting it up or sending it in a different direction.

color   The hue of an object, determined by the frequency of the light emitted from or reflected by the object. In computer graphics, color is determined by the combination of Hue, Saturation, and Value in the HSV color model, or Red, Green, and Blue color levels in the RGB model.

color calibrator   A device that is held up to the screen and uses a reference image to adjust the monitor's settings.

color depth   The amount of data used to display a single pixel in an image, expressed in bits. For example, an 8-bit image contains 256 colors or levels of gray.

color temperature   A value, in degrees Kelvin, that is used to differentiate between near-white spectrums of light.

component software A software architecture in which the core program and add-on features are all modular and interconnected, so that they can work together as if they were a single product.

compositing The process of combining different elements into a single scene. This might refer to combining still photos or bluescreen video with computer graphics backgrounds, or might be applied to any process in which separate images are combined together.

compression rate The speed at which digital video data is encoded for playback, defined in kilobytes per second (KB/s). For movies to play back properly, the target system must be capable of pulling the movie data off the storage medium and displaying it at that speed.

concave polygon A polygon that has two or more segments that form a depression or cavity in its perimeter. If any vertex of a polygon lies on the inside of an imaginary line drawn between the vertices to either side of it, that indicates that the polygon is concave. Some 3D engines have problems with concave polygons.

constraint A restriction placed on the movement of an object in IK, in order to force it to behave like a physical joint.

construction planes and grids A user-positionable plane (sometimes subdivided with a grid) that designates the point at which new shapes and objects will appear in the 3D world.

continuity In a TCB controller, continuity adjusts how tangent the path is to the control point. In filmmaking, it is the process of maintaining a smooth flow of consistency in props, costumes, action, and direction from shot to shot in a scene.

control line Also called the control polygon or hull. An (usually) invisible line that connects the control vertices and helps to define the shape of the spline itself.

control vertices (CVs) Control points that exert a magnet-like influence on the flexible surface of a patch, stretching and tugging it in one direction or another.

coordinates Two or three sets of numbers that are used as part of a grid-based system to identify a given point in space. Also called positional coordinates.

coplanar polygon   A polygon in which all the vertices lie on a single plane. Polygons that are not coplanar can cause rendering problems.

cubic coordinates   See *box coordinates*.

cut   Also referred to as a shot, it is the smallest individual piece of an animation or film. It may be a single frame, or an entire sequence. Also refers to the edited version of the entire film.

cut scene   In computer gaming, a predetermined video or animated sequence that's played to show story progression or the results of a user action.

cyberspace   In 3D graphics, the coordinate-based virtual space inside the computer's memory where 3D scenes are constructed and animated.

cylindrical coordinates   A mapping coordinate system that wraps the image around one of the object's axes until it meets itself, like a label on a soup can.

D

dataset   A collection of information that describes a 3D object. A dataset may contain 3D coordinates, material attributes, textures, and even animation.

decal   An image that can be scaled and moved around on an object independently of any other texture mapping.

default lighting   The startup lighting in a 3D program, which enables the user to begin rendering without having to define a light source.

deform/fit   A type of deform modifier that enables you to use an X-axis outline, a Y-axis outline, and one or more cross-sections to define an object's shape.

deform modifier (operation)   A means of applying transform settings to change the outline of a cross-sectional object as it's swept along a path.

deformation grid   Also known as a space warp. An object that defines an area in 3D space that has an automatic effect on objects passing through its influence. Deforms include Wave, Ripple, Explode, Gravity, and so forth.

deformation map   See *displacement map*.

depth of field   Except for motion blur, that portion of an image that is properly focused. In photography, the aperture setting controls depth of field. In 3D graphics, depth of field is normally infinite, but some products offer control over it as part of the camera settings.

designer In graphics terms, the person who develops and defines the look of a character, prop, or environment, usually as a sketch or painting.

desktop video Digital video editing and effects capability added to a computer with special video cards and software.

detach An operation that disconnects an element of a larger object, separating it into two objects. The opposite of *attach*.

diffuse color The hue assigned to an object. This is the color that is reflected when the object is illuminated by a direct lighting source.

diffuse map A mapping channel used to alter the object's color away from that defined by the color setting, usually into a pattern or image.

diffusion dither A type of dithering where the differently colored pixels are randomized to an extent, smoothing the blend.

digital camera An electronic camera that records images (onto built-in memory or tiny diskettes) that can be downloaded into a computer.

digital retouching The process of using 2D paint programs to modify photographic stills or movies.

digital sound Audio that has been converted to a binary format, allowing it to be manipulated by and played back on a computer. Music CDs use digital sound recorded in 16 bits at a 44.1KHz data rate, and all modern sound cards can provide this level as well.

digitizing The process of transforming images, objects, or sounds into a digital form that a computer can manipulate.

directional light Also called a distant light. A virtual illumination source for simulating far-away light sources such as the sun. It projects light along one axis only, and all the light rays (and hence, the shadows) are parallel.

director The person who holds the overall vision for a film or project, and is involved in the day-to-day production of that work from start to finish. The director is the manager and spearhead of the creative team.

displacement map Also known as a deformation map. A grayscale image applied to an object that actually distorts the mesh, deforming it according to the gray value. Often used to create terrain models.

distant light See *directional light*.

dither An image process that breaks gradients up into patterns of variously colored pixels. These work like the four-color printing process to simulate a wider range of colors.

dolly In film making, a wheeled platform on which a camera is mounted, and the process of moving the camera around on the floor during the shot. In 3D software, it usually means a camera movement made toward, away from, or around a subject as though the camera were mounted on a wheeled tripod.

dongle A hardware key, which is a physical device plugged into the serial port of a computer or attached in-line with the keyboard, that unlocks high-end software for use.

double-sided object An object with normals on both sides of the object's faces, allowing it to be seen from any viewpoint, even inside.

dpi dots per inch. Resolution expressed as the number of dots or pixels that the medium can display in one inch. Most computer displays are based on 72dpi, and 300–600dpi are common laser printer output resolutions.

dummy object See *null*.

DVD Digital Versatile Disc. An optical disc format for both video and computer files that features much higher data capacity than compact disc.

DVD burner Similar to a recordable CD drive, but handles one or more of the following media as well: DVD-R, DVD-RW, DVD-RAM, DVD+R, DVD+RW. Most of the DVD burners available for consumer use offer capacities of about 4.7GB.

DVE Digital Video Editing. The use of a desktop video system to edit and add special effects to video.

E

ease from A keyframe parameter that controls the acceleration of the object or event as it leaves the keyframe.

ease to A keyframe parameter that decelerates an object or event as it approaches the keyframe.

edge The boundary portion of a polygon, represented by lines that connect each of the vertices together.

edge divide A polygon-level form of *tessellation* that splits an edge by adding a new vertex.

The new vertex is connected to the others by additional edges, subdividing the original polygon.

edge extrude   Pushes a copy of the selected edge away from the original and adds polygons to fill in the gap. The result is a fin-like projection extending away from the original edge.

edge turn   Rotates the selected edge between available vertices. This is usually done to influence the normals of the polygon so that the surface appears smoother when rendered.

edge visible/invisible   Toggles the visibility of the edge. Whether an edge is visible has an influence on the normals (and therefore the appearance of smoothness) of the rendered result. Visibility also helps to define which faces in a given area belong to a single polygon.

editing   The process of assembling the various scenes created and rendered during production, turning them into a cohesive whole.

emitter   A simple polygonal shape that acts as a point of origin for particles in a particle system.

element   Object "subassemblies" usually consisting of a group of polygons. When two objects are attached, they remain selectable as elements, even though they are part of a single object.

engine   The portion of a software program that handles a specific task. A 3D engine in a game manages and updates the real-time 3D graphics.

environment mapping   A type of texture mapping that simulates ray tracing. It works by rendering multiple images from each objects' perspective and combining them into a reflection map for the object.

exclude   A feature that allows listed objects to be unaffected by the selected light source.

export   Saving a file in a cross-program or cross-platform format, like DXF.

expression   A mathematical formula or algorithm. In 3D, expressions are used to create or control animation in ways that would be difficult or very labor-intensive to do by hand.

extrude/extrusion   The process of pushing a 2D shape into the third dimension by giving it a Z-axis depth.

F

face   The area enclosed by the edges of the polygon.

face divide   An operation that tessellates a polygon just like *edge divide*, except that the user can select a point anywhere inside the polygon as the point for the new vertex to appear.

face extrusion   A process that takes a selected face or faces and extrudes them in or out from their current positions.

face mapping   An image mapping type that tries to conform the image to pairs of faces that share an invisible edge.

facial motion capture   A motion capture system designed to record facial expressions and lip movements.

falloff   The portion or range of a light source that is at a reduced or zero-intensity setting. Also, a transparency option that sets how much more or less transparent an object is at its edges. May also refer to the rate at which a light source or transparency approaches zero.

field of view (FOV)   The angle, in degrees, that encompasses everything that can be seen through a lens or virtual camera viewport.

field rendering   Output option that renders images in the same way that a television displays them: in two alternating passes, one with every odd scan line

rendered, the other with every even line. Compare with *frame rendering*.

file format   The manner in which data is organized in a computer file. Common image file formats include BMP, PICT, and TGA. Popular 3D file formats include MAX, LWO, OBJ, 3DS, and DXF.

fillet   Also called a radius edge or *round*. An arcing transition between two planes or lines.

fill light   Light source used to fill in a dark area of a scene, such as a shadow cast by the key light.

film grammar   The storytelling methodology developed by director D. W. Griffith and others to make the best use of the film medium.

first person shooter (FPS) A shooting game presented in a first-person view of the gaming world. *Castle Wolfenstein 3D* was one of the very first FPS games to gain wide popularity and kick-start the genre.

first vertex   The vertex in a shape that is used for orientation during skinning operations. Usually the one that was created first, but any vertex can be assigned as such.

flat shading/render   A display or rendering mode that shows off the surface and color of the object in a faceted manner, because the polygons aren't smoothed.

focal length   The distance in millimeters from the center of the lens to the image it forms of the subject (assumed to be an infinite distance in front of the lens). Short focal lengths produce wide-angle images, whereas long ones are used for telephoto shots.

fog   Atmospheric effect in which pixel color is shifted toward a user-specified value the farther away an object is from the camera.

forward kinematics   A manner of linking and animating objects in a top-down hierarchy; the movement of the parent affects all the children on down the chain, so many fine adjustments are often needed to position the end of the chain where you want it.

foley stage   A soundproof room filled with numerous objects and materials used to create sound effects.

forensic animation   An animated re-creation of an accident or event using whatever data (or speculation) is available. Popular for demonstrating a complex series of events in courtroom situations.

forward kinematics   The default method of animating linked objects, in which the movement of the parent object affects all the offspring on down the chain.

frame   In filmmaking or animation, a single still image that is part of a sequence. Similarly, a marker for a single image's position in an animation timeline. Also, the portion of a scene that it visible when it is viewed through a camera or viewport.

frame buffer   A portion of memory that temporarily holds the data needed to display an image.

frame rate   The speed at which film, video, or animated images are displayed, in frames per second (fps).

frame rendering   The default output option that renders the entire image. Compare with *field rendering*.

freeze   Also called *ghost* or template. A command that leaves an object visible in a scene, but prevents it from being selected or changed.

function curve   A graphical way of displaying object transformations or other animatible parameters.

G

gamma In a computer display, refers to the overall brightness of the screen. Also, a measure of brightness for all output technologies as a way of predicting their appearance when the image is viewed on a computer display.

gamut The color range that can be represented by a particular display or printing technology.

G-buffer Also called a geometry channel. Additional image channels that use grayscale images to describe the geometry, normals, textures, and other information in the model.

gel In film making, celluloid filters placed over spotlights to change their color. Sometimes used as another term for *projection map*.

geometry General term for 3D objects. Also, incredibly boring subject in high school.

geometry channel See *G-buffer*.

ghost See *freeze*.

gimbal lock A loss of rotational freedom due to the alignment of two axes in certain animation controllers.

global illumination See *radiosity*.

glow A light source setting or post-production effect that creates a soft halo of light around selected objects or materials.

gobo In filmmaking, steel cutouts that change the shape of quality of a spotlight. See *projection map*.

Gouraud shading Also called smooth shading. A display or rendering mode that produces smoothly blended object surfaces that are much more realistic than flat renderings.

greenscreen Similar to *bluescreen*, but allows the costumes or props to contain blue or purple pigments. Of course, with a greenscreen the subject can't have any green pigment.

grid Cross-hatched lines visible in the viewport, and used like graph paper for determining scale when creating objects.

grid object A 2D helper object that looks like a grid. Useful as a reference when positioning objects in 3D space.

group A command that enables the user to select a related collection of objects, then temporarily combines them into a whole.

H

helical sweep   A sweep created along a helix-shaped path. Often used to create coil spring-like objects.

hidden line   A display or rendering mode that draws the edges of an object as in a wireframe display, but only ones that would be visible if the object were opaque.

hidden surface removal
A display or rendering mode in which those polygons that cannot be seen from a particular viewpoint are ignored. Usually, the polygons can't be seen because they are obscured by other polygons that *are* rendered.

hide   A command that makes an object invisible.

hierarchy   In 3D, the parent/child relationship of objects linked together in a chain.

hotspot   The portion or range of a light source that is at the full intensity setting.

HSV   hue-saturation-value. A color selection interface used in computer graphics that enables the user to adjust hue (chroma), saturation (intensity), and value (brightness) to select a color.

hull   See *control line*.

hue   See *color*.

I

image library   A collection of royalty-free or stock images, often on CD-ROM, that are professionally photographed and scanned.

import   Loading a file saved in a cross-program or cross-platform format, such as DXF.

include   A light source option that enables the user to select a list of objects that the specified light will affect. All other objects in the scene are ignored.

instance   A type of duplicate of an object or light source in which changes to one are adopted by all.

intensity   A measure of the brightness of a light source. Also, another term for *saturation*.

intern   An often-unpaid work experience position at a company.

interpolation   The process of determining intermediate steps in a movement or shape. For example, 3D software interpolates the position of an object between two different keyframes to create all the missing frames.

inverse kinematics (IK)   A method of controlling linked objects by moving the far end of a hierarchical chain, which then causes the rest of the chain to conform.

inverted light   Also known as a negative or dark light. Makes a light source work in the opposite way, by lowering the illumination level of whatever is in range.

isoparm   Short for isoparametric curve. A curve with constant U or V values across its surface.

isotropic highlight   An oblique highlight, like the kind you might see reflected from brushed metal.

J

jaggies   Slang term for lines or areas of an image that are not anti-aliased.

K

key light   The main source of illumination in the scene, usually casting the most apparent shadows.

keyframe   Also called keys. In 3D graphics, a user-defined point where an animation event takes place. The computer then tweens the events from keyframe to keyframe. In a digital video file, it is a frame that contains the entire image, rather than only changes from the previous frame.

keyframing   The process of defining keyframes for animation.

knot   A control point that defines the control line or polygon that shapes a spline.

L

laser stereo lithography   One of the methods used to create real-world solid models from 3D data. The process involves using lasers to solidify a liquid plastic at the point where the beams intersect.

lathe   The process of spinning a 2D shape around an axis, extruding it in small steps as it is rotated.

left-hand rule   The opposite of the *right-hand rule*.

lens flare   The pattern of bright circles and rays that is seen when you point a camera lens at the sun or other bright light source.

level of detail (LOD)   Means of referring to the relative resolution of an object (low, medium, high). Term is commonly used in games where there may be two or three versions of a given object, each with different polygon counts.

light map   A texture blended with a base texture map to create the effect that illumination is falling on the base texture.

linear array   A series of objects duplicated from the original along a straight-line trajectory.

linear weighting   Animation control type in which tweening is done in a continuous, even manner, with no variation in speed or direction.

link   A hierarchical connection between two objects.

local coordinates   Coordinate system that uses the object itself as the basis for the axes.

luminosity   See *self-illumination*.

M

magnet tool   A tool designed to make 3D sculpting easier by attracting or repelling vertices when it's brought close to the object.

map   A bitmapped image, either scanned or painted, that gives a material unique qualities that aren't available by simply varying surface attributes.

map channel   See *channel*.

mapper   Short for texture mapper. A person who creates and applies materials and textures to 3D objects.

mapping   Also called texture mapping. The process of developing and assigning material attributes to an object.

mapping coordinates   A set of coordinates that specify the location, orientation, and scale of any textures applied to an object.

maquette   A small, often highly detailed sculpture that is used to help artists and others involved in production visualize a character in three dimensions. Sometimes maquettes are 3D scanned to help in creating a model.

mask   An alpha channel image. A black-and-white or grayscale element that is used to prevent certain areas of an image from being affected by a process. Called a matte in filmmaking.

massing model   A rough 3D model constructed to work out proportional and general design issues.

material   The encompassing term for all the different images and settings that are assigned to an object's surface.

matte See *mask*.

memory In computing, refers to temporary storage, like RAM.

mesh Slang term for a 3D object or scene, called that because an object viewed in wireframe resembles a wire mesh sculpture.

mesh editing Generally speaking, making revisions to an object at the vertex level.

mesh library A collection of stock or custom 3D objects.

mesh optimization The process of reducing the density of a mesh object by combining closely aligned faces.

mesh relax A command that allows vertices to drift slightly, softening tight curves and smoothing the surface.

mesh smooth A command or plug-in that analyzes a 3D object and uses splitting and averaging techniques to add additional faces. See also *subdivision surfaces*.

metaballs A form of modeling where the user builds forms out of spheres and the software blends them together into a single mass.

MIP-mapping From the Latin Multi In Parvum (many parts). A texture mapping and anti-aliasing technique that calculates the resolution of a texture map based on the object's distance from the camera.

mirror A transform that reverses an object or copies a reversed version of it along the selected axis.

modeler In CG terms, a person who builds objects in 3D.

modeling The process of creating or modifying objects in 3D. Also, the simulation of a process using computers and CG (as in modeling a weather system).

moiré A pattern that appears in video images that contain small repetitive textures, or in scans when the scanning resolution doesn't match the printing resolution. Pronounced MOR-AY.

morph Animated 2D and/or 3D technique that makes one image or form smoothly transform into another.

motion blur The smearing of an image when the subject or camera is in motion.

motion capture Any one of several processes that enable a performer's actions to be digitized and used to drive a bones deformation system for 3D character animation.

motion library   A stock collection of animated movements for bones deformation systems (usually motion captured) that offer actions such as reaching, bending, stretching, eating, dancing, and so forth.

motion path   A spline that represents the path of an object, used for reference when making adjustments to the animation.

multiplier   A light source setting that increases the intensity of the light past the RGB setting limits.

N

node   An object in a hierarchy. Also, a computer or peripheral in a network.

n-gon   A polygon with an unspecified number of sides. Also called a multigon.

non sequitur   Nonsensical words or actions, or statements that are absurd or meaningless. Also called political platforms.

non-linear editing   Editing system that enables the user to edit scenes in any desired sequence, as opposed to starting at the beginning and working through to the end.

non-planar polygon   A polygon in which one or more of the vertices are on a different plane from the others, which can result in a rendering bug.

normal   An imaginary marker (usually represented by a little line or arrow) which protrudes from a polygon face and indicates which side of the polygon is visible, and what direction it's facing.

null   Also called a dummy object. An object that does not render, so it can be used as an invisible component of a chain or as a reference point for establishing remote axes of rotation.

NURBS   Non-Uniform Rational B-Splines. A type of spline that has control points that reside away from the resulting curve, and has weights to control the curve. It uses knots that define the number of control points on a given portion of the curve.

O

omni light   Omnidirectional light. See *point light*.

opacity   The degree to which light rays cannot penetrate an object. Defines the same quality as transparency, but from the opposite end of the scale.

opacity map   A grayscale image loaded into a material's opacity channel that makes the object's surface appear to vary from opaque to transparent.

OpenGL   Open Graphics Library. A graphics description library developed by SGI and used by video cards to process 2D and 3D data for display onscreen.

operand   An object or shape being used in a Boolean operation.

optical tracking   Motion capture method where the performer is covered with little targets (usually white disks or balls), and a video camera is used to digitize their movements.

optimized palette   A palette that features the best range of colors to display a given image.

optimize   In 3D graphics, reduces the density of a mesh object by combining closely aligned faces. Also used to refer to reorganization of a hard drive to place all data in contiguous sectors.

origin point   The center point of the cyberspace universe, where the central axes meet. Identified by the coordinates 0, 0, 0.

orthographic projection   In 3D graphics, a display mode in which the viewer's location is infinitely distant from the scene, so that all lines along the same axis are parallel. Viewports such as Top, Side, Front, and User usually display orthographic views.

output   Stage in 3D production where a file, photographic slide, section of videotape, or other media is used to store the image or animation.

P

palette   The full set of colors used or available for use in an image. Usually refers to images with 256 colors or less.

palette flash   A flashing or color shift that occurs when an image's palette is altered abruptly.

pan   A side-to-side rotation of a camera around its vertical axis.

parametric coordinates   Semi-automatic mapping coordinates that can be applied during the creation of any parametric object.

parametric modeling   A 3D modeling system in which objects retain their base geometry information and can be modified at almost any point by varying the parameters that define them.

parent   In a chain of linked objects, the object that is closer to the base of the hierarchy than the object attached to it (its child).

partial lathe   A lathe operation in which the cross-sectional shape is not revolved a full 360°.

particle system   An animation module that enables the user to generate and control the behavior of a vast number of tiny objects. Used to simulate natural effects such as water, fire, sparks, or bubbles.

patch modeler   A 3D modeling system that uses a network of control points to define and modify the shape of the patch, which is usually a lattice of either splines or polygons.

persistence of vision   The tendency of the human eye to continue seeing an image for a split second after the view has changed.

perspective   The illusion that objects to appear to shrink the further they are from the viewer.

Phong rendering   A rendering method that retains the smoothness of Gouraud shading, but adds specular highlights for more realism.

photon mapping   An extension of ray tracing that can be used to efficiently simulate *global illumination* and *caustics* in complex scenes.

pitch   In flying, rotation of the fuselage up or down, causing the plane to climb or descend. Used in 3D as a way to describe X-axis rotation.

pivot point   The user-defined rotational center of an object, often the same as the point where the three local axes meet.

pixel   PI(X)cture ELement. The smallest unit of graphics that a video adapter generates, usually about the size of a pinpoint. Pixels can be of nearly any color, depending on the capabilities of the adapter.

planar coordinates   A type of mapping coordinate system well suited to flat objects. It applies a set of rectangular image coordinates from a single direction.

plug-in   An add-on feature that works within a software program. Plug-ins are popular for adding new capabilities to products without generating a new version of the software.

point   In 3D space, the smallest area that it is possible to "occupy" is called a point. Each point is defined by a unique set of three numbers, called coordinates.

point light   Also known as an omni (omnidirectional) light. A light source that casts light in all directions.

polygon   A closed shape with three or more sides.

polygonal modeling   The basic type of 3D modeling, in which all objects are made up of groups of polygons.

polyline   A line with more than one segment (at least three vertices).

post-production   That part of a film project that takes place after all the principal shooting has been completed. The editing, sound, and post effects phase.

post-production effects   Also called video post effects or simply post effects. In 3D graphics, this refers to transitions, color manipulation, or special effects applied to an animation after it has been rendered.

pre-rendered animation   Term used in computer game production that refers to animation that is generated at an earlier time, and then stored in a form that allows playback on demand.

preview   In 3D graphics, an output mode that creates a fast-rendering test animation, or a display mode that generates a simplified version of the scene in real time.

primitive   Any of a number of basic 3D geometric forms, including cubes, spheres, cones, cylinders, and so forth.

procedural texture   A type of texture that is mathematically defined. It can be used to simulate wood, marble, and other materials, but usually doesn't look as realistic as scanned textures.

producer   The person responsible for the budgets and timetable on a project. In some cases, may also be the creative lead, a producer/director.

production assistant   Usually an assistant to the producer on a project. Arranges meetings, runs errands, checks with artists on progress, updates reports, or whatever else needs to be done.

projection   Another term for a mapping coordinate method. (Cylindrical mapping is the same as cylindrical projection.)

projection map   Also called a gobo. An image added to a light source that changes the light's shape or causes it to throw a pattern onto objects it illuminates.

projector   A light source that uses a projection map or gobo.

pulling points   Slang term for *vertex-level editing*.

Q

quad A four-sided polygon commonly used in 3D programs.

R

radial array A series of objects duplicated from the original along a rotation-based trajectory.

radiosity The property that states that light reflecting off an object goes on to illuminate other objects as well. Also, a rendering method that takes into account the color and shape of all surfaces in the scene when calculating illumination levels, and produces images of near-photographic realism.

radius edge See *fillet*.

RAM random access memory. Solid-state memory that the computer uses for temporary storage.

ray tracing A rendering method in which the color and value of each pixel on the screen is calculated by casting an imaginary ray backward from the viewer's perspective into the model, to determine what light and surface factors are influencing it.

real time or **realtime** The immediate processing of input data and graphics, so that any changes result in near-instantaneous adjustments to the image.

reflection map An image or process used to create an environment for a reflective object in order to roughly simulate the effects of ray tracing on reflective objects.

refraction The bending of light waves that occurs when they move through different types of materials.

refraction mapping A material option used as a means of simulating the effects of light refraction in programs that don't offer ray tracing.

refresh rate The number of times per second that the screen image is repainted on the monitor, measured in cycles per second, or Hertz (Hz).

rendering The process wherein the computer interprets all the object and light data and creates a finished image from the viewport you have selected. The resulting image may be either a still, or a frame in an animation sequence.

resolution-independent The property of remaining smooth, no matter how much magnification or scaling is applied. NURBS-based modeling is resolution-independent.

RGB Red-Green-Blue. The three primary colors in the additive (direct light) color model. Computer monitors vary the brightness levels of red, green, and blue pixels in order to create the gamut of displayable colors.

right-hand rule A memory aid in which you position the fingers of your right hand in a way that is analogous to the X, Y, and Z axes. Another variation of the rule can help you remember the direction of positive rotation around a given axis.

roll In flying, rotation of the fuselage around its long axis, which causes the aircraft to bank left or right. Used in 3D as a way to describe Z-axis rotation. To rotate a camera around its viewing axis, making the scene appear to spin.

rotate A transform that spins an object around the selected axis.

rotoscoping The process of adding film or video to animation, either as a finished element or for use as a reference for the animated characters.

rough cut A version of an animation or film in which all the scenes are in place, but the timing hasn't been fine-tuned.

round See *fillet*.

RT3D Real Time 3D. See *real time*.

S

saturation Also called intensity. The measure of how concentrated a color appears to be. A fully saturated red, for example, cannot be any more red than it is, whereas a red with low saturation begins to turn gray.

scale A transform that adjusts the size of an object. Also, the mathematical relationship between the size of a subject in reality and the size of its representation on paper or in 3D. A typical architectural scale, for example, is 1/4"=1'0".

scanline rendering Typical rendering method used by non-ray-tracing programs. Renders the image as a series of horizontal lines.

screen coordinates An axis and coordinate system based on the computer's screen, with X being horizontal, Y being vertical, and Z being (perpendicular) toward and away from the viewer.

segment A step or division in an object, similar to the way a building is divided up into floors.

self-illumination A material channel or control that adjusts the degree to which an object appears to be lit from within. Sometimes called incandescence.

self-illumination map A grayscale image loaded into the material's self-illumination channel that creates the impression that some portions of the object are lit from within.

shader See *material*.

shadow map size A setting that adjusts the amount of memory that the system can use to create a given shadow map. The larger the map, the more refined and detailed it will be.

shadow mapping A method of creating shadows in scanline renderers that works by creating a grayscale texture map based on the lighting and mesh in the scene, then applying it to the objects at render time.

shininess The overall reflective nature of the object—in other words, its glossiness.

shininess map A grayscale image loaded into the material's shininess channel that varies the surface's reflectivity. Used for making portions of an object dull or shiny.

single-sided polygon The default type of polygons, which can be "seen" only from the side with the normal. For example, if you create a sphere with single-sided polygons and move the viewpoint inside the object to render an image, the sphere won't be visible.

skating A common problem in character animation created with forward kinematics or cheapo motion capture, in which the position of a character's feet slide around on the ground instead of remaining firmly planted.

skeleton The linked internal bone structure that can be used to deform the surrounding mesh in a bones deformation system. In humanoid 3D characters, the skeleton is a very simple version of our own.

skew A transform that forces one side of an object in one direction along the selected axis, and the other side in the opposite direction.

skinning A method of creating 3D objects by generating a "skin" over a group of (usually different) cross-sections.

smooth shading See *Gouraud shading*.

SMPTE Society of Motion Picture and Television Engineers. In video and 3D graphics, a time format consisting of hours, minutes, seconds, and frames (01:57:31:12 would be 1 hour, 57 minutes, 31 seconds and 12 frames).

snap   A feature that causes the cursor to snap from one position to another according to a user-defined grid spacing, or in reaction to object edges and vertices.

soft selection   A method of selecting vertices with a user-definable falloff value so that some vertices are influenced more than others by any transforms.

solid modeling   A special form of 3D for engineering applications that adds information about the material's weight, density, tensile strength, and other real-world facts to the model's dataset.

specular color   The hue of any highlights that appear on an object at Phong rendering levels or higher. Specular color is also affected by the Specularity setting or mapping, and by the color of lights.

specular highlight   The bright reflections of light seen on glossy objects in Phong rendering levels or higher.

specularity   A material channel or control that adjusts the color and intensity of the object's highlight, if it has one.

specularity map   An image loaded into the material's specularity channel that varies the color and intensity of the specular highlights of the surface. Useful for creating the effect of prismatic or metal flake surfaces.

spherical coordinates   A mapping coordinate system that wraps the image around the object in a cylindrical manner, then pinches the top and bottom closed to surround it.

spline   A line, usually curved, that's defined by control points. Bezier, B-spline, and NURBS are common types of splines.

spotlight   A directional light source that radiates light from a single point out into a user-defined cone or pyramid.

squash and stretch   Modified scale operations that treat the object as though it had volume. Squashing an object makes it spread out around the edges, whereas stretching it makes the object get thin in the middle.

stairstepping   The stair-like jaggedness of a computer-drawn line or object that isn't anti-aliased.

steps   The number of additional vertices generated between control points on a spline or predefined vertices on a poly.

stock mesh   Models created by others and sold singly or in collections. Using stock mesh can save an artist a great deal of time and increase productivity on a project.

storyboarding   The process of outlining a film or animation by breaking it down into a sequence of sketches that illustrate the key movements in the scene.

subdivision surfaces   A mesh smoothing operation that analyzes the lower-resolution base object and uses splitting and averaging techniques to add additional faces. The process smoothes out rough edges and emphasizes details.

sub-object operations   Editing or processing performed on only a portion of an object, down to a single polygon.

sub-polygon operations Editing or processing performed on the vertices, face, or edges of polygons.

subtractive color model   The reflected light color model in which red, yellow, and blue are the primary colors, and mixing the three together results in a muddy brown.

surface attribute   A basic material setting, such as color, shininess, or transparency, that affects all parts of an object equally.

sweep   The process of creating a 3D object by extruding a single 2D cross-section along a path.

system palette   The predefined range of colors defined by the computer's operating system software.

T

tangent point   Also called a weight. The portion of a spline control system that acts like a magnet to attract the spline in its direction.

taper   A transform that compresses and/or expands an object along the selected axis.

target   A positioning aid that enables the user to see where a camera or light is pointed from any viewport.

TCB controller Tension/Continuity/Bias controller. One of the most common methods of providing control over the keyframe control points.

teeter   A type of deformation modifier that enables the cross-section to be rotated around the X and/or Y axes, perpendicular to the path.

tension   In a TCB controller, the amount of curvature that the keyframe allows in the path before and after the keyframe.

terrain model   A 3D representation of a landscape, often generated by using a grayscale topographical map to apply displacement mapping to a grid object.

tessellate   To subdivide polygons, usually to smooth a surface.

texel   TEXture PixEL. A transitional form of texture data derived from a *texture map* and used by *RT3D* engines for calculating the color of each screen *pixel*.

texture   See *texture map*.

texture map   A bitmapped image, either scanned or painted, that gives a material unique qualities that aren't available by simply varying surface attributes.

tiling   The technique of repeating an image to cover a larger area.

tilt   The vertical equivalent of a pan, created by rotating the camera up or down around its horizontal axis.

timeline   A graph-like interface for viewing and manipulating animation events. Time is usually reflected along the X-axis, whereas animatible parameters are located on the Y-axis. At the intersection of the two axes are keyframes or other markers to indicate the type of animation event.

title safe   The portion of the screen in which text should be contained if the image were output to video. Title safe is defined by an inner perimeter that can be superimposed on the viewport.

track   Usage varies, but this usually refers to movement of the camera along a single axis, be it horizontal or vertical.

transform   A general term for an operation that alters the position, size, or shape of a object. Typical transforms include move, scale, rotate, bend, twist, skew, taper, and stretch.

transparency   A measure of the amount of light that can pass through an object. Some programs use the similar but opposing term, opacity.

triangle   A three-sided polygon, the basic polygonal shape used in 3D software. Has the advantage that it cannot become non-planar.

trim lines   Lines or curves used to cut away portions of a spline surface.

true color Full 24-bit (or greater) color, offering over sixteen million shades for accuracy and smooth gradients.

tweening Process in which the software takes control of how the object is transformed or blended between keyframes.

twist A transform that wrings an object around the selected axis.

U

unfreeze/unghost Command to remake an object that had been frozen or ghosted editable again.

ungroup Command to detach a cluster of objects that had been grouped together.

unhide Command to make a hidden object visible again.

UNIX Powerful multiuser, multitasking operating system used for servers and high-end desktop systems. Linux and IRIX are derivatives of UNIX.

user axis An axis that the user can define independently. A user axis can be at any angle, or it can be aligned to an existing axis.

UV or UVW coordinate system UV or UVW coordinates look similar to the XY image coordinate system, but they conform to the mesh no matter how it twists or bends. UVW coordinates are used for mesh objects, and shifting them allows very precise repositioning of maps on an object.

V

vacation What I'm taking after this book is finished.

value The lightness or darkness of a color (tinting or shading).

vertex A point in 2D or 3D space used to define the boundaries and position of a line or polygon.

vertex-level editing The manipulation of an object's individual vertices to change its shape.

vertices Plural form of *vertex*.

video acceleration Hardware enhancements to the video card that make it more effective for displaying digital video.

video capture The process of digitizing a video signal coming from a camera, VCR, laserdisc, or other source and saving it into RAM or as a file. Often the first step in digital video editing.

video safe (boundary) The portion of the screen that should appear on the average television if the image were output to video. Video safe is defined by an outer perimeter that can be superimposed on the viewport.

video safe colors Colors that fit into the luminance and saturation limits set for television broadcast. Colors outside this range blur and distort the video signal.

view coordinates A coordinate system that uses the viewport as the basis for the X, Y, and Z axes. These axes remain the same no matter how the user's perspective on the 3D scene changes.

viewing plane A plane surrounding the viewpoint at a perpendicular angle. It is an imaginary flat panel that defines the limits of the user's field of view.

viewpoint A position in or around cyberspace that represents the viewer's current location.

viewport In 3D software, a window that looks into 3D space.

virtual Something that doe not exist in real life but that the computer can visualize and manipulate. A 3D object is a good example. It doesn't really exist outside of the computer's memory, but the user can manipulate the object as though it did exist.

virtual memory The use of hard drive space as temporary storage when the computer system runs low on RAM.

virtual reality (VR) A computer system that can immerse the user in the illusion of a computer generated world and enable the user to navigate through this world at will. Typically, the user wears a head-mounted display (HMD) that displays a stereoscopic image, and wears a sensor glove, which permits the user to manipulate "objects" in the virtual environment.

volumetric light A type of light source with an adjustable 3D volume that can simulate the behavior of natural light in an atmosphere.

voxel VOlume piXEL. An alternative method of representing 3D objects without polygons. Voxel objects are made up of tiny cubes, usually with transparency and color.

VRML Virtual Reality Markup Language. A web browser technology that enables the user to explore simple 3D environments online.

W

weight See *tangent point*.

weld An operation that combines the overlapping vertices of shapes or objects together. Sometimes called merge, but not to be confused with the Merge command that imports additional models or lights into a scene.

wireframe A display or rendering mode for drawing objects using lines to represent the polygon edges, which makes the object resemble a sculpture made of wire mesh.

world coordinates The fundamental coordinate system of 3D space, which the user's viewpoint does not change.

X, Y, and Z

X-axis Typically the horizontal or width axis, running left and right.

XY coordinates The normal coordinate system for 2D images and shapes. The X-axis runs horizontally, and the Y-axis vertically.

yaw In flying, rotation of the fuselage to the left or right, which changes the heading of the aircraft. Used in 3D as a way to describe Y-axis rotation.

Y-axis Usually the vertical or height axis, extending up and down.

Z-axis The axis normally associated with depth. It runs forward and back.

Z-buffer Both the process and the portion of memory used to store the Z-axis data for every pixel on the screen.

zoom To change the *field of view (FOV)* of a camera so that the subject appears to grow larger or smaller. Not to be confused with moving the camera to create the same effect.

Appendix B

Contributors

Interviewees

Marco Bertoldo
marco@mondomedia.com
3ds max artist, art director

Eric Chadwick
echadwick@whatif-productions.com
http://www.whatif-productions.com
2D/3D artist

Richard Green
green@artbot.com
http://www.artbot.com
3ds max artist
Senior artist at Totally Games

Laura Hainke
cyberdogst@aol.com
3D texture artist

Bob Jeffery
sspastic@hotmail.com
3ds max artist

Michael D. Jones
mjones@DigitalArtMonkey.com
www.DigitalArtMonkey.com
3D Cinematic Artist

Kelly Kleider
kelly@kleider.net
www.kleider.net
Technical director and
freelance consultant

Andy Murdock
andy@lotsofrobots.com
http://www.lotsofrobots.com
3D Studio Max and Photoshop artist

Leila Noorani
leila_noorani@hotmail.com
2D/3D artist

Marco Patrito
Virtual Views
Via Montello, 9
1092 Beinasco (To)
ITALY
http://www.sinkha.com

Gustavo "Goose" Ramirez
goose_r69@hotmail.com
3ds max artist, animator

Eric Ronay
moonshdw@afriverse.com
http://afriverse.com/~moonshdw/
Animator, technical director

Derek Thompson
derek@derekmonster.com
http://www.derekmonster.com
Concept artist and illustrator,
storyboarding, comic art, and
character design

Cindy Hideko Yamauchi

cindy560a@hotmail.com

2D/3D artist and art director
Anime style animation and
illustration services
Marketing for anime-related
businesses

Sheldon Whittaker

sheldnz@slingshot.co.nz

Maya artist

Image and Asset Contributors

Per 'Per128' Abrahamsen

per@n-en.com

http://www.n-en.com

2D/3D Artist

Activeworlds

95 Parker Street
Newburyport, MA 01950
978-499-0222

http://www.activeworlds.com

Activision

3100 Ocean Park Boulevard
Santa Monica, CA 90405
310-255-2000

http://www.activision.com

Adobe Systems Incorporated

345 Park Avenue
San Jose, California 95110-2704
408-536-6000

http://www.adobe.com

Alias|Wavefront

210 King Street East
Toronto, Ontario, Canada M5A 1J7
800-447-2542

http://www.aliaswavefront.com

AniMagicians

Aaron Shi

3ds max artists

Laurent Antoine "Lemog"

lemog@club-internet.fr

http://www.lemog.fr.st

Maya artist

Artbeats Software, Inc.

P.O. Box 709
Myrtle Creek, OR 97457
800-444-9392

http://www.artbeats.com

Ascension Technology Corporation

P.O. Box 527
Burlington, VT 05402
802-893-6657

ascension@ascension-tech.com

http://www.ascension-tech.com

Den Beauvais

den@denbeauvais.com

http://www.den3d.com

Animation Master artist

Marco Bertoldo

marco@mondomedia.com

3ds max artist, art director

Kenn Brown
kennb@shaw.ca
http://www.kontent-online.com
Artist specializing in illustration and design of the fantastic

Eric Chadwick
echadwick@whatif-productions.com
http://www.whatif-productions.com
2D/3D artist

Jeff Cantin
tincan@pacbell.net
http://alienlogo.com/tincan/
Animation Master artist

Cody Chancellor
cody@chancellor.net
http://www.chancellor.net/
Painter and 3ds max artist

Barry 'HyPer' Collins
hyper@prcn.org
http://www.coronaleonis.com
http://www.n-en.com
2D/3D artist

Curious Labs
655 Capitola Road
Suite 200
Santa Cruz, CA 95062
831-462-8901
http://www.curiouslabs.com

Digital Art Zone (DAZ)
12401 South 450 East, Suite #F1
Draper, UT 84020
800-267-5170
http://www.daz3d.com/

Digital Illusion
Ruieta DaSilva and
Deanan Da Silva
delusion@delusion.com
http://www.delusion.com

Discreet
10 rue Duke
Montreal, Quebec, Canada H3C 2L7
800-869-3504
http://www.discreet.com

James 'Gwot' Edwards
jedwards@digitalextremes.com
http://www.digitalextremes.com
2D/3D artist and designer

Foundation Imaging
24933 West Avenue Stanford
Valencia, CA 91355
661-257-0292
info@foundation-i.com
http://www.foundation-i.com

GameSpy Industries
18002 Sky Park Circle
Irvine, CA 92614-6429
949-798-4200
http://www.gamespy.com

Mark Giambruno
OtakuShark@hotmail.com
http://www.animelook.com/mg3d
Author and 3ds max artist

Richard Green
green@artbot.com
http://www.artbot.com
3ds max artist, senior artist at Totally Games

Laura Hainke
cyberdogst@aol.com
3D texture artist

Terry Halladay
thallad@pcnet.com
http://www.pcnet.com/~thallad
*TrueSpace and Cinema 4D artist,
photographer*

Hash, Inc.
400 West Evergreen Blvd.
Vancouver, WA 98660
360-750-0042
http://www.hash.com

Akira Iketani
ubic@ai.wakwak.com
http://www.ai.wakwak.com/~ubic/
3ds max artist

InSpark, Inc.
Masa Ishikawa
(Formerly Pulse Interactive)
http://www.in-spark.net/

Interplay Entertainment Corp.
16815 Von Karman Ave.
Irvine, CA 92606
http://www.interplay.com

Michael D. Jones
mjones@DigitalArtMonkey.com
www.DigitalArtMonkey.com
3D cinematic artist

Masaru Kakiyama
kiyama@angel.ne.jp
http://www.angel.ne.jp/~kakiyama/index.htm
Animation Master artist

Jussi Kemppainen
jussi.kemppainen@dlvisions.fi
http://juzzart.cjb.net
LightWave artist

Simon Knights
SK Computer GfX
simonpk@pacbell.net
3ds max artist

Guillermo M. Leal Llaguno
Screampoint
1233 Howard Street Suite 2g
San Francisco, CA 94103
www.screampoint.com

Jared Lim
dzogchen@bigfoot.com_http://www.liquid2k.com/dzogchen
Animation Master artist

Richard Mans
richard@fuzzyrealms.com
http://www.fuzzyrealms.com
Maya artist

Momentum Animation Studios
info@momentumanimations.com
www.momentumanimationstudios.com
+61 3 9682 6255 (Australia)

Mondo Media/Mechadeus
135 Mississippi, 3rd Floor
San Francisco, CA 94107
415-865-2700
http://www.mondomedia.com

Darrin Mossor
animan@mossor.org
http://www.mossor.org
*Animation Master and Photoshop
artist*

Andy Murdock
andy@lotsofrobots.com
http://www.lotsofrobots.com
3D Studio Max and Photoshop artist

Martin Murphy
www.martinmurphy.ca
LightWave 3D, Bryce, Photoshop,
Painter, Poser, and Illustrator artist

National Center for Atmospheric
Research
P.O. Box 3000
1850 Table Mesa Drive
Boulder, CO. 80307-3000
303-497-1000
http://www.ncar.ucar.edu

Paramount Pictures
http://www.paramount.com

Marco Patrito
Virtual Views
Via Montello, 9
1092 Beinasco (To)
ITALY
http://www.sinkha.com

Vadim Pietrzynski
100605.1207@compuserve.com
3ds max artist

Carles Piles
carlespiles@teleline.es
http://www.3dluvr.com/carles
Cinema 4D artist

Pixar
1001 W. Cutting Blvd.
Richmond, CA 94804 USA
510-236-4000
http://www.pixar.com

Brian Prince
bprince@bprince.com
http://www.bprince.com
Animation Master artist

Gustavo "Goose" Ramirez
goose_r69@hotmail.com
3ds max artist, animator

Frank A. Rivera
LOGICBit Studio
LOGICBit@aol.com
http://www.LOGICBit.com
Animation Master artist

Softimage
Avid Technology, Inc.
One Park West
Tewksbury, MA 01876
978-640-6789
http://www.avid.com

Stefan M. Schmidt
stefan.schmidt@hamburg.de
sms@imagecommunications.de
http://www.imagecommunications.de
LightWave 3D artist

Adrian Skilling
adrian.skilling@dial.pipex.com
http://dspace.dial.pipex.com/adri
an.skilling
Animation Master artist

Stratasys, Inc.
14950 Martin Drive
Eden Prairie, MN 55344-2020
888-480-3548
952-937-3000
info@stratasys.com
http://www.stratasys.com

Taldren
1520 Nutmeg Place
Suite #250
Costa Mesa, CA
92626-2501
http://www.taldren.com

TruFlite
Martin D. Adamiker LLC
Tanbruckgasse 19-23/50
A-1120 Vienna
AUSTRIA
+43-1-810-9633
http://www.truflite.com

Turner Broadcasting System, Inc.
http://www.turner.com

Viewpoint
498 7th Avenue
Suite 1810
New York, NY 10018
212-201-0800
http://viewpoint.com/vpd/
vpd_index.html

Virgin Interactive Entertainment
74a Charlotte Street
London, W1T 4QN
GREAT BRITAIN
+44 (0)20 7551 0000
http://www.vie.com

Terrence Walker
Studio ArtFX
terrence@studioartfx.com
www.studioartfx.com
LightWave 3D, Aura artist

Sheldon Whittaker
sheldnz@slingshot.co.nz
Maya artist

ZINK
zink@vmall.ne.jp
http://zink.sbrain.org
*Animation Master and Photoshop
artist*

Index of Interviews

Index of Tutorials

Index

polygons, 55-56
polylines, 54
rendering, 70-75
rotation, 65-68
segments, 54
texture mapping, 58
viewpoints, 59-61

3D Studio MAX, 32

A

***A.I.: Artificial Intelligence*, 11**
accents (animation), 403
ACM (Association for Computing Machinery), 41
Add Control Point operation, 97
Add Vertex operation, 95
additive materials, 266
After Effects, 450
***Akira, Record of Lodoss War*, 35**
***Akuji the Heartless*, 503**
alias|wavefront Maya, 32
***Alien*, 488**
***Alien vs. Predator*, 504**
***Aliens*, 5**
Align command, 114, 143
***Alpha Centauri: Alien Crossfire*, 174**
alpha channels, 304, 438-439, 465-466
activating, 440
compositing with, 439
alternative coordinate systems, 63
local coordinates, 64
screen coordinates, 63-64

ambient color, 259
ambient light, 69, 325-327, 340
analyzing movement (animation), 402
angles of incidence, 324
animated maps, 318-319
animated textures, 277
animatics, 493-494
3D, 493
animation, 70, 371-372, 419
accents, 403
antics, 402
audio controllers, 401
axes, 381
behaviors, 401
Look At, 401
Point Toward, 401
bones, 386
deformations, 385-386
rigging, 386
tendons, 387
breakdown, 403
cel, 25
chains, 382
character, 402
body language, 404-405
facial animation, 405-407
motion capture, 408-410
motion libraries, 410
rotoscoping, 408
contact positions, 403
controllers, 377
deformation grids, 397-398
dummy objects, 384-385
expression controllers, 401
fluid effects, 398
forensic, 18

saturation, 262
smear, 461-462
specular, 259
subtractive color model, 262
temperature, 323
value, 262
video safe colors, 462
commercials (television), 9
complementary colors, 331
compression
codecs, 456
lossless, 456
lossy, 456
rendering, 456
**Computer Graphics World
(CGW), 42**
cones, 108
**constraints (animation
links), 383**
construction grids, 88
construction planes, 88
**contact positions
(animation), 403**
continuity, 362
control lines (splines), 92
control points (splines), 92
Bezier corner, 94
Corner, 94
Smooth, 94
Standard Bezier, 94
types, 94
control polygons (splines), 92
control vertices (CV), 85
splines, 92
conventions, 41
NAB (National Association of
Broadcasters), 42
SIGGRAPH, 41

coordinates, 50
alternative coordinate
systems, 63
local coordinates, 64
screen coordinates, 63-64
pivot point, 65
plotting, 53
left-hand rule, 54
right-hand rule, 54
rotation, 65-68
systems, effect on
transforms, 111
world coordinate system, 63
copying, 119-120, 142-143
instanced objects, 120
Corel Painter, 287
Corner control points, 94
***Cosmos*, 507**
creative directors, 22
***Creature Comforts*, 477**
cubes, 108
cubic coordinates, 293-294
cut scenes, 13
cuts (editing), 495
L-Cuts, 495
CVs (control vertices), 85
cyberspace, 50
cylinders, 108
**cylindrical coordinates,
291-292**

D

***Daedalus Encounter, The,*
27, 487**
dark light, 330
datasets, 20

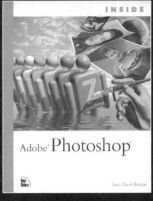

Visit Peachpit on the Web at www.peachpit.com

- Read the latest articles and download timesaving tipsheets from best-selling authors such as Scott Kelby, Robin Williams, Lynda Weinman, Ted Landau, and more!

- Join the Peachpit Club and save 25% off all your online purchases at peachpit.com every time you shop—plus enjoy free UPS ground shipping within the United States.

- Search through our entire collection of new and upcoming titles by author, ISBN, title, or topic. There's no easier way to find just the book you need.

- Sign up for newsletters offering special Peachpit savings and new book announcements so you're always the first to know about our newest books and killer deals.

- Did you know that Peachpit also publishes books by Apple, New Riders, Adobe Press, Macromedia Press, palmOne Press, and TechTV press? Swing by the Peachpit family section of the site and learn about all our partners and series.

- Got a great idea for a book? Check out our About section to find out how to submit a proposal. You could write our next best-seller!

You'll find all this and more at www.peachpit.com. Stop by and take a look today!

Publishing the Voices that Matter

OUR AUTHORS

PRESS ROOM

| web development | design | photoshop | new media | 3-D | server technologies |

EDUCATORS

ABOUT US

CONTACT US

You already know that New Riders brings you the **Voices That Matter**.

But what does that mean? It means that New Riders brings you the

Voices that challenge your assumptions, take your talents to the next

level, or simply help you better understand the complex technical world

we're all navigating.

Visit **www.newriders.com** to find:

▸ *Discounts* on specific book purchases

▸ Never before published chapters

▸ Sample chapters and excerpts

▸ Author bios and interviews

▸ Contests and enter-to-wins

▸ Up-to-date industry event information

▸ Book reviews

▸ Special offers from our friends and partners

▸ Info on how to join our User Group program

▸ Ways to have your Voice heard

New Riders

WWW.NEWRIDERS.COM

Read This Before Opening the Software

About the Cover Image

Darshine is a main character of the *Sinkha Universe* saga. Two ways of being and appearing, she is ubiquitously spaceship and humanoid in two bodies piloted by the same mind. Her dual appearance of woman and mechanism merge indiscriminately, but at the same time divide. As a result, she is a uniqu and wonderful living creature, the member of an incredibly powerful race called the Sinkha, who are not only biologically immortal, but physically invulnerable as well. Darshine was created by Marco Patrito with Maya Unlimited. Maps and textures were drawn with Adobe Photoshop.

The Sinkha Project is a fantastic saga, created by the artist Marco Patrito in the early '90s and used as a set for a multimedia novel, which was realized completely using 3D computer graphics and then distributed on CD-ROM in Europe, Japan, and the U.S. This novel has also been published on a special issue of the American magazine *Heavy Metal*. Marco Patrito is currently working to add to the Sinkha Project and plans to continue the series with new chapters in the form of printed graphic novels as well as multimedia CD-ROMs.

For complete information about the Universe and all the characters, please visit the official web site at www.sinkha.com.